Impolitic Bodies

Impolitic Bodies

Poetry, Saints,

and Society in

Fifteenth-Century England

THE WORK OF
OSBERN BOKENHAM

SHEILA DELANY

New York   Oxford   •   Oxford University Press   1998

Oxford University Press

Oxford   New York
Athens   Auckland   Bangkok   Bogota   Bombay   Buenos Aires
Calcutta   Cape Town   Dar es Salaam   Delhi   Florence   Hong Kong
Istanbul   Karachi   Kuala Lumpur   Madras   Madrid   Melbourne
Mexico City   Nairobi   Paris   Singapore   Taipei   Tokyo   Toronto   Warsaw

and associated companies in
Berlin   Ibadan

Published by Oxford University Press, Inc.,
198 Madison Avenue, New York, New York 10016

Oxford is a registered trademark of Oxford University Press

Library of Congress Cataloging-in-Publication
Delany, Sheila.
   Impolitic bodies : poetry, saints, and society in
   fifteenth-century England : the work of Osbern Bokenham /
   by Sheila Delany.
      p.   cm.
   Includes bibliographical references (p.   ) and index.
   ISBN 0-19-510988-0; ISBN 0-19-510989-9 (pbk.)
      1. Bokenham, Osbern, 1393?–1447? Legendys of hooly wummen.   2. Monastic
and religious life—England—East Anglia—History—Middle Ages. 600–1500.
3. Christian saints—Cult—History of doctrines—Middle Ages, 600–1500.
4. Christian women saints—Legends—History and criticism.   5. Great Britain—
History—Lancaster and York, 1399–1485.   6. Literature and society—England—
History.   7. Chaucer, Geoffrey. d. 1400—Influence.   8. Body, Human, in literature.
9. Christian hagiography.   10. Fifteenth century.   I. Title.
PR1840.B5L443   1997
821'.2--dc21   97-40311

9 8 7 6 5 4 3 2 1
Printed in the United States of America
on acid-free paper

Preface

More than with anything else I've written, I've been continuously aware, in the slow gestation of this book, of the help of others at every stage. The reason is partly that this Osbern Bokenham project was new terrain for me: saints' lives and fifteenth-century studies were unfamiliar areas when I began, and I was sure that both of them would be tedious. Discovering the opposite has been a pleasure, and I'm happy to acknowledge here the individuals and institutions that have aided in this discovery.

My discovery of Bokenham was serendipity, the offshoot of research on an earlier book about Chaucer's *Legend of Good Women*. The similarity of Bokenham's title—*Legends of Holy Women*—to Chaucer's struck me as possibly significant for the early reception of Chaucer's work, and it proved to be so. At the start, when Bokenham was little more than a gleam in my eye (and an unwieldy paper on the Chaucer connection, presented at the University of Washington Medieval Seminar), Michael Curley of Tacoma Pacific University encouraged this novice in hagiographical studies with kind words and bibliographical references. A release-time stipend from Canada's SSHRC (Social Sciences and Humanities Research Council) for the academic year 1987–88 enabled me to spend some months in Berkeley, California, researching and designing the project. At that point, the Bokenham material was meant to form one chapter of a work in progress, *Galleries of Women,* but it soon burgeoned indecently into two books of its own: this one and my translation of Bokenham's legendary, or set of saints' lives. The latter was published in 1992 as the inaugural volume in the University of Notre Dame Medieval Institute's new translation series—thanks to Ed Vasta of the University of Notre Dame for suggesting it—and was enabled by a renewed release-time stipend from the SSHRC in 1989–90. For both projects, much appreciation goes to my undergraduate research assistants: Ken Christensen, Barry Reid, Arlene Cook, Karen Moe, and Roberta (Bobbi) Holt and to my graduate assistant, Derrick Higginbotham. I hope they developed some affection for Osborn, or at least came to understand mine.

At home and abroad I've benefited from the hospitality and the feedback of many medievalists. In Vancouver I've been fortunate to know Jane Fredeman, DeLloyd Guth, Rhoda Friedrichs, and A. S. G. (Tony) Edwards, all of them wonderfully generous scholars in fifteenth-century studies. Their biographical, bibliographical, codicological, and just plain factual knowledge has clarified much and made for stimulating sessions at the Vancouver Medieval Symposium. Special thanks go to Simon Fraser University's Humanities Institute and its director, Jerry Zaslove, for supporting the symposium. David Fowler, professor emeritus at the University of Washington, graciously made available to me both old and brand-new material on Giles of Rome. Alastair Minnis, Carol Meale, Julia Boffey, Jocelyn Wogan-Browne, and Pam Sheingorn kindly sent manuscripts or prepublication copies of papers.

Susan Crane's penetrating commentary at the Delaware Valley Medieval Association meeting in 1989 (organized by Betsy Bowden) helped focus some of the gender issues, and Linda Georgianna's session, "Commercial Imagery," at the joint Medieval Academy/Medieval Association of the Pacific meeting (1993) at Tucson gave me the opportunity to develop my ideas on Cecelia. In 1995, Tom Hahn's interdisciplinary faculty–graduate seminar at the University of Rochester and Anna Torti's invitation to Perugia stimulated further development of particular sections of the book. Useful information was offered in discussions at LOMERS (London Old and Middle English Research Seminar) and at the Cambridge University graduate seminar in 1989. I'm grateful to James Simpson, Pamela King, and Jill Mann for making these exchanges possible.

The hospitality of David Aers enlivened my visit to the East Anglian places I've written about here and enabled me, by serendipity, to meet Martial Rose, who treated me to an unforgettable and erudite clerestory tour of the roof bosses at Norwich Cathedral. In 1993, Ralph A. Griffiths offered encouragement and valuable bibliographic help in Swansea. These trips were funded by the SSHRC and by a President's Research grant from Simon Fraser University. The book was completed during a two-year respite from teaching provided by Canada's Killam Foundation, whose Senior Research Fellowship I held in 1993–95.

Last, but far from least, I want to thank John Ganim for his sensitive and balanced reading of the manuscript for Oxford; it was all any author could want from any reader.

I also should like to acknowledge the unfailing courtesy of the staff at the British Library; the Bodleian Library at Oxford; Cambridge University Library; the library at the University College of Swansea, Wales; and Simon Fraser University's Interlibrary Loans. As always, Anita Mahoney in the word-processing office at Simon Fraser University was a marvel of efficiency. The stunning cover photo is of the *Triglyph Frieze*, by Spring Hurlbut of Toronto. I chose it because it so succinctly embodies the concept of body as architecture and architecture as body, which is one theme of this book. The photo is by Robert Keziere of Vancouver. My thanks to Joan Stebbins, curator of the Southern Alberta Art Gallery, for permission to use the photo; to the National Gallery of Canada, which owns the piece; and to Spring Hurlbut. The photos from Long Melford were taken by John Anderson of Long Melford, to whom I was introduced long-distance through the good offices of Rev. Christopher Sansbury, rector of the Church of the Holy Trinity, Long Melford. The photo of Jean Fouquet's *Virgin and Child* is shown here by permission of the Koninklijk Museum voor Schone Kunsten in Antwerp, and the passion symbols are reproduced by permission of Cambridge University Press.

The translations from Bokenham's work are mine. Those from Middle English, Latin, and French are usually mine and are specified either to me or to another translator. *Yogh* and *thorn* in Middle English have been normalized to modern equivalents; they are mingled in most manuscripts anyway. All my references to Voragine are from Graesse's edition with my translations, as the new translation by William Granger Ryan (Princeton, 1993) came into my hands only when my book was virtually completed.

Vancouver, B.C., Canada   S. D.
July 1997

Contents

Abbreviations

BL	British Library
CA	*Confessio amantis*, John Gower
CEMERS	Center for Medieval and Early Renaissance Studies
ChR	*Chaucer Review*
CT	*Canterbury Tales*, Geoffrey Chaucer
DDC	*De Doctrina christiana*, St. Augustine
EETS	Early English Text Society
EHR	*English Historical Review*
ELH	*English Literary History*
HF	*House of Fame*, Geoffrey Chaucer
JEGP	*Journal of English and Germanic Philology*
JMH	*Journal of Medieval History*
JMRS	*Journal of Medieval and Renaissance Studies*
LGW	*Legend of Good Women*, Geoffrey Chaucer
ME	Middle English
MED	*Middle English Dictionary*
MilT	*Miller's Tale*, Geoffrey Chaucer
MP	*Modern Philology*
MRTS	Medieval and Renaissance Text Society
OED	*Oxford English Dictionary*
PF	*Parliament of Fowls*, Geoffrey Chaucer
PIMS	Pontifical Institute of Medieval Studies
PMLA	*Publications of the Modern Language Association*
SAC	*Studies in the Age of Chaucer*
SEL	*South English Legendary*
SPCK	Society for the Propagation of Christian Knowledge
TC	*Troilus and Criseyde*, Geoffrey Chaucer
VCH	*Victoria County History*

Impolitic Bodies

ONE

Introductions

Is it necessary any longer to defend the much-maligned fifteenth century as, quite simply, interesting? One hopes that the recent revival of historicisms—cultural materialism, new historicism, new philology, deconstruction, canon wars, feminist history—has rendered such defensiveness obsolete; yet the fifteenth century is still often imagined as a kind of wasteland. One scholar's quip that the poets of the fifteenth century are either very important but not very good or very good but not very important (Fox, 399; cited in Fradenburg) seems curiously beside the point, for surely we can now assume the relativity and artificiality of "good" and "important" (not to mention "great"): the ways in which, and the reasons why, such terms were constructed in our author's day and in our own.

For me, it was not at first these methods—belated in the Bloomian sense—so much as an earlier historicism that sparked my conviction of the revelatory value of the minor or the marginal, whether this minor or marginal was an infrequently taught text by a canonical author or a work by a little-known writer. Here is one statement from that discourse:

> It is not the consciousness of people (*Menschen*) that determines their being, but, on the contrary, their social being that determines their consciousness. . . . In considering [revolutionary] transformations a distinction should always be made between the material transformation of the economic conditions of production . . . and the legal, political, religious, aesthetic, or philosophic—in short, ideological—forms in which people become conscious of this conflict and fight it out. Just as our opinion of an individual is not based on what he thinks of himself, so can we not judge of such a period of transformation by its own consciousness; on the contrary this consciousness must be explained rather from the contradictions of material life. (Karl Marx, "A Contribution to the Critique of Political Economy")[1]

If to some readers this reference seems hopelessly old-fashioned, to others it will appear simply as another visitation of the spectral power that Jacques Derrida eloquently invoked as an inheritance remaining "absolutely and thoroughly determinate" in contemporary intellectual life (*Specters,* 14).

3

Until my translation of his legendary was published in 1992, few modern readers knew of the Augustinian friar Osbern Bokenham. Yet his poetry is both good enough and important enough to illuminate Chaucer's work and Chaucer reception, gender studies, late-medieval European cultural history, the development of hagiography, and English political life. The friar's achievements are substantial. He made a critique of the Chaucerian sensibility that was distinctive in its time. He composed the first all-female legendary in English, with considerable artistry. Bokenham was a committed partisan of Richard, duke of York, during the period of Lancastrian hegemony when such a loyalty could be dangerous and at an earlier date than most historians have acknowledged as possible for overt Yorkist sympathies. He was in close touch with national and international politics during an especially turbulent, indeed transformative, period of English history. Finally, Bokenham is the probable translator of the first vernacular version of Claudian, hence to be connected with nascent English humanism, and his up-to-date Augustinian theology shows familiarity with the more advanced Italian humanist movement.

The center of this book is Bokenham's legendary, composed of the lives of thirteen women saints. In exploring the work and its context, I formulated the importance to Bokenham's project of three types of "body." They are the corpus of poetic and theological texts he used and critiqued, the female body he represented in his legendary, and the "body politic" of English society at a critical moment in its national life, on the eve of the so-called Wars of the Roses. How these three bodies overlap is my main theme and accounts for my title. This is, therefore, a study of fifteenth-century Chaucer reception, the theological–corporeal semiotics of the representation of the female body, the hagiographer's art, and the literary effects of fifteenth-century political history and patronage. That a single, long, late-medieval devotional work—Bokenham's *Legends of Holy Women*—should be able to encode all this without sinking into either the sentimentality or the tedium of many of his compatriots is already a noteworthy literary achievement.

Bokenham knew full well that obscurity was a likely fate for him: the limited circle of readers for which he wrote virtually guaranteed it. He acknowledges this possibility with the rueful comment in his prologue that the author's unworthiness might cause posterity to "throwyn it [the work] in the angle of oblyvyoun" (40: throw it into oblivion's corner). Here the traditional modesty topos clothes the author's anxiety about the work's controversial Yorkist political alignment. And—like other of the author's asides scattered through the legendary—it reveals an acute awareness of audience. Such awareness was just as sharply articulated by Bokenham's Cambridge acquaintance and fellow Austin John Capgrave. At the start of his life of St. Norbert, Capgrave wryly asks:

Who schal these dayis make now ony thing	Who can compose anything nowadays
But it schal be tosed & pulled as wolle? (8–9)[2]	That won't be teased and pulled apart like wool?

Comments like these have an interpellative force for the scholar, meeting them as we do in the effort of recovery that constitutes our work. Our imaginative thrust into the past duplicates and—we may like to imagine—reciprocates that of our authors into the future. In a faintly comical oscillation, our own anxieties of authorship replicate, exhume, and even fulfill theirs—as theirs do ours by provoking and shaping our scholarship. As we shall see, Osbern Bokenham was keenly aware of the imbrication of "what was past and passing and to come" (as Yeats put it). His own effort was largely one of recuperation: to recover Augustine for the present and to offer charismatic women saints as models in contemporary social life—and not for women only. Before turning to the text in chapter 2, I shall introduce the author and his works, some of his patrons, and the neighborhood. These acquaintances will affect our reading of the *Legends* and of the Claudian translation.

What we know about Osbern Bokenham is pieced together from evidence in his work and from sparse documentation. His year of birth can be inferred from remarks in the *Legends*. In his life of Margaret, which Bokenham says he began on September 7, 1443 (187–91), the author reveals his age, expressing the hope that Atropos will not too quickly cut his "fatal threed . . . Wych lachesys hath twynyd ful yerys fyfty" (248: fated life thread that Lachesis has spun out for fifty years). We later learn that Bokenham's birthday was on St. Faith's Day, October 6 (4034), and if he was anticipating his full fifty by a month, he was born in 1393. Coincidentally, he shared his birthday with another East Anglian biographer of St. Faith: Simon of Walsingham, whose Anglo-Norman life of Faith was composed about 1210 at Bury St. Edmunds (lines 52–74).

Bokenham's date of death is unknown. For a time, it was thought that he had died in 1447, the year when, according to a manuscript note, the work was copied and therefore, presumably, completed. This same note also attributes the work to Bokenham. The reason for the inference about his death was that in his opening remarks, the author expresses the wish to remain anonymous, and the EETS editor of the *Legends,* Mary Serjeantson, assumed that no one would flout such a wish during the author's lifetime. However, documentary evidence published since Serjeantson's edition shows that in 1461 and 1463, Bokenham acted as vicar general for provincial chapter meetings of the Augustinian order, so that at the age of seventy, he was alive and apparently well at Clare Priory (Roth, 2.345, 347, 351). Some months after the meeting of May 1463, in September of the same year, the wealthy draper John Baret of Bury directed in his will "to Maist' Osberne frer of Clare iijs. iiijd" (Tymms, 35: three shillings, four denarii, or pence).[3] That is the last we hear of Osbern. Baret's will was not probated until 1467, however, when it still contained the bequest to Master Osbern. Had a beneficiary died before probate, and had the executors known of the beneficiary's death, they would have removed the name. It is possible, therefore, that Bokenham's date of death was 1467 or later.

Bokenham declares that in both speech and writing he uses ordinary "language of Suthfolke speche" (4064). Suffolk might have been his native county, or he may have hailed from the village of Old Buckenham in Norfolk, a few miles north of the Suffolk line. There was a house of Austin canons at Old Buckenham, and if its records are any indication, people not infrequently took the town's name as their surname: in 1479, two of the eight canons enrolled were named Buckenham (*VCH,* Norfolk, 2.376–78). Boys could be recruited to the Augustinian order as early as the age of eleven, this having been lowered from fourteen as a consequence of the depopulation caused by the plague during the previous century. In 1424 the number of novices was still so low that no inceptor was allowed to begin university "unless he has induced one novice to join or has given at least 11s for his upbringing" (Roth, 1.302). Recruitment continued to be a problem for decades, for in 1464 the vicar provincial ruled that any friar who failed to "secure one youth for the Order and provide for his sustenance and education . . . is to be considered a rebel and must pay the fine assigned" (Roth, 2.352).

In his verse "Testament," John Lydgate gives a poignant memoir of his adolescence as a Benedictine novice at Bury, just fifteen miles north of Clare. Although Lydgate's autobiographical essay owes a good deal to Augustine's prototypical *Confessions,* it would be pedantic to discount a genuine personal factor. After an account of a normal rambunctious childhood—"the sesoun of my yeres grene" (608)—Lydgate says that he entered religion at the age of fifteen. He remained "ful of wordes, disordinat of language" (713)—a trait, we know, that took a different form in adulthood but did not disappear. He was fond of food and drink, fun loving, and impatient, and he complained about the food and disliked "contemplacionn" and "Holy histories" (728–29). In short, he was a perfectly average adolescent to whom the cloistered life did not come easily:

Of religioun I wered a blak habite,	I wore a black religious habit
Only outward as be apparence,	But only outwardly, in appearance;
To folowe that charge savoured but fullyte,	To follow that duty pleased me very little
Save ne a maner connterfete pretence;	Except as a kind of pretense;
But in effecte ther was non existence,	But in reality there was no fact to it,
Like the image of Pygmalyon,	Just as Pygmalion's statue
Shewed lyfly, and was made but of ston.	Appeared to be alive and was only made
(691–97)	of stone.

A young recruit would normally go to live at the order's establishment closest to his place of birth and, as he advanced, proceed to higher schooling in a larger city. There were numerous grammar schools in Suffolk—Thetford, not far from Buckenham, had one—and there were establishments of Austin friars at Lynn, Norwich, and Thetford as well as the priory at Clare, to mention only the more significant houses. Thetford was the last Augustinian establishment founded in England in the Middle Ages, in 1389; it was under the special patronage of John of Gaunt. The Norwich priory was a far more important center, which attracted contributions such as that of Margaret Wetherbey. In 1457 she left one hundred marks to build a new library, provided that her and her husband's names were inscribed on windows and book rests. In imitation of one at Rome, the priory church had a *scala celi* (ladder to heaven) chapel and altar, a common feature of East Anglian Augustinian churches. The Norwich chapel gave major indulgences and "was a great attraction to the devout of East Anglia" (*VCH,* Norfolk, 2.433). Bokenham's early education is likely to have been at Norwich, the diocesan center, or possibly Cambridge, as East Anglia was in the Cambridge limit (the administrative area within which mendicant friars operated).

Not all boys received the same training. Those destined for simple priestly duties had a minimal education, whereas those considered capable of administrative and scholarly work were trained for about two decades. After completing a rigorous course of biblical, classical, and philosophical studies, the successful candidate could then enroll at one of the English universities or in the English "nation" at a foreign university, with Paris particularly favored by Augustinians for the degree of *magister*. On March 21, 1423, following John Capgrave by a day, Bokenham was made *baccalarius* at Cambridge University and permitted to proceed to the level of *magister* (Roth, 1.172).[4] Since he had received permission to travel to Italy at this time but apparently did not go (Roth, 2.301–2, 1.173, n.), he is likely to have remained at Cambridge to fulfill the requirements for the highest degree. He would have acquired considerable experience in teaching younger students, in disputation, biblical explication, classics, logic, natural philosophy, and theology. From 1427 to 1463, Bokenham is referred to as "master" in those documents naming him. In this capacity he would have been entitled to privileges of travel and salary; and to personal comforts such as a servant, a private chamber, and some private possessions; to a choice of confessor; and to participation in the administration of the Order of Hermits of St. Augustine (Roth, 1.175–77).

Later Bokenham did travel abroad. In the prologue to his legendary, he mentions two trips to Italy, which is scarcely surprising, for the Augustinians prided themselves on their close connection with Rome. The 1434 general chapter was held in Mantua, and young English Austins often studied in Italy, particularly at the *studium generale* in Florence. Bokenham was in Venice, he says, about five years earlier than the present writing, that is, before he commenced the life of Margaret, or about 1438. With tantalizing brevity, he relates a harrowing experience at the hands of a Venetian tyrant:

Whan lytyl from venyse me dede dryve	When, not far from Venice, I was forced
A cruel tyraunth in-to a fen	By a cruel tyrant into a swamp
Owt of a barge, and fyve mo men. (160–62)	From a barge along with five other men.

Although Venice was a port of embarkation for the Holy Land, it was not itself a major site of pilgrimage, and we can only assume that if Bokenham had been to Jerusalem, he would have said so. He may have been in Venice on chapter business or as an observer at the 1438 Ferrara–Florence Council, whose purpose was to negotiate union with the Eastern branch of the church. It was at Venice that the Greeks disembarked, were greeted by the papal party, and stayed for several weeks. Although the English sent no official embassy to this council, there were nonetheless English envoys and observers in attendance.[5]

The safety of travelers was an especially serious problem during this council because of the fragmented Italian political situation and, consequently, competing loyalties to different ecclesiastical councils and schismatic popes. Over the entire period of composition of Bokenham's legends, the antipope, Felix V, elected at the Council of Basel in 1440, was asserting his claim, supported by the Visconti family of Milan and other European nobles. The English remained loyal to the Roman pope, Eugenius IV, who had been elected in 1431. Although he was deposed by the Council of Basel in favor of the new antipope, he remained in office until his death in 1447. Throughout this entire period, the kidnapping of English travelers, messengers, and allies was not uncommon (Harvey, 86). Apparently Bokenham's hair-raising experience in Italy was not unusual.

In the same prologue, Bokenham refers to a trip to Rome as "the laste tyme I was in Itayle" (108), which could refer to the 1438 journey or to a more recent one. It was on this last journey that rainstorms forced Bokenham to lodge at the hostel in Montefiascone, about fifty miles north of Rome. Montefiascone had a cult of Margaret, and the pious English friar writes that he occupied himself with transcribing the saint's legend, which he then brought back to Clare and eventually, at a friend's request, translated. There was also a pilgrimage to Santiago de Compostela in Spain, made in 1445 just before Bokenham undertook the life of Magdalene (4982–5117).

By 1427 Bokenham was at Clare Priory in East Anglia (Roth, 1.422). His old Cambridge colleague John Capgrave lived in the Augustinian convent at Lynn about fifty miles away. Capgrave was elected prior provincial in 1453. He too was a writer, a prolific producer of religious and historical works; Bokenham refers to Capgrave's life of Katherine of Alexandria, patron saint of Augustinian (as of Franciscan and Dominican) scholarship (6356).

Also living in Lynn was the enthusiast and mystic Margery Kempe, who died after 1439. Bokenham can hardly have been unaware of his unusual but respected countrywoman, as she was well known in the region and indeed supported by money contributions from those who sought her prayers (1.54). She also apparently served as at least an occasional spiritual counselor to nobility. Here a dynastic connection cannot be ignored, for Margery recounts her 1413 visit to Lady Westmoreland, wife of Ralph Neville and mother of Cecily Neville, who married Richard, duke of York. According to Margery's narration, "My Lady herself was well pleased with you and liked your talk" (1.54). To be sure, this visit occurred before Cecily's birth in 1415, yet it would likely have been known to those who closely followed the York connections.

Indeed, the visit might have been known from Margery's book itself, which circulated among clerical houses as an example of pious devotion. Although there is no evidence they met, it is likely Bokenham would have been among Margery's admirers, for St. Elizabeth of Hungary, whose life concludes Bokenham's series, resembles Margery in several respects, among them her married and maternal status and her crying and sobbing aloud. (Margery mentions Elizabeth as a prototype crier in book 1.62, and she may, to some extent, have modeled herself on Elizabeth, much as she did on St. Bridget of Sweden; see Cleve.) Margery was certainly well known to the Austin friars at Lynn and had a good rapport with them, for during the early 1420s she attended a service at the Lynn priory and was struck by a crying fit. Although many in the audience "were astonished at her, and cursed her most violently," nonetheless "this good man who now preached . . . said to the people, 'Friends, be quiet—you know very little what she is feeling'" (1.68). A decade later, when Bokenham was living at Clare, Margery passed through Suffolk to Ipswich, her point of embarkation for Germany. Considering both her reputation and her behavior, it seems unlikely her passage would remain unremarked by those interested in religious phenomena.

Closer to Clare, only about fifteen miles away, was the ancient and wealthy Benedictine abbey of St. Edmunds in Bury, whose abbot, William Curteis, sat in Parliament as moneylender and adviser to the king. The abbey's most famous literary resident was the poet John Lydgate (1370–1450), to whom Bokenham refers several times as part of the literary triumvirate Chaucer/Gower/Lydgate. The town of Clare fell just within the liberty of St. Edmunds Abbey, which was, "with the exception of the Crown, . . . probably the largest single landholder in West Suffolk" (Gottfried, 74, 76).

English social life was turbulent during Bokenham's lifetime, in all social classes. In 1401 the Lollard heresy had been declared a capital offense in the statute *De Comburendo haereticis*. In 1401 a priest, William Sawtre, was the first person to be burned to death under the statute, at Smithfield, London, and in 1410 at the same place, the artisan John Badby died in the flames (McNiven). Three men died as a consequence of the 1428 heresy investigation in Norwich: William White, William Waddon, and Hugh Pye (Tanner, *Trials*, 8). In 1430 several more executions by fire took place in the southeast, and in 1431 an Essex priest, Thomas Bagley, died before thousands of spectators at St. Paul's Cross in London (Thompson, 123–24). In 1440 a relapsed heretic from the days of Henry IV, Richard Wyche, was executed, but his death, far from having a deterrent effect, began to attract the kind of devotion reserved for saints until the authorities intervened (Griffiths, *Reign*, 569). Investigations and prosecutions were common among East Anglian artisans, both men and women, who read the vernacular Bible together, possessed subversive religious texts, or expressed anticlerical or iconoclastic ideas. The horror of a heretic's death was certainly equaled in the civil sphere, for the usual punishment for troublemaking and treasonous behavior was to be hanged, drawn, and quartered, with the head set in a public place and the quarters often dispersed to display as a sanguinary warning. The *Brut* vernacular chronicle mentions that in the winter of 1442–43, a woman who reproached the king about his handling of the Eleanor Cobham sorcery trial was arrested, paraded in a cart, and pressed to death with iron weights (483). Philippa Maddern mentions (with no date) the case of one Margery Tatenell, condemned to execution by burning for complicity in the murder of her husband (46, n.). She adds that

> petty traitors could be drawn and hanged, high traitors hanged, drawn and quartered, women traitors and relapsed heretics burned, penitent heretics flogged. . . . At Lydd in the fifteenth century, pickpockets and cutpurses could be nailed by the ear to a post and made to cut themselves free. At Sandwich, homicides could be buried alive. (70)

Even high-ranking ecclesiastics were not immune from rebellious sympathies. In 1405, Richard Scrope, archbishop of York, was executed for his role in leading a popular insurrection. According to Hughes, by 1419 Scrope's shrine was more popular in the north—or at least more profitable—than Becket's in the south (305–6).

During the 1430s and 1440s, large-scale public demonstrations, some more violent than others, were held in Norwich and Lynn (to mention only East Anglian sites). Some of these were the result of urban middle-class partisan politics and intraelite rivalry, whereas others protested ecclesiastical intervention in bourgeois economic life.[6] It is possible that another factor contributed to the citizens' sense of their rights in this part of England—that is, the distinctive social structures that had characterized East Anglia from the Domesday period. Although these related to agricultural life, they constituted a set of regional social practices and expectations that inevitably carried over into urban life. David Douglas showed that in East Anglia, "contractual rights existed from an early date and [were] exercised with unusual frequency," that money circulated in East Anglia unusually early and plentifully, that the village rather than the manor was the principal unit of social organization, and that there was an "absence of any organized territorial lordship throughout the district." Despite a widespread depression of the peasantry in the thirteenth century, "the social structure of Norfolk and Suffolk had not conformed to the normal manorial pattern." These, along with other "highly remarkable arrangements prevailing in medieval Norfolk and Suffolk" (204–19), cannot have been negligible in forming the social and political consciousness of East Anglian artisans and bourgeois.

Among ambitious barons and gentry, the rivalry was intense, often erupting into armed violence as groups of salaried retainers—small private armies—confronted one another. Small and not-so-small local and regional revolts were not uncommon, the most famous of the period being the so-called Cade's rebellion in Kent in 1450. For both the people and their rulers, assassination sometimes offered the easiest way to get rid of an inconvenient official or to protest his policy. In January 1450, Adam Moleyns—keeper of the privy seal and bishop of Chichester—was murdered by a group of unpaid soldiers at Portsmouth; they accused him of responsibility for the final surrender of Maine to the French two years earlier. The dying bishop is said to have accused William de la Pole, duke of Suffolk, of being the real villain. Some months later, Suffolk was impeached by the House of Commons, exiled, and then murdered at sea by the crew of the *Nicholas,* part of the fleet engaged in monitoring the Channel. His associate, Lord Say and Sele, was executed in July during the Cade rebellion. During that same momentous year, 1450, Bishop Ayscough of Salisbury was killed by a crowd while celebrating mass in Wiltshire.

Abroad, the war with France, the so-called Hundred Years War, dragged on. Henry VI was the reigning Lancastrian king during Bokenham's adult life. Like his father and grandfather, Henry VI married a French princess. But his efforts to negotiate peace were opposed by many English, who preferred an aggressive foreign policy to protect English territories in France and English commercial interests at sea. Propaganda of the period was often expressed in verse, and the rhymed "Libelle of English Policie" (1436) voices certain mercantile discontents and interests with its advice to

Cheryshe marchandyse, kepe th'amyralte,	Protect commerce, maintain naval capability,
That we bee maysteres of the narowe see. (6–7)[7]	So that we may be masters of the Channel.

Clare Priory, where Bokenham spent much of his life, might strike us as a provincial oasis amid such turmoil. Yet it was far from being an ivory tower, and Bokenham was no simple cloistered scribbler, no "drivelling monk" (as Joseph Ritson, an eighteenth-century antiquarian, rather unfairly described Lydgate). It is sometimes difficult to realize—after so much of the evidence disappeared in the Henrician reformation and the Puritan iconoclastic campaign—how very rich East Anglia was in the Middle Ages and how much of England's wealth was displayed in its ecclesiastical establishments. As Gail Gibson reminds us, Norfolk and Suffolk produced 25 percent of English cloth in the later Middle Ages (19), and Janet Becker observes that Suffolk "held the record for making the greatest number of woollen cloths in the whole of England" (9). Here is an ecclesiastical measure of England's wealth, in which two East Anglian cities figure large:

> Western Christendom in 1418 comprised 717 sees, and of these only 40 owed services in excess of 3,000 florins. It is therefore remarkable that of these 40 richest sees no fewer than 12 were in England. At the very top came Winchester, bracketed together with Rouen, and not far below came Canterbury and York, in the same class as the great German-speaking prince-bishoprics like Cologne, Mainz, Trier and Salzburg. Others in the top class might be found scattered over the vast extent of France and Spain, but concentrated also in this island: Durham, Ely, Exeter, Lincoln, Norwich, Salisbury, Bath and Wells, Coventry and Lichfield, and London. (DuBoulay, 233)

The anonymous secretary to Francesco Capello, the Venetian ambassador to England, left the earliest Venetian account of the country on record (Sneyd), and he was absolutely dazzled by England's wealth and display toward the end of the century. There are fifty-two goldsmith shops in London's Strand, he writes, superior to those in Milan, Rome, Venice, and Florence together (42). "But above all are their riches displayed in the church treasures," with the meanest parish church possessing major stocks of silver and the big monasteries "more like baronial palaces than religious houses" (29). He is particularly flabbergasted by the display at St. Thomas's shrine, where the tomb is overlaid with carved gold shields, in turn encrusted with jewels whose size, name, and provenance are proudly related by the abbot.

The Italian's impression is confirmed by Reformation inventories. Down the road from Clare, a few miles east, is Long Melford, whose parish church of the Holy Trinity is an outstanding example of fifteenth-century perpendicular style. This famous "wool church" had, besides its superb windows, substantial stores of silver and gold plate as well as pewter and latoun (brass); of rings, beads, grails, and buckles in precious metals; of coats, vestments, and altar cloths in embroidered silks and linens; and more (W. Parker, 58–60). Of course, it could not compare with an internationally known shrine like the one at Walsingham, where one might see a statue of Mary, flanked by figures of four saints—Edmund, Edward, Katherine, and Margaret—"alle clene gold," as a contemporary testified (L. Cameron, 323). Even Erasmus was impressed with the Mary chapel at Walsingham: "You would say it was the mansion of the saints, so much does it glitter on all sides with jewels, gold and silver" (Hall, 109).

To be sure, the economic picture was not entirely rosy in Bokenham's day. From the perspective of English foreign trade as a whole, the 1430s through early 1450s were a period of recovery and prosperity between two recessions or depressions (Gray, 1). The wool trade had been in a steady decline since the previous century. But this was offset by the rise of cloth manufacture and export, which increased tenfold between 1350 and 1425 and which by the 1440s both surpassed the wool trade in value and provided the largest manufacturing employment in the country (Lloyd; Munro).

Still, even the cloth industry was far from invulnerable. Paradoxically, the monetary policy that had stabilized English coinage and prosperity itself led to a serious disruption of the industry. The ban on exporting silver and gold (including bullion, coin, and plate)—a policy dating back to Edward III and even earlier—meant that the English accepted payment only in bullion or in their own relatively pure money rather than in the more debased currencies of other realms. This provoked an international boycott of English cloth, so that between 1447 and 1449, English cloth exports fell by nearly half, leading to significant unemployment in cloth-producing areas. Of course, the ongoing intermittent war with France also contributed to this crisis.

Nonetheless, Robert Gottfried points out that the region—West Suffolk—in which Bokenham and his patrons lived had to a large extent been able to avoid the economic crisis that troubled many other areas of the country. Bury, the hub and major market center of that region, was unusual in the first half of the fifteenth century because it was "growing and prospering at a time when many provincial centers were entering a period of acute economic decline" (Gottfried, 5). Its urban crises thus were primarily political rather than strictly economic, and the challenge of the bourgeoisie was played out against a backdrop of economic prosperity and expansion, not of contraction (11). For Bokenham—and his patrons, too—the atmosphere could be characterized as economically prosperous but politically worrisome. It was in many respects an age of anxiety, and I will show in chapter 8 how some of its larger social concerns made themselves felt in Bokenham's work.

The town of Clare was the administrative center of the honor of Clare: the extensive holdings of the Clare family and its descendants, which included manors in Norfolk, Suffolk, Essex, and elsewhere. The honor of Clare was one of the great Mortimer holdings, among the largest and wealthiest of Richard of York's receiverships (Rosenthal, 175, 177). Clare had been an important town during the Anglo-Saxon period. In the fifteenth century it was a prosperous town in a prosperous area, with an important regional market farmed by burgesses, an almshouse, a grammar school, and a distinguished parish church (SS. Peter and Paul) whose indulgences attracted pilgrims from the region. Although technically not a borough, Clare had many boroughlike privileges and was still in 1548 "a greate and populous towne" (VCH, Suffolk, 2.340). A rough gauge of its prosperity may be derived from the boast of the Puritan "parliamentary visitor" William Dowsing, who enumerated his destructions there in 1643:

> At Clare. Jan. the 6th. We brake down 1000 Pictures superstitious; I brake down 200; 3 of God the Father, and 3 of Christ, and the Holy Lamb, and 3 of the Holy Ghost like a Dove with Wings; and the 12 Apostles were carved in Wood, on the top of the Roof, which we gave order to take down; and 20 Cherubins to be taken down; and the Sun and Moon in the East Window, by the King's arms, to be taken down.[8]

Clare Priory was the oldest Augustinian establishment in England; it was founded in 1248 by the Clare family. It housed between fifteen and thirty men. Although one might assume that any establishment in the vicinity of Bury St. Edmunds would be swamped by its mighty neighbor, nonetheless Clare kept its end up rather well despite a comparatively small landed endowment. Friaries rarely had cartularies, but Clare did, containing transcripts of some two hundred deeds. Some of these gifts contradicted the mendicant rule about not holding property other than the site of the house, but this rule could be bent with consent of the order's officials.

Although many of the small land parcels came from local men and women, numerous mid-thirteenth-century property gifts were from Maud, countess of Gloucester and Hereford, and indeed the priory was associated from the start with the highest echelons of nobility. "The high position of the founder

[Richard de Clare, earl of Gloucester] and his posterity, coupled with the fact that Clare was the parent house of the order in England, placed this friary in a somewhat exceptional position, particularly as Clare was a favourite residence for royalty in the thirteenth and fourteenth centuries" (*VCH,* Suffolk, 127–29).

Joan of Acre—daughter of King Edward I and wife of Gilbert of Clare, earl of Gloucester—was an early donor to the priory. She was buried in the priory's church in 1305, with Edward II and many nobles in attendance. This lady had a reputation in the region as "a ful holy woman"; this is how she is described by John Capgrave. According to Capgrave, Joan of Acre was in fact very nearly a saint; the following is his account, from his *Chronicle,* of her postmortem history:

> For sche was biried in the Frere Austines at Clare, and aftir hir biriing LII. yere, at the desire of dame Ysabel of Borow, sche mad hir bare, and sche was found hol in alle membris; her tetis, whan thei were pressid with handis, the flesch ros up ageyn; hir eyeledes, left up, fel down ageyn. The clothis that were aboute hir, whech were dipped in wax and rosyn, thoo were roten; but the lynand cloth whech was next hir, that was dite with no craft, that was found clene and hool.

> For she was buried in [the priory of] the Austin friars at Clare, and fifty-two years after her burial, at the wish of Lady Isabel de Burgh, she had her exhumed, and she was found whole in all her limbs. Her nipples, when pressed by hand, grew erect again; her eyelids, when raised, fell closed again. The wrappings around her, which had been dipped in wax and rosin, were rotten, but the linen cloth right next to her body, which had not been specially prepared, was found to be clean and whole.

Indulgences of thirty or forty days were often granted by bishops to those who visited and prayed to Joan, at least partly in the hope of obtaining another English saint (Roth, 1.260). About the middle of the fourteenth century, Joan's daughter Elizabeth de Burgh, lady of Clare, sponsored Clare Hall (now Clare College) at Cambridge University. Joan's son Edward Mortimer was also buried at Clare, as were other nobles, knights, and gentry, among them Prince Lionel, son of King Edward III. It was through his first wife, Elizabeth de Burgh (not Joan's daughter but her descendant), that Lionel acquired the honor of Clare and thus the newly invented title of Clarence when he was created duke in 1362 (Powell and Wallis, 363–64).

It also was in Elizabeth's household that the young Geoffrey Chaucer learned courtly habits and acquired a foothold in the civil service, but there is no evidence that he visited Clare while in her service. Lionel's connection with the friars at Clare was close. On his wedding trip to Italy in 1368, to marry his second wife, Violante Visconti, Lionel was accompanied by Thomas Edwardstone, OESA, an Oxford master and Lionel's confessor who in 1374 was chosen prior of Clare (Roth, 1.533). On his deathbed, Lionel directed that his heart and bones go to Clare and his flesh and entrails to Pavia, near the supposed tomb of St. Augustine (Harper-Bill, 75–76).

Thus the Austins enjoyed a distinguished patronage, whose social life and aspirations they shared. They did so as neighbors—living, in Roth's vivid phrase, "at the foot of the castle" (1.259)—and the modern visitor is struck by the proximity of the priory (which still operates as an Augustinian establishment) to the castle ruins. The residents also served as chaplains and confessors. For example, two friars sang mass every day at the castle, in exchange for ten quarters of wheat and ten quarters of malt annually (Thornton, *History,* 86, *Short History,* 15). Nor did the relations between the friars and nobles end with strictly clerical functions, for some of the clerics were well-educated university men who could offer entertaining and refined conversation to while away provincial winter evenings. Equally to the point, they were trained scholars with valuable propagandistic skills (the practical uses of which are discussed in chapter 7). It was no hermitlike existence that Bokenham led among the friar hermits of Clare.

The fact that Bokenham is remembered in the will of John Baret of Bury— "successful clothier, landowner, financier and civic leader" (Gottfried, 156)— suggests that he had some familiarity with the area's provincial urban elite. The bequest, made to Osbern specifically rather than to the Clare friars as a group, indicates personal acquaintance. The amount was modest but not stingy: it was half of what Margaret Odeham left in 1492 to the entire priory at Clare, one-third what Agnes Stubbard left in 1418 to the entire priory there, and several times more than Baret left to each of the friars at Babwell near Bury (Tymms, 73, 2, 35). Baret made no provision to the Clare priory itself for repair or church art or for prayers in his own behalf, thereby supporting the likelihood of a personal rather than an institutional relationship. Since the "limitation" of Bury, covering fifty vills or subdivisions, was one of the circuits visited regularly by the brothers at Clare (Harper-Bill, 6), there could have been intermittent personal contact over a period of decades. But because the item occurs twenty pages into this long will, obviously neither the amount nor the beneficiary was of primary concern. That pride of place was held by the bequests to men at St. Edmund's Abbey with whose names the will begins. These are the powerful individuals who had most affected Baret's municipal, commercial, and personal life. Nonetheless, even with its prestigious history and connections, Clare Priory was not in the same league as St. Edmund's, and I suspect that Master Osbern, whether as confessor or beadsman or literate friend, was a relatively marginal acquaintance. Perhaps he met the busy merchant through the latter's niece, Katherine Clopton Denston, who was—as we will see—a friend and patron of the friar. Baret married Elizabeth Drury, who was Katherine's aunt (Woodforde, 111). Hence Baret was uncle by marriage to one of Bokenham's named patrons and the bequest itself may have been a favor to a cherished niece.

John Baret is not named in Bokenham's *Legends,* but several others among the local gentry and nobility are designated as patrons and friends. Of Isabel and John Hunt, mentioned at the end of the Dorothy (4976–78), I have found no trace. For the others, though, enough information survives that the figures come alive in their familial and political dimensionality, with their loyalties and tragedies, their romances, and their ambitions and rivalries.

The prologue to the life of Anne says that this legend was written "for your sake, my frende Denston Kateryne" (1466), and at the end of Anne's life, this dedication was broadened to include the lady's family:

Provide, lady, eek that Ion denstone	Provide, lady [St. Anne], also that John Denston
& kateryne his wyf, if it plese the grace	And his wife Katherine—if it please
Of god above, thorgh thi merytes a sone	God's grace—through your merits may have
Of her body mow have or they hens pace,	A son of their body before they die,
As they a dowghter han, yung & fayre of face,	As they have a young and pretty daughter
Wyche is anne clepyde in worshyp, lady, of the,	Called Anne in honor of you;
& aftyr to blysse eterne convey hem all thre. (2092–97)	And after [they die], bring them all to eternal bliss.

Denston, a village located between Clare and Bury, had close connections with the Clare family, since those who held the honor of Clare owned a large part of Denston parish. John Denston was a relative newcomer to the neighborhood, the family having then been seated at Denston Manor Hall for only three generations. John was the coroner and justice of the peace, and with other businessmen he negotiated a loan to the king. He died in 1473, after having founded a chantry college in Denston—that is, having endowed a *collegium,* or group of legally incorporated colleagues, in this case priests who would be responsible for the perpetual chanting (*cantaria*) of prayers and masses for the founder and those he designated (Cooke).

Denston did well for himself in marrying Katherine Clopton, daughter of Sir William Clopton of Long Melford. Her half brother John Clopton was soon to be an important person in the area: sheriff of Norfolk and Suffolk in the early 1450s, executor to many wealthy men, and a major benefactor of the parish church, whose patronage was held by—that is, whose priests were appointed by—the abbot of Bury St. Edmund. Between 1439 and 1446 this was William Curteys, also bishop of Rochester. In 1451 Margaret Paston advised her husband to "trust not to the sheriff for no fair language."

Despite this warning, in 1454 Clopton became engaged to a Paston. Although he and his brother-in-law John Denston met with John Paston to negotiate property, the marriage did not take place. The distrust still had not evaporated by 1470, when the Pastons are still warning one another to "be well ware of Clopton." John Clopton was Lancastrian in his political sympathies, and in 1461 he was arrested by the earl of Worcester, constable of England, along with several others—John de Vere, twelfth earl of Oxford, and his heir Aubrey, Sir Thomas Tuddenham, John Montgomery, and William Tyrell—on suspicion of having received treasonous letters from Margaret, queen of Henry VI, then in exile in Scotland. All except Clopton were beheaded on Tower Hill in February 1462. Thereafter Clopton, like so many others, toed the line; he survived into old age and died in 1498.

There is a Clopton chantry chapel in Long Melford Church, not far from Clare, where several Cloptons are buried. The church windows show a portrait of John Denston and his and Katherine's daughter, Anne, who, despite Osbern

Bokenham's prayers, remained their only heir; Anne married Sir John Brough-ton (see figures 1 and 2).

Bokenham's life of St. Katherine is dedicated to two patrons of that name, Katherine Howard and Katherine Clopton Denston.

Of kateryne Howard to gostly consolacyoun,	For the spiritual consolation of Katherine Howard
And to conforte eek of Denstoun kateryne. (6365–66)	And also for the comfort of Katherine Denston.
Also, lady, for thi katerynys two,	Moreover, lady, for your two Katherines,
Howard & Denstoun, I beseche also. (7363–64)	Howard and Denston, I also pray.

Katherine Clopton Denston's father, William Clopton, died in 1446, when Bo-kenham most probably composed his version of this legend, and perhaps it is this loss for which the friar extends the comfort of his prayers.

Katherine Howard was the daughter of William Lord Moleyns of Stoke Poges, who was killed at the siege of Orleans (1428–29); her sister Eleanor's wardship was held by Thomas Chaucer (McFarlane, 99 n.). Katherine's relation with the Clare convent was especially close: in 1445 she was given a letter of con-fraternity, a method by which the Austins acknowledged the contributions of important benefactors by extending to them a kind of lay spiritual membership (Roth, 1.212–14, 2.327). Katherine married John Howard, a strong Yorkist later distinguished in the service of Edward IV; Howard's estates were concentrated around Sudbury, Clare, and nearby Stoke. In 1461, when Howard was sheriff of Norfolk, he brawled with John Paston over elections to Parliament. After years of ambassadorial service to Edward IV, Howard was made duke of Norfolk; he was moneylender to the king, a patron of the arts, and a book collector and an-cestor of the Tudor poet Henry Howard, earl of Surrey. But Katherine did not live to see her husband's final greatness, for she died in 1465.

Katherine Howard's daughter Elizabeth is another of Bokenham's patrons, named in the prolocutory to Magdalene and in the life of Elizabeth:

. . . Seynt Elyzabeth, whos lyf . . .	. . . St. Elizabeth, whose life
I newly had begunne to ryme,	I had recently begun to compose in verse
At request of hyr to whom sey nay	At the request of her whom I neither
I neythyr kan, ne wyl, ne may,	Can, will, nor may deny,
So mych am I bounden to hyr goodnesse,	So much am I indebted to her goodness:
I mene of Oxenforthe the countesse,	I mean the countess of Oxford,
Dame Elyzabeth ver by hyr ryht name,	Dame Elizabeth Vere, to use her proper name,
Whom god evere kepe from syn & shame. (5046–56)	Whom God always keep from sin and shame.

FIGURES 1 and 2 John Denston and Anne Denston Broughton, husband and daughter of Bokenham's friend and patron Katherine Clopton Denston. Portraits in Long Melford Church, Suffolk. Photos by John Anderson, Long Melford.

And syngulerly helpe, thorgh thi
  specyal grace,
I the beseche, to dwelle wyth the there
Aftyr this outlaury, dame Elyzabeth
  ver. (9535–36)

And especially help, through your
  special grace,
I beg you, Dame Elizabeth Vere
After this outlawry [i.e., life]
To dwell with you there [in heaven].

And fynally, lady, to the trew entent

Of hyr attende wych specyally
Thy lyf to make me yaf comaunde-
  ment,
And the in hert lovyth ful affecteuosly.

I mene Dame Elyzabeth ver, sothly.
  (10609–13)

And finally, lady, hear the true
  intentions
Of her who specially
Commanded me to compose your
  legend,
And who loves you with heartfelt
  affection:
I mean Dame Elizabeth Vere.

Elizabeth Howard married John Vere, twelfth earl of Oxford, in or before 1425: both partners were very young, in their teens (see figure 3). For financial reasons, this was not the marriage the king's counselors had intended for the young nobleman, and Vere was fined two thousand pounds for marrying without royal permission. Although he was a minor and thus claimed ignorance of his guardian's failure to obtain the license, Vere lost his case and spent years paying his fine (Griffiths, *Reign*, 101). It is a convenient coincidence that this real-life love match is repeated in the life of the saint after whom the countess is named, for Elizabeth of Hungary and her German husband lived (according to the legend) an exceedingly harmonious domestic life despite opposition to their marriage. Although emphasizing the foreign couple's mutual affection, Bokenham tactfully omits from his version the element of opposition.

In 1441, the countess of Oxford accompanied her husband to Rouen, in the retinue of the duke of York, along with Isabel Bourchier and her husband (Griffiths, *Reign*, 85). As already mentioned, in 1462 she lost her husband and her son Aubrey to a charge of treason. They were executed at the Tower and buried in front of the high altar in Austin Friars, London (Roth, 2.348).

The life of St. Agatha is dedicated to Agatha Flegge.

To Agas Fleg attende, o blyssyd lady;
And hyr to purchase help swych grace,
Owt of this werd or she do pace,
That she may have deu contrycyoun.
  (8340–43)

Hear Agatha Flegge, o blessed lady,
And help her to obtain such grace
Before she passes out of this world
That she may make proper contrition.

Agatha was the wife of John Flegge, knight, administrator, and business associate of some of Bokenham's other patrons. In 1440 Richard of York appointed Flegge as keeper of his great park at Bardfield in Essex and in 1443 as the warren there. Flegge also served with Richard in France during the 1440s; he is listed as captain at Pont l'Evêque in 1441, Bernay in 1444–45, and Conches

FIGURE 3 Elizabeth Howard de Vere, Bokenham's friend and patron, daughter of Katherine Howard, also a friend and patron. Portrait in Long Melford Church, Suffolk. Photo by John Anderson, Long Melford.

in 1447 (Marshall, 235, 241). About 1447 the Flegges' daughter Joan married Sir Theobald Gorges of Somerset, another knight of York's affinity who had accompanied him to France during his first (1436) appointment there. The match was generously supported by the duke, to the tune of five hundred *livres tournois* and later two hundred *salus d'or* (Marshall, 73). Flegge and his wife Agatha jointly held from Richard several grants of land, principally in the honor of Clare, where Flegge was the duke's bailiff until at least the 1460s. He is probably the same John Flegge of Needham in Suffolk who, between 1469 and 1477, was farmer of the ulnage—that is, collector of the tax on the sale of woolen cloth (Johnson, 232; Thornton, *History,* 148).

Above all, Bokenham boasts of his friendship with the most highly placed and well-descended of his aristocratic patrons: Lady Isabel Bourchier, countess of Eu. Noble by birth, she had also married into one of the most influential families in England. She lived at Clare Castle, next door to the priory. In the prolocutory to Magdalene's life, Bokenham sketches the lively celebration at Lady Bowser's (Bourchier) on Twelfth Night, 1445, when the noblewoman commissioned the Magdalene translation. He observes her "foure sonys ying/ Besy . . . wyth revel & wyth daunsyng" (5023–24; her four young sons busy with revelry and dancing). Isabel had six sons in all, of whom three died as a consequence of the civil wars. The brief pedigree that Bokenham offers for this lady emphasizes her descent from King Pedro of Spain (5010–15; we will return in chapter 7 to this lineage). She was also doubly descended from Edward III: in the maternal line via Lionel of Clarence and in the paternal line via Edmund, duke of Langley. Her father, Richard Langley, earl of Cambridge, had been beheaded by Henry V for treason in an alleged attempt to place his brother-in-law Edmund Mortimer on the throne (the Southampton plot of 1415), and she was, as Bokenham points out (5007–8), the sister of Richard, duke of York. Besides being a literary patron of the friar, Isabel and her husband were benefactors of the priory. In 1454, for instance, Henry Bourchier was the prime mover in a donation by several people of twelve acres released to the priory in mortmain. In return, the friars were required to sing a daily mass for Duke Richard, his family, and other donors (Roth, 2.334).

Richard was landlord of Clare Priory and of the surrounding neighborhood, for on the death of the last Mortimer in 1425, he had succeeded to the Clare lands. The badge signaling his lordship of Clare showed "a black bull with horns, hooves and members of gold" (Allan, "Political Propagander," app. 3). He also succeeded, of course, to a great deal more in practice and in potential: "He was inescapably heir not only to the earldom of March but to the whole Mortimer inheritance, with its claim to the English throne. This Mortimer legacy was a real one, alive throughout Richard's minority, and it could not readily be swept under the carpet" (Johnson, 27). As lord of the honor of Clare, Richard in 1445 endowed the town of Clare with a school taught by the priest of the Guild of St. John the Baptist (Redstone, 178).

By the time of this benefaction, Richard had already been counselor to the king, twice governor of England's territories in France, and military commander there. While his sister entertained the neighborhood worthies, Richard was in Normandy. In March 1445 he met Margaret of Anjou, King Henry's controversial bride, to escort her to Rouen, the capital of English France. (In a few years Queen Margaret became York's archenemy.) He completed his term as lieutenant governor in the autumn of 1445 and returned to London in October.

Later, Richard was named protector of England during Henry's fits of temporary insanity, and in 1460 he laid formal claim to the throne on the basis of a descent superior to that of the incumbent Lancastrian. Besieged in his castle at Sandal, Yorkshire, Richard "refused to await reinforcements, saying 'he had never kept castle in France even when the Dauphin came to besiege him, and he would not be caged like a bird.' He sallied out and was killed" (Rosenthal, 175)—a kind of death by gallantry, not unlike Sir Philip Sidney's in the following century. Three years after her brother died, Isabel and her husband Lord Bourchier (by then earl of Essex) were granted a chantry by the friars at Clare "in return for their numerous benefits, especially the gift of six acres in Stonyland" (Roth, 2.347). The document was signed by, among others, Master Osbern Bokenham.

Isabel's husband, Henry, viscount Bourchier, was only somewhat less distinguished in lineage than she was: his descent from Edward III was through the line of a younger son, Thomas, duke of Gloucester. Bourchier's brother Thomas was archbishop of Canterbury and a cardinal, and Henry was eventually treasurer of England (1455) and earl of Essex (1461–81).

The circles of acquaintance and patronage surrounding Clare Priory thus comprised many who had been or would be touched by violence and intrigue at all levels of government and many who would in the coming years play a significant role during an especially disturbed period of England's national history. For the moment, as Bokenham composed his legendary between 1443 and 1447, the worst was yet to come, although as we will see in chapter 7—when some of the persons and issues mentioned here will resurface—the important issues had already taken shape.

BOKENHAM WAS NOT the only writing friar at Clare. His housemate John Bury composed a long refutation of the theological errors of the anti-Lollard but protorationalist Bishop Reginald Pecock. Bury's treatise, the *Gladius salomonis* (1457), was requested by Thomas Bourchier, archbishop of Canterbury, the brother-in-law of Bokenham's patron Lady Isabel Bourchier. Bury also donated to a Carthusian house a copy of Chaucer's *Boece*, along with assorted religious materials (Roth, 1.521).

Nor was the *Legend* Bokenham's only work: several others can be attributed to him either positively or probably. Indisputably his is the *Mappula angliae* (about 1440). It translates part of the Benedictine monk Ranulf Higden's early-fourteenth-century *Polychronicon,* an encyclopedic history and one of the most famous books in England. From Higden, Bokenham imitated the acrostic in which the initial letters of the chapters form the translator's name. There is a reference to Joan of Acre's grave at Clare ("one the sowthe side"), with the assertion that it lies whole and incorrupt, just like the many saints' bodies with

which, as Higden asserts, God's merciful pity has singularly illumined and ir-
radiated the people of England (chap. 5). Bokenham's first name appears in a
concluding Latin distich which, the author says, can be used as a prayer for his
salvation:

Cum sint Osberni data vermibus ossa sepulti,	When the bones of buried Osbern are given to the worms,
Spiritus alta petat, in pace deique quiescat.	His spirit will seek heaven, and rest in God's peace.

This work describes the advantages, marvels, geography, cities, administrative
divisions, and dialects of England. As for the marvels, "whetheir they byne alle
sothe or no, y reporte me to hem the wche byne moore experte in suche thyngys
thane y. For y wylle neither afferme hem for trewthe ner condempne hem for
fals" (chap. 5). The work ends with a rather charming "epiloge excusatorie"
apologizing for the writer's linguistic rudeness (specifically the local dialect of
his youth) and revealing the acrostic.

According to its author, the *Mappula* grew directly out of a previous project:
a compilation of saints' lives (not the *Legends*) that mentions various English
places and to which the *Mappula* is therefore intended as a *vademecum* composed "at the instaunce of my specialle frendis and for edificacioun and comfort
of alle tho the whiche shuld redene hit or here hit . . . for the more clerere
undirstandynge of the seid thyngis and otheir" (chap. 1).

This miniature literary autobiography shows an interesting sense of self and
audience, an attitude not unique to the period but probably better represented
among secular than among clerical authors (e.g., Chaucer, Hoccleve, and Christine de Pizan). The earlier hagiographical compilation may have been lost, or it
may be the prose collection entitled the *Gilte legende*. This collection exists in
eight manuscripts, all from a version made before 1438 and translated from
Jehan de Vignay's French version, the *Légende dorée,* of Jacob da Voragine's thirteenth-century *Legenda aurea*. A version of the *Gilte legende* was printed by Cax-
ton in 1483. Scholars remain divided about the attribution to Bokenham.[9]

Probably by Bokenham are two other, shorter, works. One is a translation of
Claudian's fifth-century panegyric on the soldier-consul Stilicho, *De Consulatu
Stilichonis.* According to a manuscript note, the work was written at Clare in
1445. The text, a facing-page translation or close paraphrase, gives the English in
Troilus stanzas, and the unique manuscript (BL Add. 11814), bound in white
leather, is illuminated with several Plantagenet and York badges (some with
gold) and other decorations. Certainly the syntax and the imagery resemble Bokenham's, and particularly some of the references clustered in section 22 of the
English duplicate those found in his Mary Magdalene prolocutory, also written in
1445. The other work possibly by Bokenham is "Dialogue at the Grave" (1456),[10]
recounting the genealogy and descendants of Joan of Acre. The political significance of these two apparently innocuous pieces is discussed in chapter 7.

Besides these extant works, Bokenham mentions in the life of St. Anne (2080–82) his Latin stanzaic verse treatment of Anne and her three daughters, all named Mary, but this has not been located. Another Latin work, the *Liber de angelis,* was ascribed to Bokenham by N. Toner with no argument for the attribution, nor was any argument offered by B. Hackett in denying it ("Note," 246); the attribution is also accepted by Leader. This short work exists in a unique copy at Cambridge University Library (Dd.XI.45, ff. 134v–39, item 10), and both its incipit and explicit specify "quoth Bokenhamus." This is not, however, our Bokenham but another with very different interests.

To be sure, angelology was a legitimate concern of scholastic speculation— Giles of Rome composed at least three treatises on the topic (Trapp, 248), and many other famous theologians wrote on it as well. But the *Liber* is no scholarly tract. It is a text of voodoo magic, mumbo-jumbo charms, fairytale motifs, and symbols from alchemy and astrology. With its mystical characters to be written in the blood of a sacrificed wild fowl or (if it is Monday, day of the moon angel) of a river eel; with its white wax images, its conjured black horse that will take you wherever you want to go, its guarantees of success in love and hatred, this bizarre little text could only be abhorrent to an orthodox master of theology. It could not conceivably have been composed by Osbern Bokenham of Clare.

THE WORK THAT I CONSIDER in this book, Bokenham's legendary, came after the *Mappula,* composed, according to its own statements, between 1443 and 1447. It exists in a unique manuscript in the British Library, Arundel 327. There is also a fragment of it—the opening lines of the life of Dorothy—on the last leaf of BL Add. 36983, a miscellany probably of Bedfordshire provenance (Edwards, "Transmission," 167). The fragment is without title or attribution and shows a number of minor variants from the Arundel manuscript. It suggests that at least some of the legends may have circulated separately, particularly those that, like the Dorothy, the author says were composed first, before 1445 (5040–46)—the point when, I argue in chapter 2, he reconceived his work as an artistic whole. Such circulation of short devotional booklets was typical of the period, although we know, too, that the complete work was given by Friar Thomas Burgh to his sister's convent in 1447, as the colophon informs us. The manuscript of the legendary is untitled, but Mary Serjeantson, who edited it for EETS, extrapolated her title from the author's description of his work as "divers legendys . . . Of hooly wummen" (5038–40), and I have therefore taken *Legends of Holy Women* as a working title.

Three verse forms are used in the *Legends:* rhymed couplet, the ubiquitous Troilus stanza (ABABBCC), and the Monk's Tale stanza (ABABBCBC), which occurs in some East Anglian drama of the fifteenth century and is sometimes called the Marian octave. There is a good deal of rhyme linkage between stanzas in the stanzaic portions, and the Anne prologue uses a double-reverse Marian stanza to achieve a sixteen-line unit in its celebration of Mary's mother. Some, though not all, of these complexities were highlighted by the scribe, who drew brackets, in red ink, connecting rhymed lines, a common scribal practice in fifteenth-century manuscripts. The diction and syntax are often ponderously latinate, especially when the author is reaching for a rhyme. When reading the *Legends,* it is impossible not to notice how much livelier the poetry is in those sections that use the flexible couplet form than it is in the more rigidly demanding stanzaic portions. The meter is rugged, using both four- and five-stress lines and often irregular within the line. When Bokenham apologizes for his lack of polish, he is to some extent indulging in the conventional modesty topos, for his management of rhyme and rhetoric is skilled enough, but his metrics surely warrant the disclaimer. On the other hand, his metrics are not unlike Lydgate's, or those of other fifteenth-century poets, about which scholars have spilled much ink. It is possible with Bokenham, as with Lydgate, that there is method in the madness, although I confess I have not been able to discern it.

What else do we know about Bokenham? He was an attentive reader of Chaucer, a debt to be discussed in chapters 2 and 3. He wore spectacles. At the age of fifty he considered himself old and expected to die before completing the work at hand. These details are reported by the author himself (899, 245–46), along with constant reminders of his mood and plans, travel and friends, aesthetic principles and difficulties in working (especially in translating Ambrose on Agnes; 1417–21), and even the length of time a translation took: "dayis fyve" (7367) for Katherine. This is the sort of personal tone and detail that prompted Carl Horstmann, in commenting on the *Mappula,* to characterize Bokenham as a writer whose *autoreitelkeit* (authorial vanity) could not wait for the Renaissance.

But more than egoism is at play here, for what Horstmann noticed can be set in a wider context than individual subjectivity. For one thing, a style was deliberately chosen. Some reasons for this choice are discussed in later chapters; here I observe only that such details are consistent with other aspects of Bokenham's style. There are several references to the red or bloody flux, in this work the disease of choice for minor characters. The persecutor-villains suffer from "melancholy" (a superfluity of black bile believed to cause depression and insanity) while the martyrs maintain a healthy color and a cheerful disposition. This physiology is traditional to hagiography, but not every hagiographer includes it or makes as much of it as Bokenham does. In Margaret, the author's pen is represented as a blunt-snouted animal tired from its exertions, making blots as a sign "that for the beste / Were for us bothe a whyle to reste" (905–6; that it were best if we both rested a while). In Magdalene, the naked abandoned child is seen "on chyldryns wyse besyly pleying, / And smal stonys on-to the see castyng" (6056–57; playing busily as children do, throwing little stones into the sea). We have, then, a very *embodied* figure of the author who gives us a distinctively embodied cast of characters.

This quality seems consistent with a stylistic earthiness that coexists with the elaborate latinity of syntax and vocabulary in much of the *Legends.* "Not worth a flykke!" (2957; not worth a flitch [of bacon]) says the persecutor Julian of a magician's tricks. Or, exhausted after completing the Margaret, the author writes that he feels like a weary pilgrim desiring only a little food and drink and then "his bonys aftyr in a bed to beyke" (887; afterward, to beak his bones in bed). *To beak* is to heat unseasoned wood at the fire in order to straighten it (see *Catholicon,* 29, for additional instances).

In both places, Bokenham borrows phrases from domestic and artisanal life. In doing so, he participates in an English hagiographical style already defined by the late-thirteenth-century *South English Legendary* and the earlier Katherine group, whose colloquialisms, dry humor, and vivid concreteness of detail have often been noticed, most recently by Jankovsky. Yet these stylistic features are by no means typical of hagiography—certainly not of Voragine, Bokenham's primary source. And if the author or authors of *SEL* do use homely proverbs and details or offer a personal opinion, they still do not reveal birthdays and states of health or discuss pilgrimages and social engagements.

In this regard, Bokenham's authorial—or at least narratorial—presence is closer to that of secular writers like Chaucer or Hoccleve than to most hagiographers. To be sure, in Bokenham's style, we sometimes hear the plain Suffolk village boy speaking alongside the Cambridge student of Latin classics. But we also hear the master in theology and ecclesiastical administrator well aware of a newly popular theology of the body: the international trend in late-medieval devotional literature, art and sermon that dwelled on the embodiedness, the real humanity, of Jesus.

Chapters 4, 5, and 6 show how Bokenham's corporeal semiotic carries this theology, and chapters 7 and 8 explore some of its political consequences or implications. Not least, though, what we hear at such points as the ones just adduced is the poet as such, making space for himself in the narrow room of hagiography. Bokenham's blunt-snouted pen may not have been free to engage the world at large, but I believe it performed quite well nonetheless. I find myself in agreement, therefore, with an earlier appreciator, Gordon Hall Gerould, who wrote, "Though a somewhat crabbed poet, Osbern was a poet still. . . . He was personal, just as he was classical, because he expressed the temper of his age" (188–89).

Several sorts of bodies—textual, biological, and institutional—form the organizing principle of this book. In choosing this strategy, I commit neither wordplay nor mere contemporaneity (two practices equally offensive in the eyes of some scholars). Although contemporary scholarship is indeed interested in the body and its representation and management from many points of view, that concern is far from being only modern, or even only Western (cf. O'Neill). For the Middle Ages, the metaphoricity of body was so basic, ubiquitous, and unquestioned a paradigm as to constitute what Medvedev and Bakhtin call an "ideologeme" (17, 21–25). It shared this status with the book and with the building, all three objects capable of referring to one another and to many other things as well.

Much of what Jesse Gellrich has written and compiled about the cultural function of images of book and architectural space can also be said of the body. All three can function in the mythic–ideological register because of the richness of their symbolism: what they are and what they can therefore represent. Body, book, and building are structured systems; they are or can be seen as models of orderly and harmonious arrangement, indeed of divinely imposed order if one thinks of their primordial instances, circumstances, or principles. They offer, too, images of containment—that is, frame or boundary, a clear definition of inside and outside—an order of another kind (Douglas, chap. 7). They can be thought of as instances of completion or totality. And last, each constitutes a signifying system that communicates information to those equipped to read or interpret it; one thinks here of the double meaning—textual and medical, still valid today—of *doctor*. The Latin word *membrum* conveniently encapsulates the range of metaphoricity addressed here: limb of a body, division of a treatise or sermon, chamber in a house, participant in a church or a state. As Marie-Christine Pouchelle observes, "Tout comme au moment de l'Incarnation, le verbe . . . a pris corps, la métaphore, loin de n'être qu'un artifice rhétorique, est à tout moment susceptible de s'inscrire dans le réel, et tout particulièrement dans le corps" ("Représentations," 296; Just as, at the moment of the Incarnation, the word took on body, so metaphor—far from being only a rhetorical device—is always able to be inscribed in the real and, above all, in the body).

It would be possible to cite Jacques Derrida in support of these remarks (e.g., *Of Grammatology,* 14–18), or Julia Kristeva (*Powers of Horror,* 66–67), but Virginia Woolf puts the case more poignantly, that is, more personally and therefore more uncompromisingly:

> I . . . suppose that the shock-receiving capacity is what makes me a writer. I hazard the explanation that a shock is at once in my case followed by the desire to explain it. I feel that I have had a blow; but . . . it is or will become a revelation of some order; it is a token of some real thing behind appearances; and I make it real by putting it into words. It is only by putting it into words that I make it whole; this wholeness means that it had lost its power to hurt me; it gives me . . . a great delight to put the severed parts together. Perhaps this is the strongest pleasure known to me. It is the rapture I get when in writing I seem to be discovering what belongs to what. . . . From this I reach what I might call a philosophy; . . . that behind the cotton wool is hidden a pattern; that we—I mean all human beings—are connected with this; that the whole world is a work of art; that we are parts of the work of art. *Hamlet* or a Beethoven quartet is the truth about this vast mass that we call the world. But there is no Shakespeare, there is no Beethoven; certainly and emphatically there is no God; we are the words; we are the music; we are the things itself. And I see this when I have a shock. ("A Sketch of the Past," in *Moments,* 72).

Later chapters elucidate and illustrate my foregoing remarks, for I argue that Bokenham relies on corporeal metaphor in structuring his legendary and in producing the doctrinal meaning of his text. My text, in turn, though not structured like a body, avails itself of this traditional metaphorics as a taxonomic device. The body of literary tradition comes first, in chapters 2 and 3, the written corpus with which an author must establish a relationship in order to write. My particular focus is Bokenham's ambivalence toward the work of his great predecessor Geoffrey Chaucer and especially toward Chaucer's *Legend of Good Women*. Next, in chapters 4, 5, and 6, I consider the corporeal bodies of the women saints whose legends are recounted in Bokenham's collection, with the theological and moral implications of the poet's particular representational practice. Chapters 7 and 8 turn to the living individuals—some of whom we have already met—who were Bokenham's patrons and audience. I consider their role in the "community of the realm," or body politic, and the historical situation in which Bokenham's work as a whole intervenes. Finally, chapter 9 takes up some issues of historicist and feminist theory relevant to my argument about the sexual politics of Bokenham's legendary. If his text has until now remained virgin territory, so to speak, to literary criticism and historical analysis, it is no less responsive to the methods of semiotics, rhetorical analysis, historicism, and gender-conscious scholarship than are other, more widely known texts.

The Literary Corpus

A collection of female saints' lives seems a perfectly obvious idea to us now. It seems especially so for the Middle Ages, when hagiography was what Charles Jones calls "the popular form of creative literature from the sixth through the tenth centuries" (chap. 4) and what Janet Coleman ranks high among popular genres in "the literature of entertainment and delight" (42–43) during the later Middle Ages. Curious, then, that the first free-standing all-woman legendary in English should have come as late as mid-fifteenth century, that it generated no imitators, and that the subgenre did not reappear until some two centuries later when an anonymous Jacobean author compiled a prose collection ("Lives," ed. Horstmann) showing no evidence of familiarity with the earlier work and differing from it markedly.

The time was ripe for such a project as Bokenham's. The previous century had seen the efflorescence of the *devotio moderna* and the development of a new tradition of affective piety among both laypeople and religious, with the emphasis on a personal, passionate attachment to the persons of Jesus and his saints. In this trend, women played an important role as subjects and objects of devotion, and if by Bokenham's day the new piety had somewhat abated from its fourteenth-century peak, it nonetheless remained a powerful influence in spiritual life. This was the case especially in East Anglia where Bokenham spent his life and where he might well have met both Margery Kempe and Julian of Norwich, exemplars and products of the new piety. On the Continent, women often led small pietistic or even heretical groups or banded together to perform devotion and charitable works (e.g., the Béguine movement). In England, women Lollards traveled and taught, sometimes risking their lives to do so. Norwich is the only English town known to have had communities of devout laywomen resembling the continental *béguinages* (Tanner, *Church,* 58, 64). Ann Warren shows that during the fifteenth century, Norfolk had thirty-nine anchorites (about evenly divided between men and women)—more than any other county in England except Yorkshire, with fifty-one (app. 1). The surviving East Anglian art of the period reveals intense local devotion to several women saints, a phenomenon that E. F. Jacob describes as follows:

> In Scandinavia, in England (especially East Anglia) and in parts of Germany, an emotional mysticism was claiming the attention of many who at an earlier date might have become orthodox academics or remained among the silent mortified devout. . . . The rich iconography of East Anglia in the fifteenth century points to something more than the stock work of a few firms of masons. There is a fine tangle of legend and fancy linked with the names of those popular saints of local devotion: St. Barbara, St. Dorothy, St. Edmund the king and martyr, St. Katherine, St. Margaret. It was the age of the women saints. (*Essays,* 155)

We know already that Bokenham could count on a small audience of secular women patrons among the local gentry and nobility. A secondary audience of ecclesiastical women was also present, for the endnote to the manuscript of Bokenham's legendary says that the copy cost thirty shillings and was given "onto this holy place of nunnys," although the place is not named. There was, after all, a tradition of pious books composed for nuns and devout laywomen.

Some of the best known of these texts had an Augustinian connection: the *Ancrene Wisse* (late twelfth or early thirteenth century) was composed for three anchoresses, probably by an Augustinian canon (cf. Dobson). Walter Hilton, an Augustinian canon (d. 1396), composed his *Ladder of Perfection* for a woman about to be enclosed. The *Mirror of Our Lady* was written for the Brigittine convent at Sion, which had a strictly reformed Augustinian rule (and a high level of devotional–literary activity), documented by Ann M. Hutchison. Capgrave's prose life of St. Augustine was composed for an anonymous gentlewoman born on St. Augustine's day, and his life of St. Gilbert was intended for the nuns at Sempringham.

In addition, the nuns themselves sometimes wrote. For example, the twelfth-century Benedictine nun Clémence of Barking composed a life of St. Katherine of Alexandria and may also have written a life of St. Edward Confessor. The Anglo-Norman life of St. Audrey was composed by a nun, Marie (Wogan-Browne, "Rerouting"). Continental nuns composed *Nonnenbücher,* collective biographies of the convent's members, and nuns often worked as scribes of ecclesiastical documents or liturgical compilations (Ancelet-Hustache; Van Dijk and Walker, 230, n. 1). The English Austins had two houses of nuns in Suffolk and one in Norfolk, as well as several small houses of Austin canonesses. For all these literary and social reasons, active female participation in religious life was the norm in the mid-fifteenth century.

An authoritative source, the Catholic liturgy, may also have influenced Bokenham's authorial decision. In the Sarum (Salisbury) rite, which was the standard pre-Reformation use in the south of England, the prescribed litanies for Holy Week concluded with separate lists of male and female saints. According to the *Catholic Encyclopedia* (s.v. Sarum), this was a distinctive feature of the rite: "An interesting feature of the Sarum Breviary is its inclusion of Scripture Lections for the ferias [weekdays] of Lent. The Lections, taken from the writings of the Fathers and from the legends of the saints, were often disproportionately long and obviously needed the drastic revision they received after the Council of Trent." The format was twelve or thirteen male saints followed by twelve female saints, concluding with the prayer "omnes sanctae virgines orate pro nobis" (Procter and Wordsworth, 2.251–59). We find, therefore, the following lists: For *Feria ii in Quadragesima* (Lent Monday), Mary Magdalene, Mary Aegyptica, Scholastica, Petronilla, Genoveta, Praxedis, Sotheris, Prisca, Tecla, Afra, and Editha. For Tuesday, Felicitas, Perpetua, Columba, Cristina, Eulalia, Eufemia, Eugenia, Gertrudis, Ragenfledis, Batildis, Anastasia, and Etheldreda. For Wednesday, Agatha, Susanna, Brigid, Barbara, Marina, Martina, Felicula, Julita, Sapientia, Fides, Spes, and Charitas. For Thursday, Caecelia, Fides, Austroberta, Emerentiana, Potentiana, Oportuna, Sophia, Juliana, Beatrix, Crescentia, Walburgis, and Ermenildis. For Friday, Lucia, Katherina, Sabina, Justina, Eufraxia, Fausta, Monegundis, Aldegundis, Radegundis, Pientia, Benigna, and Wallingis. And for Saturday, Agnes, Benedicta, Martha, Helena, Euprepia, Candida, Basilissa, Balbina, Ursula, Victoria, Cosma, and Sexburgis.

It happens, however, that whereas the Augustinian monks and canons tended to follow the liturgical use of the diocese in which they were located, the Austin friars were specifically committed to the Roman rite. Indeed, as Roth notes with pride, "the mighty Cardinal Protector Richard Annibaldi (d. 1276) . . . made the liturgical usage of the Papal Curia binding upon the Order" (1.191). Pfaff warns against a too-neat division among various uses in a network of factors including "provinces, dioceses, religious order, and religious houses, and the nature of certain geographical areas . . . the special liturgical role of cathedrals . . . [and variation] within the religious orders" (6). Still, in the Roman use itself (of which the Sarum and other English uses were variants), the litany for Holy Saturday includes, over the rubric "omnes sancte virgines et vidue, orate," the following twelve female saints: Maria Magdalene, Felicitas, Perpetua, Agnes, Lucia, Cecelia, Agatha, Rufina, Secunda, Anastasia, Sabina, and Petronilla (Van Dijk and Walker, 517).

I do not wish to overstate the case for Bokenham's originality in composing an all-female hagiography, for there were partial models and antecedents even apart from Catholic liturgy. Guy Philippart notes that the *liber virginum* or "legendier des femmes" was a type of early Latin legendary insofar as the sex division was a common mode of classifying lives in the Latin collections. Following this taxonomic convention, the Anglo-Saxon scholar Aldhelm divided his treatise *De Virginitate* (ca. 680) into separate sections on male and female virgins. About 1305, the Franciscan friar Nicholas de Bozon composed, in Anglo-Norman couplets, the lives of nine female saints. In one manuscript—BL Cotton Domitian A. XI— these are preceded by a similarly versified gospel version of Jesus's life. The lives in this series have been edited piecemeal, but they have not been presented or discussed as possibly a unified work. My examination of the Cotton manuscript convinces me that they might constitute a deliberate set with the *evangile* as prologue, although I am not prepared to hypothesize here whether this would have represented an authorial decision or a later scribal/editorial gathering and recension.

Finally, in 1405 Christine de Pizan compiled a set of women's legends as a short portion (about one-seventh the total) of her otherwise secular *consolatio, Le Livre de la cité des dames*. Christine's work was well known in England and could easily have been known to Bokenham. Among the mid-fifteenth-century East Anglian readers of Christine's work were Alice Chaucer de la Pole, duchess of Suffolk, who owned a copy of the *Cité* (Meale, "Patrons," 208),[1] and the Paston family, whose scribe billed them for a copy of Christine's *Othea* (Paston, 2, item 283). Another copy of the *Cité* is associated with Richard, duke of York, because its first page is decorated with the fetterlock and white rose badges of the House of York. Meale suggests that Richard could have bought it while in France or that it could have been bought for—or by—his wife, Cecily Neville, "herself a notable book-collector" (". . . alle the bokes," 135).

Although it might therefore be inaccurate to claim that Osbern Bokenham invented the female legendary as such, nonetheless it is fair to say that he reinvented it. As Philippart observes, "Chaque époque a vu naître une littérature hagiographique originale" (105), and Hippolyte Delehaye describes hagiography as a series of "textes perpétuellement rajeunis" (*Passions,* 260). I hope to show how original the Austin poet was, within the constraints of his calling and his literary genre. He chose the female legendary not as a system of classification, not to illustrate the virtue of virginity or to exhort his readers to it, and not generically subsumed within another kind of writing, but as a freestanding, carefully crafted, and distinctive instance of a very demanding genre. As with most cultural phenomena, there is no single answer to account for his choice. Rather, as this and later chapters will show, it was based on a confluence of several factors: patronage and audience, textual antecedents, theological trends, and political events of the day.

THIS WAS THE CONTEXT, and in the remainder of this chapter, I shall argue that there was also a pre-text, a model and precursor found not in ecclesiastical literature but in that of the educated laity. There was in recent English verse a well-known collection of lives of good women; it associated itself with hagiography by appropriating for its title the traditional name for hagiography, yet it was not hagiography but a parody of that genre. I am referring to Geoffrey Chaucer's *Legend of Good Women* (1386), which borrows the title of a saint's life, or legend, as well as its great theme: suffering. I have argued elsewhere that Chaucer's parody was not written at the expense of the saint's life but, rather, at the expense of the all-too-secular lives his poem portrays, lives measurable by their very distance from those of saints (*Naked Text,* chap. 1).

There is no reason to doubt Chaucer's sincere respect for hagiography, although it is not a genre he was frequently drawn to. His *Second Nun's Tale* of St. Cecelia is drawn fairly faithfully from the *Legenda aurea,* the immensely influential thirteenth-century compilation by Jacob da Voragine, archbishop of Genoa. The lost "Origenes upon the Maudeleyne" referred to in the prologue to the *Legend of Good Women* (F 428) is presumably a translation of a homily on Magdalene, falsely attributed to Origen. And the numerous references to saints used throughout Chaucer's work are a kind of touchstone from which a fictional speaker can be judged. I argue in this book that Bokenham's legendary is modeled on Chaucer's, although not in the simple, adulatory way that might be expected from one who often invokes the great trio of Chaucer, Gower, and Lydgate. On the contrary, in a curious and perhaps unique episode in literary history, Bokenham parodies his predecessor's parody in order to rehabilitate the original. If Chaucer parodies hagiography ultimately to validate it, if his aim is to expose the moral shortfall of desire, Bokenham misreads Chaucer to criticize (what he sees as) Chaucer's courtly classical *jeu d'esprit* and to revalidate orthodox hagiography in an unambiguous way.

BEFORE PROCEEDING TO the evidence, I need to consider an important objection to my argument: The kind of systematic tale-by-tale alignment of Chaucer's and Bokenham's texts that I have discerned does not seem consistent with Bokenham's somewhat haphazard compositional procedure for his legendary. This procedure is probably reflected—as Edwards observes—in the codicological features of the unique manuscript, with its three scribal hands and varied decorative styles ("Transmission," 157–62). From internal evidence it is possible to reconstruct the five-year gestation of the complete work, which was not written in exactly the order the manuscript presents.

The end point can be no later than 1447, for an explicit reference to the manuscript gives 1447 as the date when Bokenham's "son" (this could mean godson, former pupil, recruit, or younger friend) Friar Thomas Burgh,[2] of the Cambridge convent, had the text copied at a cost of thirty shillings and then gave it to his sister at an unspecified convent of nuns. The prologue to the work states that the author's inspiration for one legend—that of Margaret—was the request of a dear but unnamed friend who was especially devoted to that virgin (175–80). Perhaps this friend was Thomas Burgh, who is named a few lines farther on as recipient of "this symple tretyhs" (203–21). After some deliberation, Bokenham says, he began the project on September 7, 1443.

The next dating in the text is in the Magdalene prolocutory. On Twelfth Night (January 5) 1445, Lady Isabel Bourchier commissioned a translation of the life of Mary Magdalene. In reporting their conversation, the author reveals that he has already translated several other lives, not only Margaret's, done two years earlier, but also those of Anne, Dorothy, Faith, Christine, Agnes, and Ursula with her eleven thousand virgins. Bokenham adds that he has also recently started a life of St. Elizabeth of Hungary at the request of another noble patron, Elizabeth Vere, countess of Oxford. He thus asks Lady Isabel to defer the Magdalene project until he can complete a pilgrimage to Santiago de Compostela in Spain. Assuming that the journey was made soon after the interview, we can safely date the Magdalene and its prologue to 1445, probably the second half of that year. This leaves, therefore, the lives of Katherine, Cecelia, Agatha, and Lucy for 1445–47. We cannot know the exact order of composition of these last four, any more than of the earlier nine.

Of Bokenham's thirteen lives, then, three were (according to him) commissioned explicitly: Margaret, Magdalene, and Elizabeth. These became the first, middle, and last in the completed set, with Elizabeth relocated to the final position, although written before the five lives preceding it in the final text. (Magdalene is not the precise numerical middle, coming eighth rather than seventh in the sequence. But if lines are counted, it does straddle the midpoint of the work.) Some readers may assume that because a commissioned life is externally determined, it could not enter into the Chaucerian imitation I propose. This would be an excessively mechanistic view, however, failing to take account of actual social relations or the stubborn perseverance of creative will. For one thing, we have no way of knowing what actually went on between patron and poet, nor whether the commissioned life was initially hinted at or chosen by the poet. In other words, even a commissioned life could well fit a poet's established plan. Moreover, the author himself presumably chose the ten other lives not said to have been commissioned.

Paul Strohm has suggested that the collection "is untitled, perhaps because Bokenham did not think of it as a unified work" (161). This argument *ex silentio* is unpersuasive. The manuscript, though untitled, is not a holograph, and in any case, titles are often problematic. Chaucer's *Legend of Good Women* is a case in point. None of its manuscripts uses that title, which, as with Bokenham's collection, was extrapolated from the text (F 482–84); other manuscripts and other Chaucer works give different versions of the title (see *Riverside Chaucer,* 1179).

Furthermore, in both cases it is the text itself that requires examination, and I hope to prove that Bokenham's collection displays two types of unifying structure that can only have been deliberate: one is sequential and the other is metaphorical. The sequential ordering, or metonymic structure, is a deliberate parallel with Chaucer's *Legend,* whereas the metaphorical structure is that of the composite textual body formed by the various body parts emphasized in the legends. Does this double schema seem impossibly complex? It is no more so than the comparable double schema of Chaucer's "Absolon" ballade in the prologue to his *Legend,* a lyric that manages to combine in its short compass a double and doubly signifying onomastics: one in the semantic register and another and contrary one in the semiotic (Delany, *Naked Text,* chap. 4).

I believe that Bokenham's selection of lives and his arrangement of them in a final version were deliberately aligned with the sequence in Chaucer's *Legend of Good Women.* I do not maintain that this was his intent from the very start in 1443, but the finished product shows that at some point, it became his aim. Chaucer's own work in progress, the *Canterbury Tales,* is another instance of such evolution toward coherency: it is a collection of short miscellaneous pieces eventually incorporated into a structural framework and acquiring an internal dynamic of its own. What becomes clear about Bokenham's legendary is that the correspondences to Chaucer's mock legendary are consistent through the first ten lives, that their order follows that of Chaucer's *Legend,* and that their number is statistically far beyond coincidence.

IN CHAPTER 3 I SHOW that although Bokenham's critique of Chaucer is distinctive, his general use of Chaucer certainly is not. Bokenham several times praises the trio of Chaucer, Gower, and Lydgate in what was virtually formulaic homage by fifteenth-century writers. He also appropriates Chaucerian verse forms, as did many other poets of that century. Moreover, it is not uncommon to find secular influences, including political propaganda, permeating the pious literature composed by ecclesiastics. Hagiography itself is a deeply syncretic genre, having over the centuries incorporated Eastern and Western folktales, classical myths and legends, adventure stories, political propaganda, biographies, travel literature, and romances. Capgrave brings into his *Life of St. Katherine* echoes of Chaucer's *Troilus* and other romances, and the Brigittine nuns at Sion, near London, were evidently familiar with the *Troilus* (Colledge, 1.40, 48; Pearsall; Stouck).

The means by which a highly literate friar might come into contact with contemporary poetry were several. Personal ownership is not out of the question, for friars and monks of various orders, as well as secular priests, could and did own books, some of them as bibliophiles able to make substantial contributions to their own or another house. The fourteenth-century Austin John Ergom was one such book lover who left his massive collection to the priory at York (see Cavanaugh; Humphreys). Bokenham might well have owned one or several works by Chaucer or a collection that included a number of Chaucer's works.

We have no reason to think that Chaucer's *Legend* was held in the library at Clare Priory, even though larger Austin houses such as York did possess a fairly wide range of what looks to us like secular literature in addition to the expected patristics, scholasticism, sermons, and scriptural commentary. At the great Augustinian library in York, this nonecclesiastical material included Geoffrey of Monmouth's *Historia,* "prophecie Merlini," and other Arthurian texts; "comedie Terencie"; Aesop's fables; Dares and Dictys on the Trojan War; the *Alexandreis* of Gautier de Châtillon; the *Ilias* of Simon Aurea-Capra; Goliardic verse; virtually everything by Ovid, Juvenal, Horace, Virgil, and Claudian; as well as many works on medicine, mathematics, natural science, and astronomy. Of course, much of this material, however secular in original intent and in our view, would be grist for the predicatory mill in one way or another. Nor can we be certain what meaning might be wrung from a secular text. Julia Boffey, commenting on the association of a manuscript of the *Parliament of Fowls* with two nuns of Sion monastery in 1518, notes the poem's "countenancing of the possibility of a life of celibacy" ("Evidence"). Both Chaucer's *Troilus* and a distich attributed to Ovid made their way into a moral treatise, *Disce mori,* composed in the 1450s, probably also at Sion (Patterson). It would certainly not be difficult for Chaucer's *Leg-*

end to be seen—much as Ovid's *Ars* or *Remedia amoris* were seen—as a source of classical learning, an illustration of artful rhetoric, and an exemplary lesson on the folly of erotic excess.

In fact, the *Legend* was generally considered a morally edifying work, though perhaps caviar to the general, to judge by recorded references and imitations. Edward, duke of York, quoted the poem in the prologue (addressed to his cousin King Henry IV) of his hunting book called *Master of the Game* (1406–13): "As Chaucer saith in this prologue of the xxv good wymmen. Be wryteng have men of ymages passed for writyng is the keye of alle good remembraunce" (Spurgeon). Lydgate's list of Chaucer's oeuvre in *Fall of Princes* (1430) describes the *Legend* as incomplete because the author had been unable "in all this world to Fynde so greet a noumbre" of good women as originally intended for inclusion. This misogynistic gibe was rebuked by an anonymous lyricist represented in the Fairfax manuscript, who may have been the third husband of Alice Chaucer (the poet's granddaughter), William de la Pole, duke of Suffolk. In his verse critique of Lydgate, the Fairfax poet proceeds to imitate Chaucer's *Legend* and to praise its author for a properly positive attitude toward women (Janssen, *Edition;* MacCracken, "English Friend"). Lydgate himself twice imitated the *Legend* in his *Life of Our Lady* (1.302–9, 5.407–13), a work composed in 1421 or 1422. Obviously Lydgate had Chaucer's text readily available for consultation and considered it a suitable source for his own serious hagiography.

We know that patrons lent books to clerics and that clerics lent books to one another—indeed, this seems to have been something of a tradition at Clare (cf. Humphreys, 5). The mutual permeability of categories among lay and clerical readers and texts is evident in Julia Boffey's account of the following transaction: "Still in East Anglia, but rather later in the century [than 1473], Richard Dodyngton, a priest at Foxearth, in Suffolk, bequeathed a 'balett boke' to Sir William Clopton of Long Melford, along with his copy of *The Canterbury Tales* and 'oon prynted prymer'" (*Manuscripts*, 134).

Despite these connections and interpenetrated milieux, on the whole I think it unlikely that a contemporary, vernacular, and courtly work—even one with moral, classical, and rhetorical significance—would be owned by a small ecclesiastical library. A more plausible source for Bokenham would be the loan of a volume from a noble patron, much as Humphrey, duke of Gloucester, lent books to Lydgate (Lucas, 232), or from a member of the local gentry. As Meale points out, the buying public was coming more and more to include the middle classes ("Patrons," 202). The format could have been an anthology such as the Bodleian's manuscript Tanner 346, which dates from the 1440s or earlier (Robinson), or it could have been a booklet of the *Legend* by itself, for Chaucer's works circulated in both forms (see Meale, "Text and Book").

My reading of the alignment of Bokenham's legendary with Chaucer's text finds Bokenham working with at least the number of legends we now have and in the order we now have them. And if Bokenham's "yive feyth & ful credence"

(7875) was borrowed from Chaucer's "yive . . . feyth and ful credence" in the prologue (F 31), then he had the F prologue before him and not G, for that phrase does not occur in G. Nor does the hyperbolic adoration of the daisy that I believe Bokenham targets occur in G. Given Bokenham's rather comprehensive critique of the courtly classicizing literature of his day (discussed in chapter 3), an anthology that included Chaucer's *Legend* with F-text prologue, various Lydgate poems, some satires or parodies of religion, and assorted erotic lyrics would provide appropriate targets for the friar's analysis.

Several clear Chaucerian echoes—not to the *Legend* alone—can be found in Bokenham's legendary. Bokenham's wish to "forge and fyle" his rhetoric (408) may imitate the action of Cupid, who is seen to "forge and file" his arrows (*PF*, 212). Although this sounds like an alliterative formula, *MED* lists only these two occurrences before 1450. Bokenham's Margaret has "bent browes blake" (450), just as Chaucer's Alison has "browes . . . bent and blake as any sloe" (*MilT*, 3245–46). For Agnes, Jesus is "to me . . . a wal inpenetrabyle" (4327), much as for Criseyde, Troilus was "to hire a wal / Of steil" (*TC*, 3. 479–80). In the legend of Cecelia, Bokenham's odd term *corniculer* (7990) for the officer Maximus could come from Chaucer's *Second Nun's Tale* (8.369), although the word—referring to a horn-shaped helmet ornament—also occurs in an earlier version of the legend.[3] The Sicilian pilgrims who travel to Agatha's shrine are evoked with a syntax and vocabulary that recall their more famous English analogues:

Whan thorgh the provynce . . .
The gloryous fame dyvulged was
Of the blyssyd virgyn seynt Agas . . .
Whom for to seken wyth an holy entent
On hyr festful day mych peple went
From every plage of the seyd Cecyle,
And specyally from Syracuse . . . (9019–28)

Whan that Aprill, etc. . . . .
Thanne longen folk to goon on pilgrimages, . . .
And specially from every shires end
Of Engelond to Caunterbury they wende,
The hooly blisful martir for to seke . . . (Chaucer, *General Prologue*, 1–17)

The long "when" clause, the geographical specifications, the strategy of narrowing focus, and the words *seek, specially from,* and *from every* constitute the distinctive and memorable rhetoric of the opening lines to Chaucer's *Canterbury Tales*. No fifteenth-century reader could have missed the open and deliberate intertextuality here. Voragine—Bokenham's source for Lucy—has none of this, disposing of the journey with the single economical sentence "Lucia virgo Syracusana nobilis genere audiens famam sanctae Agathae per totam Siciliam divulgari, sepulchrum ejus adiit cum matre sua Euthicia annis quatuor fluxum sanguinis incurabiliter patiente" (30: The highborn Syracusan virgin Lucy, hearing the fame of St. Agatha spread all over Sicily, went to her tomb with her mother Euthicia, who had suffered the bloody flux for four years).

Before moving into the structural alignment with Chaucer's *Legend,* I would like to demonstrate that a principle of selectivity is indeed at work in Bokenham's collection. This will be a negative argument to preface my positive argument, for we need to grasp how many the possibilities were and why so few of them were taken up. Annie Samson contends that the selection of saints is a key consideration in "constructing a context" for the *South English Legendary.* I make the same claim for Bokenham and suggest also that selection is likely to be a major factor in understanding the work of any compiler of hagiography.

Bokenham's collection is neither alphabetical nor historically chronological in arrangement. Unlike Voragine's *Legenda aurea* (Bokenham's primary source) or John Mirk's well-known fifteenth-century *Festial*, its martyrology is not coordinated with the liturgical year, which begins with Advent (late November or early December). Nor is it, like the *South English Legendary,* coordinated with the calendar year. Unlike some collections, it is not arranged hierarchically according to degrees of sainthood from apostles, evangelists, and gospel saints down through early martyrs and confessors.

The litany lists cited earlier show what a profusion of women saints were available, and some of Bokenham's omissions might be thought surprising. For instance, he did not choose to write a life of Monica, mother of the claimed founder of his order, whose feast was established in 1388. Nor did he choose Scholastica, sister of St. Benedict who wrote another important rule. He did not write about Petronilla, daughter of St. Peter, although she was famous locally, and several of her relics were held in East Anglia. Her skull, "preserved in the abbey [at Bury St. Edmunds] was considered efficacious in sickness" (Clay, 256). Accordingly, there was a hospital of St. Petronilla in Bury, and John Lydgate composed, about 1434, a legend for "blessyd Pernell."

Bokenham also did not include the Virgin Mary, whose cult—staffed by Augustinian canons—at the prosperous shrine at Walsingham, Norfolk, was famous internationally; for English pilgrims it was second in popularity only to Canterbury. Moreover, the Virgin Mary was Clare's patron saint (Roth, 1.259). But none of the female saints distinctively associated with East Anglia appears, not even the well-known Etheldreda (Audrey), the seventh-century princess whose shrine at Ely was popular with pilgrims, or her sister Withburga, whose shrine was at East Dereham near Norwich (Williamson, 307, 309). In fact, there is not a single English saint in the collection, despite a plentiful number available and despite such a precedent as John of Tynemouth's fourteenth-century *Sanctilogium angliae,* which was reedited in the fifteenth century, probably by Bokenham's colleague Capgrave.[4]

Nor did our author choose to write about more than one modern saint, if Elizabeth, dead for two centuries, can be seen as "modern" for the time. Not even the recently canonized St. Bridget of Sweden makes an appearance, although her *Revelations* was a standard devotional tract in the fifteenth century and her newly established (1415) convent of Augustinian nuns at Sion was supported by King Henry. Bridget was famous enough that one of her prophecies was quoted in the rather unlikely context of the record of a 1445 French embassy sent to negotiate peace with Henry VI, whose recent marriage to the French princess Margaret of Anjou would—the writer hoped—be "a great cause of peace, and good opportunity for it, as Saint Brigide had said, 'Volo quod fiat pax per matrimonium'" (Stevenson, *Letters,* 1.139). Bokenham even omitted Barbara, whom he claims, along with Faith and Cecelia, as his "valentine" (8278) and who was one of the three most popular female saints depicted on East Anglian rood screens.[5] In light of such omissions and dissimilarities, I believe I can offer a convincing explanation of why Bokenham chose the saints he did and why they appear in the order they do. As we will see, the resemblances to Chaucer's *Legend* are not necessarily verbal imitations. Although verbal imitation is not absent, the dominant types of echo or parallel are imagistic and structural, as might be expected from an artful poet.

Both Chaucer's and Bokenham's collections open with a "marguerite" as the object of the Narrator's devotion. Chaucer's "marguerite" is a daisy, and Bokenham's is St. Margaret, the flower and the woman linked by their shared French name. It is also true that "marguerite" can mean "pearl," which is the connection made in *Legenda aurea,* which immediately specifies *gemma* in the very first line of its chapter on Margaret and makes no mention of the daisy. Yet Guillaume de Machaut links daisy, pearl, and St. Margaret, as does Lydgate,[6] and Chaucer acknowledges the daisy–pearl equivalence by giving Alceste a crown made of an oriental pearl (F 221–22; G 153–54), for she personifies the daisy.

Bokenham's etymology, although modeled on Voragine's, maintains a careful ambiguity. Instead of opening with the pearl association, he defers it until some fifty lines into his own account, when he does finally use the unambiguous word *gem* (291). Nowhere does Bokenham use "Margaryte-pearl" (as Thomas Usk does in *Testament of Love,* 2:4) or attribute roundness to the marguerite (as does *Pearl,* lines 5, 738). Instead, he borrows from Voragine the description of a marguerite as "whyht, lytyl, and eek verteuous" (251), qualities of either gem or flower, inasmuch as both these small white objects were thought to possess medical virtues or powers. It appears, then, that by deferring and diminishing the pearl association, Bokenham left open the possibility of recalling the daisy and thus Chaucer's poem. As if to underline this possibility, Bokenham echoes the Chaucerian text. Both Chaucer's daisy-marguerite and Bokenham's saint-marguerite are invoked as the muse of the work just begun, Chaucer's to preside over "my wit . . . my word, my werk" (F 88–89) and Bokenham's to illumine "my wyt and my penne" (333–36).

The second object of Chaucerian devotion is Alceste, companion to the god of (erotic) love and sponsor of the legends to follow. Alceste's fame was due to her willingness to die in her husband's place, descending to the underworld in his stead until rescued by Hercules. Bokenham's second life is that of St. Anne, mother of Jesus' mother and hence in lineal and physical contact with the god

of (spiritual) love. The prologue to this life is filled with a consciousness of death
and imagery of the underworld. The author claims to be moribund, anticipating
his own death and afterlife. He mentions Proserpina (1456–57), who, like Alceste, was rescued from the underworld, and Orpheus (1460–62), who, like Hercules, journeyed to Hades to rescue a woman. Mary, Anne's daughter, is invoked
as "lady of erthe and empresse of helle" (1503), a reference to the apocryphal
Eastern legend of Mary's descent to the underworld.[7] The point of contact with
Chaucer, then, is imagery duplicating the salient feature of Alceste's story.

Chaucer's first "good woman" is Cleopatra, who was traditionally associated
with three Roman leaders—Julius Caesar, Marc Antony, and Octavian—and
who committed suicide by snakebite. Bokenham's third saint, Christine, is also
associated with three Roman officials, her three persecutors: her father the prefect Urban, his successor Dyon, and the judge Julian. Christine, too, is exposed
to snakes as a means of death, but rather than bite her, they worship her. Both
stories include a major sea scene. In Chaucer it is the disastrous battle of Actium,
and in Bokenham it is the saint's triumphant ordeal in the sea, which she survives by walking on water (2550 ff.). Here the intertextual relation is of similar
motifs, but with contrasting value or outcome.

The story of Thisbe, Chaucer's second tale, narrates the engagement of a
young couple, offspring of feuding parents. Circumstances prevent the marriage
and lead to the young couple's deaths away from home. The same structural
outline constitutes the plot of Bokenham's fourth legend, that of St. Ursula with
the eleven thousand virgins. Ursula, daughter of the king of Brittany, is be-
trothed to the son of her father's enemy, the king of England. Requesting a delay
in the marriage, Ursula sets out on a pilgrimage with her companions; they are
massacred by pagans, and her fiancé is killed with them.

Chaucer's tale of Dido, his third, focuses on the bed as the key image and
locus dramatis. Aeneas's chamber has "riche beddes" (1107) on which the hero
spends a good deal of his time in Carthage; Dido tosses and turns in bed
(1165–67), and so does Aeneas (1292); their long dialogue occurs in bed; and Aeneas sneaks away while Dido is in bed, which then becomes the site of her long
lament. Repeating the image is Bokenham's fifth life, that of St. Faith of Agen,
who is stretched and bound to a "bed of bras" (3715)—a grill or "grydyl" (3728:
griddle)—and roasted. Bokenham would have found both bed and grill in his
Latin source for this legend and in visual representations of the saint, for these
objects served as her emblems.[8]

The two stories give us, therefore, two beds of torture: one the site of erotic
activity and erotic discourse and the other the site of doctrinal commitment in
word and deed. This contrasting parallelism—*cupiditas* redressed by *caritas*—
extends throughout the tale of St. Faith. Of course, the narrative may have been
meant, even in its urversion, as an anti-Dido, a deliberate contrast to an exceedingly well known classical figure. Nor need such modeling surprise us, given the
constant dialogue with the classics that shapes so much Christian writing, especially during the late classical period when many of the martyrs' stories were

composed. Michael Roberts shows that Prudentius's poem on the virgin martyr Eulalia, in his *Peristephanon* (late fourth century), not only uses Virgilian phrases but also echoes scenes and structures, several of them related to Dido as an antitype (92–97).

Thus if Bokenham parallels his Faith with Chaucer's Dido, he is not the first to have "rewritten" Dido from a Christian perspective. In its barest structure, the Faith story shows numerous similarities to the Dido episode, even apart from the bed imagery. In one of the best-known scenes from the *Aeneid,* Dido and Aeneas make love in a cave during a storm. The caves on the hillside above Agen are the refuge of Christians fleeing persecution, and from these caves comes St. Faith's convert Caprasius, with whom she is paired in martyrdom. Unlike Aeneas, the Christian hero does not flee the heroine but seeks her out, shares her *passio*. The rainstorm that forces the classical couple into their cave has its analogue in the miracles of water provoked by Caprasius's faith: dew quenching the coals of the saint's torture, water gushing out of the hill. The structure of imagery is maintained, but the image is given a different moral valence: new wine in old bottles.

Chaucer's double legend of Hypsipyle and Medea, the fourth in his set, is matched by Bokenham's version of Agnes and her devotée, Constance; thus Chaucerian sexual rivalry is replaced by Christian partnership. Amnon Linder points out that the Constantia story "forms a sequel to the well-known legend of [Agnes], and it originated as an explanation of the special veneration Constantine and his daughter showed towards her" (73). Although it does appear in Voragine as an addendum along with several other postmortem episodes, the material does not form an integral part of the narrative and need not have been included had Bokenham not had a reason to do so. As we shall see, he both amplified and abbreviated (or omitted) as he saw fit. Prominent in both narratives is the motif of the wealthy suitor. Jason, the Chaucerian seducer, seeks the "famous tresor" of the golden fleece and his wealth is an important selling point in Hercules's praise of his friend (1528–34). Bokenham's Agnes is repeatedly offered treasure, jewels, and land by a young suitor, but she declines marriage on the grounds that her present lover, Jesus, is far wealthier than anyone else. Again, shared structure and imagery become the means of ideological contrast.

For the legend of Dorothy, Bokenham's seventh, the resemblance to Lucrece, Chaucer's fifth, is the fairly obvious one of commitment to chastity. Since this is an important theme in female martyrology generally, it does little to advance my hypothesis. Nonetheless, we may note that Dorothy, like Lucrece, is Roman (many of the martyrs are not from Rome) and that the detail of feet figures memorably in both stories: Lucrece remembers to cover her feet with her dress as she falls (1859), and Dorothy is hung on a gibbet "and upward hyr feet" (4834).

Chaucer's legend of Ariadne, number six, opens in Athens. Minerva, or Athena, the patron goddess of that city, appears in an extended reference (5029–34) in the prolocutory (a kind of prologue to the prologue) to Bokenham's legend of Mary Magdalene, his eighth legend. Minerva enters Bokenham's text not in her conventional capacity as the goddess of wisdom or of war but, rather, as the patron of the art of weaving: she "hath the sovereynte / Of gay texture" (5030–31)—not a unique but an unusual portrayal.[9] The idea derives, as Bokenham notes, from Ovid's *Metamorphoses* (bk. 6), in which Athena's prowess as weaver is affirmed in her contest with Arachne. Thread figures importantly in both this and the next of Chaucer's legends, for Ariadne gives Theseus a ball of thread to help him through the labyrinth, whereas Philomela, like Athena, weaves a storytelling tapestry. Accordingly, Bokenham makes much of the brilliant clothing of his patron's children and guests, whom he delightedly observes at the festive Twelfth Night gathering at which the Magdalene was commissioned. Moreover, in foregrounding Minerva as a weaver, Bokenham necessarily reminds his reader of Arachne, a name orthographically similar enough to Ariadne that the two were often confused in medieval texts.[10] I will comment later on Bokenham's literary–ideological uses of his story of Minerva as weaver; here I shall confine myself to the observation that it provides a gentle reminder of Chaucer's *Legend*.

The life of Katherine, the ninth in Bokenham's set, demonstrates in its action the proper use of rhetoric, for its heroine is an accomplished speaker in both academic discourse and "comown speche" (6499). In Bokenham's version, though not in all others, the major episode is the saint's public debate with fifty sages and orators, and its climax is the utter silence to which her simple profession of faith reduces them. Chaucer's seventh legend, that of Philomela, is also about speech and silence. The raped and maimed heroine, tongueless, communicates by weaving the terrible narrative of her victimization at the hands of her brother-in-law Tereus. "Be ye tunglees?" (6807) Bokenham's enraged emperor baits his failed scholars, the literal body becoming figurative in its passage from Chaucer to Bokenham, and mutilation or incapacity becoming the property not of the heroine but of her opponents. Although Bokenham probably found the image in the Middle English *Seinte Katherine*,[11] it is unusual, as it does not appear in Clémence, Voragine, the *South English Legendary*, or Capgrave. That Bokenham chose to use or retain it suggests, I believe, another connection with Chaucer's *Legend*. (We will examine this image in more detail in chapter 5.)

To the legend of Phyllis, Chaucer's eighth, I have found no correspondence in Bokenham.

Both Chaucer's Hypermnestra and Bokenham's Cecelia are young brides with a secret. Hypermnestra's secret is that she is supposed to kill her husband, and Cecelia's is that she is Christian. In both cases, the secret proceeds from a male authority figure who takes precedence over the husband. For Hypermnestra this figure is a possessive and tyrannical father, and for Cecelia it is Jesus. In both cases the secret is revealed, bringing the couple closer together and honoring the marriage bond, if not in the usual way. Hypermnestra's husband escapes on their wedding night, and Cecelia and her husband vow to remain celibate. Again we find the shift from literal to metaphorical, physical to spiritual, erotic to religious, that typifies Bokenham's revision of the Chaucerian legendary.

With St. Cecelia, Bokenham apparently ends the alignment of his work with Chaucer's *Legend of Good Women.* Hypothetically, since that text is evidently unfinished, Bokenham's last three lives could correspond to a lost portion of Chaucer's *Legend.* As I read Bokenham's legend, though, the last three of his lives—Agatha, Lucy, and Elizabeth—form a peroration whose thematic is to restate an orthodox Augustinian position on the body, particularly the female body and its literary representation. For that reason I shall defer discussion of these last three lives to a later chapter. But if the presence of Chaucer's poem as hypotext to Bokenham's hypertext—I use the terminology of Gérard Genette—can be read as homage to a great predecessor, that is only half the story, for as several of my readings imply, the homage was not entirely uncritical. Next I shall take up the other side of the story, the moral scrutiny to which the Austin friar subjected his nearest literary model, and the ideological dimension to his revision.

The Friar as Critic

Although my chapter title repeats that of a book by Judson B. Allen, it designates neither the same friar nor the same criticism as his book examines. Allen is concerned with exegesis, and his focus is on what Beryl Smalley calls "the classicising group" (*English Friars,* 1) of friars. These are English Franciscans and Dominicans who, during the fourteenth century, applied to classical literature the same kind of exegetical method they used on Scripture. Osbern Bokenham's critique concerns instead the production of vernacular poetry and the literary ethics of the Christian poet. As targets for his strictures on the uses and limits of classicism, might Bokenham nonetheless have had in mind the friars discussed by Smalley? I doubt it, even though he very likely knew their work. To be sure, there was rivalry among the orders as to priority of ancient origin, with the Augustinians seeking senior status over the Franciscans and Dominicans. In addition, the Dominicans did have a reputation for too much learning, the Franciscans for perhaps too little—as St. Bonaventure put it, the Preachers put learning before holiness, and the Minors put holiness before learning (Smalley, *Study,* 258)—whereas the Austins attempted a golden mean, encouraging a certain level of study, but still suspicious of study for its own sake. Although all this might furnish a certain animus or motive, the movement of classicizing friars was finished decades before Bokenham was born, and its members were scholars and not the poets against whom our Austin inveighs.

Even if Bokenham occupied an interval between English humanisms—one clerical and defunct, the other mainly secular and nascent—nonetheless the problematic of classicism was much in evidence during the early fifteenth century, above all in Italy and particularly at Rome and Florence, the two cities with which Augustinians had special institutional connections and to which they often traveled as students, pilgrims, petitioners, observers, and administrators. In return, Clare entertained a fairly constant flow of foreign visitors, for it was one of the seven English Augustinian houses designated as destinations for foreign Austin friars on vacation (Harper-Bill, 11). We know that Bokenham was in Italy at least twice and that some English Austins went to study at the *studium generale* there. The long papal residence at Florence from 1434 to 1443 further ensured a steady stream of English clerical visitors to Italy. One Florentine humanist school was centered on Luigi Marsigli (d. 1394), an Augustinian friar at the convent of Santo Spirito and a leading light of the Florentine humanist avant-garde. Marsigli's disciples Roberto de'Rossi, a translator of Aristotle and other Greek authors, and Niccolò Niccoli (d. 1437) were well known in the first half of the fifteenth century, so there is no reason that an English traveler could not have brought back Rossi's translations to his own priory library. It is not necessary, of course, for us to establish a direct influence or contact (however possible or even likely these may be), only to define an intellectual environment for our educated, literary-minded, well-traveled English cleric.

Quattrocento humanists and their critics pondered questions such as the role of pagan literature in Christian education, the salvation of virtuous pagans, the relative weight of classical and Christian authorities, and the threat of polytheism. One humanist wrote his former teacher in 1416 to suggest a treatise against the narrow-minded, uncultured people—especially the popes—who persisted in destroying Rome's ancient architectural heritage. Somewhat earlier, Francesco da Fiano's invective *Contra oblocutores et detractores poetarum* reported that "in the presence of the Pope, an orator had delivered an address that drew heavily on pagan poets and this had caused resentment among many members of the Curia" (Baron, *Crisis,* 301). The *Invettivo* of Cino Rinuccini, on the other hand, attacked the demoralizing aspects of classicism, especially its ability to undermine civic spirit and family commitment.

The English friar's polemic against overclassicizing poets is more muted than that of his Italian contemporaries. For reasons discussed later in this chapter, it had to be. Yet this polemic does participate in the current of ideas associated with the early Italian Renaissance—as do his attitude toward the body (see chapters 4–6) and his translation of a poem by Claudian (chapter 7). Whom, then, does Bokenham have in mind?

Although Bokenham names no names, I argue that his critique targets the very authors to whom he so often pays tribute—Chaucer, Gower, and Lydgate—along with their French progenitors and English imitators. His purpose is to revalorize—against the courtly classicizers—the Christian aesthetic propounded by the claimed founder of his order. In this sense, the Austin friar-poet might well have seen himself following the founder's literary as well as communitarian path, for Augustine not only conducted a lifelong postconversion literary struggle against the seductions of classical culture but also provided a strongly polemical model of the cultural contrast using a woman as paradigm. In *The City of God* (19–21), Augustine takes up at length the case of the raped suicide Lucretia. Far from sympathizing, Augustine denounces the matron's Roman pride and self-indulgence, setting them against the proper humility of Christian women who prefer to suffer rape or martyrdom rather than to take their own lives against God's commandment. Considering, moreover, that Lucretia is one of Chaucer's "good" women, I think that a corrective impulse for the Augustinian friar's legendary must be inferred.

Other motives might be adduced as well for a criticism of Chaucer and the Chaucerian sensibility. Chaucer parodies doctrine, liturgy, and communal life throughout the *Canterbury Tales*. In particular, his ignominious scatological treatment of a friar in the *Summoner's Tale* could scarcely sit well with a learned Friar Hermit. Nor could his portraits of a venery-loving monk, vain prioress, corrupt pardoner, or randy rapist Cambridge clerks (as opposed to a virtuous and studious Oxford clerk). In fact, Chaucerian anticlerical satire continues to provoke the resentment of regular clergy even today. Here is the vitriolic assessment by a recent Augustinian scholar of the damage done to religion by Chaucer and others:

> Too little emphasis . . . is put on the tremendous harm done by the enemies of monasticism, Wyclif and his Lollards, Langland, Chaucer and their circles. By conscious exaggeration and distortion of existing faults and weaknesses common to all human beings, they created an ugly caricature of religious men and women, and consequently an aversion for the religious life, thus causing a severe dwindling of vocations. We have seen the same forces at work in our own day, for example in Nazi Germany, and it is enlightening to notice that their purpose and methods were the same. (Roth, 1.84–85)

Several factors affect Bokenham's attitude toward Lydgate. Institutional rivalry was one, for regional jurisdictional disputes were common among religious houses in the same area, and competition for land and money bequests was ongoing. Politically, the firm Lancastrian commitment of Lydgate and his establishment must have been viewed with hostility by a Yorkist convent and its inmates. Also, the old competition between monks and friars is not irrelevant to Lydgate and Bokenham. Beside the social reasons for a negative approach to Lydgate, there is also the matter of what and how he wrote. Whatever its motives, the polemical force of Bokenham's critique of his writing peers has primarily a literary focus.

This polemic and the accompanying credo are driven, as one might expect, by Augustinian theology. But by which version of Augustinian theology? A fifteenth-century writer inherited a substantial corpus of quite varied Augustinian work: not only the oeuvre of the prolific founder himself but also a great deal of newer material that displayed a broad spectrum of social attitudes and religious possibilities. Some of this newer material was written by members of the order, some by nonmembers who are labeled Augustinian by virtue of their doctrinal positions.

There was, for instance, the ultrapapalist Giles of Rome, a student of Thomas Aquinas and of the recently translated texts of Aristotle. Giles was the archbishop of Bourges, the general minister of the Hermits from 1287, and the order's major intellectual figure. As the Austins' first master of theology at the University of Paris, Giles's prestige in the order was immense. At a chapter general meeting held in Florence in 1287, Pope Clement designated Giles's work as the order's official line: "All lecturers and students shall accept and defend with all possible zeal every opinion, position or sentence that our venerable master, brother Giles, has written or shall write." (Gwynn, 38).[1]

More intellectually venturesome was Gregory of Rimini (d. 1358), another prominent Augustinian theologian and administrator. Although a strong defender of orthodoxy who polemicized against the most revolutionary thinker of the century (the Franciscan William of Ockham), Gregory was nonetheless influenced by Ockham in some respects and has been considered a nominalist by many scholars in his time and ours. The order's extreme ascetic minority is well represented by the voluntary exile and recluse William Flete. A Cambridge graduate and lecturer, Flete became spiritual counselor to Catherine of Siena, who died in 1380 and was canonized in 1461. Flete's *Remedies Against Temptations* was a well-known book of spiritual counsel in the late fourteenth and early fifteenth century, and his three letters (1380) to his Austin brethren in England urged the most rigorous discipline for the relatively relaxed English province (B. Hackett, *Flete*). A more balanced approach was taken by the canon lawyer and mystic Walter Hilton (d. 1396). Hilton's *Ladder of Perfection* was a popular devotional text among laypeople and clerics alike during the fifteenth century, as was his epistle *On the Mixed Life,* the latter characterized by what Vincent Gillespie calls a "humane tolerance" (98).

The universities produced still other versions of Augustinianism, although not by writers in the order. At Oxford during the fourteenth century, certain debates and methods comprised what William Courtenay dubbed "the new Augustinianism" or "the Augustinian revival." The new "historico-critical attitude"—as Damasus Trapp puts it—of fourteenth-century Augustinian scholars, particularly Gregory of Rimini, prompted Trapp to describe the order as "a cradle of humanism." Steven Ozment, following Trapp, adduces the names of fourteenth- and fifteenth-century Augustinians of several nationalities who can be connected with the development of humanism (18–19).

Did Bokenham participate in contemporary currents of Augustinian thought? Given the variety of Augustinian thought, the answer can only be yes and no. I believe he did use Giles's *De Regimine principum* in his version of Katherine (chapter 8), and obviously he would have been familiar with much more of Giles's work. It is likely, too, that recent controversies over grace and the immaculate conception of Mary, in which Augustinian authors participated prominently, are reflected—or at least form part of the background of—Bokenham's approach to these questions in particular lives (chapters 4 and 5).

With respect to devotional literature, Felicity Riddy proposes that Bokenham "offers Cecelia as a pattern of the mixed life of action and contemplation adumbrated by Walter Hilton and put into practise by devout women" (105). She gives as evidence these lines from Bokenham's version of Cecelia:

Now, blyssyd Cecyle, syth ye be	Now, blessed Cecelia, since you are
Lyle of hevene by chast clennesse,	Lily of heaven through [your] chastity,
Weye to the blynde by perfythnesse	Way for the blind through perfection
Of good werkys, & wyth actyf lyf	Of good works, and were endowed with
Endewyd wer wyth contemplatyf	Both active life and contemplative . . .
. . . (7432–36)	

However, these lines form part of the allegorical exegesis of Cecelia's name and, as such, are fairly faithful to Voragine's emphasis on the saint's blending of spiritual and worldly virtues. Since Voragine precedes Hilton by a century and was Bokenham's main source, it seems unlikely that Hilton is an exemplar here. Moreover, a martyr—of whatever good works—seems a far less suitable candidate as a model of the mixed life than does a more worldly saint, someone like St. Bridget or Elizabeth of Hungary.

It is in connection with Elizabeth that Carol Meale mentions Hilton along with Bokenham, in a more nuanced formulation: "The *Life* [of Elizabeth] which she [Elizabeth de Vere] requested from Bokenham, of the king's daughter who lived the mixed life of action and contemplation within the Christian institution of marriage, strikes a particular resonance in the fifteenth century when Walter Hilton's work achieved a wide circulation among women" ("alle the bokes," 138). That seems to me to strike the right balance, for much of what Bokenham writes is old—far older than the life of Elizabeth of Hungary—but becomes newly relevant in context of late medieval *devotio moderna*.

Returning to the so-called new Augustinianism, we will do well to recall Courtenay's warning that "Augustinianism at Oxford appears to have had little to do with the Austin friars" (310–11) and that many in the order did not hold the positions put forward by university intellectuals. Gordon Leff's remarks on the Augustinianism of Gregory of Rimini seem to me equally applicable to Bokenham if we can substitute "fifteenth century" for Leff's "fourteenth century" and "fourteenth" for his "thirteenth":

> We are presented with what amounts to a transposition of St. Augustine's basic doctrines to the fourteenth century. His teachings . . . are all restated in fourteenth-century terms; and it is as an Augustinian in the literal sense, of owing the essentials of his outlook to St. Augustine rather than to the thirteenth-century Augustinians, that I shall regard Gregory in this book. . . . His outlook is essentially the response of tradition to the changed circumstances of the earlier fourteenth century. (Leff, *Gregory*, 17–18)

It seems to me that, by and large, Osbern Bokenham's theology also goes back to basics, as indeed the "new" Augustinianism itself sought to do. Its hallmarks were, after all, a wider reading in Augustine's works than was common among thirteenth-century theologians, a more thorough documentation of references, and a rigorously antirationalistic elaboration of Augustinian doctrines of grace and free will.

By "basics," I mean fundamental Catholic doctrine and the best-known texts of St. Augustine. In this sense, Bokenham's work fits the generally conservative tenor of Cambridge theology as characterized by J. P. H. Clark, who observes that in the 1390s and afterward, "Cambridge men are regularly to be found on the side of orthodoxy. . . . Cambridge theology must have been content with the received wisdom, and not have sought to go beyond 'the mind of the Church'" ("Cambridge Theology," 15–16). This assessment is reinforced by

Trapp's estimate of the relatively conservative character of Augustinian theology of the same period: "The 15th-century theologians were content to 'return to the great masters,' an attitude hailed by the 'orthodox' because they mistrusted the freedom-loving theologians of the 14th century, hailed also by easy-going scholars because it was so much more convenient to study one author than ten or twenty" (215).

On the level of lay writing rather than university scholarship, Bokenham's work can be seen as of a piece with what Eamon Duffy writes about two other texts from mid-fifteenth-century East Anglia, the Brome book and the commonplace book of Robert Reynes of Acle:

> Both books display . . . a remarkably similar religion. It was a religion in which there was little evidence of the deep introspection and interiority encouraged by monastic and mystical devotional writers, concentrating rather on the objective things of religion, the observance of feast and fast, the changing pattern of the annual liturgy. . . . Neither was greatly interested in the intricacies of doctrine. (*Altars*, 75)

Of course, this does not mean that Bokenham was not acquainted with doctrinal dispute or with the work of modern Augustinian authors, whether of devotional or academic character, for his education and his administrative experience would have provided both. Rather, it means simply that these tendencies were of limited relevance to his legendary.

Two factors—one generic and one individual—were responsible for this distancing. As a genre, hagiography is usually a means of lay instruction. It must remain fairly easily accessible in order to maximize the "lay assimilation of the catechetical programme of the late medieval church" (Duffy, *Altars*, 75)—or, in fact, the church at any period. This purpose, moreover, is consistent with the missionary mandate of the Hermits of St. Augustine and their responsibility for the care of souls. As for the individual element, Bokenham has a distinctive artistic temperament. He is very much in the world, and the politics of that world—as well as some of its poetry—helped him shape his material. Nor does the absence of obvious influence from some modern Augustinian tendencies mean that Bokenham was hopelessly old-fashioned or insulated from contemporary developments in religious theory and practice. I argue in later chapters that his treatment of the body participates in both old and new tendencies and that it affirms his political vision. Nonetheless as an East Anglian, an Austin, and a Cambridge man, Bokenham expresses the refitting of old ideas to the modern world rather than new ideas that could offer a serious challenge to the old.

FOR BOKENHAM, the key Augustinian text is *De Doctrina christiana*, a guide to scriptural interpretation and, in book 4, to "the transformation of Ciceronian rhetoric for Christian orators" (Robertson and Benson, "Introduction," xiv).[2] The very opening of Bokenham's legendary hints at the debt to this particular Augustinian text. In an Aristotelian–academic prologue, Bokenham accounts for the four causes of the work in hand: efficient (the author), material (the subject matter), formal (the system of arrangement), and final (the purpose or motive for writing) causes.

Yet it is not with four that Bokenham begins but with two, for the four Aristotelian causes can be reduced, Bokenham says, to two basic questions: "what" includes the first three causes, and "why" summarizes the last. His formulation thus makes rather free with the academic–prologue genre. It undermines the usual priority of the four-cause scheme, subsuming it instead within the two larger questions. And whereas the usual division offers a double formal cause (*forma tractatus* and *forma tractandi*, or "treatise" and "treatment"), Bokenham instead doubles his final cause, giving as one "why" the desire to stimulate devotion to the saints and, as another, the wish to oblige an old friend who had requested the translation. Clearly, Bokenham feels free to revise the scholarly formulas. His ambiguity about the academic commentary tradition already appears in the revisionism of his opening words, which imitate not those of Aristotle but those of Augustine:

> Duae sunt res quibus nititur omnis tractatio scripturarum (Two are the things on which every treatment of Scripture relies; *DDC,* 1.1, my translation)

Two thyngys owyth every clerk
To advertysyn, begynnyng a werk . . . (1–2)

The intensely physical connotations of "nitor" (the infinitive of "nititur") are important to the Augustinian text. One of its most common meanings is "to kneel," as in prayer or imploring; another is "to strive or strain," particularly in the labor of childbirth—a process that, in late Roman times, was typically performed in a kneeling position. Thus the connotations evoked are of the text itself as a praying and/or generative (female) body, kneeling, as it were, on its two principles of learning and teaching ("inveniendi . . . proferendi"), as Augustine immediately specifies. The image of text as body is a classical, medieval, and Renaissance trope, certainly not distinctive to Augustine. But it is one adapted by Bokenham as an aspect of the poetic structure of his hagiography, as I will show in chapters 4, 5, and 6. Meanwhile, to return to the question of rhetoric, many other verbal echoes of the *DDC* occur in the *Legends,* and I will mention them in context of the explicitly ideological and polemical passages they inspired.

There is much conventional modesty material in the body of Bokenham's prologue: the thorny rose, corn and chaff, ale and dregs, gold growing "In foul blak erthe" (51), a pearl in its shell, and so forth. These items represent the value of the work, a value that endures despite the unworthiness of the author and his supposedly rude composition. As this list itself demonstrates, Bokenham is no stranger to the art of rhetoric. He proceeds to certify his familiarity with one of the most fashionable of the medieval *artes,* the *Poetria nova* of Geoffrey of Vinsauf,[3] even borrowing from Geoffrey the technique of illustrating rhetorically the content of his statement:

The forme of procedyng artificyal	The formal structure
Is in no wyse ner poetycal	Is not even close to poetical
After the scole of the crafty clerk	According to the school of the skilled writer
Galfryd of ynglond, in his newe werk,	Geoffrey of England's innovative work
Entytlyd thus, as I can aspye,	Entitled (as I've noticed)
Galfridus anglicus, in hys newe poetrye,	"Galfridus Anglicus's New Poetry"— [which is]
Enbelyshyd wyth colours of rethoryk	Embellished with colors of rhetoric
So plentuously, that fully it lyk	So plentifully that like it
In May was nevere no medewe sene	Was never seen any May meadow
Motleyd wyth flours on hys verdure grene;	Sprinkled with flowers on green grass;
For neythyr Tullius, prynce of oure eloquence	For neither Tully, prince of our eloquence,
Ner Demostenes of Grece, more affluence	Nor Demosthenes of Greece, never had
Nevere had in rethoryk, as it semyth me,	More wealth in rhetoric, in my opinion,
Than had this Galfryd in hys degre.	Than this Geoffrey had.
But for-as-meche as I nevere ded muse	But since I never did pore over
In thylk crafty werk, I it now refuse,	That elaborate work, I now refuse it
And wil declaryn evene by and by	And will shortly narrate,
Of seynte Margrete, aftyr the story,	According to the story,
The byrthe, the fostryng. (83–101)	St. Margaret's birth [and] upbringing.

Bokenham demonstrates Geoffrey's virtues, and the efficacy of his instruction, in the embellishment of his own language here. The purpose of the passage, however, is not to praise Geoffrey but to reject him. Bokenham's narrative will not proceed, he says, according to the "artificial" or "poetical" arrangement recommended by rhetoricians for the sake of variety, in which one starts with the middle or the end, with an exemplum or a proverb. Rather, his version of Margaret's life will have a natural arrangement, which follows the temporal sequence of events ("The byrthe, the fostryng," etc.; 101) just as the traditional versions do.

The twist noticed in this treatment of Geoffrey is paradigmatic, both paradigmatically Augustinian and also paradigmatic of Bokenham's ambivalent critical stance. Exploring the relation of rhetorical sophistication ("suavitas") to Christian truth, Augustine mentions an epistle of blessed Cyprian that includes some frivolous ornamentation. The verbiage was perhaps included, Augustine speculates, so

> that posterity might know that the sanity of Christian doctrine restrained his tongue from these redundancies and restricted it to a graver and more modest eloquence. . . . Those who admire this sort of thing think that those who do not speak in this manner . . . cannot do so, not realizing that they avoid the manner

deliberately. On that account this holy man shows that he was able to speak in this way, since he did so once, but that he did not desire to do so, since he did not do so again. (*DDC,* 4.14.31)

This, I suggest, is Bokenham's strategy too, showing that he can write in an aureate fashion if he wishes to but has chosen another style deliberately. As we will see, he repeats the point elsewhere in the *Legends.* Did he have Augustine in mind? It is hard not to think so when we note that immediately after the Cyprian passage there occur (in *DDC,* 4.15.32) two other loci that also occur in the *Legends.* Describing the Christian orator, Augustine writes that

> he is a petitioner before he is a speaker. When the hour in which he is to speak approaches . . . he should raise his thirsty soul to God. . . . At the time of the speech itself he should think that which the Lord says more suitable [than rhetorical skill] to good thought: "Take no thought how or what to speak: for it shall be given you in that hour what to speak. For it is not you that speak, but the Spirit of your Father that speaketh in you."

The biblical locus quoted here (Matt. 10:18–20) appears in Bokenham's rendition of the Lucy story (9227–37). The exhortation to pray comes in the prolocutory to Magdalene (5118–33), in which it is attributed to Plato's *Timaeus* by way of Augustine (*City of God,* 8.4).

The modesty topos reappears at the beginning of Bokenham's second life, opening the prologue to Anne. The passage is briefly mentioned by David Lawton as "splendid humbug" from which the poet "has made moral virtue out of poetic deficiencies" (766). This dismissal is too easy, ignoring as it does irony, rhetoric, doctrine, and the rest of the legendary. Contextually, the passage is surely less than splendid and more than humbug. The poet confides that if he had cunning and eloquence, "my conceytes craftely to dilate" (1402)—as did Chaucer, Gower, and now Lydgate—he would translate the life of St. Anne. Intimidated by old age and imminent death, he fears to begin. (Actually, the poet is only fifty and lived at least another twenty years.) This is another variation on the initiatory modesty topos, as Curtius notes (83–84), albeit enlivened with a personified death who "hath at my gate / Set hys carte to carye me hens" (1413–14). Recurrent minor episodes of plague made the cart a realistic image and the fear appropriate. Conventional self-disparagement now gives way to something more generally applicable: the awareness of death that enables a person to live properly:

Wherfore me thynkyth, & sothe it ys,	So I think, and it's true,
Best were for me to leve makynge	It were best for me to quit producing poetry
Of englysh, & suche as ys amys	In English, and whatever is wrong
To reformyn in my lyvynge.	To correct in my life.
For that ys a ryght sovereyn cunnynge:	For that is a supreme knowledge:
A man to knowen hys trespasce, . . .	For someone to know his faults, . . .
He may not fayle, at his partynge	He will not fail, when he departs
Owt of his lyf, to gon to blys. (1417–21)	From his life, to go to bliss.

Advancing age should prompt the writer to shape his life, not the language. As Augustine exhorted in a sermon: "The Lord wants us to sing Alleluia to Him in such a way that there may be no discord . . . in him who gives praise. First, therefore, let our speech agree with our lives, our voice with our conscience. Let our words, I say, agree with our ways, lest fair words bear witness against false ways" (Auerbach, 28). Nonetheless, Bokenham trusts that his poetic efforts will do him good in heaven if Jesus and Mary accept his intention "to excyten . . . mennys devocyon" (1438). These sentiments sound conventional enough, but they constitute the advice with which Augustine concludes his treatise:

> What, therefore, is it to speak not only wisely but also eloquently except to [observe literary decorum?] But he who cannot do both should say wisely what he cannot say eloquently rather than say eloquently what he says foolishly. However, if he cannot do this, let him so order his life [*conversetur*] that he not only prepares a reward for himself, but also so that he offers an example to others, and his way of living may be, as it were, an eloquent speech. (*DDC*, 4.28–9.61)

On that basis, Bokenham once again assures his reader that his own rhetorical roots are not in classical eloquence (1449–64) but in Christian devotion and grace (1465–80).

We come to the heart of the matter with the life of Mary Magdalene and its prefatory material. This is the longest legend of the thirteen and the only legend to have three parts rather than two (a prolocutory in addition to the usual prologue and life). It is the one commissioned by the poet's most distinguished, royally related patron. Although it is not numerically central, coming eighth rather than seventh in the set, the life of Magdalene does straddle the central position with respect to line count, occupying lines 4982–6311 in a text of 10,616 lines (whose exact midpoint would be 5308). Centrality is a numerological device common among medieval and renaissance writers (see Baybak, Delany, and Hieatt; Curtius, "Excursus," 15; Hatcher; Singleton). It is an appropriate formal statement here, for the Magdalene legend is conceptually central to Bokenham's aesthetic and doctrinal concerns.

Let me start with doctrine and the importance of Magdalene, who is distinctive among saints for a number of reasons that help explain her immense popularity. To begin, hers is the only story in this collection to narrate the life of a sinner redeemed. This makes her interesting psychologically, believable, and paradigmatic of the promise of Christianity itself. Mary's own history recapitulates that of every life from its birth in original sin to its salvation by faith. Historically, her life represents the progress of humanity from Adam's fall to redemption by Jesus' death. Mary is also the only apostle saint represented in the collection, the only one in prolonged personal contact with the adult savior and in whose narrative Jesus plays an important role in his human person. Thus the heroine possesses an aura not shared by other saints, whose experience of Jesus was either textually mediated or mystical. The fact that the New Testament itself is the primary source for the narrative adds more weight and interest. In fact, it does so within the story itself, for Mary's scriptural history precedes her in her travels. Speaking to a hermit who follows her to her cave in the wilderness toward the end of her life, Mary says,

"Hast thu ony mynd in þe gospel
Of oon Marye, most famous synnere,
Wych as Luk pleynly doth tel,
Crystys feet wysh wyth many a tere . . .

I am þat same," quod Mary tho . . .
    (6221–32)

"Are you aware, in the gospel,
Of a Mary, the most famous sinner,
Who, as Luke plainly tells,
Washed Christ's feet with many a
    tear . . . ?
I am the one," said Mary then . . .

Next, Mary is distinctive in not being tortured. (Elizabeth of Hungary is also not tortured, but her self-inflicted suffering and her abuse at the hands of her confessor lend a sadomasochistic tone to her story.) In this sense, Mary's legend displays a normality that renders it more accessible to the ordinary reader or auditor than the grotesque horror story typical of martyrological hagiography. Finally, Mary's long career as a distinguished preacher must have appealed to the many successful businesswomen who supported the "new piety" of the fifteenth century.

Given the special features of the Magdalene story and its special placement in the collection, it is apparent that Bokenham constructed an important setting for his poetic credo. It irradiates the text from the center outward, like a virtuous gem set in a ring or the powerful curative relic contained in a shrine. It is here that Bokenham addresses most forcefully the key issues of his aesthetic, administering doctrinal truth as the antidote to a potentially dangerous poetics. What is this poetics? I call it the poetics of the classicizing courtier, and although no one is explicitly named, Chaucer is a prime example of the tendency that Bokenham deplores, with Gower and Lydgate close behind.

The Magdalene material opens with a burst of classical rhetoric and astronomical erudition, giving the date on which the life was commissioned by Lady Bourchier. The passage is so elaborately aureate in diction and imagery as to approach burlesque:

Whan phebus (wych nowher is mansonarye
Stedefastly, but ych day doth varye
Hys herberwe among þe syngnys twelve,
As þe fyrste mever ordeynyd hym-selve)
Descendyd was in hys cours adoun
To þe lowest part by cyrcymvolucyoun
Of þe Zodyac cercle, Caprycorn I mene,
Wher of heythe degrees he hath but fyftene,

And hys retur had sumwhat bygunne.
By wych oo degre oonly he had wunne
In clymbyng, & drow towerd
    Agnarye . . . (4985–95)

When Phoebus (who resides nowhere
Stably but daily changes
His place among the twelve signs
As the First Mover himself ordained)
Had descended down in his orbit
To the lowest part by circumvolution
Of the Zodiac circle (I mean Capricorn,
Where he has only fifteen degrees of
    height)
And had just begun his return,
In which he had gained only one degree
By climbing, and drew toward
    Aquarius . . .

Who or what might be the butt of this parodically overblown rendition? John Gower provides a number of excellent possibilities because of his penchant for arcane modes of dating. Part I of Gower's *Tripartite Chronicle* opens with a riddling date:

Tolle caput mundi, C ter et sex lustra fer illi,

Decapitate *mundi* [lit., the world], give it [the head] three C and six lustrae,

Et decies quinque cum septem post super adde . . .

add five tens plus seven on top of that . . .

This yields MCCCLXXXVII, or 1387. An even better target, one much more similar to Bokenham's parody, appears in the first chapter of *Vox clamantis*. It is an overwrought and overlong astronomical pastiche, a cliché-ridden seasonal description establishing the date as Tuesday, June 11, 1381. This opening movement of 164 lines is translated into straightforward language later in the same book, book 1, when the author says simply, in one line, that this was just before the feast of Corpus Christi (919). Why not say so before? Perhaps the same impatient question occurred to Osbern Bokenham, for in constructing what I am proposing is a parody of Gower, he interrupts his own grandiloquent bombast with just such a question:

But in thys mater what shul I lenger tarye?

But why should I delay this business any longer?

I mene pleynly up-on that festful eve
In wych, as alle crystene men byleve,
Thre kyngys her dylygence dede applye
With thre yiftys newe-born to gloryfye
Cryst, aftyr hys byrthe the threttende
    day . . . (4996–5001)

Plainly, I mean: on that holiday eve
When, as Christians believe,
Three kings did their duty
With three gifts to glorify
Christ on the thirteenth day after his
    birth . . .

It is typical of Bokenham's style that the adjective "newe-born" is a squinting modifier. It might go with "Christ," imitating the Latin habit of separating adjective and noun, or—with a different and punning sense of "born" as "borne," or carried—it might modify "gifts." Both wordplay and Latin syntactic habits are common in Bokenham's work. The pun, therefore, he allows himself as a rhetorical indulgence, but otherwise Bokenham returns to relatively plain speaking, reformulating the date in terms of its Christian meaning: the feast of Twelfth Night. This move from overblown rhetoric to plain language and from classical erudition to Christian doctrine encapsulates the point Bokenham makes in other ways in the prolocutory. And it is a point—like so many others in the legendary—that Augustine makes as well: "Good teachers have, or should have, such a desire to teach that if a word in good Latin is necessarily ambiguous or obscure, the vulgar manner of speech is used so that ambiguity or obscenity may be avoided and the expression is not that of the learned but of the unlearned . . . . He who teaches should thus avoid all words which do not teach" (*DDC*, 4.10.24)

We next learn the reason for all this specification of date: Twelfth Night, 1445, is the occasion when Bokenham attended a celebration, doubtless at Clare Castle, sponsored by his landlord's sister: "In presence I was of the lady bowsere [Bourchier]" (5004). The prolocutory accordingly moves to a genealogy of Lady Isabel and Richard of York (discussed at length in chapter 7) and then to a description of the hostess's four young sons and other guests dancing in their gaily colored finery. Bokenham's rhetoric here takes us to the heart of his aesthetic concerns. No flowered meadow, he writes, could be more brightly colored than the dancers' clothing, for

as it semyd me	it seemed to me that
Mynerve hyr-self, wych hath the sovereynte	Minerva herself, who controls/excels in
Of gay texture, as declareth Ovyde,	Colorful weaving, as Ovid declares,
Wyth al hire wyt ne coude provyde	With all her wit/skill could not provide
More goodly aray thow she dede enclos	Better clothing even if she incorporated
Wyth-inne oo web al methamorphosyos.	The whole *Metamorphoses* in a single
(5029–34)	tapestry.

The figure of Athena earlier entered Bokenham's text, in the prologue to Agnes's life. She appears there as Pallas and is made to engage the poet in an argument reminiscent of that between the Narrator of Chaucer's *Legend* and his two critics Eros and Alceste. Bokenham's Pallas rules the verbal arts, a position evidently conferred by her supremacy in weaving and hence, by association, in the arts at large. Begging Pallas to grant him eloquence, the poet asks to be led into the meadow of Tullius (i.e., Cicero's *Rhetoric*). But he is rebuffed because, the goddess says, the freshest flowers of rhetoric have already been culled by Gower, Chaucer, and Lydgate. No Arachne he, Bokenham says he will "nevyr-more wyth hyr debate" (4601); instead, he resigns himself to plain writing "aftyr the language of Suthfolk speche" (4064).

This version of the inadequacy topos is itself a successful bit of rhetoric, as is the charming dialogue with Pallas. Moreover, this little scene occurs in a prologue composed of interlinked eight-line stanzas rhymed ABAB BCBC, in which the C rhyme of each stanza becomes the A rhyme of the next. My point is not that Bokenham disingenuously claims the plain-man persona. In fact, the tale of Agnes, though composed in Troilus stanza, does have a fairly straightforward diction. Rather, he aims to demonstrate both his capacity in aureate language and his ability to control it. He must demonstrate his rhetorical skill to prove that art is not simply rhetoric but also the control of rhetoric. He must also flash his rhetorical credentials to avoid being accused of sour grapes: that he lacks technique and therefore underrates it. The demand for control touches the ever-expansive Gower and Lydgate more nearly than it does Chaucer. But it is once again under the aegis of Athena, in the Magdalene prolocutory, that Bokenham broadens his poetic credo and his critique to include the master. The little classical reference harbors an important doctrinal and aesthetic statement.

Athena appears in the Magdalene as an artist. The word *texture,* with its double history as woven and verbal fabrication (textile/text), prepares us for a statement about art, and, indeed, the passage about Minerva continues the manifesto already begun in the prolocutory's opening movement. Bokenham's citation of the *Metamorphoses* refers to Ovid's story of the presumptuous mortal, Arachne, who challenged the goddess's supremacy in weaving. A contest takes place in which Athena produces a tapestry that pictures various divine triumphs, whereas Arachne's tapestry shows the gods in morally dubious escapades. Athena wins not by skill but by force, for in anger she destroys Arachne's masterpiece and, when Arachne commits suicide by hanging herself, transforms her into a spider (*Met.,* 6, 1–145). The story thus works as an exemplum of foolhardy human pride and insufficient respect for a deity, particularly as expressed in art. Bokenham adds that the brilliancy at Lady Bourchier's is such that not even Minerva could surpass it, even if she wove all of Ovid's text into a single pictorial fabric. In this instance, art fails, unable to compete with life. This is the dual position from which Bokenham's legendary mounts its implicit critique of Chaucer: that artists must remember divine power and that life measures art. From this perspective, no courtly classicizer can fully succeed.

After the Minerva passage, Bokenham relates Lady Isabel's commissioning of the life of Magdalene. Before writing, though, he must follow the advice of Plato, in *Timaeus,* in which Plato recommends prayer as a fitting beginning to any work (5118–33). This choice of text is especially interesting because *Timaeus* figured large in philosophical controversies of the high Middle Ages. Its version of creation is blatantly opposed to that of Holy Writ, a juxtaposition that agonized many Christian philosophers over the preceding three centuries as they sought, in a variety of ways, to confront the problem of opposed and mutually exclusive authoritative texts: classical philosophers versus Scripture, eternity of the cosmos versus a magical moment of creation, rationalism versus faith in Scripture.

Such questions were far from unknown in Bokenham's day. In 1277, Giles of Rome, whom every Austin was obliged to read, participated in the controversy surrounding the condemnation of philosophical propositions in Paris. Besides criticizing the condemnation, Giles also composed the treatise *De Erroribus philosophorum* (On the philosophers' errors)—a volume held (in 1318, at least) in the Clare Priory library (Harper-Bill, 88). The seminal error of all the rationalists, from Aristotle through Averroes, Avicenna, and Algazel, was precisely their belief "that nothing came to be in a different state from that in which it had been except as the result of a preceding motion" (cap. 1.3); that is, the eternity of time, motion, and the cosmos is the basis of every other error. There were other channels for these ideas as well, for the problem of rationalism erupted again in the fourteenth century in the work of William of Ockham and his numerous followers at various European universities. The Franciscan's work was engaged by, among others, the Augustinian Gregory of Rimini, and a new round of condemnations took place at Avignon and in Paris. Like many others, Gregory called for the separation of faith and reason, for each has objects specific to it. Moreover, as long as university students and teachers continued to comment on Aristotle's *Physics,* the ancient Greek cosmology would remain an issue.

For Bokenham, however, this was not a problem. Serenely he observes that if pagans were capable of such piety as Plato displays, how much more ought we Christians to do (5134–39)? He is quite willing, therefore, to follow Plato's advice about prayer, producing a prayerful sermon on the Creation, the Fall, and redemption (5143–5213). It is an exemplary lesson in the proper use of classical learning as a stimulus to Christian devotion, not as a substitute for it. Although Bokenham does not quote St. Paul's famous dictum that "all that is written is written for our learning" (Rom. 15:4), his method effectively illustrates it. Even more to the point for my purpose is Augustine's elaboration on this Pauline statement, in *De Doctrina christiana,* 2.40: the interpretation of "despoiling Egyptian gold" which, as Smalley comments, "really boils down to the proviso that a Christian, when studying the classics, must remember that he is a Christian" (*English Friars,* 40).

Like any proper ideologue, Bokenham is not content merely to display the right, he must also correct the wrong. In Augustinian terms, "The defender of right faith and the enemy of error should both teach the good and extirpate the evil" (*DDC,* 4.4.6). Bokenham's prayerlike sermon therefore modulates into a polemic against, first, the abuse of classicism and then the abuse of courtly rhetoric, for these aesthetic practices are contrary to the moral principles just enunciated. Regarding classicism, the poet writes:

Where-fore, lord, to þe alone I crye	So, lord, to you alone I cry
Wych welle are of mercy & of pyte,	Who are the well of mercy and pity,
And neythyr to Clyo nor to Melpomene,	And not to Clio or Melpomene
Nere to noon othir of the musys nyne,	Or to any other of the nine muses
Ner to Pallas Mynerve, ner Lucyne,	Or to Pallas Minerva, or Lucina,
Ner to Apollo, wych, as old poetys seye,	Or to Apollo who, as ancient poets say,
Of wysdam beryth both lok & keye,	Carries the lock and key of wisdom,
Of gay speche eek & of eloquncye;	Of colorful speech and of eloquence;
But alle þem wyttyrly I denye,	But all these I deny utterly,
As evere crystene man owyth to do,	As every Christian ought to do,
And þe oonly, lord, I fle on-to. (5214–24)	And I flee, lord, only to you.

Bokenham was not the only or the first writer of his period to make such a declaration: Gower, Lydgate, John Walton, and John Hardyng also offer instances of the trope.[4] In fact, the rejection of the muses became a poetic topos in the early Christian era, a subset, as it were, of the larger topos, "Contrast between Pagan and Christian poetry," as Curtius labels it, adding, "It [the rejection of the muses] is an index of the rise and fall of ethical and dogmatic rigorism" (235). Yet if the protestation of exclusive religious loyalty has a somewhat formulaic character, it should not vitiate the sincerity of our poet or detract from his distinctive project, for the sentiment is integrated into his work at every

level. Furthermore, if the topos meant anything in the late Middle Ages, it is because some classicizing writers did invoke paganism too liberally for the taste of
those with more austere sensibilities, thus provoking once again the confrontation with a major intellectual rival that characterizes Christian history from the
start. An anonymous classicizing clergyman of the late fourteenth or early fifteenth century drily records his own encounter with rigorism:

> I rede in haly wryte, I sey noght at I red in ovidie, noyther in oras. Vor the last
> tyme that I was her ich was blamyd of som men word, be-cause that I began my
> sermon wyt a poysy. And ter-vorn, I say that I red in haly wryt, in the secund book
> of haly wryt, that I suppoise be sufficiant inowgh of autoritee, that wen the childyr
> of that Israel wer in the land of Egipt . . . (Grisdale, 22)

> I read in Holy Writ—I don't say that I read in Ovid or in Horace, for the last time
> I was here I was criticized by some people because I began my sermon with po-
> etry. And therefore I say that I read in Holy Writ, which I assume is of sufficient
> authority, that when the children of Israel were in the land of Egypt . . .

Chaucer is an obvious candidate for reproach here, perhaps *the* obvious candidate for reproach. Although the classical invocation was used by all and
sundry in Bokenham's time, nonetheless it was Chaucer who had effectively introduced it into English literature. The classical deities and figures he invokes
include Morpheus, Venus, Apollo, and various muses in the *House of Fame;*
Tisiphone, Venus, Calliope, Mars, Furies, fates, Clio, and various muses in
Troilus (*TC,* 3); Mars and Polyhymnia ("Anelida"); Socrates and Fortune ("Fortune"); and the queen of the furies ("Pity").

Far more offensive to orthodoxy, though, must be Chaucer's invocation of an
inanimate object: the daisy in the *Legend of Good Women,* hyperbolically and
blasphemously addressed by the first-person Narrator as

the clernesse and the verray lyght
That in this derke world me wynt and ledeth.
           . . . ye ben verrayly
The maistresse of my wit, and nothing I.
· ·
Be ye my gide and lady sovereyne!
As to my erthly god to yow I calle,
Bothe in this werk and in my sorwes alle. (F, 84–96)

Later, Eros tells the Narrator that the daisy is his "relyke" (F 321). As muse,
mistress, saint, and even deity, the daisy is revered out of all proportion. Behind
Chaucer's hyperbole stands the new courtly poetry of Machaut, Deschamps, and
Froissart. It is perhaps from Deschamps's *Lai de franchise* that Chaucer derived
the most blasphemous phrase in the passage cited—"erthly god"—for Deschamps refers to his daisy as "la déesse mondaine" and had called Chaucer himself "d'amours mondains Dieux en Albie." Evidently it was a fairly common
locution at the French court: Deschamps also calls Machaut "mondains dieux

d'armonie," and Machaut promises to worship his lady "comme dieu terrien" (Lowes, 620–21).

But this matter of muses, invocations, and epithets is only the tip of an iceberg. It is the symptom of a classicizing spirit especially blatant in Chaucer's *Legend,* in which devotion to classical sources is even more troublesome than in other late-medieval works. The reason is that the *Legend* praises ten women so true in love that half of them commit the deadly sin of suicide, and nowhere does the author condemn their act. Moreover, the "love" portrayed in at least some of the tales is plainly lust compounded by poor judgment, and in some instances, it is lust for an ethically unworthy partner at that. Bokenham offers something formally similar but ideologically opposite: a gallery of portraits of women who died for the right reason, not in despair but in faith and hope, not for erotic passion (*cupiditas*) but for love of God (*caritas*). In so doing, he reasserts the proper duty of Christians and the central lesson of the claimed founder of his order.

In the matter of invocations and muses, Chaucer shares the spotlight with many, among them Thomas Usk, whose prologue to *The Testament of Love* invokes Aristotle and David; or Charles of Orléans, a prisoner of war in England between 1415 and 1440, who in various lyrics calls on Cupid, Venus, Fortune, Danger, Death, Clotho, Lachesis, and Atropos.

Far more eminent is Lydgate, who begs Mars, Othea, Clio, and Calliope for their "grace" (*Troy Book,* prol. 1–62) and elsewhere invokes Niobe ("Complaint of the Black Knight") and Lucina ("On the Departing of Thomas Chaucer"). Even in his "Exposition of the Pater Noster," Lydgate displays ambivalence: hope "doth my brydel leede / Toward Pernaso, to fynde there som muse" (15–16), although once arrived there, the poet dares not call on Euterpe but hopes to find sufficiency in Jesus.

More problematic is Lydgate's classicizing hagiography, the *Life of St. Alban and St. Amphibel,* in which he manages "to introduce the humanistic world of antiquity into the religious sphere, to sing the praises of Christ as Orpheus, Hercules and Achilles, to make the Romans and Trojans progenitors of the Saints, or to invoke the Muses in a religious legend" (Schirmer, 172). No doubt Lydgate takes advantage of a long exegetical tradition that glosses Hercules and Orpheus as types of Christ, so that one might interpret Lydgate's apparent classicism here as, instead, an extremely exuberant figuralism. And even though Lydgate's enthusiasm for classical material often seems as unrestrained as his syntax or his overwrought vocabulary, it is also surely relevant that some of this enthusiasm originates in a desire to please an influential patron. John Whethamstede commissioned the *Alban;* he was abbot of St. Alban's and a member of the neoclassical humanist circle of Humphrey, duke of Gloucester. Nonetheless, these circumstances would not mitigate the offense to a rigorous contemporary reader—particularly a reader with a political ax to grind as well as an aesthetic and doctrinal one. Nor do such considerations lessen the sense of incongruity when Lydgate advises the reader to "lat pale Aurora condute yow and dresse / To holy churche, of Cryste to have a syght" ("On the Mass," 23–24). That Lydgate himself felt the tension between his two referential systems is suggested in his "Misericordias domini," in which he ostentatiously bids farewell to classical subject matters before embracing "hooly writ" as a preferred source of poetic material.

How, then, is the Christian poet to use classicism? As Smalley remarks of her "friar doctors," "The answer is that it was a matter of where to draw the line" (*English Friars,* 40). Every university graduate would have read a fair amount of classical literature and science. It is a question central to the Augustinian project, and this is the Augustinian response:

> But we should not think that we ought not to learn literature because Mercury is said to be its inventor, nor that because the pagans dedicated temples to Justice and Virtue and adored in stones what should be performed in the heart, we should therefore avoid justice and virtue. Rather every good and true Christian should understand that wherever he may find truth, it is his Lord's. . . . He will repudiate superstitious imaginings and will deplore and guard against men who ". . . changed the glory of the incorruptible God into the likeness of the image of a corruptible man, and of birds, and of four-footed beasts, and of creeping things." (*DDC,* 2.18.28)

Although this perspective enjoins a certain flexibility or compromise, it simultaneously elucidates the rigor according to which both Chaucer and Lydgate might be said to have crossed the ideological line.

After dealing with the matter of invocations as symptomatic of overenthusiastic classicism, Bokenham takes on the question of courtly style, particularly as manifested in the courtly love lyric. He will pray only to God, he says,

Not desyryng to have swych eloquence	Not desiring to have such eloquence
As sum curyals han, ner swych asperence	As some courtiers have, or such difficulty,
In uttryng of here subtyl conceytys,	In uttering their subtle conceits
In wych oft tyme ful greth dysceyt is,	In which there is often much deceit,
And specyally for there ladyis sake	And especially for their ladies' sake
They baladys or amalettys lyst to make,	They like to make ballades and amulets
In wych to sorwyn & wepyn thei feyn	In which they pretend to sorrow and weep
As thow thee prongys of deth dede streyn	As if death's prongs constrained
Here hert-root, al-be thei fer thens;	Their hearts, though they be far from it.
Yet no-for-than is here centens	Yet nonetheless their message is
So craftyd up, & wyth langwage so gay	So elaborately worked up, and in such lively language
Uttryd, that I trowe the monyth of may	Uttered, that I believe the month of May
Nevere fresshere enbelshyd the soyl wyth flours	Never more freshly embellished the soil with flowers
Than is her wrytyng wyth colours	Than is their writing [embellished] with colors
Of rethorycal speche both to & fro.	Of rhetoric back and forth.
(5225–39)	

We know that the target of this polemic is not nobility per se or courtly manners; the setting, after all, is Lady Bourchier's. Nor is it polished language per se, for Bokenham readily composes in courtly stanzaic forms such as the Troilus stanza or the Monk's Tale (Marian) stanza. The issue is, rather, the abuse of eloquence or the ethics of composition, just as earlier it was not the use of classical studies but their abuse. Even more, it is the abuse of signs. The test case chosen here is the courtly love lyric, which fails the test more disastrously the more successfully it achieves the poet's desire. Like any of the world's goods, language can be enjoyed, used, or abused, as Augustine reminds us:

> To enjoy something is to cling to it with love for its own sake. To use something, however, is to employ it in obtaining that which you love, provided that it is worthy of love. For an illicit use should be called rather a waste or an abuse. (*DDC*, 1.4)

> He who is foolish and abounds in eloquence is the more to be avoided the more he delights his auditor with those things to which it is useless to listen so that he thinks that because he hears a thing said eloquently it is true. This lesson, moreover, did not escape those who sought to teach the art of rhetoric. They granted that "wisdom without eloquence is of small benefit to states; but eloquence without wisdom is often extremely injurious and profits no one." (*DDC*, 4.5)

Beside seduction, another way in which the courtly lyric or romance abuses the linguistic sign is in its development of a language of the religion of love. With its vocabulary of service, devotion, grace, passion, divinity, saints, judgment, bliss, and so on, this poetic language represents a perversion of devotional language to erotic ends. In Augustinian terms, it is the language of *caritas* turned to the aims of *cupiditas,* the referentiality of its signs not only ambiguous but deliberately misleading.

Egregious in this respect are two in the revered trio of famous English authors: Geoffrey Chaucer and John Gower. I briefly discussed Chaucer's *Legend* for its potential to offend the religiously minded. In like fashion, his *Troilus* displays a continuous stream of parodic references that turn the language of orthodox religion to the uses of eroticism. These culminate in an ineffably vulgar statement by the Narrator when after the first consummation by his principals, he comments on the happy conclusion of the good-natured tiff between Pandarus and Criseyde: "What! God foryaf his deth, and she al so / Foryaf, and with here uncle gan to pleye" (3.1577–78: Delany, "Techniques"). Even if one believes, as I do, that Chaucer meant in both *Troilus* and the *Legend* to expose the religion of love for its bad taste and bad judgment, it nonetheless is not hard to understand how a moralistically inclined reader such as the Austin friar might hesitate to grant the separation of author, narrator, and character that such an interpretation requires. (The "querelle de la Rose" shows how lively that critical issue remained in the early years of the fifteenth century, even though the author–character distinction was a well-understood literary principle; cf. Minnis.)

Gower's *Confessio amantis* is structurally an extended parody of the institution of confession. Although it does convey a good deal of perfectly acceptable morality, the priest and "holy fadir" to whom Amans confesses is Genius, Venus's "oghne Clerk." Genius is thus committed to the rule of Eros, according to whose principles he is shriven and pardoned. Gower defines his book as one that "stant betwene ernest and game" (8.3109)—between serious didacticism and erotic allegory—but not every reader will accept that mix. Moreover, Gower's extended attack on mendicant friars in *Vox clamantis* (4.16–24) can scarcely have endeared him to the clerical reader, as he blames friars for all the usual vices as well as for recruiting children.

Any number of minor or anonymous texts might offend a member of the clergy. One such piece is the so-called Lover's Mass or Venus's Mass, a blatant liturgical parody. The poem was published in about 1450, in the beautifully produced anthology of Chaucerian and other works known to us as Bodleian Library MS. Fairfax 16. The text probably circulated independently for a period of time before that, as did most of the other material in the manuscript. The poem parodies the Catholic mass, its eight portions corresponding to sections of the mass. The "Introibo" announces the poet's advance to "the famous Riche Auter / Of the myghty god of Love" and his intention to sacrifice there. The "Confiteor" reiterates the poet's "ful gret repentaunce" that he did not start earlier in the service of love. The "Kyrie"—written in a more intricate form than the rest of the poem—cries mercy, for danger and disdain, the poet says, "Causen myn herte: of mortal smerte: dyspeyre." A joyful outcome is prayed for in the "Gloria in excelsis" and the "Oryson." The poem concludes with an "Epystel in prose," a mock-legal document of enrollment in a religious order: "ffrom the party of the por plentyff in love wyth many yers of probacon professed to be trewe / To all the holy ffraternite and Confrary: of the same bretherhede / And to all hospytlerys and Relygious / nat spotted / nor mad foul wyth no cryme of Apostasye . . . Elthe / : and long prosperyte" (Hammond). Pilgrims, writes the poet, like to count up the distance and the places passed so that they can "take to hem force / vigour / and strengthe / myghtyly Wyth oute feyntyse / to parforme / and manly to acomplysshe / the Resydue / and the remnaunt of her labour."

To the same stimulating end, the poet reminisces about the years and circumstances of his love life, as well as the love literature he has read (including Ovid's *Heroides* and Chaucer's *Troilus* and *Legend*). The sexualized vocabulary describing the pilgrim's aim suggests that for the poet, the labor referred to for himself is neither pilgrimage nor that of completing the poem. He concludes at last with a request for pity from his brother lovers in their "devout observaunces." A poem could scarcely be better calculated to offend a priest, whether secular or regular.

To conclude my discussion of Bokenham's polemic, I offer some observations on his word *amulets* ("amalettys": 5230). It would have been an odd word at the time, for Bokenham's use of it is the earliest English instance recorded in the *OED,* and in French it is not documented until the middle of the sixteenth century. It appears, therefore, that although Bokenham could have found the word in Pliny, he is creating it in English. Equally interesting is Bokenham's pairing of the word with *ballades* ("baladys or amalettys"), as though amulets were a literary genre and not small objects to be worn on the person and possessing protective powers. In fact, though, these two definitions were not, at least in late-medieval French, mutually exclusive, for sometimes the protective object was in fact a text. Its format consisted of a piece of parchment folded many times, with the cutout corners forming, when the sheet was unfolded, a series of lozenges, on each of which a portion of text was written. Often the text was a life of St. Margaret, although sometimes it might be magic spells or diagrams.[5] I imagine it was the latter Bokenham had in mind—a love spell—in pairing the amulet with the courtly ballade.

Last, *amulet* is the word that Robertson chose when translating Augustine's "ligaturae" (*DDC*, 2.20.30). I wonder whether Bokenham might not have made the same choice, for the Augustinian passage in which "ligaturae" occurs is directly relevant to Bokenham's concerns in the passage just cited. It targets "the worshiping of any creature or part of any creature as though it were God." This does not refer to human lust but to works of magic and prognostication "which the poets are accustomed to mention [*commemorare*]." Yet the Augustinian warning can easily apply to the religion of love and the accompanying lyric–romantic fetishization of the female body and its parts as practiced in courtly poetry. That practice would come under the friar's critique farther on in his legendary, as we will see.

Reverting to the modesty topos in his Magdalene prolocutory, Bokenham admits that it would be foolish for him to aspire to a courtly eloquence appropriate to neither his age nor his "degree" (5245; social position, as a humbly born friar living far from court). His prayer ends, therefore, with a modest request:

That I kunnyng may han suffycyently	That I may have skill adequately
To serven the devocyoun of my lady	To serve the devotion of my lady
Aftyr hyr entent, that is to seyne,	According to her desire, that is to say,
That I may translate in wurdes pleyne	That I may translate in simple words
In-to oure langwage oute of latyn	Into our language out of Latin
The lyf of blyssyd Mare Mawdelyn. (5249–54)	The life of blessed Mary Magdalene.

This restores to its original function the language of religious devotion, cleansing the linguistic signs of their social–erotic accretion. To serve a lady is to attend "to hyr goostly confourth" (5255) and therefore to the spiritual comfort of a larger audience, "them generally wych it redyn shal" (5256).

I propose that another sort of restoration is under way as well here: a generic one in which, again, both Chaucer and Lydgate are culpable. Chaucer parodied the saint's life in his *Legend of Good Women*, and Lydgate used the genre for fairly immediate and rather transparently self-serving ends (using "self" in its corporate and not individual sense). His short "St. Austin at Compton"—subtitled "Offre up yowre dymes"—is an unabashed effort to intimidate stubborn laypeople into making a ready and generous donation of tithes. His "Legend of

St. Gyle" relates the angelic origin of abbatial liberties and franchises. Although Bokenham would certainly have wanted to defend both tithes and liberties, he may well have perceived a need to cleanse hagiography of its courtly ironic and its bureaucratic accretions to return to the fundamentals of faith.

Moving from the Magdalene prolocutory and prologue into the legend proper and the Katherine following it, we move from theory to practice. If the introductory material sets its sights on the uses of rhetoric, the two long legends center on specific speech acts, discussed in chapter 5.

T HE CRITIQUE LEVELED BY the Austin friar at his great predecessor-poet is an indirect one. It had to be, for several reasons. Most obvious to us is that Chaucer was already revered as a great poet. Although rigorous, Bokenham was no ascetic zealot, no proto-Puritanical parson such as Chaucer had portrayed, rejecting rhyme and meter, alliteration and fable, as mere "draf out of my fest" (*CT*, X, 35) in favor of a prose penitential tract as the only way to embody "moralitee and vertuous mateere" (38). The Austin friar is himself too good a poet, too self-conscious, and too heavily influenced by Chaucer to produce a reductive or fanatical polemic of the "Quid cum Jesum Aeneas?" type: he is no St. Gregory, Tertullian, or Peter Damian. This exclusionary extreme is not the Augustinian tradition in any case, for Augustine's recommendation about the world's good, including pagan culture, was, as we have seen, not renunciation but proper use (and see Bolgar; Murphy, chap. 2). In this sense, Bokenham has a tradition to draw on for his critique of the classicizing courtly poets of his own era. Yet the critique seems, in the end, a rather quaintly obsolescent or wistfully nostalgic gesture, coming as it does at a moment when classical humanism was firmly on the agenda. This could not have been evident in England at the time, given the relatively feeble influence of the Gloucester circle and other classically inclined individuals. Nonetheless, Petrarch and Boccaccio were already authorities, and their works were part of many monastic libraries. Ficino was a younger Italian contemporary of Bokenham, and Pico and Machiavelli were born in Osbern's last years. If Bokenham insists on holding the line, it is because he correctly senses a threat.

There is also a more worldly and more political register of tactical considerations for the fifteenth-century scholar-poet who would criticize Chaucer. The Chaucers were doing very well in Bokenham's day, for the poet was father and grandfather to some very considerable people in fifteenth-century England. They in turn were related to and allied with some of the most powerful, even dangerous, individuals in the realm (see figure 4). The poet's son Thomas,[6] who died in 1434, was an influential person during the first half of Bokenham's life. Thomas Chaucer had some minor land interests in East Anglia, although the real center of his life was Oxfordshire. His wife was Maud Burghersh, daughter and coheir of John Burghersh, a cousin of the duchess of York and a grandniece of Henry Burghersh, bishop of Lincoln and treasurer and chancellor of

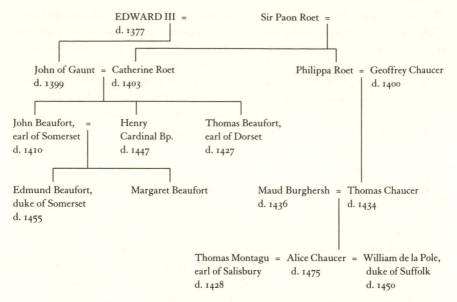

FIGURE 4 Some important Chaucer connections in Bokenham's day.

England. Through his marriage, Thomas Chaucer held land in Suffolk, and for a time he owned the manor of Gresham in Norfolk.

Thomas Chaucer seems to have inherited his Chaucer grandfather's proclivities or even his actual business, for the poet's father was a vintner and his son was, after 1402, butler for the royal household. In this capacity, he purveyed wines for the king's various castles and armies as well as for the court, and he was also responsible for collecting the tariff on imported wines. (In a period of intermittent war with France, the office of butler must have been particularly lucrative.) During his lifetime, Thomas Chaucer sat on many royal commissions, including the one that investigated Oxfordshire after the Oldcastle revolt of 1415. Like his father, he served as a minor diplomat, with royal missions to Germany, France, and the Low Countries, and John Lydgate composed a heartfelt farewell poem for his good friend: "On Thomas Chaucer's Departing" into France.

Thomas Chaucer's career was probably aided more by his relationship with living nobility than with a dead courtier-poet. His mother was the French noblewoman Philippa Payne de Roet, whose sister Katherine Swynford was John of Gaunt's longtime mistress and, from 1396, wife. Their offspring, the legitimized Beauforts, were movers and shakers in the kingdom. The most eminent of them was Henry Beaufort, chancellor under Henry IV and Henry V, bishop of Lincoln and of Winchester and, from 1426, cardinal. Beaufort referred to Thomas Chaucer as "dilecto consanguineo" (beloved cousin) in granting him the lifelong constableship of his castle at Taunton (Ruud, 8)—one of many such lucrative perquisites and sinecures Chaucer enjoyed during his lifetime.

Another Beaufort, Edmund, became earl of Dorset and duke of Somerset. He was a rival of Richard, duke of York, in court circles under Henry VI and supplanted Richard as governor of England's French territories just at the time when Bokenham was composing his legendary. In the intrigue-ridden atmosphere of the late Lancastrian court, the Beauforts were allied with William de la Pole, duke of Suffolk, against Yorkist ambitions and critiques of the regime.

In local and parliamentary politics, too, Thomas Chaucer was an important figure. He was the executor of many wills and held the guardianship and marriage of many young people. Sometimes these lucrative grants came about through the generosity of a noble patron, and at other times, through friendship with members of the provincial gentry. Among his many benefactors were the Stonor family, who lived near Chaucer's estate at Ewelme and who were also landlords and friends of the family of John Fortescue, chief justice to Henry VI and an important Lancastrian propagandist (see chapter 7). Thomas Chaucer was sheriff of Oxfordshire and Berkshire (1400–1404). He was elected no fewer than fourteen times to the Commons from Oxfordshire and was five times speaker for the Commons, at which he acted as "mouthpiece"[7] for the interests of his relatives the Beauforts.

Thomas's daughter Alice Chaucer achieved even more brilliant social status through her advantageous marriages to nobility. As one biographer summarizes her career, "she lived to be the wife and widow of three . . . men, two of whom were of great military and political prominence in English history; she was the friend and confidante of royalty; she became the mother-in-law of a king's sister" (Anderson, 24). Like her grandfather's famous Alison of Bath, Alice made her fortune by a childhood marriage to a wealthy old man; she was a rich widow at the age of eleven. She next (after a lapse of several years) married the earl of Salisbury, a famous military commander in the wars with France. Her third, last, and most notorious spouse was William de la Pole, earl and duke of Suffolk. In chapter 2 we encountered him as the likely composer of courtly verse that was possibly meant for Alice in 1429.

It is easy for us moderns to assume that this match was advantageous primarily for the Chaucers: a leap into the nobility for a middle-class family. Yet this was already a very wealthy and influential middle-class family. John L. Watts points out that Suffolk's territorial dominance in the Thames Valley came through his inheritance of the Chaucer lands and that the earl also acquired through the marriage a "ready-made following in an area highly convenient for anyone planning to spend a lot of time at court"—connections that included the powerful Beauforts and that would "come to prove the basis of [Suffolk's] rule" (*Domestic Politics,* 183). Suffolk eventually became one of the most hated men in England, widely perceived as the counselor responsible for England's capitulations to France and the loss of English territories there. He was impeached by Parliament and assassinated at sea in 1450. His death was commemorated in numerous exultant popular songs decrying him as a traitor. While Bokenham wrote, however, Suffolk was still in favor as the king's chief minister and confidant of the queen.

In the late 1440s, then, to criticize Chaucer was to criticize the near ancestor of extremely family-conscious people who were in a position to do something about their displeasure. I do not mean that Bokenham's head would necessarily have rolled as a penalty for tactless literary criticism, although it was a time when heads did roll, sometimes for sharp remarks interpreted as subversive or treasonous. One such case occurred in 1444, when Thomas Kerver, a gentleman from Reading, was tried for having "wished and desired" the king's death, engaged in "traitorous imaginings" of it, and said that England would be better off if the king had never been born. Kerver narrowly escaped execution (Meekings). Although such precedents would certainly induce caution among critics of the regime, I think that other consequences of tactlessness might have been more likely for the friars at Clare: perhaps fewer political favors for Augustinians, fewer land bequests to Clare or to other Austin houses by friends or would-be friends of the offended parties, a tax imposed here and there, a liberty interfered with, and so on. Given the Augustinians' pro-Yorkist tendency and particularly the Yorkist patronage and partisanship at Clare, it was wise to be careful.

As a close friend of Geoffrey Chaucer, explicitly addressed and praised at the end of the *Troilus,* John Gower must to some extent share the aura of his exalted friend. Even apart from this reflected posthumous glory, Gower had independently established himself as a friend of the Lancastrian dynasty with his *Tripartite Chronicle,* a violently anti-Ricardian tract that fulsomely praises the Lancastrian usurpation as divine intervention. Adding insult to injury, Gower portrays the friars who advised and confessed Richard as a pack of vice-ridden, fraudulent scoundrels (1.188 ff.).

If Gower was safely dead when Bokenham wrote, Lydgate was not. A similar sense of tactical caution would have to affect any critique of Lydgate, who was a protégé of the king's uncle, Duke Humphrey of Gloucester, and a propagandist for the Lancastrian regime. Several of Lydgate's poems were commissioned by a king or noble. One scholar describes him as "a kind of poet laureate" (J. Miller, "Literature to History," 64), and Lucas comments that "he must have been a considerable financial asset to his abbey" (236) because of generous payments from patrons. Lydgate composed mummings for festivals at court and probably designed pageants for the 1432 entry of Henry VI into London on his return from France (Doig, 110, 114).

Not unlike the Chaucers, Lydgate performed minor diplomatic tasks, occupying "a senior post on [the duke of] Bedford's administrative staff as a kind of liaison officer" (Schirmer, 116). He spent several years (1426–29) in Paris on Bedford's behalf and was sought after as a propagandist by other powerful men whom he met either in Paris or through his friend Thomas Chaucer. Bury St. Edmunds was intimately linked with king and government. Its abbot, William Curteis, sat in Parliament and financed and advised the king. Gloucester, brother to Henry V, was arrested and died at Bury in 1447 during a Parliament held there. Lydgate was thus a fairly significant person because of his connections, so that with regard to him as well as to Chaucer, the network of political affiliation dictated a discreetly indirect approach.

In *The Anxiety of Influence,* Harold Bloom wrote of "an age before the great flood" of printed literature—from Homer to Shakespeare—when a master like Geoffrey Chaucer "moved his ephebe only to love and emulation and not to anxiety." It is easy to recognize the naïveté, perhaps the wishful thinking, of this estimate. Nonetheless, it is rare to find a negative critique of Chaucer during the fifteenth century. If we grant that a negative critique of Chaucer is indeed what Bokenham made, then we must recognize it as a minority report, unmatched until the last years of the century when the Scottish poet Robert Henryson challenged narrative authority with his famous "Quha wait gif all that Chauceir wrait was trew?" (*Testament of Cresseid*) or until early in the following century when, also in Scotland, Gavin Douglas reproached Chaucer for exactly the opposite fault that Bokenham does, though in the same work, the *Legend of Good Women.* Douglas blamed Chaucer for not remaining true enough to Virgil, whose light Chaucer professed to follow in retelling the Dido story in his *Legend.* What was too much classicism for Bokenham became too little for Douglas (see *Eneydos,* written in 1513).

In Bokenham's midcentury legendary, then, we witness an act of literary reception in which an English reader subtly constructs his literary past—but not in a shape resembling that imposed by most other writing readers, whether scribes, editors, commentators, or poets. The reinvention analyzed here was not performed by someone who was, or even aspired to be, a member of what Seth Lerer calls the *familia Chauceriana* (18). Indeed, Bokenham's version of the precursor would almost inevitably be doomed to marginality as long as the "star-maker machinery" of the Chaucer–Lancastrian establishment remained in place, its legacy culturally dominant in a consensus only now starting to be deconstructed.

In defining the terms in which a moral–theological critique of Chaucer could be made, Bokenham may strike us as odd in another way. This is, after all, just the critique that Chaucer tried to preempt in his retraction to the *Canterbury Tales* and, earlier, in the so-called epilogue to *Troilus*—the two places where Chaucer seems to try to establish, in his own voice, his ideological bona fides. Moreover, we have learned, through the work of D. W. Robertson and others, to integrate with other facets of Chaucer's sensibility the strong Augustinian current in his work. Why does the Austin friar ignore or minimize this current rather than emphasize and celebrate it?

One reason is surely that the *Legend of Good Women*—the text that Bokenham used as a structural model—is not one in which this current is readily discernible, cloaked as it is in a rhetorical veil of dream vision, wordplay, and irony. Whatever its kernel of truth, its shell could only give offense to someone like Osbern, not least in presenting itself as a parody of the saint's legend. At another level, though, perhaps it is Harold Bloom who helps us understand the phenomenon, for we might look at Bokenham's approach to Chaucer as a "creative misprision" enabling him to distinguish himself from a precursor whose influence dominated the fifteenth century. However we explain it, Bokenham's legendary stands as evidence that tradition may oppose as well as imitate; indeed, it may do both in a single act.

Impolitic Bodies I

Head, Feet, Face, Womb

Obsecro autem vos, fratres, per miserationem Dei,
ut exhibeatis corpora vestra hostiam vivam, sanctam, Deo placentem.

> (Rom. 12:1; Augustine,
> *On Christian Doctrine,* 4.20.40)

I beseech you, therefore, brethren, by the mercy of
God, that you present your bodies a living sacrifice, holy, pleasing unto God.

> (trans. Robertson)

Even though the selection and ordering of the first ten saints in
Bokenham's legendary were influenced by Chaucer's *Legend of
Good Women,* the fifteenth-century poem still has an ethos and an aesthetic of its
own. It has what the Middle Ages called, in French and English, *sentence:* an
inner meaning or form not identical with the narrative. I described the negative
expression of this *sentence* in chapter 3, as an Augustinian polemic against the
abuse of rhetoric and of classical culture by the courtly classicizing trend in recent English poetry. In this and the next two chapters, I discuss the positive axis
of the Augustinian ethos as expressed in Bokenham's poetic procedure.

To develop a fuller *sentence* than the recommendation of patient humility and steadfast faith, Bokenham—trained as he was in logic, literature, and
preacherly technique—fleshes out the narrative skeleton of his chosen genre
with a great deal of additional and often original material: dialogue, incident,
description, and commentary. Of course, he also omits or alters material found
in other renditions. This is the flexibility of hagiography that makes it amenable
to various kinds of criticism, including those I use here: semiotic, historicist, and
gender conscious. Bokenham's hagiography is distinctive for, first, its politics, to
be discussed in chapters 7 and 8, and, second, its success in constructing a theological semiotic of the (female) body.

Most of the individual lives that Bokenham retells center on a particular
point of Catholic doctrine. In this way, the poet crystallizes a tendency already
pronounced in his main source, the *Legenda aurea* of Jacob da Voragine. That

massive text can be seen as a cumulative history of the Catholic Church and a defense of its doctrine: "La légende apparait donc comme un moyen de représentation doctrinale ou de figuration apologétique" (Boureau, 207; see also Reames). Most of Bokenham's lives also concentrate on a particular part of the body. This appears to have been a deliberate structural technique, for the groupings appear in order through the poem: Margaret, Anne, and Christine (Bokenham's first, second, and third saints); Magdalene, Katherine, and Cecelia (numbers eight, nine, and ten); and Agatha, Lucy, and Elizabeth (eleven, twelve, and thirteen). I therefore devote a chapter to each of these groups, together with the body parts and the doctrines they emphasize. Four of the lives—Ursula, Faith, Agnes, and Dorothy; numbers four through seven—do not participate in this scheme because theirs is a different but not unrelated thematic, that of the couple, which I have chosen to omit from this study.

I will proceed, therefore, once again through the legendary, this time with the *sentence* in view.

Head, Feet, and the Somaticized Text

They do not die easily, these zealous adolescents (aged eleven, fifteen, and eighteen) who are flayed and burned and drowned and maimed and shaved and insulted and disemboweled and roasted and have their tongues and breasts torn off, their guts and bones exposed, and are then proposed to, whereupon they answer spiritedly: no. Their endurance is superhuman—indeed, surreal. They survive ordeals that would kill any of us ten times over.[1]

Yet there is a moment of truth that no saint survives, for the coup de grâce is, most often, decapitation. Considering the vast ingenuity of torture and its lethal apparatuses, it is curious that decapitation accounts for so large a proportion of martyrs' deaths. To take two samples closest to hand: Five of Bokenham's ten martyrs die of decapitation, and the same proportion holds for the *South English Legendary* in which, by my count, seventeen martyrs are decapitated and another seventeen die by various other means—burning, stoning, crucifixion, stabbing, hewing to pieces, roasting, drawing by horses—even though these other means have failed with those who are finally decapitated. It is as if this violation of physical integrity, unlike any other, is universally acceptable to God as a cause of death. He could, of course, intervene miraculously in decapitation, as in any other offense against the body, but generally he does not.[2] For dramatic purposes, there has to be something to which the saint is terminally vulnerable, something that generic convention understands as finally mortal. Otherwise, a legend could continue indefinitely, and the concept of martyrdom would lose its meaning. Decapitation is thus what stands between the saints and Roadrunner, who truly is immortal—and, for that reason, comic.

Scholars since the sixteenth century have noticed the prevalence of decapitation after numerous more horrible but less efficacious torments: "seul le glaive est invincible" (de Gaiffier). They have offered an ingenious variety of narrative explanations, including the one I just made: that the faithful could never have become martyrs had God suspended the natural effect of steel. Others have proposed that since the sword was the symbol of political power, God wanted to show that public order was to be maintained; that mutilation might interfere with resurrection, whereas decapitation leaves the rest of the body whole and thus resurrectable; that God intended a celestial reprobation of the barbaric inventions to which tyrants often had recourse.

These diegetic reasons for decapitation—locating motivation within the narrative itself—are supported by several other reasons, among them the social significance of different forms of punishment. In Europe, decapitation was considered the most honorable form of execution. It was otherwise for the Turks, for in Islamic culture, decapitation was "une mort infâme" (Stahl, 69), used for slaves and persons of low status, whereas important people were strangled. Christian society, though, decreed that thieves were hanged, profaners burned, aristocrats decapitated, and peasants stabbed. Many of the early martyrs were of noble blood or gentle rank, so that the method of execution may simply have been the most appropriate to a victim's social status. A detailed study correlating social rank and means of death would be necessary to corroborate this hypothesis.

Ancient medical theory—prehistoric and classical—may be relevant to the question, too. Many early cultures believed that semen was produced in the brain, to travel down the spine and be ejected from the genitals; both women and men were believed to produce seed. Hence the head was the source of fertility and of the life principle itself, and therefore, it was physiologically more important even than the heart.[3] This is no doubt why, as Stahl points out with ample documentation, the skull was the most prized saintly relic of all—with second place going to the right hand. Indeed, this perspective prompts the speculation that hagiographical decapitation might be a sort of back formation: Because the head was so highly valued—indeed coveted, as booty in war and devotional object in peace—many hagiographers provided, in their narratives, the object of special devotion. A fifteenth-century French life of St. Barbara relates that when Charlemagne requested and received the saint's body as a gift from the pope, her head was kept in Rome:

> Toutes foiz il retint le chief par devers luy car il ne vouloit mie que la sainte cité de Rome, laquelle est le chief du monde, fust privee d'aucun especial joel de tant glorieuse vierge. (Williams, 176)

> Nevertheless he [the pope] kept the head, for he did not want the holy city of Rome, which is head of the world, to be deprived of the special gem of such a glorious virgin. (My translation)

Ideologically, there is also something to be said about decapitation as the high road to martyrdom. It has to do with all that the head not only is but also means in classical and Christian thought. Because the head is the seat of rationality, it represents the principle of rule. To be separated from it is deadly in the figurative as well as the literal register, fatal to the body politic as well as to the personal body.

Plato's philosopher kings are the head of the body that is his republic, and it is instructive to trace St. Paul's use of the imagery of the body politic. In Romans 12 and 1 Corinthians 12, the church is a body, but there is no mention of a head; a relatively democratic concept of the group seems to prevail. In Ephesians 4:15–16 and 5:23, Jesus is specified as head of the ecclesiastical body, and the second locus relates this scheme metaphorically to the marital relation; principles of hierarchy have come to define church and marriage. By Colossians 2:19, the head is defined as the source of the life of the rest of the body, and in Colossians 3:18–22, its metaphoricity is extended to include not only the subordination of wife to husband but also that of child to parent and slave to master. The hierarchical principle now characterizes every area of life, and so it comes down through Christian tradition.

The *South English Legendary* explains that every human being has three types of soul. Two are located in the liver and the heart, and they are principles of growth, sensation, and movement, held in common with the rest of creation. The third and supreme soul is the distinctively human one created for Adam in paradise. It is of angelic nature; it enters the human body at the end of the fourth month of gestation; and its place is "in the childes brain anhei. that the hexte lime is" (d'Evelyn and Mill, 2.427, l.766).

Decapitation is the final, effective ordeal for martyrs, not only for biological reasons but also for ideological ones. To treat decapitation as merely another narreme, another avoidable torment, would be to minimize the importance of the hierarchical value system that the Catholic Church had come to exemplify and civil society to accept. The rest of the body may be indiscriminately abused in an orgy of sadistic polymorphous perversity, but the head retains its headship.

IT IS NOT, HOWEVER, with heads that Bokenham begins his legendary, but with feet, and a particular foot at that. This is the foot of St. Margaret, the first saint in the set, and we are introduced to her foot in the prologue to her life, which also serves as the prologue to the collection as a whole. The foot makes its appearance in the author's account of the four causes of his poetic endeavor, as a subcategory of the fourth, or final, cause: authorial motivation or intention. Love of St. Margaret was a motive for writing, Bokenham asserts; hence the importance of her foot, which can be beheld at an old priory of Dominican canons near the author's birthplace. This foot lacks "the greth too only / And the hele" (141–42), but these are at a nunnery in Reading (Berkshire). Yet it is an efficacious foot even without its great toe and heel, for it imparts protective virtue to any brooch or ring that touches it and is vowed to its shrine. He experienced, Bokenham tells us, the power of Margaret's foot only five years earlier in Venice, when a ring previously touched to the relic protected him in a dangerous situation (160–70). If the power of the head is metaphoric, that of the foot is metonymic.

We encounter a single foot again at the end of Bokenham's text, the foot of St. Elizabeth, protruding from under the royal bedclothes as she, queen of Hungary, sleeps with her loving husband the landgrave. A lady-in-waiting has been instructed to waken Elizabeth gently during the night by shaking her foot, so that the queen can perform her nightly prayer and meditation. This ritual of the foot becomes the center of a charming and—in another generic context—*fabliau*-like anecdote. One night, however, the lady shakes the wrong foot, waking the landgrave instead of Elizabeth. But so kindly and discreet a man is he that he pretends it never happened. This episode is imitated from Voragine, but again it is important to realize how selective Bokenham is with even his main source. This is especially true in the case of Elizabeth who, as a modern saint, generated an immense amount of official and unofficial documentation.

The chapter devoted to her in the *Legenda aurea* is, at nineteen pages, one of the longest in that compilation, and Bokenham (like other hagiographers) is selective. He omits, for instance, the episode in which Elizabeth's gift of rich clothing backfires when the impoverished recipient, overjoyed, falls to the ground as if dead. He also omits such miraculous episodes as Elizabeth's feeding a poor man with fish she catches in a pond where no fish were ever caught before, or her restoration of sight to a blind child. Some other hagiographers (e.g., Bozon) include these incidents. But if Bokenham omits them, by the same token the foot episode is left out of various other versions (cf. Karl). The important point here is that for all its conventionality or predetermination, any saint's life is constantly reshaped. That is, the hagiographer's rigorous freedom is to compose a life consistent with his or her own aims.

It seems, then, that Bokenham chose to frame his work with the image of a foot at either end or—imagining text as body—on either side of it. He thus establishes a pair of pediments on which to construct his architecture of the female body. My associations here depend on metaphor rather than wordplay, for *pediment* does contain the root meaning "foot."[4] Yet one need not rely only on etymology to justify the move from body to architecture to text (or, indeed, among them in any order), for—as I indicated at the end of chapter 1—these objects served, for Christian writers, as privileged and often interchangeable metaphors. Are we entitled to see the physical–textual feet in Bokenham's legendary as pediments in an architecturally constructed text? Might the friar-poet have thought of his edifying text as an edifice (from Latin *aedifico*: "to build, establish, or strengthen")? One can only show a context of possibility.

Hugh of St. Victor, following Gregory the Great, referred to Scripture as "a building, in which, after the foundation has first been laid, the structure itself is raised up; it is altogether like a building, for it too has its structure" (6.4.140). Hugh goes on to elaborate the image, describing in detail the mason's tasks and then applying them to the study of Scripture:

Pay attention now! I have proposed to you something contemptible to gapers but worthy of imitation to those who understand. The foundation is in the earth, and it does not always have smoothly fitted stones. The superstructure rises above the earth, and it demands a smoothly proportioned construction. . . . The foundation which is under the earth . . . stands for history, and the superstructure which is built upon it . . . suggests allegory. . . . Here is the whole of divinity, this is that spiritual structure which is raised on high, built, as it were, with as many courses of stones as it contains mysteries. . . . See now, you have come to your study, you are about to construct the spiritual building. Already the foundations of history have been laid in you: it remains now that you found the bases of the superstructure.

For a Neoplatonist like Hugh, these and numerous other resemblances are not just metaphorical but real, in that "the soul is put together out of all the parts of nature" (1.1); thus there is a genuine resemblance of substance linking various areas of the cosmos, and similars are apprehended by similars. Moreover, to fail to apprehend these resemblances is not simply a failure of imagination, according to Hugh, but more seriously a failure of intellectual perception.

Holy Writ as well as far more recent textual productions, including secular ones, were represented as a building. Augustine's *City of God* and Christine de Pizan's *Livre de la cité des dames* announce themselves as architectural texts, both about a city and built up like a city. Perhaps the most famous instance of the metaphor occurs at the opening to the *Poetria nova* of Geoffrey de Vinsauf. Presenting the writer as an architect, Geoffrey emphasizes the importance of a vision of the whole work:

If a man has a house to build, his impetuous hand does not rush into action. The measuring line of his mind first lays out the work, and he mentally outlines the successive steps in a definite order. The mind's hand shapes the entire house before the body's hand builds it. Poetic art may see in this analogy the law to be given to poets. . . . Let the mind's interior compass first circle the whole extent of the material. . . . As a prudent workman, construct the whole fabric within the mind's citadel; let it exist in the mind before it is on the lips.

Likewise, "the cosmic Book was the ideal *sine qua non* of medieval architects, who imagined that they were copying it as vast encyclopedias in stone when they designed cathedrals across Europe and Britain from the eleventh century to the fourteenth" (Gellrich, 35).

The analogy of body as building appears in two of the most privileged medieval discourses. One of these is medical lore. Marie-Christine Pouchelle documents a long tradition of anatomical/architectural analogy in Roman, Arabic, and medieval culture: body as city, city as body, body as fortress or castle, body as ship, and so forth (*Corps et chirurgie,* pt. 2, chap.3; also see Cornelius). The other is religious discourse, with its gospel, Pauline and Augustinian injunctions to think of the body as temple or altar (e.g., John 2:19–21; 1 Cor. 6:19; *DDC,* 3.14.22). For Augustine, in fact, the architectural image—specifically for the female body—goes all the way back to Genesis. There we read that "the

Lord God then built up the rib, which he had taken out of the man, into a woman" (Gen. 2:22). The Latin reads, "Et aedificavit Dominus Deus costam quam accepit de Adam in mulierem," and it is on the architectural image "aedificavit" that Augustine focuses his attention in his commentary on Genesis: "Why was it not said 'He formed' or 'He made,' as it was said with respect to all the preceding works? But the text says, *The Lord God built the rib,* as if there was a question of a house rather than a human body" (9.13). Obviously, this locus would have been part of a young Austin's university education in biblical commentary, so that in building it into his own text, Bokenham, far from innovating, continues an already authoritative tradition. This tradition was fed as well from the classical side, for Plato's *Timaeus* employs architectural imagery in recounting the creation of humankind: chamber, apartment, wall, citadel (sec. 70A).

For the high and late Middle Ages, the body most frequently invoked as architectural space—whether temple, palace, dwelling, mansion, *aula,* or tower— was that of the Virgin Mary; this was a common topos in the frenzy of naming that constitutes much of the literature of mariolatry. Instances close to Bokenham in time and place come from Lydgate (e.g., *Life of Our Lady,* 2.544–50, 1663, etc.) and from "The Prophets" pageant in the N-town plays:

"I am Salamon the secunde kynge
And that worthy temple for sothe made I
Which that is fygure of that mayde yinge
That xal be modyr of grett messy [messiah]." (Block, lines 39–42)

Bokenham's Lucy employs the trope, describing herself as the dwelling place and temple of the Holy Ghost (9375–76).

Equally available to an educated man was the idea of text as body, a well-known patristic and, later, academic commentator's trope. A twelfth-century Ovid scholar commenting the story of Phaedra advises his reader "hanc fabulam require in corpore" (look up this story in the body [of Ovid's work]). Carrying on this tradition, Bernard Silvestris viewed the *Aeneid* as an allegory of the ages of a human being. Accordingly, he was able "to impose a biographical order on the plot of Vergil's text, whereby the temporal aspects of the plot of the *Aeneid* represent a biographical paradigm of the body" (Desmond, 130). Thus in Bernard's reading, the text of the *Aeneid* becomes really a *corpus,* a somaticized text. An anonymous English preacher of the late fourteenth century represented the Old and New Testaments as two women (Grisdale, 25–26), and the late-fifteenth-century German scholar Gabriel Biel described the Scriptures as two breasts "mercedem laborantibus promittentia" (promising reward to laboring [people]; Obermann, *Harvest,* 112). Nearer home, John Capgrave, dedicating his *Chronicle* to King Edward IV, relates his desire to collect dispersed scriptural writings: "My laboure was to bringe hem into o body" (1).

The reciprocal version of the text-as-body metaphoric equivalency—body as text—is expressed by Chaucer's Wife of Bath, who enjoys the "glossing" of her *corpus* by a clerkly husband. However, it is the universal signifier, the body of Jesus, that most prominently exemplifies the metaphor in various genres. As Word made flesh, it seems fitting that Jesus should be likened to text, whether epistle, book, or legal document. Numerous instances can be found in drama, lyric, and devotional literature. My three examples come from the fourteenth century: a sermon, a prose compilation by Pierre Bersuire, and a Middle English poem. They represent Christ's body as a letter, a book, and a charter:

> Mankynde, whan a was dampned to everlastyig prison, hath ned to send a messager to the hie lord of hevene, that a wold be goodliche & gracius to him. But who was best to be this ambassiatur & tis messager? Truliche the lordes owne sone, Crist Him-silf. . . . This messager never recused it nor deneyd it, but mekeliche & wilfulliche offred up this letter, that was his owne bodi, to the vader of hevene. Ye. this letter & tis charter was gayliche writen with divers letters, vor the vi voghels [six vowels] e this letter wer Cristes vi wondes that a suffred o the cros, whan a was nailed terto, the consonauntes wer other wondes that Cristes bodi was fulfild with, whan a was betyn & scorget abowte te piler. This was a precius letter & comfortable to mankynd. (Grisdale, 77)

> For Christ is a sort of book written into the skin of the virgin. . . . That book was spoken in the disposition of the Father, written in the conception of the mother, exposited in the clarification of the nativity, corrected in the passion, erased in the flagellation, punctuated in the imprint of the wounds, adorned in the crucifixion above the pulpit, illuminated in the outpouring of blood, bound in the resurrection, and examined in the ascension. (Bersuire, *Repertorium morale,* cited in Gellrich, 17)

> Streyght I streyned on the rode
> Streyned to drye on a tre
> As parchemyne ought for to be
> Hyreth now & ye shul wyten
> How this chartre was wryten
> Upon my face was made the ynke
> With Iewes spotel on me to stynke
> The Penne that the lettres was wyth wryten
> Of scorges that I was with smyten
> How many lettres ther-on bene
> Rede and thu myght wyte and sene
> .V. thousand .iiij c. fyghfty and ten
> Wondes on my bothe blac and wan
> To shewe yow al my love-dede
> My silf y wol this chartre rede
> Ye men that goth by the way
> Abideth & loketh wyth youre ey
> And redeth on this parchmyn. (*Charter of Christ,* lines 78–96 in Spalding)

Every martyr, in his or her *imitatio Christi,* seeks to become a similar text, with similar lessons inscribed on his or her body.

What should we make of this digression on metaphorics and ideologemes? I believe that Bokenham deliberately produced a somaticized text; that is, he meant his text to be seen as a body, specifically a female body, at first fragmented but finally reassembled. This and the next two chapters show that both the fragmentation and the final reintegration have important doctrinal meaning. So, I propose, does the particular bodily part emphasized in each legend. This suggests the reversibility of the body–text image: not only is the text (like) a body, but the individual bodies portrayed also are (like) texts. Although we know that hagiographical text is all they are, this is not the sense I have in mind. Rather, I mean that the bodies portrayed in Bokenham's legendary are like texts because they signify specific messages or lessons. They become—whether through their ordeals (plot) or through poetic representation (rhetoric)—signifying systems. To some extent, this is out of Bokenham's hands; it is what he has inherited from the literary corpus of hagiography. But whether he invents, enhances, or omits, he is always conscious of the signifying power of the bodies he portrays.

These are not the only advantages of the body metaphor, however. A collection of saints' lives might be extremely boring: it is, after all, much the same story told over and over again. Christine de Pizan confronted this problem in her collection of exemplary female lives, and not just in its hagiographical portion. The figure of the city (derived equally from Geoffrey of Vinsauf as from Augustine) enabled Christine to escape or at least to relieve the merely agglutinative and repetitive nature of her material. It enabled her to follow Geoffrey's organicist precept about the vision of the whole, even while committed to a genre that contradicts an organicist aesthetic. (This genre I call the *gallery* [*Naked Text,* chap. 5]—a term useful because it is equally applicable to hagiography or secular lives and to series of lives composed in any style or period.) Similarly, the body figure offers Bokenham a principle of coherent internal structuration. It serves as an aesthetic counterweight to the monotony inherent in hagiography, giving him a way to write different stories rather than the same one thirteen times and also a way (alongside the Chaucer alignment) of grouping or arranging those stories.

Let us return now to feet and heads. The preceding discussion amounts to saying that I think it far from accidental that the image of a single foot appears both near the beginning and near the end of Bokenham's text. In view of the aesthetic principles elucidated in chapter 3, I think we can understand, too, why Bokenham chose to begin with feet rather than heads. The blazon of the (usually female) body is one of the most prominent and memorable descriptive conventions in courtly lyric and romance. It invariably begins with the head and works downward, for precisely the reasons just explained. What is highest is best and comes first. Although I doubt that Bokenham would want to challenge the hierarchical principle per se, he does, as we have seen, explicitly refuse what he considers to be the deceptive aspects of courtly eloquence. As I have already suggested and will argue later, the courtly/erotic fetishization of the female body is one of the most insidious aspects of poetry—and indeed of social life—that Bokenham wishes to refute in his own poetic practice. To reverse the courtly/erotic order of representation is thus to offer an imagistic version of the whole doctrinal point. It lets the work start with a solid foundation, as it were—feet, the lowest part, in touch with the earth (as John of Salisbury noted in his version of the body politic)—just as the progress through life to a high point of virtue and salvation starts with the solid foundation of humility.

Face

Another convention that Bokenham scrutinizes—and makes the reader scrutinize—is *descriptio*. What is interesting about his handling of description is that he uses it in order to refuse it; examines it, as it were, and then drops it. Description is, of course, one of the most important conventions in erotic and even nonerotic poetry. In hagiography, however, it is normally effaced. Young and virginal female saints are said, generically, to be beautiful; this is often, after all, what brings them to the attention of an amorous pagan tyrant and leads to their martyrdom in defense of their choice of virginity over marriage. Yet hagiography rarely, if ever, describes a female saint. She is not, after all, so much an individual as an exemplary figure. What matters about her is precisely not the body but the force of will. Generic convention, therefore, leads us to expect no description of the saints in Bokenham's series.

In fact, only one of them is described: Margaret, the first. Placement is important here, and so are the moves, for clearly Bokenham wants to deal with this matter of *descriptio* early on and then to remove it from the agenda. The sequence opens with one stanza of conventional hyperbolic and completely abstract praise of the young woman's beauty (400–406); there is no description. Two stanzas of equally conventional refusal to provide a description follow, since, the author says, he cannot compete in descriptive technique with Boethius, Ovid, Virgil, Geoffrey de Vinsauf, Gower, Chaucer, or Lydgate (!). Despite this elaborate disclaimer, we do get the description five stanzas later. It is unique in hagiographic tradition because of its detailed specificity, and it is Margaret's face as seen through the eyes of the prefect Olibrius:

And whan he sey hyr forheed lely-whyht,	And when he saw her lily white forehead,
Hyr bent browys blake, & hyr grey eyne,	Her curved dark brows and gray eyes,
Hyr chyry chekys, hyr nose streyt & ryht,	Her cherry cheeks, her straight nose,
Hyr lyppys rody, hyr chyn, wych as pleyne	Her ruddy lips, her chin—which gleamed
Pulshyd marbyl shoon, & clovyn in tweyne,	Like polished marble and had a cleft—
He was so astoynyd of that sodeyn caas	He was so astonished by the sudden event
That unnethe he wyste wher that he was.	That he scarcely knew where he was.
(449–55)	

Here, then, is conventional rhetoric, a rather skillful blend of popular and courtly topoi, including (among the latter) the top-to-bottom progression down the face. The poet lets us know that he is perfectly capable of writing in this way when he chooses to. After all, Augustine himself was for the judicious deployment of rhetoric, for

> who would dare to say that truth should stand in the person of its defenders un-armed against lying, so that they who wish to urge falsehoods may know how to make their listeners benevolent, or attentive, or docile in their presentation, while the defenders of truth are ignorant of that art? . . . While the faculty of elo-quence, which is of great value in urging either evil or justice, is in itself indiffer-ent, why should it not be obtained for the uses of the good in the service of truth? (DDC, 4.2)

Therefore Margaret's appearance is quite delightful, with her cleft chin and—like young Alison in the *Miller's Tale*—bent black brows. These details produce a somewhat more individuated portrait than many. Yet—as is so often the case with medieval individualism—the individual has its prototypes, in this instance, in a text long antedating Chaucer's. Geoffrey of Vinsauf's model exercise for describing a beautiful woman includes eyebrows that "re-semble in dark beauty the blackberry, and a lovely and milk-white path [sep-arating] their twin arches," as well as the chin "smoother than polished mar-ble" (3.563–80) that Bokenham gives his Margaret. Even the echo of Chaucer's Alison is not the only connection with courtly poetry about country matters, for when Olibrius sees Margaret she is pasturing her nurse's sheep. The episode thus represents a moment of *pastourelle* inserted into hagiography. The scene is not original to Bokenham, but he expands it far beyond his source in *Legenda aurea*.

The prefect is smitten and amazed. On recovering from his "swow" (460; swoon, trance), he offers to wed the girl if she is free or, if she is a serf, to buy her as his paramour. The idea regarding legal status and social rank is in Voragine, but it also recalls the concluding lines of Chaucer's description of Alison as

a prymerole, a piggesnye,
For any lord to leggen in his bedde,
Or yet for any good yeman to wedde. (*CT*, 1, 3268–70)

Is this, then, love that Olibrius feels for Margaret, transfixed as he is by the sight of her? No, because "he lokyd no ferthere than in hyr face" (456). There is a nice ambiguity to this line, for it is followed by the subordinate clause, "where of natural yiftys plente was I-now" (457). Together the lines constitute high praise for Margaret's beauty. Yet they also tell us that the prefect is vulnerable to appearances, to the superficial and evanescent qualities of things and persons. It is a mistake that we do not want to duplicate. Margaret's physical beauty can stand for beauty in general; the details are irrelevant, for there always are attrac-tive people aplenty. And *descriptio* can stand for rhetoric in general: the poet is capable of it but does not want the fresh colors of rhetoric to seduce his reader at the expense of the spiritual core.

Margaret's legend does not end with her death. The stanzaic narrative is interrupted at that point (line 868) by a break of seventy lines in rhymed couplets, in which the author rests his weary pen and body, as tired as a pilgrim. The image of pilgrimage prepares us for the last portion of Margaret's story, the transferal or translation (*translatio,* "carrying over") of her corpse to Italy in the tenth century. Peter Brown refers to *translatio* as the inverse and complement to pilgrimage, the movement of relics to people rather than the movement of people to relics (*Cult,* 88). Many legends include the *translatio* as part of the saint's story; for example, in Bokenham's collection, Faith and Magdalene also are moved.

Brown evokes the peculiar intimacy of reliquary metonymy, observing that the saint—often called "the invisible friend"—becomes part of an "imaginative dialectic" of resurrection: "For how better to suppress the fact of death, than to remove part of the dead from its original context in the all too cluttered grave? How better to symbolize the abolition of time in such dead, than to add to that an indeterminacy of space?" (*Cult,* 78). Such "indeterminacy of space" appears in both the separation of the parts from the whole and the transferal of the body or its parts from place to place during the years or centuries after death until the remains are brought to their final tomb. England was full of relics, and it is fitting that we are taken into Bokenham's devotional work by way of a local relic such as Margaret's foot, for such an object—a finger, a tooth or bone fragment, a shred of cloth that the saint had worn—might be for many people their nearest and most intense link with devotional life.

On route to its last interment at Montefiascone, Margaret's body begins to be distributed when a rib is offered to hallow a church (1103). The narrative evidences a somewhat cavalier attitude toward body parts, which appear and disappear without explanation. We are told, for instance, that Margaret's corpse was originally carried along with the body (1003, 1324) or the head (1131–32) of St. Felicity—an unexplained association—but when Margaret is exhumed for the last time, there are also found three sweet-smelling ribs of SS: Cosmo and Damian (1326–27), who had not been mentioned previously. But we are never told how Margaret's foot came to England.

Womb

Feet are not the only body motif framing Bokenham's legendary; childbirth is another. Margaret's miraculous escape from the "womb" (ME: belly) of a dragon qualifies her to become the patron saint of women in labor (841–44), although she is figured as the infant rather than the mother. This is not inappropriate, however, for it is in infancy that Margaret becomes a Christian. Her parents, patriarchs of paganism in Antioch, gave her to a wet nurse who was secretly a Christian. Thus Margaret drew in Christianity with her (surrogate) mother's milk, and when her biological mother died, she chose to remain with her spiritual mother. She was in this sense thrice born: from mother, nurse, and dragon. From the social perspective, the ancient practice of farming out a child to a hired wet nurse was one "that the church had tried to stop as far back as the eighth century" (Goody, 154; also cf. 37). Margaret's biological parents thus get the punishment they deserve: loss of their child.

The second life in the series is centrally about childbirth, this time literally rather than metaphorically. It is the story of St. Anne and her husband Joachim, parents of the Virgin Mary, and the miraculous late-life conception of this hitherto sterile couple. The next ten lives are of virgins, but the last is of St. Elizabeth, a married woman with children. This framing repetition of childbirth imagery should not be taken as a celebration of the family. On the contrary, the family as a social institution is shown to be as unreliable, fragile, and fragmented as the physical body itself. The birth that Bokenham wants to validate is the one into faith.

Anne and Joachim are a Baucis and Philemon couple, for

Lyche to lyche ever doth applie,	"Like to like" always applies;
As scheep to scheep & man to man,	As with sheep and man to man,
Pertryche to pertryche & swan to swan	Partridge to partridge or swan to swan,
So vertu to vertu is agreable. (1639–42)	So virtue is liked by virtue.

"Birds of a feather flock together": it is a law of nature, and in consorting so well together, Anne and Joachim demonstrate their virtue and their participation in the order of created nature. This is, after all, the thematic center of the tale: the reproduction of one's kind, the physical nature that human beings share with every other animal. Yet this is precisely what Anne and Joachim cannot fulfill, for they are a barren couple. When Bishop Issachar publicly reproaches Joachim for their childlessness, Joachim leaves home for the wilderness. There, questioned by an angel, he poignantly confesses:

"I wante the argumentes of a man;	I lack the evidence of manhood,
& whan men be reknyd I am lefth behynde;	And when men are counted I am left out;
For no maner isseu may I han . . ."	For I can't produce any offspring.
(1833–35)	

Joachim lacks the social evidence of adulthood and virility, the family that will create him as patriarch.

While Joachim is in the wilderness with his sheep, Anne is in her orchard observing a sparrow feed its young (a scene taken from the *Protevangelium* of James). The two scenes effectively balance each other, each partner unable to do what the animals do so easily, each desiring nothing so much as the fruit (a constantly reiterated image in this tale) of their "nature" (a word of multiple meanings in Middle English, including sexuality, nature, and genitals). On her part, Anne suffers no such erosion of her self-respect as Joachim does, no questioning of her womanhood because God has "shut her womb" (1813–14, 1873–74). The lack of offspring is not presented as the fault of either partner, although in some other versions, Anne blames herself. Here, Anne is saddened but essentially philosophical about her barrenness. She regrets her inability to share the natural experience of all animals, addressing God as follows:

"O lorde almyhte, whiche hast overe al Soverente, & to evere creature, Fyssh, ful and bestis, bothe more & smal,	O almighty lord, who has sovereignty Over everything, and who to every creature Large and small, whether fish, fowl, or beast,
Hast grauntyd be kyndly engenderrure To ioyen in the lykenesse of ther nature, And in ther issu, iche aftyr his kynde,	Has granted through natural engendering To enjoy reproducing their kind And in their offspring, each according to its nature,
To worshyp of thy name wyth-owten ende!" (1763–69)	To worship your name perpetually.

She goes on to say that if she had a child, she would offer it to God's service, and in response to this, an angel appears, promising good tidings and "fruht of thi body" (1788).

There is a theology in all this. These are the people through whom Jesus took a natural created form. Hence we are asked to see them in their full naturalness, which they share with the rest of *natura naturata*. The strong current of natural imagery suggests that the *annonce fait à Anne* in no way diminishes her animal nature and furthermore implies that Mary was conceived in the natural way.

The sticky point here is the doctrine of immaculate conception, which held that Mary was conceived without original sin and therefore could not have been sexually conceived. Controversy regarding the immaculate conception of Mary developed partly as a consequence of a particular formulation in a version of the early Greek–Christian *Protevangelium,* in which the Anne material is first found. One manuscript family of the text gives a different verb tense—"has conceived" for "will conceive"[5] in the angel's announcement to Joachim. Some theologians maintained that the conception of Mary occurred at the moment of Anne's and Joachim's kiss—asexually—at the Golden Gate in Jerusalem, when she met him returning from the wilderness and they exchanged news of their angelic revelations. Others held that Mary was conceived in original sin but then was immediately cleansed, or later sanctified, in the womb. The theological difficulty lay in the universality of Christ's redemption, for if everyone were contaminated by Adam's sin (as St. Paul maintains in Romans 5:12) and if Jesus redeemed everyone from original sin, then Mary, too, was tainted with original sin. Accordingly, if Mary were completely exempt from original sin, she could not be redeemed by her son.

This is why Aquinas, Bonaventure, Albertus Magnus, and many others could not agree with the idea of the immaculate conception of Mary. The *Vita sancte Marie* by the thirteenth-century Franciscan Thomas de Hales takes a plainly naturalist position, as does its late-fourteenth-century Middle English translation, *The Lyf of Oure Lady*. In these texts, "Ioachim autem genuit sanctam Dei genitricem"; "Barpantera gendrede Ioachim and Ioachim gendrede the hooly modir of God" (Horrall, 33). When the couple meet at the Golden Gate, Anne has not yet conceived, although they are "prolis promisse certitudine se-curi," "sikir of the certeinte of the child bihight [promised]." Anne conceives only after the joyful couple have gone home and "abedin" God's promise. There appears to be a pun here, with the word *abed* embedded in *abided* (39). John Lydgate took a clearly maculist stance when he wrote, of Anne's conception of Mary,

And she conceyved, this fayth full trwe wyf
By Ioachym, the holy frute of lyfe. (*Life of Our Lady*, 1.125–26)

It is significant that among the forty or so manuscripts of this work, none shows a variant replacing "by" in line 126 with "of," which would alter the syntax (to "wife of Joachim") and at least enable the possibility of an immaculist position. Another fifteenth-century ecclesiastical poet, John Audelay, composed two poems on St. Anne. In one of them he speaks to Anne about Mary, "the moder of Messee . . . thou consayvyst clene be Ioachym that hole man" (13–14; Messiah's chaste mother you conceived by Joachim, that holy man"). In the other he twice uses the phrase "betwene you two" (i.e., Anne and Joachim) to speak of the conception of Mary. Obviously, the position is maculist, even aggressively so. As for the Augustinians, they "generally insist on the absolute universality of original sin,"[6] although one or two Augustinians did express themselves on the other side. Foremost among Austin maculists were Giles of Rome and Gregory of Rimini, the latter arguing that Mary was conceived in sin but not born in sin. (Gregory discussed the matter in his sentence commentary, of which the Austins at York owned two copies.)

Does Bokenham take a position? Not explicitly, and the key moments in his narrative remain somewhat vague, in contrast to such explicit formulations as those just given. Rosemary Woolf has suggested that the efflorescence of literature in praise of Anne during the high and later Middle Ages is a consequence of the debate over immaculate conception (293–97). Her discussion takes for granted that this literature supports the new doctrine. However, Woolf underestimates the tenacity of commitment to the older doctrine, and so she does not consider that the new Anne literature could be used as effectively for the maculist position as for its rival. Clearly, the doctrinal thrust of any Anne text must be determined by its exact formulations.

The doctrine was still extremely contentious when Bokenham was writing. It had been officially declared as doctrine only a few years earlier, in 1439, at the Council of Basel, after more than a century of bitter controversy. This doctrine was by no means easily or universally accepted, especially not by the Dominicans, who continued in the position of their great doctor, Aquinas. They called the council a "synagogue of Satan" and the new doctrine its first diabolical off-spring. The council's ruling did not end debate on the question, for decrees in 1482, 1483, and 1503 forbade further discussion, on pain of excommunication. Only in 1854 was the immaculate conception of Mary declared Catholic dogma, and some Catholics today consider it a theological error.

It can scarcely be surprising, then, to find in about 1450 a range of positions on the question. For instance, one Middle English life of St. Anne (R. Parker) specifies that in his absence, Anne conceived without Joachim's help; both the angel and Anne tell Joachim so (200, 275). Clearly, this would require divine in-tervention and therefore would support the immaculist position. A shorter life similarly has the angel inform Joachim that "thy wyff is with chyld" (Ms. Bodl. 10234, line 169, in R. Parker). On the other hand, a third short life has the angel promise Joachim a child "of hys begetyng" (Ms. Trin, Coll. 601, line 356, in R. Parker), which specifies natural conception, hence a maculist position. Mirk's rendition of "De Concepcione beate Marie" (his homily 4 in the *Festial*) is clearly not immaculist: "shall conceive" is the verb used throughout. In homily 57, "De Nativitate beate Marie," the homilist says that God gave them "fryte of hur bod-ies by grace more then by kynd" (245; fruit of their bodies, by grace more than by nature). Both partners play a role in generating this fruit, and I take the last phrase to mean that the conception was miraculous because it was belated, not that it was without original sin.

Bokenham seems to cover both bases. At the start of his life of Magdalene, he does refer to Jesus' mother as "mary wyth-owtyn synne" (5265), but this evades the touchy question about how and when she became sinless: whether *ab ovo, in utero,* or at birth. In the life of Anne, the angel tells Joachim that "a daughter she hath" (1887) and that this daughter will be filled with the Holy Ghost "from hyr modir wombe" (1892)—a formulation clearly compatible with the Thomist po-sition of sanctification *in utero* but also possibly applicable to sanctification *ab ovo.* When the couple meet at the Golden Gate, Anne says only that "to con-ceyvyn I am made able," and the birth occurs nine months later (1976, 1987). The constant stream of natural imagery seems to align Bokenham's version with the maculism common to his order. So does the series of Old Testament late-life conceptions that the angel recites to Joachim—Sara, Rachel, and the mothers of Samson and Samuel (1875–85), all of them accomplished by divine intervention but through natural process and producing no exemption from original sin. The poet's apology for any possible "heresye / A-geyn the feyth" (1444–45) in his pro-logue to this legend probably alludes to an implicit maculism in conflict with the recent conciliar ruling.

THE QUESTION OF PARENTS and children, already adumbrated in the first two lives, comes to a head in the third life, that of Christine. The hero-ine is only twelve years old when the action occurs, and much of her behav-ior partakes of the insolence and even violence of that passionate age between childhood and maturity. The story, without a prologue, pulls us directly into a tale of father–daughter conflict. The prefect Urban of Tyre, considering his daughter's adolescent beauty, locks her in a tower, there to perform her pagan religious duties until a suitable husband can be found. Eventually he becomes the first of Christine's three persecutors. In this sense, Christine's story can be seen as an extension of that of St. Barbara: Barbara is also locked in a tower by her father, a wealthy official who beheads his daughter upon her conversion to Christianity.

The imprisoned princess is a conventional motif in secular poetry, particularly chivalric romance and *lai*. Think, for instance, of the immured ladies in Marie de France's *lais* "Yonec" and "Guigemar." Structurally identical to the story of Christine is the *chanson de toile* of Audefroi le Batard, "Bele Ydoine." Here another beautiful and stubborn adolescent, pining for the man she loves, is beaten with a horse bridle for her sullen behavior and then locked in a tower for three years. Other spouses are offered and refused. Like Christine, Ydoine eventually gets the man she is committed to by way of a test or ordeal, a tournament that he wins. Bokenham heightens the parallel to chivalric romance in his vocabulary here: besides the tower (which is standard in the story), Urban is "mayster off knychtys" (2110), and Christine is called "to hevenly chevalrye" (2428). The overlap of hagiography with romance and other genres has been affirmed by many scholars. One English collection, the *South English Legendary,* is explicitly meant as an alternative to romance:

Men wilneth muche to hure telle. of bataille of kynge	People like to hear stories of kings' battles
And of knightes that hardy were. that muchedel is lesynge	And of brave knights—stories that are mostly lies.
Wo so wilneth muche to hure. tales of suche thinge	Whoever likes to hears tales of such things
Hardi batailles he may hure. here that nis no lesinge	May hear about brave battles here where there is no lying,
Of apostles & martirs. that hardy knightes were	Tales of apostles and martyrs who were brave knights,
That studevast were in bataille. & ne fleide noght for fere. (d'Evelyn and Mill, 59–64)	Who were firm in battle and did not flee for fear.

Although Bokenham is more subtle and probably less rigidly doctrinaire than this anonymous author, nonetheless his deliberate introduction of the romance vocabulary does serve as a curiously jarring reminder of, and contrast to, secular priorities in art and in life.

As is the habit of young women in towers, Christine does the opposite of what her jailer intends. Meditating on nature from her tower window, she is graced with a revelation of God's goodness and becomes a Christian. Her father at first tries persuasion, beginning with a parental lecture-cum-interrogation in the generic form that has survived these many centuries: Dear, why are you not doing as you've been taught? Do you know how much I've sacrificed for you? And finally: Do as you're told or you'll be sorry (2237–50). Their subsequent argument centers on the doctrine of the Trinity, for Urban fails to understand why, if his daughter can worship what he sees as three deities, she cannot worship more.

This doctrinal point is present in all versions of Christine's ordeal, as is the fact that Christine has three persecutors. However, Bokenham has amplified these givens to foreground triplicity as the theological theme of this legend. It is placed third in his series; he carefully emphasizes the story's tripartite division; an angel warns Christine in her tower that she will be tormented thrice (an incident present in *SEL* but not in Voragine); in one of her ordeals, Christine invokes the three Old Testament "children" saved from the flaming furnace (2719; Dan. 3:8–30); she converts three thousand pagans by her example (2801–20; *SEL* has three hundred; 262); she is confined in an oven for three days (as in *SEL*, whereas Voragine has five: "per quinque dies . . . permansit"); and she recapitulates the doctrine of the Trinity three times, with both her father and the judge Zyon (2835–42) and then again in her ordeal (2895). But Christine does not just preach the Trinity, she exemplifies it. If, as Foucault writes, "the body is the inscribed surface of events . . . , totally imprinted by history," (148), this is especially true of Christine. Because she is tortured three times, she becomes an emblem of trinity—her body the site of intimate knowledge of three in one.

The other religious point the legend makes concerns the severance of family ties. Christine formally renounces her parents, in the ultimate version of what Freud called "family romance": the replacement of real parents "by others of better birth . . . replacing the real father by a superior one" (Freud, 224). Bokenham constructs a long pathetic scene of the mother's visit to Christine in prison. With torn clothing and ashes on her head, the mother begs Christine to recant:

"O doughtir Cristyn, have mercy on me Thi wrechid modyr, for the al oonly	"O daughter Christine, have mercy on me Your wretched mother, for you are the only one

I have and no mo, wych awtyst to be
The lyght of myn eyn; thynk, dowghtir,
    that I
	I have and no more, and you ought to be
	The light of my eyes. Remember, daughter,
	    that I

Ten monethis the bare in my body,
And wyth grete peyn in-to this world
    the brought." (2411–16)
	Bore you ten months in my body
	And brought you into the world with
	    great pain."

Christine replies that Christ, whose namesake she is,

"is my fadir, he is modir also . . .
Wherefor go hense, & labour nomore.
Clepe me not doughtyr; here I the forsake."
  (2426–36)
	"is my father and mother too . . .
	So go away and don't bother any more.
	Don't call me daughter; I forsake you
	    now."

The next day Urban calls her before him, threatening that if she fails to sacrifice to his gods, he will torture her and never call her "daughter" again (2457–58). This, she replies, would be the greatest favor: "I not hou for me thou myght more do" (2462; I don't know how you could do more for me).

Spiritually she is no longer theirs. Physically, though, she is flesh of their flesh and throws it in their faces—literally:

Whyl these tormentours so cruelly dyde schrape	While these torturers so cruelly cut
Cristynnnys sydis & hir flesh dyde race,	Christine's sides and tore her flesh,
A gobet ther-of, as she had lyst to jape,	She took a chunk of it, as if wanting to play,
Sche threu, thus seying, in-to hir fadir face:	And threw it into her father's face, saying
"O ould shreu of yll dayis that pace,	"O old shrew who pass evil days,
Syth thou deysryst flessh for to eet,	Since you wish to eat flesh,
Seke no forthere nere in noon other place.	Seek no further nor elsewhere.
Have of thine own & faste gyne to frete."	Have your own [flesh] and gobble it
(2467–74)	up."

When Urban determines at last to kill his daughter, she prays for him to die "aftyr his meritys" (according to his deserts). That same night, Urban dies a horrible death of swollen entrails and goes to hell. Hearing the news, Christine kneels in a devout prayer of thanksgiving.

At the very end of this legend, Bokenham reminds us of his own efforts to generate this wayward child, his version of Christine. He prays for the saint's mercy

on-to the translatour	on the translator
Wych thi legend compyled, not wyth-out labour	Who compiled your legend, not without labor,
In englyssh tunge . . . (3126–28)	In the English language.

It is not unlike Christine's mother's appeal for mercy earlier on, and the reminder of birth explicit there is punningly latent here in the reminder of the author's "labor." Late in the next century, this was Sir Philip Sidney's favored image of the creative process, but already in Bokenham's time and earlier it was associated with both childbirth and writing.[7] This is, however, a protective attitude toward his own work that we noticed in the Austin friar, as in his earlier concern that his first big hagiography be understood and in his production of the *Mappula* to assist the previous work through the world of readers. Bokenham cannot afford an *envoi* to his exotic tale—this is the wrong genre for it— but plainly he feels that his art deserves appropriate notice, and this is the closest that hagiography can come.

FIVE

Impolitic Bodies II

Tongue, Mouth, Language

If an incident is worth telling, it is worth repeating: this sometimes seems to be an aesthetic principle in pious literature. Christine flings a gobbet of her flesh into her persecutor-father's face, taunting his figurative voracity by giving it literal translation: eat this. With her third torturer, the judge Julian, Christine repeats the episode with another part of her body. When Julian has her breasts cut off and her tongue cut out, Christine spits a piece of the severed tongue into the tyrant's face with such force that he is blinded. The lack of a tongue does not prevent her gloating, "Yet have I speche, & thou wurthyly / Off thine oon eye has lost the sycht" (3081–82). Christine's tongue thus literally becomes a weapon. But such grotesque literality is not the most meaningful use of the tongue, and so Bokenham takes up other dimensions of tongue and mouth later in his legendary.

Three more lives in the collection, the eighth, ninth, and tenth—those of Mary Magdalene, Katherine, and Cecelia—focus on the apparatus and practice of speech, with a carefully constructed decreasing literality. The language theme is latent in all of them by virtue of plot, for Mary preaches, Katherine debates publicly, and Cecelia argues cleverly. Nonetheless, it is Bokenham's poetic skill and ideological intent that foregrounds and orchestrates this theme into a "language group." Although he inherits plot, the shaping of narrative is distinctively his own.

THE LEGEND OF MAGDALENE is the only one in Bokenham's collection that has three parts. As indicated earlier, this is the central story in a number of ways: it is mathematically central, doctrinally central, and commissioned by the most socially exalted patron. Whereas the other legends have at most a prologue to the life, this one has, in addition, a prolocutory, or prologue to the prologue, containing the commissioning scene and the literary polemics discussed in chapter 3. The tripartite structure confers greater dignity to this already important material. Perhaps it mimes the structure of the painted or carved triptych screen often found in church art or that of the "conventional *dispositio*" of the formal academic treatise: proposal / invocation / narration (J. B. Allen, *Ethical Poetic,* chap. 3).

Moreover, the word that Bokenham has chosen, or invented, for this extra section—*prolocutory*—is interesting. The office of prolocutor was a specifically ecclesiastical one; in fact, it was the ecclesiastical version of the speaker in the House of Commons, for the prolocutor led the convocation, or representative assembly of English clergy. The convocation usually met to discuss royal requests for ecclesiastical subsidy, which since the Third Lateran Council in 1179 had been considered "a serious menace to the church" (Kemp, 57). By the fifteenth century, convocation discussions usually centered on who should collect taxes (usually a tenth) from the clergy. In coining the word *prolocutory* for the opening movement of his life of Magdalene, Bokenham thereby inserts a deft reminder of the clergy in their sociopolitical collectivity. In this sense, the life of Mary is not only hagiography but also ecclesiastical genealogy, for Mary, as one of the first and most famous preachers contemporaneous with Jesus and certainly the only female one, is the mother of them all.

Once again, it may seem that this story is what any hagiographer must recount in a life of Magdalene. Yet once again, such determinism proves inadequate, for not every version of Mary's life dwells, as Bokenham's does, on her oratorical career in southern France after Jesus' death. Christine de Pizan, for example, omits it completely from her exceedingly brief notice of Magdalene in the third or hagiographical section of her *Livre de la cité des dames.* Christine mentions only the saint's steadfast commitment to Jesus (Curnow, 3.2.263) and, in two earlier references (1.10.33, 34), her compassionate weeping and her selection by Jesus as the first to announce his resurrection. Although this last reference occurs in a place where Christine wants to vindicate female speech from misogynist slander, it seems to me that Bokenham offers by far the stronger antimisogynist case. Even apart from the structural or symbolic ways in which this is accomplished, Bokenham does, after all—as Christine does not—give voice to his female saints, a powerful, extended, and effective voice. Clearly, Bokenham has made a conscious artistic choice in this matter, and for the period it is a daring one. The Catholic Church forbade preaching by anyone not properly ordained, ipso facto, any woman.

The enthusiast Margery Kempe records a frightening experience in this regard. Arrested at York, Margery is brought to the archbishop's chapel, "and many of the Archbishop's household came there scorning her, calling her 'Lollard' and 'heretic,' and swore many a horrible oath that she should be burned" (1.52). This was no mere idle threat, for in 1401, by the decree *De Comburendo haereticis*—intended specifically to combat the growing and subversive Lollard influence—heresy had become a capital crime in England. The climate was tense in the next decades, with numerous denunciations, investigations, trials, and abjurations. In Norwich between 1428 and 1431, sixty men and women were interrogated, and in another investigation, also in Norwich and also in 1428, at least three were burned. A fourth burning occurred at Chelmsford in 1430, and others, not recorded, may well have taken place (Tanner, *Church,* 140).

One of Bokenham's brothers at Clare, John Bury, earned credentials as a scourge of heretics by sitting as a commissioner at some of these trials (Tanner, *Trials*). Although extant records of the heresy trials do not specifically refer to unlicensed preaching, whether by men or women, nonetheless the question played an important part in Margery Kempe's arrest and interrogation at York.

Although she passes an examination on the articles of faith, still the archbishop's clerics complain that "'the people have great faith in her talk, and perhaps she might lead some of them astray.'" She is then required to swear "'that you will not teach.'" Margery refuses, whereupon "a great cleric quickly produced a book and quoted St Paul for his part against her, that no woman should preach. She, answering to this, said, I do not preach, sir; I do not go into any pulpit. I use only conversation and good words, and that I will do while I live." Given the intensely repressive social climate of the time, it seems courageous for a writer to draw as strongly as Bokenham does the image of the talking, arguing, teaching, and preaching woman.

In another discursive register—less grim but scarcely endearing—women's speech is criticized by ridicule. Female loquacity is probably the best-known reproach in the literary arsenal of medieval misogyny and social satire. As one "proverbial couplet" has it:

There ben women there ben wordis
There ben gese there ben tordys. (Robbins, 394)

Women produce words as naturally and as easily as geese do turds; women are like geese (silly, spiteful, bottom heavy, salable, consumable, flocking together, etc.), and their words are about as valuable as goose turds. This is masculinist ecclesiastical culture in its "popular" guise, and it is another instance of what such a portrayal of women as Bokenham's confronted.

Magdalene's story narrates the making of a preacher. Perhaps this is one reason that its prolocutory and prologue seem to be written with Augustine's *De Doctrina christiana* at hand, for it is basically an *ars praedicandi* cast into narrative form. After Jesus' death, Mary and a company of cobelievers are driven out to sea in a rudderless ship. They arrive in Marseille through God's Providence, and there Mary begins her career as a preacher. She is remarkably effective:

Alle that hir herdyn awundryd were,	All who heard her were astounded,
What for hyr beute on that o party,	Partly because of her beauty,
And for the facundye wych she oysyd there,	And because of the fluency she displayed
And for the swetnesse eek of hyr eloquency,	And because of the sweetness of her eloquence
Wych from hyr mouth cam so plesauntly	Which came so pleasingly from her mouth
That thei haddyn a very delectacyoun	That they were truly delighted
Stylle to stondyn & here hyr predycacyoun.	To stand still and hear her preaching.
(5787–93)	

There is a special reason for Mary's effectiveness:

And no wundyr thow that mowth sothly	No wonder if indeed that mouth—
Wych so feyr kyssys & so swete	Which so often and so devoutly had bestowed
So oftyn had bredyd & so devothly	Such fair and sweet kisses
Up-on cryst oure salvatourys feet,	On Christ our savior's feet
Dyvers tymes whan she hym dede mete,	Often when she met him—
Past othir swych grace had in favour	Had, more than any other [mouth], the grace and favor
Of goddys wurde to shewe the savour. (5794–800)	To demonstrate the savor of God's word.

The immense volume of Magdalene literature in the Middle Ages is elaborated from several fairly tenuous gospel statements. In fact, the medieval idea of Mary Magdalene is a composite, combining in one figure the several Maries mentioned in the New Testament.[1] What stands out, though, is Mary's physical contact with Jesus, particularly with his feet. At his feet she sits (Luke 10:39); his feet she weeps on; kisses; dries with her hair; anoints (Luke 7:38–46); and anoints and wipes with her hair (John 11:2, 12:3).

It is Mary's direct oral–pedal contact with Jesus that creates her as a preacher. The preceding stanza is elaborated from a sentence in Voragine ("Nec mirum, si os, quod tam pia et tam pulchra pedibus salvatoris infixerat oscula, caeteris amplius verbi Dei spiraret odorem") and appears elsewhere, for example, in Bozon's Magdalene (lines 146–49). The locus provides a convenient instance of Bokenham's art, for he shapes his stanza to mime its meaning. It begins with a mouth in the first line of the stanza. In the second and third lines, we discover that this is a kissing mouth; and in the mathematically central fourth line of the stanza, appear the savior's feet, the object of the kissing.

The physical presence of Jesus is a turning point accomplishing a transformation—in the stanza, in Mary's life, and in world history, for these feet are the means by which the kissing mouth becomes the preaching mouth. In the last line of the stanza comes the end, or *telos* (final cause), of the process, God's word, whose savor (taste or odor) delights not sense but spirit. The metaphysical savor of gospel erases any lurking distaste that may accompany the idea of foot kissing. In its transformative process, then, the stanza imitates the working of divine intervention via the body of Jesus—whether in history or the preacher's career or any individual life. Once again, there is an Augustinian precedent. An anonymous fifteenth-century preacher writes, "And skillefulliche may love be likened to a fote, for thus seith Seynt Austyn, 'Pes meus, amor meus—my fote is my love'" (Ross, item 14). The reference is to Augustine's *Enarratio in Psalmum* ix: "Pes animae recte intelligitur amor. . . . Amore enim movetur tanquam ad locum quo tendit" (The foot of the soul is correctly known as love. For by love, it is moved to the place where it is heading).

Not everyone in the late Middle Ages shared a positive perspective on foot kissing. However, the reluctance that Bokenham would have been aware of did not originate in hygienic or aesthetic hesitation but, rather, in motives of status. It was the custom for those who entered the presence of the pope to kiss his ring and his foot. In 1438 (when Bokenham traveled to Italy; see chapter 1) the Council of Florence convened, its main purpose to negotiate unity with the Eastern Church. The first stumbling block came when the Greek patriarch refused to kiss the foot of Pope Eugenius IV. This nearly scotched the council before it began, but a compromise was reached when Eugenius yielded on this point. The English were strong supporters of Eugenius, even though they sent no official embassy to this council, and the Augustinians even more so. I mention this incident to indicate how many layers a hagiographical motif might have or how a motif might acquire new meaning in new circumstances. Here, doctrine, art, and current politics reinforce one another.

In embracing the savior's feet, Magdalene does more than show her devotion. For scriptural commentators, she also makes a doctrinal point. "The head means the Godhead of Christ," declared St. Cyril of Jerusalem, but the feet were symbolic of his humanity. As Leo Steinberg shows, it was Jesus' genitals that played this role in fifteenth-century painting, to display unequivocally the incarnation or "humanation" of Christ. For medieval theologians, though, it was his feet:

> The nature of Christ is two-fold; it is like the head of the body in that He is recognized as God, and comparable to the feet in that for our salvation He put on manhood as frail as our own. (Eusebius, in Steinberg, Excursus XVIII)

> Whoever calls the head of Christ his divinity, and the feet his humanity, he does not stray from the truth. (St. Maximus Confessor, in Steinberg, Excursus XVIII)

> If it seemed right to St. Paul to describe Christ's head in terms of his divinity, it should not seem unreasonable to us to ascribe the feet to his humanity. (St. Bernard, in Steinberg, Excursus XVIII)

The same symbolism might be applied to human beings generally, as an anonymous preacher did at the beginning of the fifteenth century, albeit with a more negative tonality than in preceding examples:

> We se wel, that the pekok whan a loketh abowte on his fair vetherus. his und-irliche prowd & miche ioie makis of hem, but whan a lokez doun & seith the vowlnes of feet. than a take gret sorw to him & wext hegeliche a-schamed of him-silf. Truliche rith tus schuld eche man e this world do, whan a hath be-hold the gaie vetherus o myrthe & prosperite o this world. than let him take hede of his feet, that is to seie his endyngday. the whiche is nat onliche wretchid. but also per-lus. (Grisdale, 63)

> We observe that the peacock, when he gazes on his beautiful feathers, is wonder-fully proud and makes much joy of them, but when he looks down and sees the foulness of feet, then he takes great sorrow and grows highly ashamed of himself. Truly, everyone in this world should do exactly the same when he has beheld the

gay feathers of mirth and prosperity. Then let him take heed of his feet, that is to say, his last day, which is not only wretched but perilous.

Magdalene's is the legend that most fully expresses the incarnation of Jesus. It does so inherently because Mary was an "apostoless" in whose legend Jesus physically appears as a character in his historical presence and also because the heroine was in close physical touch with him. Accordingly, Bokenham's treatment forces us to be always aware of the embodiedness of Jesus through Magdalene's continual attention to his physical needs: "She mynystyrd hym & hys in there nede," (5505) and blessed are those chosen "hym to feden in hys bodily nede" (5526); numerous other places might be cited.

The emphasis on physicality in this tale is not limited to the relationship of Jesus and Mary Magdalene. Instead, Bokenham's distinctive treatment of this famous story exudes a general physicality, often of a calculatedly repulsive kind, for instance, the flux that Mary's sister Martha suffers for twelve years (5511–12) and the twice-stressed stench of Lazarus dead and raised (5636, 5649). Toward the end of the tale, when Mary has become a hermit living in a cave, there is a cluster of reminders of physicality: "bodyly counfort" (6160), "bodyly eerys" (6168), "bodyly food" (6171), "bodyly eye" (6179), and "beryn up a body" (6181). These occur when Mary is dying, to remind the reader of what was at stake theologically from the start of the tale and, indeed, as I argued in chapter 4, in its prefatory material as well. On one hand, the relation is between body and soul in every individual life, and on the other hand, the relation is between physical and spiritual components in the difficult doctrine of incarnation, which occupies the center of Bokenham's religion, just as this legend occupies the center of his text.

Ｋ ATHERINE'S LIFE DEMONSTRATES the lesson of the Magdalene material just preceding it, albeit in another register. Christian rhetoric is used to persuade its recipients of Christian truth. Katherine is no "apostoless" but an Alexandrian princess converted in secret to Christianity. Although Bokenham omits the story of her conversion—related at length by Capgrave, among others—he sends the reader curious about this matter to

My fadres book, maystyr Ioon Capgrave,	The book of my father, master John Capgrave,
Wych that but newly compylyd he. (6356–57)	That he very recently compiled.

Yet Katherine, too, becomes a preacher, and a successful one. Like Bokenham, Katherine is an accomplished speaker in two modes of discourse: the academic style and ordinary speech. She is a highly cultured woman in a city that prided itself on its culture, and she is learned in the seven arts "wych be clepyd lyberal." She is educated

So profoundly, that greth ner smal
Was no clerk founde in that cuntre,
What-evere he were or of what degre,
But that she wyth hym coude comune.
(6394–97)

So thoroughly that no major or minor
Scholar could be found in the land,
Of whatever occupation or rank,
That she couldn't communicate with
him.

Katherine is therefore able to address the emperor in high-flown philosophical terms appropriate to his station and her own, "by many sylogysmys & by many an argument" (6493). The emperor accuses her of "treccherous sotylte" (6657; treacherous subtlety) and sophisticated argument "by poysye, / By rethoryk or ellys by phylosophye" (6693–94). Yet she is also capable of "comown speche" (6499), and it is with a simple profession of faith that she succeeds in reducing to silence the fifty orators hired to debate with her:

Of yow I ask leyser & space
Myn entent pleynly for to declare,
Wyth-owte rethoryk, in wurdys bare
Or argumentatyf dysceptacyoun.
For treuly I mak a protestacyoun
That syth I am in crystys argumentys

I ask you for time and place
To declare my aims fully,
Without rhetoric, in simple words
And without argumentative debate.
For truly I affirm
That since I am instructed in Christ's
    arguments,

Instruct, I for-sake alle argumentys
Of seculer kunnyng, & of phylosophye,
And othir thyng to kun I now denye

I forsake all arguments
Of secular knowledge and of philosophy,
And I now renounce knowledge of any
    other thing

Than hym wych welle is of alle vertu
And of al kunnyng, my lord cryst Ihesu.
    (6760–70)

Than him who is the well of all virtue
And of all knowledge, My Lord Christ
Jesus.

She then proceeds to outline (very briefly) the fundamentals of the faith.

Katherine's victorious tactic is *sermo humilis,* the Christian stylistic tradition treated centrally by Augustine in *De Doctrina christiana* and studied by Erich Auerbach (chap. 1). Her plain homiletic style is as much an *imitatio Christi* as her death will be, for Christ adopted a lower style, as it were, becoming human in order to address humanity.

Not only did God accept a lower ontological status in taking on human nature, but also he adopted a low social status within it as the son of a carpenter who chose to minister to both the poor and the prosperous. He consorted with humbly born disciples and taught in a simple style that all could understand. Yet, despite stylistic modesty, Christian discourse achieves its own sublimity through content, a redefined sublimity that casts aside the classical system of literary decorum with its three levels of style. The reason is that "a Christian orator's subject is always Christian revelation, and this can never be base or in-between" (Auerbach, 35). In Augustine's words:

Among our orators, . . . everything we say, especially when we speak to the people from the pulpit, must be referred, not to the temporal welfare of man, but

to his eternal welfare and to the avoidance of eternal punishment, so that everything we say is of great importance, even to the extent that pecuniary matters,
whether they concern loss or gain, or large or small amounts of money, should not
be considered "small" when they are discussed by the Christian teacher. (*DDC,*
4.18.35)

This is the aesthetic Augustine reinvented from its scriptural foundations.
Indeed, Auerbach observes that Augustine was its major theorist and also the
best Latin witness to it because of his own history: "Before his conversion [Au-
gustine] had been one of those highly cultivated men who thought they would
never overcome their distaste for the style of the Bible" (48). The confrontation
of Christian with pagan–classical culture is arguably the major Augustinian
theme, treated in sermons, Bible commentaries, the *City of God,* and the *Confessions.* As might be expected, this confrontation plays a central role in *De Doctrina
christiana,* which expounds the training of the Christian—in sharp contradis-
tinction from the classical—orator (i.e., the training of the preacher). For there
is, Augustine writes,

> a kind of eloquence fitting for men most worthy of the highest authority and
> clearly inspired by God. Our authors speak with eloquence of this kind, nor does
> any other kind become them. Nor is that kind suitable for others. It is suited to
> them, and the more it seems to fall below that of others, the more it exceeds them,
> not in pompousness but in solidity. (*DDC,* 4.6.9)

This, then, is the Augustinian principle that informs Katherine's speech to
the fifty pagan orators, and there can be no question of its success. It is interesting, therefore, to observe the metaphorics in Augustine's figuration of the successful discourse of the Christian orator. When the "subdued style" does resolve
difficult questions, set forth basic principles, and demonstrate an adversary's
error, "it excites such acclamations that it is hardly recognized as being subdued.
It does not come forth armed or adorned but, as it were, nude, and in this way
crushes the sinews and muscles of its adversary and overcomes and destroys resisting falsehood with its most powerful members" (*DDC,* 4.26.56).

Augustine avails himself here of the rich multiple wordplay in the word
members. The image of the combative nude body, its victory reversing the
usual fate of the naked and unarmed Christian martyr, calls for "limbs" as the
primary meaning. However, this book of the *Doctrina* begins with an analysis
of the rhetoric in some Pauline epistles, and much of this analysis consists of
the enumeration of *membra,* or clauses in a given sentence (4.7.13–20). Finally, at
another metaphorical level, the word *member* can only evoke the conceptual–
linguistic pun at the heart of the Pauline figuration of the Christian congre-
gation: members of one body with Jesus as its head. In the preceding passage,
then, the "most powerful members" of the church are precisely its orator-
preachers, exercising their "most powerful member" (limb or organ), the
tongue, to produce "powerful *membra,*" or clauses to win the victory over paganism and error.

This is what Katherine does as well. Her language is a body, a *corpus,* a site molded by literary, aesthetic, doctrinal, and (as we will see in chapters 7 and 8) political discourses. At the same time, her physical tongue is a weapon, the only one she has, and, from a spiritual perspective, an extremely effective one. Christine's tongue was literally a weapon: spat out forcefully, it blinded the persecutor. Does Bokenham show an explicit consciousness of the tongue in his legend of Katherine as well? I think he does.

Although the thematic emphasis in Katherine's story is on speech acts rather than the apparatus of speech, nonetheless the tongue does make a single appearance in Bokenham's version. It is not, however, her tongue that is in question. In fact, it is curious that Katherine does not have her tongue cut out, for she offends through that organ more specifically than any other saint because of the debate episode. Nonetheless, maiming of the saint's tongue is not part of the Katherine story in any version. Rather, the organ or organs in question here belong to the fifty defeated orators. When the emperor Maxence sees that his fifty hired speakers have been won over by Katherine's sermon, he rages at them:

"O ye lewed knavys, what eyleth yow?	"O you ignorant knaves, what's wrong with you?
Wher is your pompous phylosophye now?	Where is your pompous philosophy now?
Wher is your bost & your avauntyng	Where is your boasting
That ye madyn at youre fyrst comyng?	That you made when you first arrived?
Why stonde ye thus stylle? be ye tunglees?" (6803–7)	Why do you stand still this way? Are you tongueless?"

As mentioned in chapter 2, the text in which Bokenham is likely to have found this reproach occurs in the early Middle English *Seinte Katherine,* when the emperor says to his scholars, "Nabbe ye teth ba ant tunge to sturien?" (465; haven't you got both teeth and tongue to move?). Indeed, the earlier life gives a good deal of prominence to the tongue, using the image seven times in various contexts. (Most of these instances were evidently added by the English poet, for they do not appear in the Latin source, which is also printed in the d'Ardenne edition, or in French or Italian versions of the tale.) If Bokenham was influenced by *Seinte Katherine* in this regard, he made the tongue image far less pervasive than in the thirteenth-century text but, by the same token, more sharply focused and more powerfully effective in its single appearance in his own legendary.

Katherine has what the scholars lack: the power of persuasive speech, figured by the materialist emperor as the organ of speech. Only by acquiring the faith that inspires the saint's speech can the scholars redeem their lack. Until they do, they are, in effect, emasculated, reduced by a heroic woman to the silently passive, stereotyped "female" role. Katherine, however, assumes the "masculine" or leadership position by exercising an organ that is an upwardly displaced version of the male sex organ. (Such displacement is well recognized in medieval medical lore,[2] rationalized there not only by similarity of shape—a metaphorical link—but also by social causality or association—a metonymic link: possession of the lower organ enables use of the upper one.) Obviously, Bokenham is trying to undercut the rigid gender-role divisions that underlie such facile representations.

The three stories considered in this section thus show a carefully graduated movement away from physicality. Christine's tongue, torn out, becomes a physical weapon. Her ability to speak even after this maiming is a miracle, a transcendence of the merely physical; it is in much the same vein as her walking on water or her ability to resurrect the dead. Nor was Bokenham the first to concentrate on the apparatus of speech. This part of Christine's story echoes the legend of Romanus as told by the fourth-century Christian poet-apologist Prudentius in his *Peristephanon*. Because this martyr gives unusually lengthy harangues, his mouth is specially tortured, and there is a ghoulishly detailed scene of the excision of his tongue. The operation does not, however, prevent further speech, for "Christum loquenti lingua numquam defuit" (10.928; Tongue never failed him who spoke of Christ). The point is repeated in another story, that of Cyprian, of whom the poet writes:

> incubat in Libya sanguis, sed ubique lingua pollet, sola superstes agit de corpore, sola obire nescit. (13.4–5)

> His blood rests in Africa, but his tongue is potent everywhere; it alone of all his body still survives in life, it alone cannot die. (trans. Thomson)

A similar movement, made explicit, appears in Magdalene, whose mouth evolves from erotic kissing to pious kissing and is finally transformed by contact with Jesus into the vehicle of gospel. Katherine's faith serves the same transfigurative function, turning academic rhetoric into the handmaiden of faith (to borrow an image from scholastic discussions of the relationship of faith to reason). Even more radically, Katherine's faith enables her to produce a new style genuinely appropriate to the content of her new faith.

Cecelia's life, the last in this series about the production and use of language, is the most abstract in its concerns. Indeed, the concept of the abstract is itself the theme, opening areas of perennial interest to philosophy. How is the abstract mediated for and by the material world, and what are the means of exchange in this mediation? Put in these terms, the notion of the abstract can be appreciated in its relation to language theory, which was an important branch of scholastic philosophy. Even more simply, the point of the Cecelia might be said to be dualism: the philosophical basis of Christianity.

L IKE CHRISTINE AND KATHERINE, Cecelia is aggressive in her use of language, displaying the insolence that hagiography often permits the woman martyr. Cecelia's verbality, though, is in a different mode than Katherine's: her debates are not public, and she plays clever language games with her persecutor:

"Of what condycyoun art thou?" quod he.
"A ientyl wumman born, & noble," quod she.

"What is your position?" he said.
"A noble gentlewoman," said she.

"I aske," quod he, "of thi relygyoun & thi byleve."

"I am asking," he said, "about your religion and your belief."

"Thy askyng," quod she, "ys lewyd, I preve,
That two answers sekyth to oon questyoun . . . ."

"Your asking," she said, "is ignorant; proof:
You request two possible answers to one question . . . ."

"Knowyst not," quod he, "of what power I am?"

"Don't you know my power?" he said.

"Yis, yis!" quod Cycyle, "I knowe yche deel,
And what youre powere ys I can tel weel.
Alle youre power, as yt semyth to me,
May wele to a bleddyr lyknyd be . . ."

"Oh, yes," Cecelia said, "I know every bit
And can say what your power is.
All your power seems to me
Comparable to a bladder [balloon] . . ."

"Wyth iniuryis thou begunne, & hast perseveraunce
In the same, quod Almache; quod she sothly:

"You began with insults and you keep on

The same way," said Almachius; she replied,

"Iniurye may not be seyd propyrly
But wyth wurdys of deceyt yt uttryd be."
    (8105–27)

"Insult may not be correctly said to exist
Unless it be uttered with deceitful words."

This rather tiresome stichomythia also characterizes the prefect's dialogues with Cecilia's two converts: her husband, Valerian, and her brother-in-law, Tiburtius. Such rapid-fire dialogue is distinctive in Cecilia's story, and not only in Bokenham's version. It is stylistically appropriate precisely because of the language theme because it makes apparent the notion of language as exchange. After a frustrating interview with the two men, the prefect Almache exclaims, "Where-to we / That cerclyn aboute in batayle verbal?" (7962–63). He puts his finger on the very spot, for the "verbal battle" of linguistic exchange is emblematic of even deeper structures in the tale.

Exchange and release from it are important motifs in this legend. The newly-wed Cecelia requests release from the sexual obligations of marriage, claiming to have a guardian angel who prevents her participation in this socially approved exchange between persons and families. Valerius offers to believe his wife's story in return for a vision of the angelic lover, and the trade-off is made. When Cecelia is widowed by the martyrdom of her husband, Valerius, the prefect requisitions her goods and property, but Cecelia preempts this appropriation by removing her goods from the economic cycle of exchange and instead distributing them to the poor as a free gift.

The imagery of commercial exchange is especially striking in the short sermon made by Cecelia to the officers who escort her to her ordeal and who weep in pity for the noble young woman. Cecelia converts these officers by convincing them that her death is no loss but, rather, a lucrative exchange with a hundred-fold profit. The soldiers' belief would, she says, earn the same spectacular reward, and she urges them to make this deal with the businessman God. Here is Bokenham's version of the passage (which in Voragine is considerably terser):

"That I now rather to deye chese	"That I now choose rather to die
Than to sacryfyse, ys not to lese	Than to sacrifice is not to lose
My youth, but a commutacyoun	My youth, but a commutation
Of wysdam it ys, as ye se moun;	Of wisdom, as you may see;
Lych as a man comenaught [covenaunt] ded make	Just as if a person made an agreement
Erthe to yivyn & gold to take,	To give earth and take gold,
Or ellys to chaungyn an ould rottyn hous	Or to exchange an old rotten house
For a ryal paleys of stonys precyous.	For a royal palace of precious stones.
But now of you I aske a questyoun:	But now I ask you a question:
For ych peny if ye receyve shuld moun	If for every penny, you could receive
At a market or a feyr an hool shylyng,	At a market or fair a whole shilling,
As many as thedyr ye ded bryng,	As many [more] as you started with,
Wolde ye not spedyn you thedyr hastly?	Wouldn't you hurry there?
I trowe ye wold! now serys, treuly	I believe you would! Now sirs, in fact
God of hys goodnesse hath up set	God in his goodness has set up
In hys courht abovyn a bettyr market;	An even better market in his court above,
For to every thyng that to hym is soulde	For to everything sold to him
The reward ys ordeynyd an hyndyr-foulde,	Is ordained a hundredfold reward
And ther-to lyf that nevere shal cees.	And, besides, eternal life.
Now thynke ye not this a noble encrees,	Now don't you think this a fine profit,
An hundyrd for oon, wyth hys addytament?	A hundred for one, with his bonus added?
Hou trou ye? seyith your entent."	What do you think? Speak your mind."
Quod they ych oon, "we byleve veryly."	Every one of them said, "We believe."
(8071–93)	

Not every version of Cecelia's life contains this sermon or the incident about the attempted sequestration of Cecelia's wealth and property. Chaucer omits both of these economic narremes from his extremely abbreviated treatment of the legend in his *Second Nun's Tale,* as did his likely source for the portion of the tale in which it occurs (Reames, "Recent Discovery"). Perhaps such attention to finances struck some readers as repulsively materialistic, despite its gospel echoes (Matt. 19:29; Mark 10:30). The sermon might even have been considered theologically suspect, for the commercial metaphor is at odds with one of the most basic Christian doctrines, the definition of grace as an absolutely free and unmerited gift of God. Hence it implicitly contradicts the emphasis, in what Courtenay calls "the new Augustinianism" of the late Middle Ages, on divine action and initiative in the matter of grace, a strong anti-Pelagian position maintained "often at the expense of human effort and human merit" (308–9).

The reference here is to an important controversy of the mid-fourteenth century, in which Augustinianism played the central role. One participant was Gregory of Rimini, who was elected general of the Order of Friars Hermits in 1357. Since Gregory's work was to some extent influenced by the very scholar it aimed to refute—William of Ockham—it "raises the curious problem" (as Etienne Gilson remarked) "of possible collusions between nominalism and a certain Augustinianism" (502). Also engaged in the debate was Thomas Bradwardine, chancellor of St. Paul's, king's confessor, archbishop of Canterbury, and Oxford theologian. Although not a member of the Augustinian order (he was a secular priest), Bradwardine put forward an ultra-Augustinian position against the "pestilential Pelagians" (Leff, *Bradwardine,* 2) of his day, whose skepticism and (relatively) human-centered psychology made them, in his view, dangerous to orthodoxy. Indeed, Bradwardine's term "Pelagian" refers to one of St. Augustine's most important opponents, the British-born monk Pelagius, who challenged what he saw as excessive pessimism in Augustine's theories of sin and grace. Leff, who identifies William of Ockham as the most important of the fourteenth-century "Pelagians," summarizes Ockham's position on grace and merit as follows:

> Since by God's absolute power habits are unnecessary, the Holy Spirit can accept the natural act of a created will and so actions of hope and faith themselves can be natural and yet gain supernatural reward. This acceptance by God of natural acts . . . means that a man, by acting, can gain from God, and that natural deeds carry a very rich potential worth. (Leff, *Bradwardine,* 204)

In the preface to *De Causa Dei,* Bradwardine deplores precisely the commercialistic implications of his opponents' theories: "If they happen to give a place to grace, or perfunctorily declare that it is necessary, they still boast that they can deserve it by the power of their own free will, so that in this way grace may not seem to be a free gift at all but rather something that is sold" (Obermann, *Bradwardine,* 28).

The strict view is that human beings do not deserve the gift of salvation, nor can they earn it, although they can manifest its presence. What this means for the literary artist, hypothetically at least, is that representationally, grace is outside the loop of exchange. It cannot be bought or traded and thus cannot be represented as a mercantile transaction. Cecelia's little sermon stubbornly represents salvation not as a gift but as a regulated commercial investment. Moreover, it shows humanity, not God, taking the initiative in this exchange.

There are other ways to approach the locus, however. R. A. Shoaf examined the role of commercial metaphor in Christianity, especially of *commercium* as "a crucial concept, generating a nearly inexhaustible supply of imagery for the relationships between God and man" (9). This imagery achieves its meaning not through the notion of grace but, rather, through the concept of philosophical dualism on which Christianity is predicated. Jesus is the archtrader or merchant because he exchanged himself for humanity, ransomed or redeemed (bought back) humanity from sin with the free gift of his body and his love. This is why Augustine was able to refer to Jesus as merchant (*mercator*) or celestial bargainer (*negotiatore caelesti*):

> Attendite omnes homines, utrum ad aliud sint in hoc saeculo, quam nasci, laborare et mori. Haec sunt mercimonia regionis nostrae, ista hic abundant. Ad tales merces Mercator ille descendit. . . . O bone Mercator, eme nos. Quid dicam, eme nos, cum gratias agere debeamus, quia emisti nos! (sermon 130.2 in Shoaf)

> Mark this question everyone: whether there is anything else in this world than to be born, to labor, to die. These make up the merchandise of our world, these things abound here. For such pay did that Merchant descend. . . . O good Merchant, buy us. What am I saying, buy us? when we ought rather to give thanks, that you have bought us.

> Haec enim mira commutatio facta est, et divine sunt peracta commercia, mutatio rerum celebrata in hoc mundo a negotiatore caelesti: venit accipere contumelias, dare honores, venit haurire dolorem, dare salutem, venit subire mortem, dare vitam. (*Enarrationes in Psalmos,* 30.2)

> For this marvelous exchange was made, these divine transactions accomplished, this alteration of affairs in our world consummated, all by the heavenly Merchant: He came to receive reproaches, to give honors; he came to drink grief and sickness, to give health and salvation; he came to undergo death, to give life. (Shoaf, 10–11; cf. also Augustine's sermon 80.5, in Steinmetz)

Jesus is thus the great mediator between two levels of reality, the physical and the spiritual. Moreover, he represents, uniquely and simultaneously, the principle of exchange and the liberation from exchange: redemption and grace at once. From this perspective, Cecelia's commercialistic sermon takes its place as one of various literary techniques deployed in a multilayered exploration of dualism and the transcendence of dualism, for the imagery of commerce concretizes the dualism inherent in Christian philosophy and therefore in Christian narrative.

It is Tiburtius, the brother-in-law, who most succinctly expresses the doctrinal lesson of this tale. Before he dies, Tiburtius baits his persecutor with a philosophical riddle. He refers to other martyrs who

"wyth her hool herte despysed wyshly
That semyth to be sumwhat in apparence
And ryht nowht ys in very existence,
And ther-ageyn han foundyn & wyth
deth boht
That most veryly is & yet semyth nouht."
(7908–12)

"with their whole heart despised, certainly,
What, in appearance, seems to be something
But in its real existence is nothing,
And on the other hand found and with death bought
What most truly is and yet seems nothing."

What seems to be and is not, he explains, is the world; what most perfectly is, but seems not, is the fate ordained after death.

This oscillation between temporal and spiritual levels of meaning accounts for Cecelia's notorious insolence. Cecelia herself calls attention to the language theme by reproaching the tyrant for asking a question capable of two answers (8108–9). Because it is about dualism, this narrative relies rhetorically and structurally on patterns of doubleness to represent the subjective or cognitive experience of dualism. If the story of Christine is patterned in threes to emphasize its trinitarian lesson, so Cecelia's is patterned in twos to express dualism.

The strategy is especially prominent in the structure of inner and outer spaces governing the wedding scene that opens the tale. The first of these spaces is sartorial. Cecelia wears a hair shirt next to her skin, but over it, clothing of white and gold "the werd to blynde" (7470–71; to deceive the world). Next, psychological exteriority and interiority—sensual perception and intellection or will, objectivity and subjectivity—are contrasted when Cecelia hears the organ sing a wedding march, but "covertly in hyr inward mynde," she sings a solemn prayer for chastity. This is the incident that made Cecelia the patron saint of music, because it is about a musical event, the wedding march, and—more important—because it demonstrates the "inner ear" essential to the work of every composer and musician. For a musician, this is the awareness of tonality, so internalized that it enabled the deaf Beethoven to continue to compose. For Cecelia, it is the spiritual awareness enabling her steadfast and active faith.

We are then made aware of duality in another register: inner and outer architectural spaces, beginning with the wedding-night discussion of the newlywed pair, in which Cecelia reveals her secret commitment:

The derknesse of nyght	Night's darkness
Of the maryage day had flemed the lyht,	Had chased away day's light,
And ych man to his loggyng was go,	And everyone had gone to his house;
Valeryan & Cycyle to her chaumbyr went tho,	Then Valerian and Cecelia went to their chamber
Where whan thei were in her secre sylence,	Where, when they were in their secret silence,
Thus Cecylye to hym uttryd hyr sentence. (7483–88)	Cecelia thus revealed her meaning to him.

The couple retire in privacy, but Cecelia's confession requires Valerian to leave this enclosed, intimate space: he must reenter the public world to find Pope Urban, who will baptize him. Specifically, he has to go three miles down the Appian Way and ask further directions from poor people sitting in the street (7543–54). These detailed and explicit instructions, given by Cecelia, create for us both the dangerous urban setting that surrounds the marriage chamber and the social threat surrounding any individual conversion during the period of persecutions. When Valerian returns to the chamber, an angel brings twin garlands for the couple. Almost immediately thereafter, a second man enters the narrative: Valerian's brother "cam & at the dure dede cal" (7702). He, too, must make the trip to Urban; the same directions are given, and once again we visualize the warm, safe bedroom versus the hazardous, poverty-ridden cityscape. The brothers later convert Almache's officer Maximus, who, for the third time in the tale, produces the image of inner and outer architectural spaces. He does so in a context that provides a spiritual gloss on the two previous narrative instances. At the brothers' execution, Maximus swears that he sees angels escort their souls into heaven. These angels, he says, are brighter

"than evere was mayde wych in fressh wede	"than ever was any maid who, in new clothes,
Owt of hyr chaunnbyr ded procede	Came out of her chamber
Ageyn hyr spouse, hym in to fette." (8043–45)	Toward her spouse to bring him in."

Interiority and exteriority thus constitute an important axis of symbolic meaning in the tale.

Pairs both imagistic and structural repeat this dualism throughout the story: sexual binarism, the marital couple, the pair of brothers, the two angelic garlands with which Cecelia and Valerian are crowned, the white lilies and red roses of which these garlands are composed, and the two martyrdoms of first the men and then the woman.

Of course, the conclusions of these pairs, oppositions, and exchanges is that they are ultimately to be resolved in faith, which is the bridge between inner and outer, spiritual and sensual. What happens to Cecelia's body is therefore significant, for she is the one saint in Bokenham's collection not immediately dispatched by decapitation. Three sword strokes do not suffice to kill her immediately, and since this is the legal limit, she can be given no more (8231–39). The saint survives for three days "half-deed" (Chaucer, *CT,* 8.533; Bokenham, 8235) or "half a-lyve . . . half quik & half ded," as *SEL* has it.

In fact, Cecelia is both living and dead, a liminal–transgressive figure linking two worlds normally distinct and opposed. She becomes an emblem of the theology of her tale. If Christine's body, in her three ordeals, is an image of trinity, so Cecelia's living–dead body is the visible site of passage between physical and spiritual levels of reality. Her body is a bridge, just as her preaching is a bridge in the linguistic realm, or language itself is a bridge between people, between the physical and psychological levels of human existence, and between the present perceptible and the absent invisible. Similarly, her property serves as a bridge to *caritas,* and marriage is a bridge between two individuals, recreating them (theoretically) as "one flesh."

Music, of which Cecelia is the patron saint, is the bridge between immediate and absolute realities. We hear music sensually and produce it physically. It is, by nature, ever changing, a product of time (successive moments, tempo) and violence (the impact of hand or tool on metal, strings, or stretched skin). At the same time, music participates in the abstract absolute because it is the product of unchangeable mathematical laws—numerical proportions and intervals—such as govern the cosmos itself. And as with any sensual or physical phenomenon, including language, the pleasure of music may be an end in itself or may conduce to a "higher" reality. Thus music is inherently like language, polyvalent in partaking of two worlds. This is just the paradox Augustine addresses in the last chapter of *De Musica,* that the physical (a tone) creates the mental (a sensation, then a memory) and hence is a superior truth (though not of a superior kind). How can this be? Augustine emphasizes the interdependence of body and soul, but his main argument is an analogy with the incarnation of Jesus:

> Be rather amazed at the body's being able to make anything in the soul. . . . And yet, it has a beauty of its own, and in this way it sets its dignity off to fair advantage in the eyes of the soul. And neither its wound nor its disease has deserved to be without the honor of some ornament. And the highest Wisdom of God deigned to assume this wound, by means of a wonderful and ineffable sacrament. . . . And so it is not surprising that a soul operating in mortal flesh feels the passion of bodies. . . . The true in the body is better than the false in the soul. (332)

Cecelia's half-dead body both is and represents the resolution of "opposites" or of paradoxes, in a vision such as is revealed to Valerian in his conversion: a vision of "o lord & oon feyth ther-to, / O baptem . . . & o god also" (7625–26; one lord and one faith as well, one baptism and one god also). This is the unity to which duality finally reduces, and with it sex, money, and language (or marriage, commerce, and rhetoric, to name the systems in which these means of exchange participate). This is the unity represented by the body of Jesus. Cecelia's commerce is with eternity; she is "sapiens negotiatrix" (Connolly, 183: "a smart negotiator"),[3] able to participate in what the *New Catholic Encyclopedia* calls "the economy of salvation," "God's salvific economy."

Even in its urversion, the *passio* composed in about 500, the Cecelia story is a skillful, dramatically rendered meditation on sophisticated philosophical themes, presented as a martyr's legend. I am tempted to write "disguised as a martyr's legend," but surely the point of this story is that every philosophical or spiritual theme comes to us in some physical form. The consequences are that appearances require interpretation and that the all-important themes are capable of representation—a comforting message (indeed, a salvational one!) for hagiographers and scholars alike. Although Osbern Bokenham inherited Cecelia's story, it is to his credit that he was an astute enough reader and an able enough poet to notice and enhance what he found in his sources, producing an artful revision of an already artful prototype.

Impolitic Bodies III

Breast, Genital, Gut, and All

The last three of the thirteen lives in Bokenham's collection form a coda, concentrating more densely some of the themes of the body already introduced in the other lives. In an appropriate stylistic adjustment, the eleventh and twelfth lives, those of Agatha and Lucy, display a sustained and sometimes revolting creatural naturalism not dwelled on elsewhere. Although specific hideous torments are inflicted on each martyr as her legend's skeletal plot requires, these are named but not wallowed in with any particular rhetorical *amplificatio*. With Agatha and Lucy, however, we do get an *amplificatio* both of torture and of what is usually perceived as distasteful or disgusting about the human body: its wounds and diseases, wastes and ejaculations. *Coda*—the word I just used in its literary sense—can be spelled in Latin as *cauda,* "a suffix, ending, or tail." The word *taille* provided Chaucer with a nice pun at the end of the *Shipman's Tale* in which a free-spending libertine wife uses it to mean both a tally stick and her own rear end. Bokenham himself does not introduce either a Latin or an English version of this word into his text, but his thematic concerns at this point justify my association, as I hope to show.

Breast

St. Agatha's iconographic attribute is the breast. She is often represented holding a breast in a pair of pincers or with a sword driven through her breasts; occasionally she is depicted with the flesh hook that was used to rip her breasts (Milburn). Although the removal of breasts is not unique to Agatha—Christine's breasts were also cut off, and milk flowed out instead of blood (3011–18)—it is the distinctive central feature of Agatha's ordeal and her sanctity, and it is only Agatha whose breasts are restored to her body. Accordingly, Bokenham makes every effort to amplify his references to this part of the saint's body.

The consul Quincian does not merely order Agatha's torture but urges the torturers as follows:

"Touchyth hyr a lytyl from the herte
Up-on hyr pappys & doth hyr smerte,
And let hyre knowyn what ys peyn."
　(8587–89)

"Touch her near the heart
On her breasts and make her hurt,
And let her know what pain is."

The torturers oblige:

And thei anoon hyre gunne to streyn;
Sum wyth pynsouns blunt & dulle
Hyr tendyr brestys begunne to pulle
Ful boystously; summe in here hondys
Browhtyyn brennyng hoot fyr-brondes,
And therwyth hyr pappys al to-brent;
Sun wyth yirnene forkys out rent
The flesh ther-of, that gret pyte
How the blood owt ran yt was to se
On every syde ful pleneuously.
And whan this was doon, he gan to cry
And chargyd hys tormentours in al hast
Hem of to kutten & way to kaste
Wyth-oute pyte or reuthe, allas!
　(8590–8603)

Then they began to force her.
Some with blunt, dull pincers
Began to pull her tender breasts
Very crudely; some in their hands
Brought burning hot firebrands,
And burnt her paps therewith;
Others with iron forks tore out
The flesh of them, so that great pity
It was to see how the blood ran out
On every side very plentifully.
When this was done, [Quincian] shouted
Commanding his tormentors quickly
To cut them off and throw them away
Without pity or mercy, alas!

To this diabolical sadism, Agatha responds with a spirited denunciation:

And whan a-wey was kut both flesh & fel,

Agas thus seyd: "o wrecchyd & cruel

And cursyd tyraunth, hast thou no shame
A-wey to kuttyn that on thy dame
Thou dedyst soukyn for thi fostryng
Ere thou koudyst etyn, whyl thou were
　ying
And ere thou wyt haddyst or dyscresyoun?
Where-fore me semyth greth confusyoun
It awt to be to every man
Thus to dysfyguryn a wumman
As thou hast me in thi fersnesse. (8605–15)

And when both flesh and skin were cut
　away,

Agatha thus spoke: "O wretched and
　cruel

And cursed tyrant, have you no shame
To cut away what on your mother
You sucked in your nursing
Before you could eat, while you were
　little
And before you had sense or judgment?
So I think it should be a
Great shame to every man
To disfigure a woman like this
As you have [disfigured] me in your
　fierceness."

She adds that despite the loss of her breasts,

"In my soule al hool wyth-ynne
Pappys I have wych fro me tuynne
Thou nevere shalt moun wyth no peyne,

"In my innermost soul, unharmed
Breasts I have that you will never
Be able to separate from me with any
　torture,

Where-wytht I fostre & susteyne   And with them I nurture and sustain
Al my wyttys ful dylygently."   All my faculties very diligently."
     (8619–23)

Afterward, when Agatha has been thrown back into prison, an old man appears to her. He claims to have been present when Quincian "dede rende / From thi brest thi pappys cruelly" (8654–55; cruelly ripped your breasts from your chest). He says that her answer tormented the tyrant more than the pain did her and offers to cure her with his ointments, for "they mounn wele be recuryd ageyn / And maad al hool" (8659–60; they [her breasts] can be healed and made whole again). Agatha refuses. At first the old man thinks this is from sexual modesty, and he tries to allay her fear by reminding her that he, too, is a Christian. She replies that she is neither afraid nor embarrassed, for the doctor is so far advanced in age and she herself so horribly mutilated that both of them are beyond either feeling or provoking lust (8673–80). Her reluctance comes, rather, from the determination to accept nothing except from Jesus. When the old man reveals that he comes from Jesus—he is St. Peter—the breasts are miraculously restored.

In Bokenham's day, the female breast was even harder to ignore than it is today. Naked breasts were in vogue among noblewomen after about 1429 for events of high frivolity, and even though it is unlikely that many were seen at festivities at provincial Clare Castle, anyone with Bokenham's connections would have been aware of this courtly fashion. Thomas Gascoigne was a somewhat eccentric but well-respected cleric and chancellor at Oxford. In his *Dictionaria theologica,* compiled between 1433 and 1457, Gascoigne deplores the fashions of his day in the tone of Chaucer's Parson some decades before. Men, Gascoigne scolds, wear tights and slashed capes that shamefully exhibit their thighs and genitals, and women's naked breasts (actually he writes "chests," *pectora*) present many occasions for sins of word and touch (144–45, s.v. *Ornatus*). King Henry VI was known for his innocence and even prudery, but his courtiers were not; they "introduced a bevy of unclad dancers into a Christmas Ball," which Henry fled, crying "Fy, fy, for shame!" (James, *Henry*).

In France from 1444 onward, even more scandalous events were taking place at the court of Charles VII. The king's young mistress, Agnès Sorel, was particularly notorious for displaying her naked breasts. Sorel was, as Margaret Scott puts it, "the inventor of new shock tactics in dress at the court" (26), and her example was imitated and denounced by many. Scott's comment is based on the words of a contemporary, Georges Chastellain, chronicler to Philip the Good of Burgundy. Chastellain wrote that Sorel was the producer and inventor ("produiseresse et inventeresse") of whatever could lead to ribaldry and dissoluteness in matters of dress (4.366). Jean Jouvenal des Ursins, archbishop of Rheims, in 1445 wrote to his brother Guillaume, just named chancellor of France, that Guillaume should advise the king to correct various feminine sartorial faults in his household, including "ouvertures de par devant, par lesquelles on voit les tetins, tettes et seing des femmes" (Champion, 39; front openings through which one sees the teats, nipples, and breasts of women).

The breast was thus something of a cause célèbre in French moralistic circles during these years, and the issue can only have been exacerbated by the scandalous painting of Sorel as a bare-breasted Virgin Mary, completed in 1449 by the famous portraitist and illuminator Jean Fouquet (see figure 5). There is little chance that this juicy gossip could have escaped the ear of parties in England attuned to court matters and the conduct of the war, particularly given the constant marital, diplomatic, and cultural exchanges between France and England. Furthermore, the "wronged" queen of Charles VII, Marie of Anjou, was the aunt of Margaret of Anjou, who married Henry VI and became queen of England in 1445. A biographer of Agnès Sorel remarks that when Charles entered Paris in 1435, "the pamphlets of the English . . . repeated only one thing": the scandal of Agnès, the immorality of Charles's court (Dorliac, 80).

FIGURE 5 The French king's mistress, Agnès Sorel, as the Virgin Mary. Portrait by Jean Fouquet, about 1449. By permission of the Koninklijk Museum voor Schone Kunsten, Antwerp.

Bokenham's rhetorical inflation of the breast thus can be read as a topical allusion to courtly fashion, but that is far from being its whole purpose. Bokenham was not mainly a social satirist or even a sharp commentator in the Gascoigne mode, but a propagandist for the faith in its fifteenth-century Augustinian version. Next I look at his treatment of the breast as an extension of the polemical position that I described in chapter 3.

Certainly the legend of Agatha, as written by Bokenham, succeeds in demystifying the female breast as a focus of sexual attraction. The constant attention to this part and the continual reference to the saint's breasts as "them" tend to reify the breast as a functional object whose primary use is nursing, as Agatha reminds her persecutor. Moreover, the breast becomes an object in that it can be separated from the body and thrown away like any scrap of meat. It is tempting for ultrafeminists to view Bokenham's amplificatory procedure here as merely another instance of masculine sadistic fantasy. Because I address this question at some length in my last chapter, I confine myself here to asserting that Bokenham's aim is the reverse: he intends to expose masculine sadistic fantasy as precisely that, whether in its hagiographical or its lyric manifestation.

Paradoxically, the separation and fetishization of body parts are practices shared by persecutor and lover—one in action and the other in representation only. Penetration of the female body provides a metaphorical association between erotic and persecutory action, an association already articulated in Prudentius's fourth-century telling of the ordeal of St. Agnes. Eroticizing the executioner's sword, Prudentius has the martyr say,

hic, hic amator iam, fateor, placet:	This lover, this one at last, I confess it, pleases me.
ibo inruentis gressibus obviam,	I shall meet his eager steps half-way
nec demorabor vota calentia:	and not put off his hot desires.
ferrum in papillas omne recepero	I shall welcome the whole length of his blade into my bosom,
pectusque ad imum vim gladii	drawing the sword-blow to the depths of my
traham. (*Peristephanon* 14.74–78)	breast. (Trans. Thompson)

Prudentius does not use the word *vagina* (literally, "sword sheath"), but he hardly needs to, for the saint's heated rhetoric and sword imagery already call it to mind. Bokenham offers no such eroticization of weaponry or torture, for in his text the only figurative husband is Christ. If for Bokenham the persecutor is somehow related to the erotic lover, the connection is more subtle than Prudentius allows.

The torturer's procedure may neutralize the lover's passion, but in a way also imitates it, for the rhetorical device of the descriptive catalog or blazon of female charms reduces and fragments its object. Like a sadistic one, a thoroughly sexualized or aestheticized view of the body singles out a particular biological feature for scrutiny while ignoring the individual's integrity as a physical and moral being. Thus Geoffrey of Vinsauf offers two blazons, one of a woman's body and another of her attire, as if the two systems were equivalent, both of them merely aesthetic. "So let the radiant description descend from the top of her head to her toe, and the whole be polished to perfection" (3.598–99), he advises. Joseph of Exeter's description of Helen of Troy in his *Yliados* takes this process to extreme grotesquerie, for Joseph's description does not limit itself to appearance but penetrates to the body's interior:

> In like manner her inner nature has secretly adorned the glorious world of her inner parts, inhabiting her generative chambers and governing the city of her viscera. Her heart is the prime mover and chief governor of the inner works. Her loquacious lung refines the modulations of her tongue. Her spleen dispenses laughter by a little opening. Her comely little gall-bladder is set afire by quick anger. . . . An itching in her tender liver gently titillates her even when she is calm. (Miller, "Blazons," 379)

Particularly egregious as an illustration of the catalog method is an anonymous poem contemporary with Bokenham, "How a lover praiseth his lady" (ed. Hammond). The poem appears in the manuscript anthology known as Fairfax 16, which was published about 1450 and was an assembly of booklets whose contents had been composed at various times over the previous seventy years. In fact, praise of a lady is only part of this odd poem, in which the lady makes her appearance only after 190 lines of prefatory material. The sensibility is one of scientific analysis, orderliness, and thoroughness. The piece opens with a detailed astronomical specification (1–14). It then moves to a garden geometrically ordered ("cast by geometrye / By euclyde ys . . . eye": 33–34), filled with medicinal plants and tended by medical authorities mythic, classical, and medieval: Apollo, Hippocrates, Galen, and Avicenna (90–94). Social satire enters in the form of a miniutopia, for near the garden is a city that has religion without envy, lordship without extortion, commerce without greed, marriage without instability, and ideal human types constituting a brief estates satire (150–90). There follows a digression on the poet's rhetorical inadequacy (212–43) and then—my point—the long-awaited main topic, a lengthy variant of the conventional blazon of female charms.

This listing renders each part in very full "anatomically correct" detail, as if in a dissecting laboratory; it is so methodical as to approach burlesque or grotesquerie. The head is not only admired but also measured; the wit within is certified free of mania ("Ther was no mannye": 254) or any "furious mocion" (255). For the lady's golden hair, the poet appeals to Chaucer's Absolon ballade in the prologue to the *Legend:* her hair is fairer than that of "yong absolon / Estrild [presumably Esther]. Eleyne. or fresshe Polexene" (261–62). We get a rather ghoulishly detailed description of the eyes and their physiological structure (308–9), the blonde, arched eyebrows (316–19), and the correctly proportioned forehead (321–31). The lips are described with a conceit seeming to anticipate Donne: they "wyth chyld ben by maydenhede / Swol" (346–47). Nor does the enthusiastic poet fail to pay homage to the lady's epiglottis ("pyglote," 348), tongue, and, apparently, sublingual salivary glands (348–55). We are reassured that the teeth are not only even, small, and white but "without out ake or putre-faccion" (359). The neck receives seventeen lines of description (362–78). Ver-bally, at least, the author cops a "fele" of his beloved's "appul brests" (384), "so lyte so white so hard so rounde" (386). We learn that her nails are naturally red, "not peynted as in spayne" (408) and that she has a twenty-inch waist (413–14). Last of all comes

the paleys of venus the quene
The goolden cloyster of maydenhode I mene
Naturys celle storer of mankynde. (432–34)

The poem ends with a review that breaks down the lady's body into a classifica-tion system different from the hierarchical. Now she is reduced to a set of fifteen beauties, listed in series of threes: three white (all over, teeth, eyes); three red (nails, lips, cheeks); three long (neck, sides, fingers); three round (breasts, arms, and "anothir thing which I speke not of at all"; 457); and, finally, three little (ears, mouth, and feet).

In few love poems is the strategy of fragmentation deployed quite as trans-parently and methodically as in "How a Lover," and few love poems can pro-voke in the reader as strong a desire to reassert what Augustine calls "the force and power of integrity" of the body (*De Genesi contra Manichaeos,* 1.21). Given its medical–scientific orientation, it is a fairly short step from the poem to the dissecting table that lurks in the subtext to its raptures. Even though I do not want to posit any sadistic intention and suspect the poet may well have been a doctor—perhaps even doctor to the obviously quite young girl he so intensely admires—the lack of aesthetic control here is less innovation than extension, of a rhetorical habit already widely practiced. It merely allows the tendency al-ready implicit in the blazon to come to the fore, laying bare (so to speak) what many lyricists and romancers were already doing in better taste.

In Bokenham's text, the link between the sadistic and erotic fetishization of the female body is articulated by Christine. When her breasts are cut off in her third ordeal, the saint thanks Jesus

| "That thou vouchysd-safe every letting from me | "That you allowed every corporeal hindrance |
| Of my body awey kut for to be." (3022–23) | To be cut from me." |

This relief—appearing in neither Voragine nor Christine de Pizan—comes in part because the breast is a source of pleasure for women. As Aucassin rather obnoxiously remarks to his Nicolette,

Li amors de la femme est en son oeul et en som le cateron de sa mamele et en som l'orteil del pié; mais li amors de l'home est ens el cuer plantee.

Woman's love is in her eye and in the tip of her breast and in her toe; but man's love is rooted in his heart. (Prose XIV)

The martyr is grateful also because the breast is a source of pleasure, both aesthetic and erotic, for men, and so it inserts the bearer into the whole social complex of erotic and reproductive relations as subject of gaze, action, and appropriation. This position does not in every case force compliance with social norms, but it may well require serious resistance, as Christine's earlier relationship with her father shows. For the saint, the loss of her breasts thus translates into a welcome loss of much that could constitute an obstacle to perfect devotion.

The violation of physical integrity was not, in Bokenham's time, limited to either hagiography (in the sadistic dimension) or lyric poetry (in the erotic). The perception that the songs we sing, the poems we read, and the language we use teach us how to feel about many things, including women, was by no means foreign to the intensely value-conscious Middle Ages. Robert Mannyng of Brunne makes the point in his treatment of the Second Commandment, which forbids taking the Lord's name in vain, in *Handlyng synne:*

Thou mayst be lore, seyth seynt Austyn,	You may be lost [damned], says St. Augustine,
Gyf thou were ever so fole hardy	If you were so foolish
To swere grete othys grysly,	As to swear great grisly oaths
As we folys do al day,	As we fools do continually,
Dysmembre Ihu al that we may (664–68)	Completely dismembering Jesus.

Chaucer's Pardoner denounces oath swearers for blasphemy, for in swearing by the various parts of Jesus' body, they have "Cristes blessed body al torent" (*CT,* 6, 709; torn Christ's blessed body to pieces). These injunctions against swearing as dismemberment of Jesus' body participate in a widespread topos in late-medieval sermons and pious art, both literary and visual, which represented the swearer as archetypal persecutor of the archetypal martyr (Cave, fig. 26; Owst, 414–25; Ross, no. 17; Woodforde, 185). This is the tormented and dismembered body at the center of medieval religious consciousness: *the* hegemonic image of the period displayed in every crucifix and pietà (see figure 6). Ribs torn, hands nailed, blood flowing, and heart exposed and often represented separately: it was an image, according to the preachers and moralists, duplicated with every casual conversational oath (by God's body/blood/bones, etc.).

We need to recall, too, that the visualization of detached body parts was linked not just with religious doctrine—not in a culture in which the amputation of head, hand, tongue, eyes, or genitals was a possible penalty for various treasonous or "immoral" acts, in which the ceremony of amputation was a ritualized public event, and in which a severed head or hand or extruded guts might be placed on public display for weeks as a warning.

The fourteenth-century lawyer Oldradus de Ponte describes a case in Avignon in which he defended a Jewish man married to a Christian woman (this constituted adultery, whereas casual sexual relations between a Christian and a Jew did

FIGURE 6 Passion emblems of dismembered body, in church roof boss. Source: C. J. P. Cave, *Roof Bosses in Medieval Churches* (1948). By permission of Cambridge University Press.

not). Oldradus lost, and the Jew was tortured and castrated. The lawyer's melancholy comment is, "I saw the physical evidence of the excision before the palace" (Zacour, 70). After the 1450 Cade's rebellion in England, the heads, quarters, and limbs of executed rebels were distributed for display to towns all over England (Griffiths, *Reign,* 648). In 1460, the head of Clare Priory's landlord, Richard of York, was displayed at the gates of the city of York, decorated with a paper crown. Nor was dismemberment of the corpse a punishment reserved just for rebels. It was, in fact, part of the normal rites of disposal for nobility, who often died far from home and to whose bodies several places might have a special claim. The corpse of a king or noble might be boiled to remove the flesh from the bones, which then could be easily transported without fear of putrefaction. Or the body might be eviscerated for embalming, with head, heart, viscera, and body buried in different places. Despite an outraged prohibition of this practice by Pope Boniface VIII in 1299, it continued during the Middle Ages and afterward, throughout Europe and in England (E. Brown, "Death").

If oath swearers can be accused of verbal sadism, how much more vulnerable to the charge are the lover poets who rip apart the female body in their verse! And for the critic of such verbal tactics, what more effective way to deflate the lyric–erotic overvaluation of a lump of fat than by asserting its biological use, showing the worst physical practices of fragmentation, and re-presenting the body part completely estranged? That, I believe, was Bokenham's rhetorical tactic in an overall strategy to rehabilitate femininity for theological and political purposes.

THE DEMYSTIFICATION AND ALIENATION of the body continue in the next legend, that of Lucy. The terms are different: primarily those of disease and copulation. The first half of the story assaults us with a long, digressive description of the saint's mother's dysentery. This is a traditional detail and necessary to the plot, for the cure of this disease motivates the women's trip to Agatha's shrine where the mother is cured through her daughter's devotion to Agatha. Traditional as it is, though, Bokenham innovates: what Voragine says in half a sentence, or Bozon in three words ("une privé maladie") Bokenham expands to more than thirty lines (8985–9018). It is truly a purple passage that invokes the top medical authorities, includes medical speculation on the red or bloody flux, the balance of humors, the "excoriation of guts," and other theoretical and empirical features of the disease.

The second half of Lucy's story turns from disease to copulation. After her mother's cure, Lucy's Christian tendency is revealed, and she is condemned to a brothel. Again, Bokenham amplifies considerably. The judge Paschasius orders her sent to the brothel where

". . . wylt thou or nylt, folwe the lust   "Whether you will or not, you'll have to
Of evere comer thedyr nedys thou must   Go along with the lust of every comer
Of nature aftyr the condycyoun." (9249–51)   According to what is natural."

The multiple corruptions of the sex act—immorality, disease, and semen—are combined in the judge's prediction:

"And whan thou thus wyth corupcyoun	"And when you are thus befouled
Defoulyd art, I undyr-take	With corruption, I guarantee
The holy gost wyl the forsake." (9252–54)	The Holy Ghost will forsake you."

We are lectured on the business mechanics of prostitution:

Anoon to hys presence he ded calle	Then he called before him
Of the cyte the Ruffyens alle;	All the ruffians of the city:
Wych been men that synfullye	These are men who sinfully
Wummen ben customyd to selle & bye,	Are accustomed to buy and sell women
And to setten hem to ferme at the bordelhous,	And send them out to work at the bordello,
Ther to gete wyth her craft vycyous	There to earn with their vice-ridden trade
Her lyvyng & her maystres ther-to,	Their living and that of their masters,
Greth peyne to suffre lesse thei so do. (9285–92)	Suffering serious punishment unless they do so.

The judge's instructions to the pimps and bordello keepers are also quite detailed. They are to proclaim throughout the city that a young virgin is available to satisfy the fleshly lust of whoever comes and "at hys owe lykyng" (9301: "at his [the customer's] personal wishes"); and she is to be "exercysyd / . . . Tyl she be deed for werynesse" (9305–7); that is, dead from multiple rape.

Both sections of the Lucy story, then, reduce the body to sheer functionalism. The body is a foul bag open at either end, site of disease, emitter of black or red evil-smelling fluids, vessel of humors and semen. That is half the story's *sentence*. The other half is that the requisite miracles are performed so that Lucy remains untouched. She cannot be taken to the brothel because she is miraculously fixed to the spot where she stands, and nothing—not even teams of oxen—can budge her. This is the physical manifestation of her immovable will, as she herself points out when questioned, for the Holy Ghost has supplied her with "swych wychte" (9352; such weight) that not even ten thousand men would be able to move her. The poet compares the saint to "an hyl / Rotyd . . . both fyx & styl" (9325–26; a hill, permanently and immovably rooted), but she herself speaks the image revealing the scriptural sources of her faith and her discourse, that of the solid and weighty building:

"by the vertu	"through the power
Of the holy ghost I hys dwellyng-place	Of the holy spirit, I his dwelling place
And hys temple am made, by a specyal grace." (9374–76)	And his temple am made, by special grace."

Lucy is unable either to die or to move from the execution spot until priests administer the eucharist and all bystanders have answered "amen" (9432–38).

She is interred on that very spot, "beryd in the same place" (9442), and a church is quickly ("hastyly") erected over her grave ("there-ovyr"). As stable after death as before it, Lucy now cannot be moved or translated as so many other saints were. In this exact place her body will remain for all time, "abydyng the daye of the greth assyse" (9445; awaiting the day of the great judgment). The temple to which she once metaphorically compared herself is now metonymically the sign of her ordeal, marking the place. The only translation that Lucy can undergo is verbal, and Bokenham gently reminds us of this fact in wordplay, bringing himself into the concluding prayer in his capacity as "translatour / Of thi legende," who hopes to be rewarded by the saint herself.

Lucy's bodily immovability is emblematic of her immovability of will. The latter means that even if she had been taken to the brothel and raped, Lucy would not have been defiled, for

defoulyd shal nevere the body	never shall the body be defiled
Wyth-owtyn assent of the soule be. (9256–57)	Without assent of the soul.

This is straight Augustine:

> For the sanctity of the body does not consist in the integrity of its members, nor in their exemption from all touch. . . . And thus, so long as the soul keeps this firmness of purpose which sanctifies even the body, the violence done by another's lust makes no impression on this bodily sanctity, which is preserved intact by one's own persistent continence. (*City of God,* 1.18)

Accordingly, Augustine goes on from this principle to mount an indictment of Lucretia of Rome, who committed suicide after being raped by her husband's friend Tarquin. The argument counterposes to Lucretia's pride the examples of Christian humility offered by just such martyrs as Lucy:

> We maintain that when a woman is violated while her soul admits no consent to the iniquity, but remains inviolably chaste, the sin is not hers, but his who violates her. . . . [Lucretia] burned with shame at the thought that her patient endurance of the foul affront that another had done her, should be construed into complicity with him. Not such was the decision of the Christian women who suffered as she did, and yet survive. They declined to avenge upon themselves the guilt of others, and so add crimes of their own to those crimes in which they had no share. . . . Within their own souls, in the witness of their own conscience, they enjoy the glory of chastity. In the sight of God, too, they are esteemed pure, and this contents them; they ask no more; it suffices them to have opportunity of doing good, and they decline to evade the distress of human suspicion, lest they thereby deviate from divine law. (*City of God,* 1.19)

This potential for immovable will is present in every Christian. It is the still center—the soul, perhaps—of this tale whose literary body is an intense and revolting naturalism.

As recounted by Bokenham, the stories of Agatha and Lucy alienate the body; they defetishize it by stripping it of its association with beauty and erotic desire. Simultaneously, they aim to refetishize the body in the direction of functionalism and, consequently, to redirect our attention to the necessary subordination of all nature to the Christian imperative. A visual representation of the fully refetishized female body is the bare-breasted Virgin Mary nursing her son, a common motif in Italian art of the fourteenth and fifteenth centuries (Miles, "Bare Breast"). When we have this image in mind, we can begin to appreciate the breathtaking audacity of Jean Fouquet's 1449 portrait of Agnès Sorel as a bare-breasted virgin. The genius (some might say diabolical genius) of that representation is its intense compression into a single image of the antithetical socioideological forces of court and convent. Though the portrait is a version of a well-known scene—the *virgo lactans*—it is a conspicuously immodest one. The child is not nursing; the balloon-like breast is proudly displayed; the portrait emphasizes the contrast between full bosom and tiny waist. In this way, it imposes on the viewer a constant oscillation of perception and response; it is a deeply destabilizing work of art, then or now.

Yet it might be argued that the Fouquet portrait can be read in another way: that it perfectly embodies the same delicate balance sought by the Austin poet. Such possibility of argumentation is indeed the very oscillation of response that I mean. It is a precarious equilibrium that Bokenham seeks in his legendary, as it intends both to undercut a lyric–erotic exaltation of the body and to condemn a purely sadistic demystification of it. On one hand, the body must be depreciated, but not so far as to slander a creation of God. On the other hand, the body must be appreciated as God's work, but not so far as to elevate it beyond reach of traditional doctrinal restrictions. The proper balance is that the body must be respected, its appropriate claims met, and its appropriate subordination understood.

This is the position maintained in the Augustinian intellectual tradition and in its rule, for the Austins—unlike some other orders—were not ascetics. In his study of the Austin canons, J. C. Dickinson brought out "the spirit of judicious moderation" (178) that typified the order in contrast to other more extreme communities. To be sure, evangelical poverty was a highly controversial topic among the orders. During the thirteenth century, it prompted a reform movement within the Augustinian order, and again in the fourteenth century, a reform tendency arose in response to antimendicant attacks led by Richard Fitzralph on behalf of secular clergy (Mathes, 59).

Nonetheless, the essential character of the Austins' *regula* remained fairly stable, its devotion never based on absolute poverty but, rather, on the communal life. Unlike Eastern ascetics, Augustinians did not cultivate bizarre techniques of afflicting the body. Unlike Cistercians, they did not require silence. Unlike radical Franciscans or those in any order who accepted the ideas of William of Ockham, they did not believe in the complete refusal of worldly goods as the most genuine form of apostolic life. Instead, the Austins permitted their members, and particularly their masters in theology, a range of privileges and creature comforts. They did not abstain completely from meat or wine; they did not forbid the wearing of linen. They encouraged humanistic studies within reason. Every Austin friar was entitled to the *peculium:* personal objects, money, or valuables to be placed in the common coffer, to be used for the common good only with the friar's consent and to be returned to the common coffer after use (Roth, 1.230). The fact that Bokenham is labeled *master* in documents naming him indicates his, and the order's, refusal of extremes even originating in the ranks, for a few untypically rigorous Friars Hermits called for renunciation of that title and its material benefits so as to maintain the correct level of poverty. This was standard practice at Lecceto, where the ascetic William Flete felt more at home than in worldly England, and at several other Italian houses. Indeed, Flete formally renounced his own *magisterium* when he withdrew to Lecceto, where Augustine himself was said to have visited (Gwynn, 141), and his 1380 letter to the masters of theology in the English province hints that they ought to do the same.

The Austins approved of cleanliness and good health. Indeed, in the interest of health and the balancing of humors, bloodletting was permitted four times a year (Roth, 1.237). It was just this emphasis on a balanced and sensible treatment of the body that led Derek Brewer, in a now generally accepted hypothesis, to posit the Augustinian origin of *Ancrene Wisse.* In a text written nearly two centuries after the *Wisse* and also for a woman about to be enclosed, the Augustinian canon and mystic Walter Hilton advised that "hunger and physical distress greatly hinder spiritual progress":

> If you desire to attain purity of heart, you must resist unreasonable bodily desires, but you should not attack their natural origin, such as hunger, which you are bound to feel and to satisfy at proper times. You must strengthen yourself against it by taking the medicine of food in the same way as you would take the proper medicine against a bodily ailment, so that you may serve God in greater freedom of body and soul. (*Ladder of Perfection,* 1.75)

Farther on, Hilton expands this recommendation:

> One who loves God is well aware that he must sustain his bodily life with food and drink for as long as God wills. . . . If possible, he will choose the kind of food that is least troublesome and maintains his bodily strength, whether meat and fish, or only bread and ale. . . . He would rather make use of the best and most costly of food if this interfered less with the custody of his heart, than to take only bread and water if it involved more disturbance. (*Ladder of Perfection,* 2.39)

Hilton's view is very much in line with the perspective established a generation earlier in the *Vitasfratrum* (1357) of Jordan of Saxony, provincial of the Saxon–Thuringian province of the order. Jordan's general principle was that scandal (*mala singularitas,* lit., "bad reputation") arises from two extremes: accepting more than is necessary to communal life or accepting less; this applies to food, clothing, personal property, and penance (Mathes, 107–8).

Far from being innovative, these late medieval sentiments are consistent with the opinions of the claimed founder of the Augustinian order. They may express an attitude newly or recently more popular than before among clergy and laity, but that attitude is recognizably and, in its ensemble, distinctively Augustinian. J. P. H. Clark observes of Hilton that "it is above all a deliberately conservative

Augustinianism which pervades his writing" and that he displays "indications of a conservative strand in Cambridge theology in the mid-fourteenth century, the time and place where Hilton apparently received his intellectual formation" ("Image," 204). A recent scholar singles out the body as "the cornerstone of [Augustine's] theology" (Miles, *Augustine,* 131) demonstrating that even though Manichaeism left a residue of mistrust of the body in some of Augustine's early work, the theologian moved definitively away from dualistic formulations to offer a well-integrated version of the relation of body and soul. Indeed, Augustine's ongoing polemic against the radically dualistic Manichees, who saw matter as the Kingdom of Darkness, required a comparatively balanced view of human nature. Thus Miles observes that if in early dialogues Augustine represents the body as a servant to the soul, the *City of God* (15.7.2) refigures the relationship as that of spouses (Miles, *Augustine,* 124). The mature works, she claims, struggle to close the gap between body and soul that the earlier writing left open.

Yet significantly, even in an early work like *De Musica,* in which the image of the soul as a servant is prominent, the body is still extravagantly praised because God honored it in assuming it. Besides being assumed by God, the body was created by God and therefore is good, as Scripture says and as various theologians had reiterated. "What an honor for the clay," rhapsodized Tertullian, "a glory to the earth . . . a greater glory for the flesh. . . . If the body is the servant of the soul, it is also her associate and coheir" (in Cornélis, 202–5). Augustine continues this line:

> And *Thou, O God, sawest every thing that Thou hadst made, and behold, it was very good.* Yea we also see the same, and behold, all things are *very good.* Of the several kinds of Thy works, when Thou hadst said "let them be," and they were, Thou sawest each *that it was good.* Seven times have I counted it to be written, that Thou *sawest that that which Thou madest was good.* And this is the eighth, that Thou *sawest every thing that Thou hadst made,* and behold, it was not only *good,* but also *very good.* (*Confessions,* 13.43)

For Augustine, the tension between body and soul is no chasm but natural to the whole person, to be managed by virtuous behavior rather than by physical self-affliction (*De Continentia;* Miles, 62). The senses are not to be depreciated, for they are the body's agents on behalf of the soul (*De Trinitate;* Miles, 30). "What is soundness of body? It is to be insensible to nothing. . . . Therefore, not to be devoid of sensation like a stone or a tree or a corpse, but to live in the body without being sensible of its weight—this is to be sound in body" (*Serm.* 277; Miles, 39). Sexuality, though not lust, was created by God before the Fall, so that Adam and Eve could have united and reproduced themselves—albeit without libido—in Eden:

> I do not see what could have prohibited [Adam and Eve] from honorable nuptial union and the bed undefiled even in Paradise. God could have granted them this if they had lived in a faithful and just manner in obedient and holy service to

Him, so that without the tumultuous ardor of passion and without any labor and pain of childbirth, offspring would be born from their seed. . . . Those who had begotten children would remain in the prime of life and would maintain their physical strength from the tree of life which had been planted in Paradise. (Augustine, *Genesis* 9.3, trans. Taylor)

Why did Adam and Eve not "come together in nuptial union"? Tactical reasons: God, foreseeing the Fall, did not order them to do so (*Genesis,* 9.5). In propounding these views, Augustine went against the usual opinion (Tatian, Chrysostom, Gregory of Nyssa, Ambrose, Jerome; cf. Brown, *Body and Society,* chaps. 4, 14, 19) that there could not, on principle, have been any sex in Eden. Taylor, translator of the passage from the *Genesis* commentary, writes that Augustine "came to a balanced view of human sexuality which is remarkable in a writer of that period" (266).

To return to our women saints, I propose that Bokenham's treatment of the body is designed to manifest the order's, and the founder's, distinctively balanced view of sense and spirit. I argue in chapters 7 and 8 that this traditional Augustinian attitude toward the body serves Bokenham well in constructing the sexual politics of his legendary.

The concluding movement of the poem shows tradition in the making. Lucy, a Sicilian, is Agatha's countrywoman; she worships at Agatha's shrine, and her powers are affirmed by the earlier saint. Thus the devotional tradition is handed down not only from text to reader, but—even before textuality—also from saint to saint in local oral transmission. We, as readers, are witness to tradition in the making. Just as Magdalene is able to identify herself as an already scriptural figure, already textualized, and thus to recreate the pretextual moment, so Lucy, too, creates that moment for herself and Agatha. That the tradition continues into the modern era is demonstrated by the last life in the series, that of St. Elizabeth of Hungary (d. 1231).

E LIZABETH'S LIFE SEEMS to contradict the ethos of the body just sketched, for although Elizabeth is not tortured, her self-imposed privations and those imposed by her harsh confessor Master Conrad constitute a lifelong ordeal potentially extending to self-mutilation. After her husband's death, when Elizabeth's uncle wants her to remarry in violation of her vow of chaste widowhood, she threatens to cut off her nose so that no man will want her. Although this is not a unique motif in hagiography, its shock effect is considerable here. Equally shocking to modern ears is Elizabeth's renunciation of "al delectacyoun / Of hyr chyldryn" (10293–94: all delight in her children):

"I as dung now despyse
Al temporal thingis, & my chyldryn here

To me than othir mennys be no more dere."
  (10299–301)

"I now despise as dung
All temporal things, and my children here

Are no dearer to me than other people's [children]."

Just as Christine found parents in Jesus, so Elizabeth finds children in the many poor and sick she nurtures. She is particularly concerned about caring for poor and ill children, who—Voragine writes—called her mother and tried to follow her home as children follow their mother. Bokenham renders this in a much-expanded version:

Pore wummens chyldryn also usyd she	Poor women's children she was accustomed also
In that place to kepyn ful many oon,	To shelter there, many of them,
To wych she shewyd as grete cherte	To whom she showed as great charity
As she modyr had be to hem everychon.	As if she had been mother to them all.
And whanne she cam, sume to hyr runne anoon	When she arrived, some ran to her
As chyldryn to the modyr, & sume dede crepe,	As children to their mother, and some crawled,
And eftsoons whan she awey dede goon,	And when she went away,
As she here modyr had ben thei ganne wepe.	They wept as if she were their mother.
(10017–24)	

This new "family" is created by the saint's acts of *caritas,* not by the lustful act of *cupiditas.* No other saint in the collection displays such consistent lifelong asceticism, which is clearly not offered as a norm of holiness but as one of several possible ways to worship. It imports into this legend, in particularly uncompromising terms, the otherworldly component of the Christian dialectic. What the poet does explicitly recommend as a model is not the saint's self-deprivation but, rather, her patience, humility, and obedience, virtues available to both sexes and all classes (9834–45).

If Elizabeth's asceticism cannot be imitated by many, her attitude can. She is no recluse but lives in the thick of social and domestic life. As the daughter and wife of rulers, Elizabeth has many opportunities for self-indulgence, yet her life is dedicated to charitable works, especially care of the sick. The naturalism of the two previous tales resurfaces here as Bokenham expands every detail of the saint's self-abasement, including the "stynkyng exalacyoun" of "mennys corrupcyouns" in the hospitals where she works while her maidens stand by, unable to endure the patients' breath (10009–16). Elizabeth's virtue is to maintain the proper spirit in both prosperity and adversity. In this sense, her life is genuinely exemplary: no melodramatic exotica set in the distant Italian or Egyptian past but as contemporary as someone like Margery Kempe, whose married status and fits of crying might be recognized in the life of the Hungarian saint.

FROM HEAD TO FOOT, with face, mouth, tongue, womb, breasts, flesh, and guts in between, Bokenham offers a collective anatomy of these impolitic bodies of women whose strength and assertiveness ensure their death and—in the spiritual and literary dimensions—their life. Curiously, hands are not prominent in this anatomy; I suppose that his, the writer's, supply the lack.

Besides achieving their own entry into eternal life, the saintly woman confers life as well: the eternal life of the soul that, at the end of each legend, the poet asks on behalf of his patrons, himself, and all devout. Yet the Augustinian valuation of the body suggests that we should not forget the life that every woman can confer, whether saint or not: biological life.

It is not only in the stories of Anne and Elizabeth that physical generativity is acknowledged and honored. I believe it is subtly present in the number of lives that the poet chose to include in his array. There are thirteen, the number of months in a year measured in months of twenty-eight days, the length of a menstrual cycle. This is the calendrical calculation that Bokenham uses in his life of Christine, whose mother so poignantly reminds her wayward daughter, "I / Ten monethes the bare in my body" (2414–15): the ten-month figure is correct only when a month is four weeks, or twenty-eight days, long. Lest such awareness of female reproductive biology seem inappropriate to a friar-poet, we need to remember how much attention was paid by scholastic philosophers to matters of natural science, particularly those posing the crucial question of matter and form. Accordingly, Augustine addressed the topic of embryology, as did Avicenna, Aquinas, and a host of less famous writers. Among the works of Giles of Rome—works that every Austin was required to read, teach, and defend—was the treatise *De Formatione corporis humani in utero* (On the formation of the human body in the womb).[1] Given the attention to number that is evident at many other points in Bokenham's poem, the number of lives is likely also to be significant.

Biology is not the last word, though, but only the first. As in other places in this legendary, biological fact is open to doctrinal interpretation. Another important set of thirteen with special relevance to hagiography is the number of primary apostles, including St. Paul. An apostle is a missionary (literally an envoy), and all thirteen primary apostles were believed to have died as martyrs in various lands. In this sense, they are the first imitators of the prototeacher and protomartyr Jesus. The significance of this number was commemorated in the number of members admitted in 1415 to the new monastery at Sion, the only religious house in England that professed the reformed order of St. Augustine. It accepted eighty-five, representing the thirteen apostles and seventy-two disciples (Aungier, 21). If Mary Magdalene is often referred to as *apostoless* (as Bokenham has the countess of Eu do in her commission request, line 5068) then the complete array can be seen as a female apostolate, teaching by word and example.

The coexistence of physical and symbolic (or historical–literal and spiritual) interpretations of a given text is a key principle in Augustinian hermeneutics. Although this coexistence is by no means confined to Augustinians, it should come as no surprise in the work of a consciously Augustinian artist. If the biological meaning of thirteen constitutes the literal level of interpretation of Bokenham's set of female saints, and the activities of the apostles are its ethical or

moral level, what about the third and fourth levels of medieval allegorical interpretation, the allegorical and tropological (often collapsed into a single doctrinal
statement)? What is the ultimate significance of Bokenham's literary remem-
berment of the female body? To be sure, it can be read as a semiotic trope coun-
tering with wholeness the dehumanizing fragmentation of the body portrayed
in martyrology and implied in erotic lyric. It can be read as a reminder of
women's reproductive function (so central to the political crises of the day, as I
show in chapter 7) and as a reminder of the apostolic calling enacted by some
Christians. Yet an even more encompassing theological issue is represented in
the fragmentation and reconstitution of the human body: Christian eschatology,
death, and resurrection. How do Bokenham's saints, separately and together,
make a statement about the future life?

Every saint was already, in hagiographic theory, a limb of a corporate body.
This is true of every Christian, of course, but the sense in which it is even more
particularly true of saints is expressed in a ninth-century life of St. Gregory composed by a monk at Whitby. The writer offers an apologia or justification for
possible inaccuracies in his account:

> It should offend no one at all that the ordering of these events is irregular. . . .
> And neither should anyone be offended if any of these deeds were actually done
> by some other of the saints, since the holy apostle, through the mystery of one
> body with its members the saints, by comparing it with the living body has so
> brought them into union that we should attribute to each member the works of
> the other in turn. And the office of, for instance, the eyes and the ears benefits the
> hands and feet in common. . . . Therein, we know that all of the saints are
> through charity of the body of Christ, whose members are in common. Hence if
> any of these things which we have written were not of that man [i.e., a specific
> saint], . . . we should little doubt that they too should be in so great a man; for
> . . . with all living things what is discovered in one should always be attributed
> to the others. (Jones, 118)

This mutual attributability of deeds and virtues is not, in this passage, common
to all Christians but only to saints, who have a special relation to Christ above
and beyond that of others, because they strive to imitate him in virtue or martyrdom. In this view, then, a saint's death is the joining (or rejoining) of a limb to its
body. For other Christians, that reassemblage occurs on an individual level, for
each person can anticipate, in the resurrection of the body, a new and better
unity of his or her imperfect, putrefied, or otherwise disassembled body.

Resurrection theory was controversial virtually from the start of the Christian era. Inherited from various late Jewish tendencies, the resurrection of the
body was celebrated in the Pauline epistle 1 Corinthians 15, after which it was
elaborated by many writers, including Augustine, in what became "a central occupation" of his old age (Miles, 99; also see Cornélis; Dewart; Heinzmann). The
physical resurrection of Jesus was not to be denied (as the Manichaean leader
Faustus did) or seen as unique (as Origen and others argued) or limited to the
just (as the Jews maintained) but, rather, was exemplary for all humanity, a uni-

versal promise. Moreover, the resurrected body was not an immaterial version of the lived body (as the Gnostics maintained) or some etherealized perfect shape. In 543 and 553, Origen was posthumously condemned for having taught that the resurrection body would have the most perfect form of all: spherical, like the form of the stars, but this interpretation of his work seems to have been a misunderstanding (Chadwick; Festugière).

Contrary to all this, what came to be mainstream orthodoxy taught that the resurrected body would be the same body as during life, complete in all its parts, lacking only concupiscence and corruption. The last book of *The City of God* is devoted to the resurrection of the body, in great detail. What about aborted fetuses, dead infants, cannibalism, obesity, or deformities of excess or deficiency (chaps. 12–20)? The solution—a paean to the theology of reassemblage—is that the risen body

> will consist of the remains in the sepulchre, augmented by whatever parts of the body may have been lost in life, and by all that has suffered decay after death. All this will be transformed from its former condition as a natural body into the new condition of a spiritual body, and will be invested with incorruptibility and immortality. And, even though by some accident of life or by the savagery of enemies the whole body has been reduced to dust and thrown to the winds or scattered on the waters so that not a trace of it seems to be left, nothing in fact will escape the omnipotence of the Creator, and not a hair of its head will perish. (*City of God*, 22.21)

Even thirty years earlier, in his defense of Genesis against the Manichees (and again in *Confessions* as well), Augustine had sung the praise of physical integrity. Explaining why God considered his creation to be not only good but very good, Augustine observes that this is precisely because of its wholeness and completeness:

> For every beauty that is composed of parts is much more praiseworthy in the whole than in a part. In the case of the human body, if we praise the eyes alone, or the nose, or the cheeks, or the head, or the hands, or the feet, and we praise the remaining beautiful parts individually and by themselves, how much more should we praise the whole body to which all the members, which individually are beautiful, contribute their beauty? If a beautiful hand . . . is separated from the body and loses its attractiveness, the other members are also ugly without it. The force and power of integrity and unity are so great that many good things are pleasing only when they come together. (*De Genesi contra Manichaeos*, 1.21)

The speculations and arguments of the apostolic and patristic periods continued through the high Middle Ages. Among the *auctores* who contributed to the elaboration of resurrection theory was Giles of Rome. For Giles, as might be expected, the resurrection body will have all it needs for integral and perfect being ("esse integrum et perfectum"; cf. Nolan, 113).

Bynum sees a shift in emphasis in thirteenth-century resurrection theory, with "the ultimate victory not the immortality of the soul but the exact reassemblage of body parts" ("Bodily Miracles," 85). In view of the strong emphasis on reassemblage during the patristic period, certainly in Augustine's work, which became hegemonic, it would be more accurate to see this shift in emphasis as a revival rather than an innovation. Bokenham would have absorbed it from both sources, the modern and the ancient, and he treats it with, again, typical moderation.

Clearly, Bokenham does not share Guibert de Nogent's radical revulsion of the fragmentation of bodies. Whereas Guibert criticized both the translation and the division of saints' bodies as obscene (Bynum, "Bodily Miracles"), Bokenham does not recoil from narrating in considerable detail the translation of St. Margaret from Antioch to Italy (869–1400), a story in which the body of another virgin, Felicity, and the sweet-smelling ribs of SS. Cosmos and Damian are also discovered (1322–30). One of Ursula's attendants is translated, albeit unsuccessfully (3468–3502; the corpse returns to its original spot in a convent). Faith is translated (3993–4020), as are Mary Magdalene (6298–6304) and Katherine (7346–57). We recall the satisfaction with which Bokenham relates his rescue from a tight spot due to his previous touching of "hyr [Margaret's] foot bare" (169) with his ring and the pride with which he informs the reader of the presence in local establishments of that foot and its separated toe and heel (133–43).

"If corruption or fragmentation," writes Bynum, "or division of body (the transition from whole to part) is the central threat [to survival], resurrection (the reassemblage of parts into whole) is the central victory" ("Bodily Miracles," 77). And so it is for the impolitic bodies represented by the Austin friar: those supremely tactless, rebellious adolescents; those nonconforming citizens; those determined virgins and controlling wives who constitute his array of female saints.

The resurrection of the body is, for the Augustinian poet, humankind's final hope, as it was the martyrs', to live again and to live in triumph. I discuss the narrower social significance of his collective portrait in the next two chapters.

SEVEN

The Body Politic

During this Parliament [of 1428], some women
from Stokkes came to the Parliament chambers,
along with some other women from London, re-
spectably decked out, bearing letters to the duke
of Gloucester, the archbishop, and other lords then
still alive. The tenor of the letters was to censure
the duke of Gloucester who, not wishing to rescue
his wife [Jacqueline, countess of Hainault] from
the affliction of imprisonment in Burgundy, but—
his love grown cold—let her remain in servitude
and [who] moreover publicly lived with an adul-
teress, to his personal ruin, that of the kingdom,
and that of the efficacious order of marriage.

(Riley, 20, my translation)

Despite their gesture of solidarity and their concern for the
welfare of individuals, the state, and the social institution of
marriage, the women of Stokkes[1] and London set aside certain complications
when they petitioned Parliament in the Gloucester case. Jacqueline already had
a husband—John of Brabant, count of Hainault—when she married the English duke in 1422. The new couple claimed, of course, that this previous marriage was invalid, and they sent to Rome for an annulment. The considerable
European lands that Jacqueline would bring into England's sphere of influence
helped create popular support for the match. The monk-poet John Lydgate,
probably commissioned by Duke Humphrey of Gloucester himself, did his part
to encourage public approval, by writing poems to celebrate the union. But
Jacqueline soon became a pawn in the disputes over her land inheritance and, as
a consequence of Gloucester's ill-advised invasion of Hainault, was taken prisoner by Philip of Burgundy. Gloucester found consolation with Eleanor Cobham, a lady-in-waiting of his wife, and when in 1428 a papal bull finally declared Jacqueline's first marriage valid, Humphrey was able to make his
mistress the duchess of Gloucester. The women of Stokkes and London were
not the only ones to protest. The mayor and aldermen proposed to Parliament
the rescue of Jacqueline, and in this lost cause even the obliging Lydgate took
sides against his patron with his "Complaint for My Lady of Gloucester."

What the incident suggests is the extremely public nature of the private lives of those who ran the kingdom. This is an ancient topos in medieval and renaissance thought ("the king's two bodies"). It was felt especially acutely in England while Osbern Bokenham compiled his legends of holy women on the eve of the so-called Wars of the Roses,[2] the series of factional rivalries and, eventually, dynastic disputes that had everything to do with marriage and reproduction, adultery and illegitimacy, lineage and genealogy. Although reproduction was far from chaotic, it displayed enough irregularities, insufficiencies, and superfluities to cause difficulties of succession and rule. The sons of Edward III, with their numerous progeny, occupy us in this and the next chapter; most important to my purpose are the lines of John of Gaunt and Lionel of Clarence.

We could describe the third quarter of the fifteenth century as a moment when the body politic seemed to risk dismemberment. Toward the end of it— closer than he knew to the desired resolution—Bishop Russell preached a homily for the 1483 Parliament of Richard III:

> The gospelle of Luc . . . [tells] of a woman that had x. dragmes [drachmas, coins], and oone of them was lost . . . . Owre womanne that hath lost oone of her x. dragmas ys *nostra respublica,* whyche ys ferre fallen from her perfeccion, and gretly astoned of the falle and decaye, of the gret hurt and brusere that she nowe seeth yn the membres of the public body of Englonde. (Chrimes, *Constitutional Ideas,* 182)

Both the image and the sentiment had been common enough in England for decades. The image itself was a commonplace of European culture, the prototype Plato's *Republic* with its parallelisms between social community and human individual (see Barkan, chap. 2; Hale; O'Neill). It remained important to political discourse in Bokenham's day. He would have found it, among many other places, scattered throughout the immensely popular *De Regimine principum* (ca. 1280) of Giles of Rome, the major Augustinian *auctor* of the two centuries following his death. (I suggest in chapter 8 what other uses Bokenham made of Giles's treatise.) Christine de Pizan's *Livre du corps de policie* (Book of the body politic), composed between 1404 and 1407, also used the body as a structuring metaphor (much as she used the city in the 1405 *Livre de la cité des dames*). Christine has the prince as the head, the knights as arms and hands, and "the universal people" as the stomach, legs, and feet.

Some twenty years after Bokenham completed his legendary, the king's justice and Lancastrian loyalist Sir John Fortescue used the body politic in defense of a moderate monarchy, with Augustine and Aristotle as his authorities (*De Laudibus*). Even corporate municipal life used the ancient trope:

> For the fourteenth-century London alderman Andrew Horn, for example, the mayor required reverence from his burghers and subjects because his authority rested on divine, as well as human, election; he was the head and they the mem-

bers. Moreover, the idea persisted that, just as the person of Christ as its head constituted the corporate identity of the church, so it was the person of the mayor as head which gave a town the corporate identity which, for example, enabled it to plead or be pleaded at law. (Mervyn James, 11)

This and the next chapter show that for Osbern Bokenham, as well as for Bishop Russell, the body politic might be sexed female. What I mean by this in connection with Bokenham is something less obvious than the explicit image of a woman, even though that image, I have argued in the preceding three chapters, is present in the somaticized text of the legendary. Here, however, I turn to genealogy and reproduction, governance and morality, and Bokenham's vision of the relevance (or irrelevance) of sex and gender to social life and the moral life.

In England, military confrontation between competing dynastic factions did not begin until 1455, but other kinds of serious violence had started long before, creating an atmosphere of fear and danger. Several ecclesiastical and secular lords were murdered by angry masses; numerous riots broke out; factional dispute in the king's council was constant; brawls and depredations by members of one or another noble retinue were common; and Jack Cade staged a temporarily successful, multiclass rebellion in 1450, demanding legal and financial reforms and the recall of Richard, duke of York, from semiexile in Ireland.

The general scandal and incompetency of Henry's reign—it has been called (perhaps hyperbolically) "the most calamitous in the whole of English history" (Wolfe, 37)—must have made York seem like a viable alternative during the late 1440s when Bokenham was working on his collection. I do not necessarily mean an alternative to Henry in the 1440s, although Richard's lineage would at any time have made that an obvious possibility, but at least an alternative to other, more favored magnates. "Must have done" is a phrase usually to be mistrusted in scholarship or biography, but I think it is justified here, in view of other evidence.

In this chapter I contend that Bokenham did practice a partisan Yorkist politics that he expressed in his hagiography and that he or other inhabitants of Clare Priory expressed elsewhere. In bending his pious work to the uses of a mild propaganda, Bokenham in no way betrayed the genre, for hagiography had for centuries been allied with polemical or political projects: to authenticate territorial claims, to raise funds for ecclesiastical construction, to strengthen clergy against lay or rival ecclesiastical infringement of their privileges, to ensure an institution's economic well-being by "proving" its claim to a given relic as an attraction for donors and pilgrims, and to provide a focus for national or local identity and stability (particularly for women and the poor). As Jacques Le Goff observed, "Il n'ya pas de récit innocent. Et celui sur les saints est un des moins innocents qui soient" (Préface to Boureau, vii). The patronage outlined in chapter 1 already provides a prima facie case for a Yorkist orientation; this is supported by factors external to the hagiography and, more important, by distinctive representational strategies in the text itself.

LYDGATE'S ABBEY, the old and magnificently wealthy Benedictine foundation at Bury St. Edmunds, was strongly Lancastrian in its political sympathies. Bokenham's establishment at Clare was Yorkist. The English Austins had generally a pro-Yorkist reputation, as suggested by the following anecdote about the battle of Blore Heath (September 23, 1459). When the battle was interrupted by darkness, the Yorkist commander (Richard Neville, earl of Salisbury) was able to withdraw safely because of a faithful Austin friar's subterfuge:

> But the Erle of Saulysbury hadde ben i-take, save only a Fryer Austyn schot gonnys alle that nyght in a parke that was at the backe syde of the fylde, and by thys mene the erle come to Duke of Yorke. And in the morowe they founde nothyr man ne chylde in that parke but the fryer, and he sayde that for fere he a-bode in that parke alle that nyght.[3]

If the order generally exhibited Yorkist sympathies, the more so did Clare, whose landlord Richard became in 1432 when he acceded to the honor of Clare, along with his other properties. Here we do not need to relate possibly apocryphal anecdotes like the one just cited, for the documentary evidence demonstrates a fervent commitment to Richard at Clare, at an earlier date than historians usually concede. One of these, a passage from Bokenham's legendary, appears in the elaborate prolocutory to his life of Magdalene, which had been commissioned in 1445 by Richard's sister Lady Isabel Bourchier. She, we are told, is

Doun conveyid by the same pedegru	Descended by the same pedigree
That the duk of york is come, for she	As the duke of York, for she
Hys sustyr is in egal degre,	Is his sister of equal rank,
Aftyr the dochesse of York clepyd Isabel,	Named Isabel after the duchess of York,
Hyr fadrys graunhtdam, wych, soth to tel,	Her paternal grandmother, who, to tell the truth,
In spayn kyng Petrys dowtyr was,	Was daughter to Spanish King Peter
Wych wyth a-nothir sustyr, so stood the caas,	And who, with another sister,
The royal tytle of spayne to englond broht,	Brought the royal title of Spain to England.
And, for the fyrste sustyr yssud noht	Because the first [older] sister didn't give birth,
But deyid baren, al stood in the tothir,	But died barren, everything depended on the other,
By whhom the ryht now to the brothir	Through whom the [royal] right now has come
Of seyd dame Isabelle, to seyn al and sum,	To the brother of that same Dame Isabel, namely
The duk of york, syr Rychard, is come,	To the duke of York, Sir Richard:
Wych god hym send, yf it be hys wyl.	God sent it to him if it be his will.
(5006–19)	

First we must disentangle the network of names: Pedro the Cruel, king of Castile (d. 1369), had two daughters, both of whom married English princes. Costanza (1354–94) was John of Gaunt's second wife, through whom John acquired title to Castile and Leon. Isabella (1355–93) married Edmund of Langley, duke of York, a match insisted on by Edward III to keep the Castile claim in the family. Their son Richard was earl of Cambridge, father of Bokenham's patron Isabel and of her brother Richard, duke of York (see figure 7).

It is an odd pedigree with which to praise an English lord and noblewoman whose exalted English ancestry included Edward III in both their paternal and maternal lines (through Edmund of Langley and Lionel of Clarence, respectively). Moreover, contrary to Bokenham's assertion, Costanza of Castile was not barren. She bore John of Gaunt two children: John, born in 1374, who died in infancy, and Catalina (1372–1418), who married Enrique III of Castile and Leon. This couple, in turn, bore a son who ruled as Juan II (1405–54) during Bokenham's lifetime, indeed during the poet's pilgrimage to Spain in 1445, when this very passage was composed. (One of Juan's offspring, Isabella, known as "the Catholic," married Ferdinand of Aragon to become half of the best-known Spanish royal couple in history: the patrons of Christopher Columbus.) Why should Bokenham make such a gross error, and why should he so ardently wish his patron to take the throne of Castile when Richard had such good title to that of England?

The answer lies in Richard of York's specific familial ambitions during the spring and summer of 1445, when he was negotiating the future of his eldest son

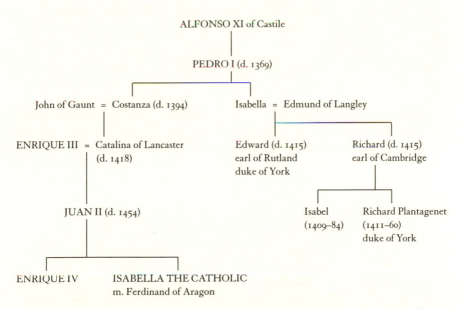

FIGURE 7 The Castilian pedigree and connections of Isabel Bourchier and Richard, duke of York.

and heir, Edward (the future Edward IV). He was in correspondence with Charles VII in hopes of arranging a betrothal to one of the French king's infant daughters.[4] The projected match with a French princess may itself have been viewed as preparation for an even higher aspiration: Edward's possible occupation of the throne of Castile. Or conversely, the Castilian claim might have been seen as enhancing the young Edward's desirability as a royal match. Pugh notes that early in July 1444, Richard spent twelve pounds for a copy of the Treaty of Bayonne made in 1388 between John of Gaunt and his Castilian father-in-law, in the hope, or belief, that it provided for the reversion of the Castilian crown to Isabel and her descendants in the absence of an heir in Costanza's line (123–24). Again in 1445, ten pounds was paid for a copy of the articles made between John of Gaunt and Juan, count of Trastamare (Marshall, 53). In 1445, Juan II had not yet entered the second marriage that produced the famous, or infamous, Isabel. His first marriage produced only one son, Enrique IV, who in 1445 was twenty years old and married—but a virgin, as was his young wife. He was known in Spain as Henry the Impotent (T. Miller, 28–29 and chap. 7). In the sense that at this moment Costanza's line seemed about to die out, she could technically be said to be "barren" in the long run; thus the title might revert to her sister's line and therefore to Richard and his heir.

These topical references explain the oddly insistent way in which Bokenham dated the Magdalene material in the opening lines of its prolocutory:

The yer of grace, pleynly to descryve,	In the year of grace—to define it plainly—
A thowsand, fourhundryd, fourty & fyve,	One thousand four hundred and forty-five,
Aftyr the cherche of Romys computacyon	According to the computation of the Roman Church
Wych wyth Iane chaungyth hyr calculacyon . . . (4981–84)	Which changes number with Janus [January] . . .

Why did Bokenham feel it necessary to describe the church's calendrical method, which begins the year in January? Precisely because a then-common nonecclesiastical method of dating began the year in March. But the genealogical material to come a few lines later, and the marital negotiations they support, represents a specific "window of opportunity" for which it seems the poet wanted to get the dates exactly right.

That window closed in 1451 with the birth of Isabel of Castile. In later years, though, when Richard's son had come to the throne as Edward IV and had chosen a wife of his own liking, the Castilian line once again became relevant. The heir to King Henry IV Trastamara of Castile (1454–74) "was a daughter of uncertain legitimacy, so that the house of York might hope . . . to press a claim to Castile and Leon,"[5] and indeed this assertion became part of Edward's propaganda, even though he eventually renounced the claim in a treaty with Henry IV.

The genealogy so obligingly inserted into the Magdalene prolocutory reveals the close attention paid by the Austin friars at Clare to the family matters of their landlord, to whose success their own was inevitably tied. This concern required, as is evident here, a correspondingly close attention to matters of state, both domestic and international, that could affect the fortunes of York (however these might be defined at a given moment). That such meticulous attention should be paid to a magnate's genealogy by his beneficiaries ought not to surprise us. J. R. Lander has suggested that genealogy would have to have been common knowledge

> in many a late-medieval farmhouse, manor house and castle. Families were interested in their pedigrees for very practical reasons. In the complete absence of any system of land registration, a grasp of genealogy was the essential basis of property ownership. A secure title lay in the proven, secure descent of a manor, and evidence culled from the memories of friends and neighbours was often a decisive factor in the verdicts of inquests. ("Family," 27)

Those with a dynastic ax to grind counted on this widespread interest in genealogy at all levels of the population. Pedigree workshops churned out document after document for kings and nobles during this period, many of them pictorial and many beginning with Adam or legendary British history. Alison Allan observes that whereas Lancastrian pedigrees are in Latin only, Yorkist ones are in Latin but with English versions as well, a phenomenon she interprets as "evidence of a positive intention to make the genealogy intelligible to the entire literate population" ("Political Propaganda", 272). Bokenham's Castilian genealogy for his patron Lady Isabel Bourchier thus represented both neighborly concern and political hope, a hope ended five years later with the birth of another Isabel.

Was it a hope only for Castile? The claim to Castile incorporates Richard's descent from Edward III through Edmund of Langley—not Richard's strongest line to the English throne, but a reminder of something still tentative and dangerous in 1445, something that made itself heard more insistently in another poem from the same year.

THE SECOND DOCUMENT regarding Richard was also composed in 1445, although historical evidence suggests later in that year than the Magdalene prolocutory, which can safely be dated to the first half of 1445. This second piece—anonymous but probably by Bokenham—is a facing-page translation of Claudian's fifth-century panegyric on the soldier-consul Stilicho, *De Consulatu Stilichonis;* it exists in a unique manuscript (BL Add. 11814). The Claudian scholar Alan Cameron points out that it is probably the earliest vernacular version of Claudian in any language and one of the earliest English translations of a late-classical writer other than Boethius.[6] A note in the same hand as the manuscript says that the work was "translat & wrete at clar" in 1445. The English is in an unrhymed line of (usually) seven stresses, probably in an attempt to imitate a classical meter. The document opens and closes with stanzaic envoys added by the translator, which are in Troilus stanza (ABABBCC) but with an irregular number of stresses per line, from five to seven. The manuscript has five color- and gold-illuminated badges showing devices of relatives of Richard of York, including the fetterlock of Edmund Langley, Richard's paternal grandfather and first duke of York; the falcon of his father, Richard, earl of Cambridge; the white rose of Clifford, also belonging to Langley; a white hind lodged on green ground for Joan Plantagenet, mother of Richard II; and a fiery dragon, the standard borne by Edward III at Crécy. The illuminations thus proclaim this text to be no innocent scholarly translation but a sharply partisan document, asserting a royal right and a particular succession. As we will see, the words sustain that visual message.

This was not the first time that a classical text had been used as an instructive parallel to contemporary politics. On the Continent, more than eighty years earlier, Petrarch used the genre of ancient pastoral eclogue for current political allegory with his twelfth "bucolic song," entitled "Conflictatio," whose battling shepherds represent the kings of England and France at the battles of Crécy (1346) and Poitiers (1356). Nearer home, in 1422, after the death of Henry V, John Lydgate composed *The Serpent of Division,* a prose treatise retelling Roman history, and especially the life of Julius Caesar, as a warning against civil strife. This, the first lengthy narration in English of the Caesar story, was commissioned (like so much of Lydgate's output) by Duke Humphrey of Gloucester. The stanzaic envoy specifies that "this litill prose declarith in figure" the damage done to Rome. It urges "ye lordes and pryces of renowne" to make

A merowre toforne in youre resoun
Of Pompey and Cesar Iulius . . .
And for teschewe stryf and dissencion
Within youreself beth not contrarious,
Remembring ay in yowre discrecion
Of Pompey and Cesar Iulius.

For the Claudian translation, the very choice of text opens possibilities of contemporary political analogy. To appreciate how clever a choice it was, we must recall the propagandistic content of Claudian's work and its historical referentiality, for the late-classical work offers striking analogies with Richard's situation and its plot makes much of Britain. The poem is in four sections, in the first two of which Stilicho is taught Aristotelian and other virtues and then rejects several vices. In part 3, the personified provinces of the Roman Empire one by one beg Stilicho to assume leadership of the empire. Last, in part 4, Rome itself exhorts him, and Stilicho is made a consul by Rome. When Britannia speaks, she addresses Stilicho as an important military hero in the fourth-century Roman conquest of Britain, a general who has defended Britain from the Scots, Picts, and Saxons.

Richard of York was also a military commander, having just concluded, in 1445, a five-year term as lieutenant general of England's forces in northern France; hence the translator describes Richard as "the defense of England" in his opening stanza. This connection is hard to miss when we observe that the translator changes Britannia's "ne pictum timeam" (254: "I shall not fear Picts") to "I shulde not fere batile / . . . of picardy" (277): Picardy was the contested region in northern France closest to England.[7] The third stanza of the translator's introduction explicitly connects Stilicho's story with that of Richard:

Marke stilichoes life. whom peoplis preysed
with what labouris. of the regions wide.
And Rome hir selfe. the consulat he vpreised
ffor now the parlement pierys. wher thei goo or ryde
Seyen the duke of yorke hath god vpon his side. (15–19)

Observe the life of Stilico, whom nations praised—
through what efforts of the far-flung provinces
and of Rome herself he improved the consulship:
for now the Parliament peers, whether [or wherever] they walk or ride,
say the duke of York has God on his side.

What may we make of this juxtaposition of two military leaders?

Claudian's poem is more than a panegyric on the career of a military man, the virtuous Stilicho. It is an exhortation to power. Stilicho was an ambitious man who married into the imperial family and ruled briefly as regent for the emperor's younger son in the western portion of the empire. Lacking the proper lineage to be emperor, Stilicho would have to look to usurpation or allow his dynastic ambitions to be fulfilled through his son, who was of royal status through his mother. Stilicho's rival and chief obstacle was the praetorian prefect of the eastern portion of the empire, Rufinus, who spread rumors about Stilicho's treasonous ambition. Thus the poem translated at Clare, along with Claudian's numerous other poems on behalf of Stilicho, included themes all too familiar to fifteenth-century English politics. Dynastic ambitions and rivalries, usurpation and royal connections are as central to the earlier moment as to the later one. The theme of matrilineal entitlement was important to both men as well, for just as Stilicho's claims and ambitions were legitimated through his wife, so Richard's strongest claim to the throne, his descent from Lionel of Clarence, came through a female line.

The rhetorical climax of Claudian's fiction is Rome's effort to persuade Stilicho to take the consulship. A marginal gloss at line 325, near the start of Rome's speech, reads "deo gracias Ricarde." The tag comes after the lines in which Rome exculpates Stilicho from slanderous accusations and rumors that Rufinus may have started:

The commoun Rumour of foltysh people . nevir of this sclaundir gladyd
In such rebukys no feith is had . of credens nevir cam letter
The to accuse and in this parte . thi grettest worshippe groweth (323–25)

Popular gossip never rejoiced in this slander;
No faith is had in such rebukes; no letter of credence ever came
To accuse you, and in this region your substantial reputation grows.

The profession of trust thus marked by the marginal gloss is expressed by Rome, to which Augustinians were distinctively linked and that carried special prestige

as site of the papal court. At the same time, it is articulated as a specifically regional attitude, one that would be fairly common in the neighborhood of Clare,
Richard's oldest and wealthiest seat.

The last portion of Rome's speech argues that Stilicho—although until now
excluded from the consulate by his lineage ("servage and lowe birth"; 359)—
ought now to take up the office to provide continuity and preserve the virtuous
old ways:

> Wherefore the rulying of our lawe . thou owist to the[e] to take
> That this olde worship perissh not now . which haven of worshippe was . . .
> than olde worship defendyd
> Al hevynesse shal be put a side. (344–55)

> Therefore you ought to take on rulership of our law
> so that the old honor—the very haven of honor—should not perish . . .
> then, old honor defended,
> all gloom will be put aside.

These sentiments were especially germane to English dynastic concerns, for the
Lancastrian usurpers were often portrayed as interrupters of a legitimate and
benign reign, and the notorious baronial violence of the era was deplored as another symptom of the injustice of Lancastrian rule.

Rome then goes on to prophesy a glorious future for Stilicho's offspring. The
language in this section duplicates much of that found in Bokenham's 1445
Magdalene prolocutory and elsewhere in his legendary. It thus constitutes
strong, though not conclusive, stylistic evidence for his authorship. The robe offered to Stilicho is spun by Lachesis (*DCS*, 370), and "lachesis fatall" appears
again in the translator's epilogue. It is Lachesis who, Bokenham writes, spun his
life thread (*LHW*, 248). Rome displays "precious yiftes and roobys hevy . the
which minerva wrought" (*DCS*, 375). It is in Bokenham's Magdalene prolocutory that Minerva also appears as the weaver of vivid garments (*LHW*, 5030)
rather than as the more usual goddess of war or wisdom.

Lucina will comfort the "labors" of Stilicho's wife "in her childyng" (*DCS*,
377). Lucina is one of the deities refused as an object of invocation in Bokenham's Magdalene prolocutory (*LHW*, 5218). Rome gives a sketch of the infancy
and childhood of Stilicho's son Eutherius, his "tendir laughyng . . . &
wepyng" (*DCS*, 381), the "manly precepts" of his adolescence when "he rulyd
and turnyd his hors atte wille" (387). From the Magdalene prolocutory, we recall
the scene at Lady Bourchier's with her four young sons: "Besy . . . with revel
& wyth daunsyng" (*LHW*, 5024). The maternal theme recurs in the legend itself
when Magdalene performs miracles enabling first the conception and then the
survival of a royal child, and here, too, we are given a charming stanza-long
view of the little boy running naked on the beach and throwing pebbles into the
sea (6053–59). Again, for both authors, the maternal theme was an important
one, given the lineage in each case.

These rhetorical resemblances cannot be considered definitive evidence of authorship, for they are not unique references. But they are not commonplace, either, especially in combination. Thus Lucina is invoked as a patroness in Virgil's Fourth Eclogue and is mentioned by both Augustine (*City of God,* 4.11) and Chaucer; Lachesis appears only once in Chaucer (*TC,* 5.7) but not in Augustine or Christine. Minerva as weaver is not found in Chaucer (in which she is associated, in her many appearances, with wisdom or war) or in Christine's *Cité* (in which Arachne is credited with inventing weaving) or her *Othéa* (in which she is the goddess of war and wisdom) or Augustine (in which she invents crafts generally but not weaving specifically). The point is, then, that this is a specific collocation of classical references distinctive to the two texts under consideration. These references show an imagistic and thematic cluster in two works composed at the same time and place and displaying the same political loyalty. As such, they substantially strengthen the likelihood of Bokenham's authorship.

Besides a hero, there is also a villain in Claudian's work: Stilicho's opponent and rival, Rufinus.[8] There was certainly a Rufinus figure in Richard's life in the autumn of 1445, although he was neither Henry VI, as Cameron suggests (430), nor the earl of Suffolk, as Griffiths proposes (*Reign,* 704, n. 54).[9]

For Richard of York, 1445 was not a good year—not, at least, in its second half. The long war with France was winding down, and England was clearly losing. Approaching the end of his five-year term as lieutenant general of England's forces in northern France, Richard and his supporters expected a renewal of the appointment, but it was not to be. In August and September, an important visitor from home was in Normandy: Adam Moleyns, king's councillor and diplomat, keeper of the privy seal, dean of Salisbury, and soon to be consecrated bishop of Chichester. Moleyns was chief negotiator with the French, now mandated to discuss extending the truce then in force and, apparently, to evaluate Richard's performance. Evidently, Moleyns was not satisfied (Ferguson, 28; Reeves).

In October, when Richard arrived in England to attend the Westminster Parliament, he was under a political cloud and, though enormously rich, in financial straits. He had lent large sums of money to the government and was unable to collect much of what was owed to him. At the end of his term in Normandy, this amount came to a staggering £38,666, of which £12,666 was written off (Harriss, "Marmaduke Lumley," 146). His consequent inability to pay some of the expenses and salaries of his command in France caused resentment and disciplinary trouble among the troops. To make matters worse, Richard was accused by Moleyns of embezzlement, mismanagement, and favoritism. Richard complained to the council about the "sclaindereux langaige" that had been deployed concerning his "demenyng on the tother side of the see," and he also accused Moleyns of having fomented trouble and recruited witnesses against him while in Normandy some months earlier (Johnson, 52–53; Reeves, 245–49). Richard's administration was audited and investigated, with the assistance of officials brought over from Normandy. Eventually he was exonerated, but the controversy was sufficiently damaging that Richard lost his post. In December

1446, he was replaced as lieutenant governor in Normandy by Edmund Beaufort, marquis of Dorset.

Among the men defending Richard was a prominent member of his affinity, Sir William Oldhall, a Norfolk landowner, councillor in France, and chamberlain to York between 1444 and 1456. Oldhall had a particular connection with Clare, for his "most significant post . . . was the stewardship of the honour of Clare in Suffolk, at a fee of £156 yearly, with an additional 20 marks for the constableship of Clare castle" (Marshall, 60). In 1447 Oldhall was also granted a rent-free, lifelong lease of meadow, pasture, and castle garden on Richard's estate at Clare (Roskell, "Oldhall," 2.186).[10] It seems likely, then, that the disastrous episode in Richard's career would have been followed especially closely by his clerical friends and tenants at Clare Priory and that it would have had special resonance in the neighborhood. Indeed, given Osbern Bokenham's attested presence at social events in the castle, there is no reason that he could not have heard the bad news from Oldhall, if not from the landlord himself or his sister, during the fall or winter of 1445.[11]

Given Richard's troubles in 1445, it is legitimate to wonder what—besides loyalty to a landlord—might offer a basis for linking him with Claudian's Stilicho, who is represented as an effective and widely loved ruler. In fact, there were strong parallels, certainly for one disposed to find them. Richard's tenure in Normandy, if checkered from the military viewpoint, was successful in other ways. Although his first tour of duty (1436–37) was fairly uneventful, he did respond to complaints about pillaging and other offenses committed by undisciplined English soldiers. In 1436 he summoned local representatives to Honfleur to investigate these grievances and managed to reestablish some control of the troops and of the local administrators (Burney, 145, 193).

York's second tour (July 1440 through September 1445) began as something like a triumphal return in that he was able to negotiate conditions and to exercise almost unlimited authority. As Pugh puts it, "He returned to Rouen virtually as viceroy" (119). On arriving, Richard conducted a detailed inquiry into a range of serious complaints: desertion because of lack of pay, raiding of food, robbery, and, above all, absentee officership. Again in 1444, stray troops were ravaging the Coutances region, and Richard had them rounded up. Burney comments that "credit . . . must in this period go very largely to Richard duke of York, without whom the whole system would very likely have fallen into complete ruin" (189). Richard was therefore "remembered in Normandy as a ruler who had dispensed justice and he can be given credit for the concern that he undoubtedly showed for the welfare of the inhabitants of the duchy" (Pugh, 188–89). Johnson concurs overall: despite various shortcomings, Richard "restored effective authority in a province all but lost to rebellion, and sustained business confidence in a continued English presence. This was an honourable achievement" (50). And in 1443–44, the gross failure of the Guyenne campaign led by Richard's rival, Somerset, can only have made Richard look good by comparison.

Thus Richard's tenure in France could easily provide analogies with the Stilicho story in both its positive and negative dimensions—that is, with Richard as the heroic Stilicho and Moleyns, perhaps less obviously, as the slanderous opponent.

Let us return now to the translation to observe how it refracts these events. If Claudian's poem is an exhortation to power, what is the position of power to which the poem "writ at Clare" exhorts Richard of York? As we will see, it occupies a position at once provocative and carefully ambiguous.

THE CLAUDIAN TRANSLATION is preceded by a prologue—technically an envoy—of three stanzas in which the translator apostrophizes his text. In the opening stanza, he asks it to pray so that

the high prince sett not ferre aside	the high prince may not neglect
Nobil doctryne thurgh thyn imprudence	Noble doctrine through thy imprudence—
Which of al Engelonde is namyd the defence	He who is named the defense of all England,
In loonge labourys. ful like to stilico	Much like Stilicho in his long labors:
Assemblabil in rest. god graunte him be also	God grant him also to be similar in rest.

This opening stanza is already subtly provocative. What is the textual imprudence that might prompt a prince to set aside noble doctrine, and what is this doctrine? We must fill in the blanks here, but I take "thyn imprudence" to be Claudian's validation of ambition, and the conflicting doctrine to be the conventional Christian–Stoic lessons of patience, social responsibility, and noblesse oblige. The translator thus holds two conflicting ideas in balance, rejecting the idea of rebellion as imprudent while simultaneously reminding his audience, or indeed Richard himself, of the possibility of advancement. A similarly subtle balancing act is performed in the last line of this opening stanza. If York is to be similar to Stilicho in rest, as he is in labor, he must presumably come to occupy higher office than the just-completed term in France: Stilicho did, after all, become consul.

The second stanza of the prologue urges the treatise to show itself to "his highnes"—surely another provocative phrase, given its royal connotations, for only one purpose:

That be thi remembraunce. vertue moote him please
Aftir whom grace folowith. soon from heven sent
Which in loonge tymes. makith right sure ease.

That by remembering you, virtue may please him
After whom grace follows, sent soon from heaven:
Which in difficult times gives reliable comfort.

Again the translator protests nothing but the most virtuous intentions: the text is a reminder of virtue for someone gifted with divine grace. Yet the reference to grace is ambiguous. Does this grace follow every virtuous person, or is it the distinctive divine aura surrounding those of royal blood, specifically those predestined for the throne? It alleviates tedious times; does this consolation come from the sureness of salvation or the contemplation of an elevated earthly destiny? It is carefully phrased to simultaneously open and close subversive possibilities.

Stanza 3 brings in Richard by his title, ending with a fulsome assertion of his divine guidance, perhaps even divine right:

> ffor now the parlement pierys. where thei goo or ryde
> Seyen the duke of yorke hath god upon his side
> Amen. amen. blissed Ihesu make this rumour trewe
> And aftir. feele peryles. this prince with Ioie endewe.

> For now the Parliament peers, whether [or wherever] they walk or ride
> Say the duke of York has God on his side.
> Amen, amen, blessed Jesus make this rumor true
> And after many perils this prince with joy endow.

The reference to "Parliament peers who say [Richard] has God on his side" might seem more appropriate to a later date, specifically 1451, when Richard was nominated in Parliament as the heir. However, this occurred in the House of Commons, not of Lords, and the peers were by no means receptive to the nomination at that time. The phrase could allude to Richard's royal right, although no claim had yet been made. Far likelier is the latent image of a judicial duel in which God vindicates the innocent. In view of Richard's ordeal at the end of 1445, it is appropriate that this duel has a parliamentary venue. In 1445, few peers would have wished Richard to the throne, but many would have wanted him acquitted of Moleyns's accusations. The stanza ends with a religious vocabulary that seems overstated for the immediate situation: two "amens," the assistance of Jesus, and a joy whose capital initial in the manuscript links it visually with Jesus, who will bring about the desired joy by making true the "rumor" of Richard's having God on his side. The tonality here seems far more appropriate to kingship than to simple exoneration from charges of financial mismanagement.

The poem closes with a short epilogue, again an envoy. It exhorts the "lytyll tretys" to follow ("swe") Claudian "evyn as hys chyld," for Claudian is one of the virtuous pagans who, whether or not he can be saved, can certainly instruct. "Love not hys lawe / love weel hys word," the poet at once cautions and encourages his reader. Both caution and encouragement are much in the vein of Bokenham's chastising of overclassicizing Christian poets (see chapter 3). They are equally typical of traditionally moderate Augustinian attitudes toward learning. With this respected pagan author, Bokenham finds common ethical ground:

> Oure feyth and hys be not as oon they goo in dyvers sutys .
> Yet eche assentyth . that pure honour merces est virtutis.

> Our faith and his are not the same; they walk in different clothing.
> Yet both of them agree that real honor is the reward of virtue.

The image of clothing here seems to locate religious difference at the surface as a matter of mere form or appearance. Yet if we read these "sutys" as suits of livery, denoting what in Bokenham's day was the sign of loyalty to a great landlord, then the difference in clothing might well be one of life and death, as, given the violent rivalries and short tempers of the time, it frequently was. The clothing image can then be seen to operate as an accurate miniallegory, meaningful on both social and spiritual levels. The poetic sensibility here, though not necessarily unique to Bokenham, is typical of his work, and so is the theological position espoused in this passage.

To deny the salvation of virtuous non-Christians or pre-Christians was the orthodox norm, but not everyone agreed with it, and the question had been controversial since the early Christian era. In regard to the pagan philosophers, Augustine had concluded that human understanding does not reach so far as to know their ultimate fate (cf. Turner, 180). Some later scholars—Abelard and Aquinas, for instance—devised intricate arguments to the effect that intuitive or implicit belief is sufficient for pagans' salvation.

An even more radical extension of this position was held by an important Augustinian of the generation after Bokenham. Giles of Viterbo (1469–1532), vicar general, prior general, and cardinal protector of the order, held that even knowledge of the Trinity can be had by natural human powers and that Plato wrote so well of the Trinity that Scripture could hardly add more (O'Malley, *Giles,* 23–39). A much harder line was taken by Walter Hilton, who, in *The Ladder of Perfection,* denounced scholars "who say that Jews and Saracens can be saved by keeping their own law . . . and in that faith they do, as it seems, many good works of righteousness" (2.3). For Hilton, virtue and intention were not sufficient for salvation. For another fourteenth-century writer, Thomas Bradwardine, virtue was the product of grace; hence a pagan has no true virtue, cannot carry out a good action, and can only perform sinful works—an opinion, Leff observes (*Bradwardine,* 155), not in keeping with Catholic tradition or dogma.

Nominalists came up with a far more generous position, arguing first that natural goodness can exist without grace, although it cannot win eternal life, and second that since God is omnipotent, he can save an unbeliever if he wills to do so. Bokenham's recommendation of Claudian's words and his tolerant attitude seem to incorporate this approach, although whether he is indebted for it to Aquinas or to Ockham is impossible to know, for both were respected *auctores* in university curricula and monastic libraries.

The last words of the epilogue offer the following wish on behalf of Richard:

My lord off yorke most tendurly graunt good ihesu thys
Preeude in hys herte: how evyr honor merces est virtutis.

To my lord of York, please gently grant, good Jesus, this [to be]
Proved in his heart: how honor is always the reward of virtue.

It seems to me, then, that the Claudian translation is probably by Bokenham, that it affirms loyalty in the crisis Richard faced during the autumn of 1445, and that it exhorts him to hope for the best. Would this "best" include the crown, as some formulations in the poem seem to hint? Some historians are reluctant to believe that Richard could have had royal aspirations much before he formally laid claim to the throne in his 1460 parliamentary petition or before 1456 when the factional intrigues of Queen Margaret and her party were particularly effective against Richard or, at the earliest, before 1451 when it was proposed in Parliament that Richard be formally recognized as the heir presumptive.[12]

But the matter could hardly have been so certain as to permit precise dating. The dynastic question had been on the agenda from 1399 onward, and the usurping house of Lancaster constantly attempted to fortify its claims and to discredit those of competitors with stronger credentials. Griffiths observes that during the 1440s, Henry and his advisers were ignoring York as a possible heir and instead were advancing the Beaufort, Holand, and Stafford families, precisely because York's claim was better than the Lancastrians'. Appreciation of

> the parlous dynastic situation of the Lancastrian royal family . . . was certainly strong by 1440 . . . reflected in the buoyant business of pedigree production. Pedigrees from Adam and Eve or Noah especially proliferated during Henry VI's reign . . . which pointedly exclude all reference to the line of Lionel of Clarence. . . . There is no reason to doubt that Richard of York's sense of dynasty was as strongly developed as the king's. ("Sense of Dynasty," 25)

Pugh shares this view, remarking that by 1460, when Richard finally formally pressed his claim to the throne, "there can be little doubt that he had long regarded himself as the rightful king of England" (86). Richard's most recent biographer writes, "He was inescapably heir not only to the earldom of March but to the whole Mortimer inheritance, with its claim to the English throne. This Mortimer legacy was a real one, alive throughout Richard's minority, and it could not readily be swept under the rug" (Johnson, 27).

Lander observes that about 1450 Richard began to use the surname Plantagenet—"now heard again in England for the first time for about 300 years"— and comments that his purpose "apparently was to emphasize the purity of his own descent from Edward III in contrast with the doubtfully legitimate Beauforts" (73). These opinions and observations have nothing to do with temperament or psychology, only with facts of reproductive and political history. Moreover, it little matters what Richard himself thought or when he thought it (as if we could do more than guess), as long as others considered him fit for power, as evidently they did at Clare. Cameron notes a similar problem in assessing Claudian's relation to Stilicho: "What official organ, even today, does not on occasion overreach itself, whether through excessive enthusiasm or defective information, and embarrass its party?" (46). That the Claudian translation remains so cautiously ambiguous both prevents a firm conclusion and stimulates it—for what is the purpose of such ambiguity if not to protect a writer while provoking an audience? The piece is certainly partisan, for it is clearly related to the events of autumn 1445; beyond that, though, all is inference.

THE THIRD DOCUMENT executed at Clare and demonstrating Yorkist sympathies was produced eleven years after the two just discussed. Like the Claudian translation, this document is anonymous but probably is by Bokenham. Unlike the translation, it makes no effort to drape partisanship in classicizing guise. The "Dialogue at the Grave of Dame Johan of Acres" (ed. Barnardiston),[13] its unique manuscript dated May 1456, is a brief catechism "bitwix a seculer askyng, and a frere aunsweryng" questions about the genealogy of one of the early donors to Clare Priory, who had died in 1305 and was buried at the priory (see chapter 1). The manuscript consists of an English and a Latin version, with the English in the ubiquitous Troilus stanza. In its entirety, the piece comes to only eighteen stanzas. Its tracing of the Clare family culminates in Richard, duke of York, "this Prynce myghty" with his numerous offspring both dead and alive. After rehearsing this impressive pedigree, the dialogue wishes Richard long life and ends with the hope that "with virtue and victorie god hym [Richard] avaunce / Of al his enemyes."

It is once again, therefore, an embattled Richard we glimpse in the "Dialogue," and not without reason, for 1456 was another particularly trying year for him. The preceding few years had seen deteriorating relations among magnates of the realm. Since 1450 Richard's grievances had mounted. Queen Margaret seems to have considered York a threat to the inheritance of her son Edward, born in 1453, or possibly to her own influence. Her antagonism was partly responsible for the series of humiliations that York endured early in 1455. His finances were not in good shape, despite—indeed, because of—his important services to the crown, some expenses for which were not reimbursed. In 1454 Richard complained to Parliament that he had had to sell properties and pawn jewels to meet expenses, and there is evidence that he died heavily in debt (Bean, 182, 197). Just a year before the "Dialogue" was written, in May 1455, Richard had participated in an ominous incident that some historians call the start of the Wars of the Roses: a military clash at St. Albans with supporters of the king, in which Richard's principle rival, Somerset, was killed and the king himself was slightly wounded. Richard apologized for this episode on bended knee.

The year 1456 saw intensified factional wrangling and worse. In February, York resigned, reluctantly and at Queen Margaret's insistence, the powerful position of protector that he had briefly held during one of Henry's episodes of mental illness. In May, one of York's French friends, the treasonous duke of Alençon, was arrested. In this way, comments Scofield, "the duke lost the ally in France on whose support he had been counting, while the Earl of March [Richard's son Edward] lost the second French bride his father had courted for him" (1.24). In September, "York was in London, at the bishop of Salisbury's house, where he was treated to a particularly savage propaganda spectacle. The heads of five dogs were impaled outside his lodgings in Fleet Street, each carrying a scurrilous verse in its mouth. Their message was as direct as its presentation was brutal. The son of a traitor, York deserved to die" (Johnson, 176–77).

In October, Margaret managed to drive the Yorkist ministers from court, and

York and his allies were censured by the king's council. In December he was physically attacked in Coventry by the young duke of Somerset and was saved by the mayor of the town (Johnson, 177). Like the two other documents I discussed, the "Dialogue" ardently supports Richard, though without specifying in what capacity. As in the two earlier documents, the lack of specificity is less significant than the presence of partisanship. The descent of Dame Joan of Acre was a powerful reminder to both enemies and friends of Richard's illustrious lineage and therefore his potential future. It also offered encouragement to the duke himself during an especially bleak and difficult time.

I STATED EARLIER THAT Bokenham's partisanship is not deduced from external factors alone or from explicit references to Richard of York, but also from representational strategies in the text of Bokenham's legendary. Here and in the next chapter I consider more subtle literary forms of political partisanship than those cited so far. The most important of these is the most obvious: that Bokenham's legendary is a collection of *female* lives. In chapter 2 I examined various cultural factors and texts contributing to his choice. Now I want to look again at its distinctiveness, which may be easier to appreciate when we consider that only 17.5 percent of all the saints revered and canonized between 1100 and 1700 were women; in the preceding centuries, the number was even less (Weinstein and Bell, 220).[14] Despite the cultural factors conducing to an all-female collection, therefore, it was not an obvious or an inevitable choice. Bokenham's legendary emphasizes the capacities and effectiveness of women at a moment when these qualities had particular political importance.

Commenting on certain writings of fifteenth-century jurist Sir John Fortescue, the historian Charles Kingsford wrote, "The direct historical interest of these pieces is not great; they turn chiefly on the right of females to transmit a succession" (*Historical Literature,* 168). I will have more to say about Fortescue later, but for the moment I wish to concentrate on what Kingsford identifies as the uninteresting crux of the works in question: the right of females to transmit a succession. This right or ability was central to York's strongest hereditary claim and therefore to some of the propaganda against that claim. The reason is that the Lancastrian claim was carried in an all-male line via John of Gaunt and his male descendants, but the Yorkist descent from Edward III by way of Prince Lionel of Clarence relied at two points on women: Richard's mother, Ann Mortimer, and his great-grandmother Philippa. This was the genealogy Richard chose to emphasize in his 1460 petition to Parliament for the throne (see figure 8). He could have used, and often had used, another line of descent from Edward III, that of Edmund of Langley, which did not pass through females. But because Lionel was an older son than Edmund, the rule of primogeniture made the Lionel descent a stronger claim. This is why Richard's title was superior to that of the Lancastrians: beside being usurpers, they descended from John of Gaunt, a younger son of Edward III than Lionel. Indeed, Richard's claim was

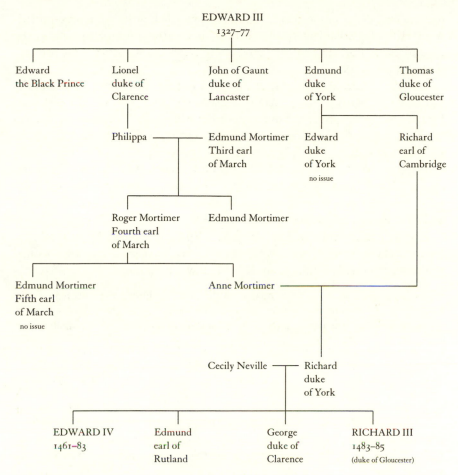

FIGURE 8 The matrilineal (Lionel) claim of Richard, duke of York, to the throne of England, and some of Richard's progeny.

strong enough to convince Parliament, which at last, in 1460, consented to Richard's accession—but made it inapplicable during Henry's lifetime. Soon after winning his legal case before Parliament and, in principle, securing the throne for himself and his heirs, Richard was killed in a skirmish at Wakefield.

By the middle 1400s, the questions of female succession and female transmission of right to rule had a history of nearly a century in English political life. They had been placed on the agenda at the start of the war with France in the 1330s and again in 1399 with the usurpation of Henry IV. Against Henry's legitimist rivals was directed the parliamentary statute of June 1406, which entailed the succession to Henry's sons and their male issue (Jacob, *Essays,* chap. 6). Some months later, the statute was repealed when it was pointed out to the king that his own claim to the crown of France depended on Isabel, mother of Edward III, and Parliament requested that "the restriction be removed on the ground that it limited unduly the prospective rights of succession of the princes" (Lapsley, 327, n. 2).

Decades earlier, the capability of this same Isabel to acquire and transmit the right to rule had become a major propaganda point for both English and French, remaining so for the duration of the war. A flood of material was released on both sides covering various aspects of the conflict: chronicles, debates and dialogues, invectives, epigrams, and letters and treatises in Latin, French, and English. With respect to Edward's dynastic claim, the English indignantly asserted Isabel's right to the French throne in the direct royal line while the French derided the idea that a woman could transmit what she never possessed and what French custom had never permitted.

Female exclusionism was not, in fact, a legal principle in French political theory of the fourteenth century. On the contrary, the generally acknowledged principle, expressed by King Louis X in 1314, was that

> raisons et droiz naturez donnent que en deffautes de hoirs males, les femelles doivent aussi bien heritier et avoir successions es biens et possessions des peres de cui elles ont estè procrèes et descendues en loyal marriage comme font li malle.

> reason and natural law instruct us that in default of male heirs females should inherit and have succession to the goods and possessions of the fathers of whom they are procreated and descended in legal marriage, the same as do the males. (Potter, 237)

Although there had been no reigning French queen, this was "an accident of genealogy" that could not be taken "automatically to constitute a custom of the realm" (Potter, 236). To be sure, there is a single-sentence article in Merovingian and Carolingian legal compilations banning a woman from inheriting ancestral land. This custom was preroyal, prenational, and even prefeudal, so there was no serious reason to apply it to the kingdom (which is not personal property) of France (which is not coterminous with Salian territory), and no fourteenth-century theorist did so. What, then, provoked the eventual articulation of the so-called Salic law?

Female exclusionism began empirically as a tactic in fourteenth-century French nationalistic realpolitik. It was asserted, opportunistically and without elaboration, in context of a series of French dynastic crises. According to a summary in Giesey's "Juristic Basis,"

> In 1316 Louis X died without a male heir . . . and rather than cede the throne to his daughter [Joan of Navarre, a small child at the time], it was passed in turn to his two younger brothers, each of whom also died without male issue; then, in 1328, the direct Capetian male line having become extinct, the crown was awarded to their first cousin Philip, of the collateral line of the Valois. In the process a direct male Capetian of distaff descent was passed over. . . . To explain the exclusion of women there was invented a century later the myth of the

Salic law. . . . Nor, indeed, would the Salic Law have had to be adduced if the male of distaff descent excluded in 1328 had not happened to be the English king [Edward III]. (11)

It was opportune for the French to invoke female exclusionism in 1328 because Philip Valois, who became Philip VI of France, was only a nephew of Philip IV, whereas Edward III of England was a grandson through his mother, Isabel, and thus was a direct descent and had a superior claim (see figure 9).

As John Le Patourel points out,

> The idea that Edward should assume the title is known to have been suggested by a deputation from Bruges as early as 1328. He actually used it on letters patent dated 7 October 1337. . . . The assumption of the French title had been under discussion between Edward and his allies for some months at least before January 1340 [when he formally assumed the title king of France at Ghent]. (180)

In 1339 Edward proceeded to enforce this claim by invading France, thus unleashing the war that lasted throughout all of Chaucer's lifetime and most of Bokenham's. Edward's propagandists naturally had to address the question of female inheritance, as did Philip's—indeed, it was an even more important issue to the French because "the majority of Frenchmen were, as far as action went, at least apathetic about the identity of their ultimate ruler and even about his nationality" (Lewis, 7). In fact, many were pro-English. Nonetheless, the dynastic propaganda on both sides remained without specific reference to the so-called Salic law, which, according to Potter, was first mentioned very briefly in France about 1358 but not elaborated until about 1415 in the work of the jurist and political theorist Jean de Montreuil (Potter, 247). In this sense, the Salic law was an invention of the early fifteenth century, designed to legitimize the pragmatic exclusionism that was already established in France and that had been revived

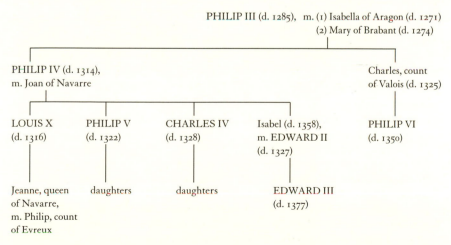

FIGURE 9 The matrilineal claim of Edward III of England to the throne of France.

more importantly, but still pragmatically, to block a valid English claim to the French crown.

Not surprisingly, the propaganda that flooded out on both sides operated perfectly well without the Salic law. Its tone was already set in an epigram composed in 1339 regarding Edward's assumption of the arms of France.

Rex sum regnorum bina ratione duorum;	I am king of two kingdoms by a double reason:
Anglorum cerno me regem jure paterno;	Of the English I consider myself king by father right;
Jure matris quidem rex Francorum vocor idem.	By mother right I am called king of the French.
Hinc est armorum variatio bina meorum,	This is the double design of my arms.
M. ter centeno cum ter denoque noveno. (Wright, 26)	One thousand three hundred plus thirty nine. (My translation)

A few years later, an invective against France written in 1346 offered considerable development of these sentiments. This poem survives in three manuscripts, "which suggests that it enjoyed a certain vogue, and may have been known in clerical and even governmental circles" (Barnie, 8). It is indeed a "gesta bellicosa," as one manuscript describes it. Despite its valorization of female descent, the invective counts effeminacy in its repertoire of insults against Philip of France. Its linguistic exuberance can be appreciated from the comical rhyming wordplay in this typical line: "Si paleas valeas, Valeys, depone timorem" (If you are worthy of the contest, Valois, drop your fear). On the question at hand, here is what the invective has to say:

Mater Ysabella nostri regis, generosa,	Our king's mother, Isabella—generous,
Prudens, formosa, virtutum lucida stella,	Prudent, beautiful, shining star of virtue,
Regis francorum Philippi filia cara,	Dear daughter of the French king Philip [IV]—
Nupserat Anglorum regi, pacis via clara.	Married the king of England, the obvious way to peace.
Ejus tres fratres sine semine morte ruerunt,	Her three brothers fell dead without [male] issue.
Lex, Deus, et patres sibi regni jura dederunt.	Law, God, and ancestors gave title to the kingdom.
Quicquid juris habet mater proli pia donat;	What the pious mother has, she gives to her child.
Proles non tabet, sed matris dona coronat.	The child is not weak but crowns the mother's gift.
Est Judaeorum Christus rex sub vice matris,	Christ was king in the maternal line,
Ergo Francorum rex fiat aper vice matris. . . .	So the boar [Edward] may be king of the French in the maternal line. . . .
Karolus imperator, rex patricius, dominator,	Emperor Charles, highest king and ruler,

Coelitus instructus, subito de corpore ductus,	Instructed by angels when suddenly led from the body,
Audivit dici per responsum Lodewici,	Heard it said by Louis's reply
Quod rex regnaret sua filia quam generaret.	That through his [Louis's] daughter should reign a king whom she would bear.
Nomine materno rexit, sed jure paterno.	He should reign through the mother, but by paternal right [or law].
Ergo magnifico credamus in hoc Lodewico.	Hence we believe this lord Louis.
Ergo, Philippe comes, apro redda sua jura. (Wright, 34–35)	Hence, Count Philip, return his title to the boar. (My translation)

Here the English propagandist cleverly turns an old French legend against the French. He bases his support of Isabel's right on the *Visio Karoli III*, written in 900 or 901 and originally intended to justify royal succession through the female line. The story relates the dream of Charles the Fat, great-grandson of Charlemagne and emperor from 885 through 888. The sleeping emperor is guided by an angel first to hell and then to heaven where he meets his uncle Lothar and his cousin Louis. They ask Charles to pass the throne to Louis's grandson through his daughter Ermengard, since Charles has no direct heir. Although this succession did not occur in 888, when Charles the Fat was deposed, it did take place some years later. In October 900, the man in question, another Louis, had himself proclaimed king at Pavia; in February 901, he was crowned emperor at Rome. A few years later, he was blinded by a rival and has come down through history as Louis the Blind.[15] Michael Curley comments that

> the *rechauffage* of [the "Prophecy"] during the mid-fifteenth century should be understood as a response in *genre* to the French reliance on prophecy as a powerful tool of propaganda in their disputes with the English. . . . English publicists followed this *littérature de circonstance,* and attempted to undermine some of its conventional juridical and pseudo-historical props . . . the so-called Salic Law, for example. (337)

The text consists of Latin verse with a Latin prose commentary. Chapter 5 is devoted to two scriptural precedents concerning women's property rights. One narrates the ruling of Moses in an inheritance dispute between a dead man's daughters and his brothers. Moses rules as follows: "The claim of the daughters of Zelophehad is good. You must allow them to inherit on the same footing as their father's brothers. Let their father's patrimony pass to them. Then say this to the Israelites: 'When a man dies leaving no son, his patrimony shall pass to his daughter'" (Num. 27:7–8). The other instance of mother right is, of course, Jesus' lordship, although as we will soon see, this political–theological point varies according to the particular writer's dynastic politics.

Some prominent chroniclers of the period saw the "woman question" as central to the Hundred Years War. Jean le Bel, for example, is unequivocal about cause and effect. After the death of the last directly descended Capetian king, he writes, the twelve peers and other lords of France gave the kingdom to Philip of Valois

> et en osterrent la royne d'Angleterre, qui estoit demourée seur germaine audit roi Charles derrainement trespassé, pour ce qu'ilz dient que le royaume de France est sy noble que il ne doibt mye aler par succession à femelle. . . . Et firent celluy messire Philippe couronner à Rains l'an de grace MCCC et XXVIII, le jour de la Trinité, dont puis aprez sont venues grandes guerres et dissolutions au royaume de France. (Vol. 1, chap. 17, p. 92)

> and excluded from it the queen of England, who was still blood sister to the said king, Charles [IV], recently deceased, because they said that the kingdom of France is so noble that it must never go by succession to a female. . . . And they had this Sir Philip crowned at Rheims in the year of grace 1328, the day of the Trinity, as a result of which great wars and disasters came to the kingdom of France. (My translation)

Jean Froissart borrowed liberally from his fellow Hainaulter le Bel, taking much the same line while expanding the material rhetorically. In his chapter entitled "Cy commence loccasion dont la guerre meut entre les roys de france et dangleterre" (Here begins the incident that provoked the war between the kings of France and England), Froissart writes,

> Et furent tous trois roys de france apres la mort du roy phelippe leur pere par droicte sucession lung apres lautre sans avoir hoir masle de leur corps engenre par voye de mariage. Si qu'apres la mort du derrenier roy Charles les douze pers de france ne donnerent point le royaulme a leur seur qui estoit royne dangleterre pour tant quilz vouloient dire et maintenir et encores veulent que le royaume de france est bien si noble q'l ne doit mie aller a fumelle [femelle] ne par consequent au roy dangleterre son aisne filz. Car ainsi comme ils veulent dire le filz de la femelle ne peut avoir droit ne succession de par sa mere venant la ou sa mere na point de droit. Si que par ces raisons les douze pers & les barons de france donnerent de leur commun accord le royaume de france a monseigneur Phelippe nepheu iadis au beau roy phelippe . . . & en osterent la royne dangleterre & son filz qui en estoit hoir masle & estoit filz de la seur du derrenier roy Charles. Ainsi alla le royaume de france hors de la droicte ligne ce semble a moult gens. De quoi grands guerres en sont meues et venues & grans destructions de gens at du pays au royaume . . . car cest la vraye fondacion de ceste histoire. (Vol. 1, f. ii)

> And they [i.e., the three sons of Philip le Bel] were all three kings of France after the death of King Philip [IV], their father, by correct succession one after the other, without having a male heir of their bodies engendered by means of marriage. So after the death of the late King Charles [IV], the twelve peers of France did *not* give the kingdom to their [the kings'] sister, who was the queen of England, for they declared and maintained, and still do, that the kingdom of France is so very noble that it can never go to a female or, consequently, to the king of England, her elder son. For as they declare, the son of the female can have neither claim nor succession through his mother, coming whence his mother has no claim. So for these reasons, the twelve peers and the barons of France gave, by their agreement, the kingdom of France to my lord Philip [Valois], nephew to the

former King Philip the Fair . . . and they excluded the queen of England and her son, who was male heir and was son of the sister of the late King Charles. Thus the kingdom of France went outside the right lineage, as it seems to many people. From this, great wars were provoked and great destruction of people and territory in the kingdom. . . . For this is the real foundation of this story/history/chronicle. (My translation)

A few chapters farther on (f. 15, v), Froissart repeats the story, intensifying the wrong that has been done. He portrays the dying King Charles advising his barons that they "donnassent le royaulme a celluy qui avoir le devroit par droict" (should give the kingdom to the one who ought to have it by right). Shortly after his death, the king's wife bears a daughter, so that there is in fact a direct (female) heir who could hypothetically assume the crown after a prolonged regency. Thus Froissart shows the barons' decision for Philip of Valois to have been doubly antifemale.

Another important and well-known prose document of the period is the rather deceptively named *Somnium viridarii* (1376) or, in its French translation (1377), *Le Songe du vergier* (ed. Chatillon). The work is no erotic dream vision but a long debate between a knight and a priest about papal versus royal power. It has been called "le plus important et le plus fameux des ouvrages de droit public" in late-medieval France (Coville). It touches on many topics, including female succession and transmission of rule. In the Latin original, the cleric defends polygamy and divorce against the knight, but the French reverses these positions.

Arguing for the succession of a woman and her son, the cleric adduces the practice of other kingdoms such as Spain, Aragon, and Sicily, and he cites scriptural precedent (Num. 27). He goes on to a more radical critique of secular laws and customs, for these are sometimes "iniques & desraisonnables" (wicked and irrational). Barring women from inheritance is one such law. Moreover, it runs contrary to common law, which says that there is no difference between men and women with respect to inheritance. Anyone who posits exclusionary differences between men and woman is blaming nature for the sexual difference necessary to conserve the race. Yet even if we grant that public matters are better handled by men than by women, this is no argument against the son of an entitled woman. Furthermore, the current king of France, Philip, is a more distant relation of the royal line than are the kings of England and of Navarre, and this is offensive. The book of Genesis is brought into play via the law of levirate (the duty to marry a deceased brother's widow), which shows that the offspring of such a marriage, male or female, represent and are legitimate heirs of the dead father.

The knight replies that the law has traditionally defined the son as the father's representative and heir; that a right never acquired cannot be transmitted; that patrilineal descent is proper; that a male heir can better defend the kingdom than a female can; that the levirate was intended to ensure male heirs; that women are not only inconstant by nature but also have, in general, nine other major moral faults—indeed, "femme est une beste qui n'est pas ferme ne stable" (woman is an animal neither firm nor stable), and even the completely virtuous Virgin Mary neither came to spiritual government nor will judge at the day of doom.

Unequivocally on the French side is a set of four anonymous anti-English tracts composed between 1418 and 1422 (ed. Pons). The two that emphasize the lineage issue are not of governmental provenance, and the distribution of their manuscripts suggests that in their time they exercised "une certaine influence" (Pons, 11). The tract entitled *Débats et appointements* begins with the Trojan origins of France and French history to the present and continues with long dialogues between Truth (*Vérité*) and France. In the opening historical survey, the accession of Philip Valois occupies more than one hundred lines (about 13 percent of the total 747): clearly, it bulks large in the author's mind. Against Edward's claim, the author asserts an ancient law—he does not call it "Salic"—so old that "il n'est memoire du contraire" (there is no memory of the contrary: lines 320–26). Thus "de ce nul ne doit faire aucune doubte, mais doit fermement croire qu'ils ont faulse et dampnable cause" (from this no one ought to have any doubt but ought to believe firmly that they [the English] have a false and damnable cause; 342–43).

The second text in this group that I wish to cite, the *Fluxo biennali spacio*, is a dialogue between a Frenchman and an Englishman. The debate starts with the Englishman's justification of the war on the basis of the Isabel lineage, to which the Frenchman replies, "Filia est in hoc regno incapax" (line 1; in this kingdom a daughter cannot rule). The Englishman promptly proceeds to cite the by-now conventional incident in Numbers 27, which is immediately refuted by the Frenchman on the equally traditional grounds that Zelophehad (Salphat) was a man of low birth and so the issue was not succession to a kingdom. Moreover— and this argument appears here for the first and last time in the century-long polemic—the English themselves excluded a woman from the throne: Matilda, the daughter of Henry I, in 1135.[16] It's news to me ("hoc michi novum"), confesses the Englishman; "Lege hystorias" (Read [your own] history), retorts the Frenchman before proceeding to relate the well-known story about how an angel appeared to King Clovis with a sacred ampulla of chrismatic coronation oil. Because this oil confers the character of priesthood, it can never be applied to a woman (lines 35–49).

I introduce this material not to suggest that the Hundred Years War was fought to vindicate the rights of women to inheritance or to anything else; that would be a naive and anachronistic position. I do contend, though, that in the writing of many propagandists on both sides, the question of women's nature was indeed at the heart of the devastating conflict that occupied English and French history for so long. Even as late as 1459, after the end of the war, one chronicler, Noël de Fribois, justified his discussion of the English claim by admitting that so many had already written on this topic it might seem unnecessary, but nonetheless his treatment would be distinctive (Lewis, 5). Lewis claims that the appeal of these treatises "seems to have been felt at all levels of literate society" (5): bourgeois, chivalric, and noble.

Barnie comments that "it is the fashion to minimize the importance and seriousness of Edward's pretensions to the crown of France—the dynastic issue" (4) in favor of feudal-territorial issues such as the control of Guyenne. He also notes Edward's opportunism regarding the principle of female succession rights (6). Le Patourel, however, unequivocally attempts to rehabilitate the claim to France as a genuine good-faith issue, on the grounds that Edward's chances of achieving it were fairly good until 1359 and that the claim "was meant more seriously and deserves to be taken more seriously than it has been by historians during this century" (173). Yet whether the "real" motive of a given event is serious or cynical is not always the primary question in cultural studies that it must be in political analysis. Sometimes the significant phenomenon may be the effectiveness of propaganda rather than its accuracy. The war may "really" have been about English territories in France or about French aspirations to a centralized nation-state, but there can be no question that for many contemporaries the dynastic–reproductive issues loomed large, finding their way into propaganda of various kinds—including, I believe, hagiography.

In Bokenham's time, political circumstance returned the principles of the so-called Salic law to the realm of dynastic considerations, where they had begun more than a century earlier in France. After 1437, the busy ecclesiastical lawyer Thomas Bekynton—soon to be bishop of Bath and Wells—was secretary to the young Henry VI. In 1435, at the Congress of Arras, the French had offered to cede important territories in return for England's abandonment of its claim to rule France. Although the bargain was rejected, the issue remained alive, and Bekynton compiled for the king the materials concerning the English title to the crown of France.[17] The collection is a series of legal documents, most of them from the time of Edward III. They are striking in their ingenuity, resembling the big fourteenth-century Ovid commentaries with their variegated argumentation and twists and turns of logic and interpretation.

The collection opens with a letter from Pope Benedict to the young Edward III, urging him not to claim the title to France and not to be misled by perverse and fraudulent counsel. Philip has been a decent king; he is your relative; you will lose; everyone is astounded at your naïveté and vanity. As for the female line, "ponamus ante oculos mentis tuae" (we place before the eyes of your mind) the fact that the French succession has never admitted it, and therefore it cannot admit Edward. Oppositional documents justifying the English assert that France belongs to us "iure ligittimo" and complain that the French king is the invader ("intrusor"; Charles seized Guyenne in 1324). A woman may well be excluded "ut regno salubrius consulatur" (that the kingdom may be better governed), but her son must be admitted (ff. 112b–113a). Augustine is quoted to the effect that a woman's sex is not a vice but a fact of nature (f. 113; not attributed, but to *City of God* 22:17), and the document refers, interestingly, not only to the French exclusion of women but also to their hatred ("odium") of women. The

case of the Virgin Mary and Jesus is cited as an "excellentissimum legittime suc-
cessionis exemplum" (most excellent model of legitimate succession) imposing
silence on those who claim the contrary (f. 113b).

One document dismisses the pope's opposition by observing that the pope
cannot rule in temporal matters (f. 124a), but another letter from Edward III
follows the formulas of piety, greeting "devota pedum oscula beatorum" (with a
devout kiss, the foot of the blessed) and complaining that Philip not only
usurped the throne of France but also invaded the English-held territory of
Aquitaine and stirred up the Scots to rebellion (ff. 133b–35a). Several French
documents in the Harley manuscript, attacking Edward's claim, reiterate the
French custom according to which no woman has ever ruled or transmitted rule
in France ("succesdast onques ne donast droit" etc., f. 33b) and assert bitterly
that the English should never have set foot in France (f. 34b). Also included in
the collection are extracts from the *Somnium viridarii* that could serve either
side, and Petrarch's twelfth eclogue appears with Latin glosses explaining its application to war episodes during the mid-fourteenth century (55 ff.).

What this interesting assemblage shows—especially in conjunction with
the other material discussed—is the continuity over a century, from the 1330s
through the 1430s, of the explicit and intense awareness of the political consequences of ideas about female nature and abilities. The question is most often
addressed in an empirical or opportunistic rather than a principled manner, but
it is no less important for that reason. In all, the documents discussed here suggest a fairly constant level of awareness against which an all-female legendary
might acquire special significance.

The "woman question" was brought forward into the 1460s, forcefully and
explicitly, in the work of the eminent jurist John Fortescue. From 1438, this
worthy was the justice of the peace in several counties, including Norfolk and
Suffolk. He advanced to become an adviser to Henry VI, chief justice of the
King's Bench from 1442 to 1460, and a prominent Lancastrian propagandist.
Bokenham may have become acquainted with Fortescue's name (and quite possibly his person, considering Fortescue's position in East Anglia) in 1441, when
the lawyer represented the Crown in a suit against an Augustinian monastery in
Edington (Wiltshire). The establishment claimed a tax exemption granted by
Edward III (Kantorowicz, 173; Plucknett, 168, n. 10). (This kind of assault on
traditional ecclesiastical liberties is allusively protested in Bokenham's hagiography, as we will see in the next chapter.) By 1450, Fortescue was sufficiently unpopular to be mentioned among other Lancastrian advisers and administrators
in the sarcastic political song, "For Jack Napes sowle, placebo et dirige," said to
have been composed by Cade's rebels while gloating over the assassinations of
the duke of Suffolk and of Moleyns (Furnivall, 10).

Fortescue composed several English and Latin treatises upholding the Lancastrian succession, trying to demolish the York claim by proving the invalidity
and impropriety of female rule or transmission of rule. Even though these
works were written more than a decade after Bokenham had completed his leg-

endary, their arguments were drawn from standard sources such as Scripture, patristic commentary, Aristotle, and Aquinas. The arguments circulated among clerics and barristers and were commonly taught at the universities and the Inns of Court. As a Cambridge graduate and an official in an important international order—particularly at a time when the ruling English dynasty wanted to establish its credentials—Bokenham would be familiar with the arguments on the question.

Fortescue's *De Natura legis naturae* attacks the Yorkist claim in broad terms. Seeking to ground legality (*lex regis*) in the law of nature, he brings to bear on a hypothetical case all the resources of traditional theology and philosophy. His hypothetical case is this: A king dies without a son. He has a daughter and a brother, and the daughter has a son. Which of the three should inherit the kingdom? In other words, "could the female descendants of Lionel, Duke of Clarence, possess and, possessing, transmit, a valid claim to the throne of England?" (Jacob, "Fortescue," in *Essays,* 111). Fortescue's document repeats much of the material found in treatises of the century before, although with opposite conclusions in the interest of Lancastrian genealogical propaganda.[18]

The second half of the treatise takes the form of a lengthy courtroom drama pleaded before Justitia herself. (The author immediately notes that it is "no obstacle to [Justitia's] power that women are by law excluded from the judicial office; for although the word justice (*justitia*) be of the feminine gender, she herself is not a woman, nor of the female sex"; chap. 1). The piece deploys many tired old arguments and a few clever new legalistic ones. Its methods will be familiar to anyone who has looked into the papalist side of church–state polemics of the high Middle Ages. The final judgment is for the king's brother, because women may neither possess nor transmit rule.

The family dynamics are repulsive. The son denigrates his mother with sarcasm, condescension, and filial machismo ("I laugh at these two notions of my mother," "the pious simplicity of a woman," etc.). His position, not surprisingly, is that a woman can transmit rule but not exercise it herself. The uncle must then hoist his grandnephew on his own petard, showing that the nephew's attack on his mother's right redounds against the nephew, because if women cannot rule, they cannot transmit rule, either. From this thesaurus of misogynistic theory, I select a few samples:

> The Lord often, among the weighty words of his threatening, says [to idolaters] that he would not leave of them *mingentem ad parietem* [anyone who pisses against a wall; 1 Sam. 25:22, 34]. Now this action is the action of a man, and not of a woman, the Lord thus distinguishing the sons of those wicked men from their daughters, as the male dog is distinguished from the female, a distinction which he certainly would not have made if the female, like the male, could have succeeded to those kings ordained to destruction. (chap. 5)[19]

> Nature works nothing except with suitable and the fittest instruments; art, therefore, which imitates nature, works not otherwise. Who ever hunts hares with

cats? Nature disposes greyhounds for the fields and the pursuit of hares, but cats for staying at home to catch mice. It is a shame, as though a man should hunt game with cats, to draw away from home, for the purpose of governing nations, the woman whom nature has fitted for domestic duties. Nature did not make a woman a fit instrument for that purpose. An artificer is not so inconsiderate as to cleave wood with a mattock, nor a sailor so careless as to entrust the oar to the hands of one with the palsy. . . . Behold, then, a sufficient cause why a woman cannot succeed in a kingdom. (chap. 9)

Next comes a long argument showing that Jesus was not king of the Jews in right of his mother, but only of Joseph, Mary's husband (chap. 11). Scripture shows that Joseph was a true heir of King David; however, he was not Jesus' father, and thus Jesus could not have been king of the Jews "by hereditary and temporal right of succession" but, rather, through appointment by God to that position. As for Mary, gospel does not assert a royal lineage for her, and although we believe her to be a descendant of King David, too, Jewish law excluded female succession during the life of a male heir (in this case, Joseph). We will see later that the Yorkists were at pains to give a different view of the holy family.

Another chapter contends that exceptional women cannot be considered representative of the sex and that, in any case, most exceptional women were not morally admirable. Furthermore, the existence of remarkable women, even those who have ruled successfully, has no bearing on the topic, for "it is reason that corrects facts, but facts never change reason; for facts alone may show what has been done, but it is reason alone which informs us what ought to be done. Therefore, if the arguments which we have urged are valid, they cannot be disproved by bygone facts" (chap. 22). The preeminence of man over woman is likened to the preeminence of soul over flesh (chap. 63). This hierarchy is said to be replicated in both nature and heaven, "for the life of the citizens of heaven above, to whose society the Church prays that we may come, is a social life" (chap. 65).

Even in Fortescue's more famous *De Laudibus legum angliae,* written between 1468 and 1471 and not especially concerned with dynasty, the masculinist principle is strongly restated:

The offspring born of a woman is the progeny of the husband, whether the mother is free or servile. . . . Is it not . . . more convenient that the condition of the son should follow that of the father rather than that of the mother, when Adam says of married couples that "these two shall be one flesh" which the Lord explaining in the Gospel said, "Now they are not twain but one flesh." And since the masculine comprises the feminine, the whole flesh made one ought to be referred to the masculine, which is more worthy. (chap. 52; in Chrimes, 103)

Although Bokenham cannot have known Fortescue's treatises on dynasty when he wrote his legendary, they represent the range of argumentation that his hagiography opposes. The friar's method is not a logical refutation of philosophical premises, and in the last analysis, Bokenham would probably have wanted less to abandon those premises outright than to adjust them to a more liberal interpretation. His argument remains a poet's argument: implicit, empirical, a fortiori: If real women have effectively done God's work and transmitted the highest truth, then they are, in principle, able to transmit a merely temporal rule. To choose to compile an all-female hagiography was the first step in the statement of a complex and forward-looking social vision.

Was Bokenham the only one? Is there nothing else to meet the sort of argument that Fortescue published in 1460, arguments that French theoreticians had, after all, published much earlier and that circulated throughout the century as part of the learned man's intellectual and political vocabulary? Unfortunately, much of the period's propaganda has not survived, incorporated as it was in ephemeral newsletters, handbills, or ballads.

But fifteenth-century propaganda does surface in surprising places and genres, as we have already seen. One of these is the chronicle of John Hardyng. It is a work notoriously difficult to date, for it exists in two main versions, compiled and revised over a period of some two and a half decades (1440–65) and adapted to different patrons as power changed hands.[20]

The question of Hardyng's politics is murky, for his career was complicated with respect to political loyalties. His early patron, Sir Henry Percy ("Hotspur"), fought against Henry IV, on behalf of a Lionel-descended (i.e., matrilineal) Mortimer claim to which Hotspur was related by marriage to Lionel's granddaughter. This did not prevent Hardyng from serving all three Lancastrian Henries later on, although not necessarily because of any principled loyalty. His 1440 mission to Scotland on behalf of Henry VI (a mission on which Hardyng forged documents relating to England's claims in Scotland) did not produce a satisfactory reward, and Hardyng spent the next decade and more trying to augment it with a manor at Geddington in Northamptonshire, a hope at last disappointed. "Since he was trying to inveigle Henry into giving him his reward," comments Antonia Gransden, "it is not surprising that [Hardyng] sought to please him by presenting the Lancastrian view of history" (137). Hardyng was also constable to Sir Robert Umfraville, who died in 1436 and with whose biography the Lansdowne manuscript closes. Umfraville, too, seems to have had a wavering loyalty to the new dynasty, for he was apparently considered a possible partner in the 1415 Southampton plot against Henry V (Jacob, *Fifteenth Century,* 147).

In view of this fluctuating career, I think it hazardous to assert that Hardyng was ever "Lancastrian" in any other than the shallowest, most empirical, or opportunistic sense. Insofar as any more thoughtful loyalty emerges from his text, it appears to be Yorkist. One might suggest, given Hardyng's history, that the accession of Edward IV did not necessarily make Hardyng a Yorkist or force him to change sides but that it perhaps offered the appropriate occasion for a long-standing anti-Lancastrian tendency to come into full bloom.

That, at any rate, is what we have in the second, printed version of his chronicle. The text, dedicated to "My lorde of Yorke," is explicit that Henry

IV "kyng Rycharde deposed wrongfully" (18). It gives (as Bokenham did in 1445) the Pedro genealogy justifying Richard's and, later, Edward's title to Spain. Hardyng, too, skips Costanza's offspring, saying that since the first male heir of either Spanish sister (Costanza or Isabella) would be king of Castile, therefore "To you, my lorde of Yorke, this dooeth appent, / For your uncle Edwarde ws first heire male, / To whome your father was heire without faile." The prohemye to this version, however, offers a far more powerful kinship: the Lionel descent, and in it Hardyng explicitly validates the female transmission of right. He apostrophizes Richard in rehearsing the pedigree. Anne Mortimer—great-great-granddaughter to Edward III—married the earl of Cambridge, who

gatte of her your selfe as I have red.

Why should ye not then be her verraye heyre
Of all her lande, and eke of all her right,
Sith Iesu Christe, of Iude lande so feire,
By veray meane of his mother Mary bryght
To be kyng claymed tytle and right?
And so did name hym self kyng of Iewes:
So by your mother the right to you acrewes. (17)

The same theological parallel appears later on when Hardyng displays the history of England's claim to France. A genealogical chart shows that Edward III was king of France "ex jure matris," and the accompanying stanza, repeating the war propaganda of a century earlier, says that Edward's son, Prince Edward, who died in 1367,

was the first of Englyshe nacion
That ever had right unto the croune of Fraunce
By succession of bloode and generacion,
Of his mother without variaunce,
The whiche me thynketh should be of most substaunce;
For Christ was kyng by his mother of Iudee,
Whiche sikerer side is ay as thynketh me.

As if recognizing the provocation of this material, Hardyng quickly disclaims any motive for mentioning this pedigree other than desire to offer complete information to the reader. Nonetheless, these matrilineal sentiments ("always the surer side, I believe") are not isolated in the chronicle, for the printed version of the entire work is a heavily distaff-loaded history, replete with women heirs, women military leaders, wise women lawgivers, women peacemakers, women strategists, and women rulers. One might object that these are merely the data of British history, especially its legendary component, and thus have no relevance to the state of the woman question in Hardyng's time. But historiography is always selective, and it is striking how often the role of a woman or of "feminytee" is foregrounded through the ages in Hardyng's representation.

This orientation is obvious even from the opening stanzas, for Hardyng does not begin his history with the tale of Brutus leaving Troy (the one familiar to readers of *Sir Gawain and the Green Knight*). Rather, he substitutes for this traditional story of *translatio imperii* a "femininity prologue," a mythic tale that, despite its bizarre features, is ultimately based on the anthropological history of matriliny, matrilocal marriage, and female leaders among the ancient cultures of the British Isles.[21] Hardyng's prologue tells of three sisters, daughters of the king of Syria, who discovered England and named it Albion after one of them. At home, the sisters' plot to murder their husbands is discovered, and they are sent away by ship to England. There they inseminate themselves with the heat of imagination, attract incubi, and bear giant offspring, although Hardyng assures us this was only for the best of motives: "For to fulfyll the werke of womanhed, / And bryng forth frute, the land to rule and lede" (29). On his belated arrival, Brutus would have to defeat these giant offspring.

This prologue imitates the *Brut,* but it is particularly useful to the orientation displayed throughout Hardyng's *Chronicle*. "This chronicle is not trewe," Hardyng observes of the fanciful Albion story, because there was no king in Syria at that time. Farther on, he opts for both versions—England is named Albion after its white cliffs or after an alien princess—"And so both waies maye be right sure & trewe" (chap. 6, 30). Although this both/and formulation resembles that of the conventional skeptical–fideistic nonresolution of a problem often seen in late-medieval scholasticism, the underlying motive here is less philosophical than rhetorical. That is, the "femininity prologue" is a useful trope for Hardyng because it introduces the role of women, which is part of his propagandistic aim to vindicate.

Like Bokenham's revisionist legendary, Hardyng's revisionist history (at least in its latest version) displays a gendered politics in service of the house of York. Returning now to Bokenham's text, I will show how it politicizes the tractable material of its genre.

EIGHT

Sexual–Textual Politics

Anyone in the fifteenth century who was seriously interested in the English succession would have been conversant with the difficulties created by the birth of eight sons to Edward III, several of whom survived and had offspring of their own. Erudite propagandists, whether secular or ecclesiastical, were among the seriously interested, not least because ecclesiastical houses were often asked to produce pedigrees for nobles and monarchs. During the Lancastrian era, this industry reached new levels of output precisely because of the multiplicity of convincing claims to royal lineage. Our Austin friar's familiarity with the details of his princely patrons' pedigree—and indeed with the genealogy of others whose fortunes might affect Richard—is built into the prolocutory to his life of Magdalene, commissioned by Richard's sister (see chapter 7).

Genealogy is not, however, the only site where sex and politics meet. Beside the territorial claims, inheritance disputes, and wars created or justified by genealogical classification, other aspects of sexual politics (broadly defined) include attitudes toward nature and the body, the display of sexist or misogynistic attitudes, the production of discourse by women—particularly political discourse—and the rhetorical choices of male authors representing female characters. In this chapter, I investigate Bokenham's management of these issues.

THE LIFE OF ANNE, Bokenham's second saint, is inherently a genealogical story because of Anne's unique daughter and grandson. Anne's role as the forebear of Mary and Jesus required that she herself occupy an illustrious place in the holy-family history. Yet neither of the two scriptural attempts at tracing Jesus' genealogy—Matthew 1:1–17 and Luke 3:23–38—go through Mary and Anne; rather, they show the descent of Joseph, which Matthew takes back to Abraham and Luke, to "Adam, son of God." This patrilineal pedigree, illustrious as it may be, creates difficulties inasmuch as Jesus is not related by blood to Joseph but only to Mary. Thus it is Mary who must be ennobled with a suitable descent. One approach was offered by early Christian hermeneutics of the Hebrew Bible. In the reverse logic of Christian exegetics, Mary's descent is said to be from David because of scriptural prophecies predicting the birth of a leader from a young woman (mistranslated "virgin") of David's line. Moreover, since Mary's parents, Anne and Joachim, make no appearance in Scripture, their existence had to be invented.

Their story was told in the early Greek apocryphal *Protevangelium of James,* perhaps modeled on the Old Testament story of Hannah in 1 Samuel 1–2. From the Greek fiction, it was elaborated by Latin authors. This text is the ultimate (though not necessarily the immediate) source of Bokenham's narrative of Anne's life. Yet even here, no genealogy is given; it had to be created by patristic writers, particularly St. John of Damascus, whom Bokenham cites twice (1526, 1541). John explains the cultural and legal reasons that scriptural genealogies give only the male line. Because it was not customary for the Hebrews to give the pedigrees of women and because Jews were required to marry within the same tribe, "consequently it was sufficient to show the descent of Joseph" (362).[1] John provides a brief pedigree for Joachim, asserting his descent from David via the line of Nathan, but makes no mention of Anne's line or even of her parents' names. In other words, he provides a "matrilineal" descent for Jesus by bringing in Mary, but Mary's line is still reckoned patrilineally, so that the apparent "matrilineal" genealogy is rather severely limited to a single generation (Jesus to Mary, whose royal blood is through her father, Joachim). This became the standard account, used and acknowledged by Voragine and many other writers. The *Vita Marie* of the thirteenth-century Franciscan Thomas de Hales also gives these patrilineal lines, as does its late Middle English translation: Joachim's descent from David is summarized, as is Joseph's, but there is no mention of Anne's ancestry (chaps. 1, 10).

It is likely, as some scholars have suggested, that attention to Anne was a consequence of the late-medieval development of the doctrine of the immaculate conception of Mary (see chapter 4). In England, the cult of Anne had a political stimulus as well, for her feast, though already popular, was officially promulgated there in 1382 to celebrate the marriage of Richard II to Anne of Bohemia. Late in the fifteenth century, the fictional Anne's mother, Emerentiana, in turn became the object of attention particularly in the Low Countries and Germany, thus extending backward yet another generation the ever-proliferating family of Jesus.[2]

Given the gospel origins of the savior's pedigree and the lack of other information, Bokenham can do little to augment the matrilineal dimension. Of necessity, the ancestry he traces is that of Joachim and Joseph, and at the same time, he does all he can to make his reader aware of the maternal role. Following the method of Matthew, who names several mothers, rather than that of Luke, who presents a completely male lineage, Bokenham names David's wife, the mother of his four sons: "bersabee, / Whilom the wyf of wurthy urye" (1521–22). He also names both of Anne's parents: "ysachar hyr fadyr / Was clepyd, & nasaphath hyr modyr" (1516–17). Anne is often mentioned as the daughter of Issachar (e.g., Higden's *Polychronicon* 2:44 or Mirk's *Festial,* 215), but the mother's name is both rare and variable.

The *Acta sanctorum* (33.236), under its entry for July 26, the feast of St. Anne, says of her parents, "nomina eorum incerta esse . . . procul dubio nihil certi de illis eorumque nomine affirmari potest" (their names are uncertain . . . doubtless nothing factual can be affirmed about them or their names). Numerous traditions are cited, among them the Stolonus and Emerentiana parentage, Issachar and Nasaphat, Mathan and Mariam, and some omitting the mother's name but citing an Isaac or Garizim as the father. It is interesting to note, therefore, that the pair chosen by Bokenham is found in two other texts quite close to him in place and time. The N-town *Mary* play lacks a genealogy, but the manuscript notes to the play do provide these names of Anne's parents (Meredith, 87). So do several of the poems honoring St. Anne in the notebook, dated 1470 and after, of the scribe and local official Robert Reynes, of Acle near Norwich (items 46–49 in Louis). It seems, then, that Bokenham availed himself of a late and possibly a local tradition in his naming here, rather than the far more widespread patristic and patrilineal tradition that omits (or, rather, fails to invent) Anne's mother.

Bokenham expands the conventional explanation for the absence of mothers from Scripture (1525–38). His formulation here is interesting:

Also for more cler undurstongynge	Also for clearer understanding
Of this genealogyal descencyon,	Of this genealogical descent,
I wil ye wyte that for no thynge	I wish you to know that by no means
The olde law wold suffre permistyon	Would old law [Judaism] allow the mixing
Of sundry kynredes, for whiche conclusyon	Of different kinship lines, so that
Ioachym toke anne of hys ny alye,	Joachim took Anne from among his near kin,
And ioseph was streyned to wedde mary. (1532–38)	And Joseph had to wed Mary.

The heavily laden and usually derogatory term *old law* is perhaps a clue to intention. Jewish endogamy was replaced by Christian exogamy (the degrees of kinship forbidden to Christian marriage). Since this custom of old law has been replaced by a better one of new law, perhaps the Jewish custom of denying matriliny also should be superseded by a better one.

These are the sorts of latitude available to any hagiographer and also the ways in which every hagiographer conveyed a point of view. Some of Bokenham's distinctive shapings of his material are more blatant than the ones discussed here, but others are more subtle. Let us proceed once again through the set, now with a view to the social vision it incorporates. I use the term *vision* deliberately, for if the motivation is partisan, the net result will be broader than that, conveying a sense of England's mythic past and its ideal future. As with my theological–semiotic reading in chapters 4 through 6, not every legend is equally relevant to the thematic.

IN SOME INSTANCES, the revisionary point has to do with gender. For example, the salient episode in Margaret's story is the saint's encounter with her adversary, the force of evil. It appears first as a dragon, which swallows the maiden but bursts because of the cross she is wearing; then it appears as a demon whom she throws underfoot and interrogates about his origins and activities. Obviously, this episode leaves room for a certain amount of imaginative improvisation, yet the one point that seems to survive is the demon's chagrin at being vanquished by a young woman. In Mirk's *Festial,* it is the saint's youth and apparently inferior social status that chafe, but in most versions it is specifically the sex of his antagonist that humiliates the demon.

The early Middle English *Seinte Marherete* makes much of this at the end of the demon's homily on correct female behavior, and both the *South English Legendary* and Lydgate in his "Legend of Seynt Margarete" have the demon say that he could tolerate being beaten by a man but not by a girl. The same sentiment is voiced by the devil in Nicholas Bozon's Margaret. It seems to be equally conventional in the legend of Juliana (cf. Bozon, ed. Learned; *SEL*). The sexism here lies in the premise that women are morally weaker than men; hence they are unworthy opponents of the devil. But because this sentiment is expressed by a demon, perhaps it is meant to be rejected by the reader. An equally possible interpretation is that the demon, an expert in sin, knows who is most likely to fall. In any case, Bokenham cuts through this interpretive ambiguity by omitting the sexist lament altogether. His Margaret is not to be seen as exceptional to her sex in strength and virtue but, rather, as representative. Therefore the misogynistic comment, though traditional to the story, would undercut his purpose.

Bokenham's life of Faith contains a functionally similar omission. Pamela Sheingorn observes that some English versions of that story—those of Simon of Walsingham and the *South English Legendary* (ed. Horstmann), both from the thirteenth century—eroticize the saint's body by having her stripped naked before her ordeal and then stressing her nakedness ("Crystis wyf"). This important detail has narrative significance in motivating and magnifying the miracle in which a white dove descends during the saint's torture and clothes her in a magnificent white robe. Furthermore, it helps intensify the *cupiditas/caritas* tension already inherent in the story by virtue of the bed/grill image and the couple motif. The Provençal poem even refers to Caprasius as the saint's "druz," borrowing the lyric–erotic word for lover to restore it to its original meaning of "faithful friend." As I argued in chapter 2, it was precisely this oscillation between erotic and doctrinal registers that made Faith's story a possible antithetical parallel to Dido's. Yet even though it is open to ideological interpretation, justified by the narrative, and rationalizable as a temptation that the reader must resist, the nakedness of the young martyr does create the possibility of an unredeemed moment of voyeuristic pleasure. It can become the tiniest invitation to lubricity, and Bokenham's omission of it eliminates that possibility.

It also does more. Faith's story is one of a few in which the persecutor does not offer marriage or concubinage but virginity—pagan virginity. Faith is given the option of becoming a virgin priestess of Diana, much as Agnes is offered the position of vestal virgin. What this does is take sex off the agenda. It redirects the focus of the story and of the saint's determination, back toward faith and away from physical chastity. The problem with chastity, of course, is that it can become a rather misleading virtue in emphasizing a primarily sexual axis to devotion rather than an ideological one. In suppressing the motif of Faith's nudity, Bokenham is consistent with his procedure elsewhere. The point is made once again (as with Elizabeth, the married and maternal saint) that spirituality—not sexual condition—is the main thing.

Faith is not the only martyr whose nudity Bokenham suppresses or minimizes. Voragine has Christine led "nudam" through the city by her second persecutor; Bozon has her father strip her nude for beating (line 45); but Bokenham's Christine is at no time said to be without clothing, despite the unusual number and variety of her torments. The saint to whose story nudity is necessary—and not merely a matter of rhetorical discretion—is Agnes. She is explicitly condemned to be paraded nude through the town en route to the bordello where she will be condemned to serve all comers, but her long hair miraculously conceals her entire body. Voragine is quite clear: "Tunc praefectus jussit eam exspoliari et nudam ad lupanar duci" (Then the prefect ordered her to be stripped and led naked to the brothel). Bozon expands this sentence considerably, to a dozen lines in which much is made of the saint's nakedness, and the word *nue* appears three times (105–17).

Bokenham, on the contrary, does not use the word *nude* or *naked* in regard to the saint. Instead, he has the judge order her to be—not the racy *stripped* (a word used in this sense since the thirteenth century) but the far more neutral *spoiled* or *despoiled* (i.e., *deprived,* without specifying what she is being deprived of). Only when the saint's hair grows to cover her does Bokenham use the word *nakedness*—but by now she is covered, not naked, and so again the slight invitation to lubricity has been avoided. The only other instance of a naked martyr in Bokenham's legendary is Agatha, laid "al nakyd" on a bed of coals (8783). Otherwise, it seems that he attempted to restore some dignity to the tormented woman saint and to control as far as possible the reader's response.

Bokenham's treatment of the Ursula legend is fairly faithful to Voragine's, and that source already contains two episodes that tend to redress the misogynistic tilt of the ecclesiastical establishment. Not omission, therefore, but expansion is the Austin's rhetorical tactic here. The first instance of ecclesiastical sexism in the Ursula story occurs when the cardinals at Rome attempt to persuade Pope Cyriacus not to follow the troop of "quasdam mulierculas fatuas" ("a feu fonnyd wommen," 3319; a few foolish little women) as his angelic vision has told him to do. This episode is somewhat expanded, and the next one is amplified quite exuberantly. This is not part of the tale proper but an addendum; it narrates a conflict of power between an abbot and an abbess in Cologne, years after the massacre of the company of virgins. The abbess, in possession of the body of one of the virgin martyrs, gives the corpse to an abbot on condition that he will enshrine it honorably in a silver coffin. When he fails to do this, the offended corpse miraculously goes back to its first home. Then, when the abbot runs to beg it back again, he is refused possession by the abbess. This story (not much longer in Voragine's telling of it than the summary I have just given) becomes five Troilus stanzas in Bokenham's treatment, with the abbess voicing a resoundingly firm, four-line refusal to "Syr abbot" (3449). Both the expansion and the holy woman's reprimand are original with Bokenham.

Another opportunity for sexist comment arises in the Magdalene story when the saint first preaches to pagans at Marseille. Voragine does not comment specifically on her sex; rather, he writes that she is admired for her "specie . . . facundia . . . dulcedine eloquentiae" (her appearance, fluency, sweet eloquence). "Specie," with its frequent meaning of shape, form, figure, or contour, might seem to open the way to questions of sexuality, sex, and gender. This possibility is taken up by Nicholas Bozon, who writes that the pagans are astonished

Ke nule femme sout si parler   That any woman could speak so
Ke ses paroles percent lur quer.   That her words pierced their heart.

Bokenham preserves from Voragine the second and third nouns intact: "facundye . . . swetnesse eek of hyr eloquency" (5789–90), but for the more troublesome "species," he unambiguously gives "beute" (5788), foregoing any comment on sex or gender.

BESIDES THE GENDER-RELATED POLITICS of Bokenham's version of the Faith story, a territorial and partisan theme also emerges. Faith's life is one of several that Bokenham tells us he completed between 1443 and 1445 (cf. line 5043). The site of Faith's passion was Agen, located in the southern French province of Lot-et-Garonne in Aquitaine, and her body was later translated to another town in that area, Conques. For the English, and especially for an Englishman devoted to the welfare of Richard, duke of York, that part of France was of prime importance at just the time when Bokenham composed his Faith.

Aquitaine came to the English in 1154 as a consequence of the marriage of Eleanor of Aquitaine to the duke of Normandy, who became Henry II of England. Normandy and Aquitaine (or Guyenne) were thus the two strongholds of English influence in France, the most loyal to England and the last to be reconquered by Charles VII. Guyenne was an important commercial partner of England, providing much of England's wine, produce, and woad (a dye), the last especially important to the cloth industry but, by the fifteenth century, no longer cultivated in England (Wilson, 206). The area was also an important conduit for many Spanish products. In return, England sent cloth, hides, fish, and corn. The Gascons had little desire to become part of France, not least because they operated in much more favorable conditions than would be possible under the tax-obsessed French regime: "They considered France a foreign country and French a foreign tongue" (Labarge, 180).

During the 1330s, conflict over the duchy of Guyenne had been a catalyst touching off the Hundred Years War, but the region and its trade prospered at this time. The region was a particular focus for English patriotic feeling. Froissart testifies that in the battles of Poitiers and Navaretta, England's patron saint was invoked in the popular battle cry "St. George for Guyenne!" Aided by the lack of effective political and military leadership among the English, both at home and in France, Charles had already, in the 1440s, begun a lengthy administrative reorganization to unite France under a centralized government. Agen was a central point in his 1442 campaign for the invasion of Guyenne (Vale, *English Gascony,* map 3), and when Bordeaux finally fell to the French in 1453, after a long resistance, many of its merchants emigrated to England.

Richard of York's paternal uncle Edward, earl of Rutland and duke of York, was a lieutenant in Guyenne from 1401 to 1404. His death at Agincourt in 1415 brought the duchy of York to the four-year-old Richard. But the Lancastrians were widely resented in Guyenne, partly because the deposed Richard II had been born in Bordeaux and, more important, because Lancastrian policy—beginning with John of Gaunt, created the territory's overlord in 1390—had always threatened, or seemed to threaten, traditional Gascon privileges and autonomy. The story of Faith in its geographical setting is thus full of familial and dynastic associations for Bokenham's patron. But in his own career, the patron had even more recent and more painful associations with the place.

In 1443, John Beaufort, earl and then duke of Somerset, was named commander for Guyenne. This appointment was seen by Richard and his circle as an error and an insult, clearly prejudicial to his own authority in France. As Vale puts it, it meant that Richard was "removed from supreme command" (*English Gascony,* 127). Even worse was the financial pressure and humiliation Richard had to endure during this period, for while he went begging to the royal council for money to pay his soldiers in Normandy, the limited funds that were available were channeled instead to Somerset for the Guyenne campaign. The entire country was well aware of this campaign, for loans to finance it were requested or commandeered and commissioners were sent out to the shires "with instructions for 'stirring and inducing the people of the said shires by all ways and means that they can . . . for aid of men, victuals and ships for the relief and succour of Guyenne'" (Vale, *English Gascony,* 126). Richard's supporters were doubtless gratified when Somerset's leadership proved a complete fiasco.

Perhaps Bokenham's life of Faith helped rub Lancastrian noses in the dirt, its setting inevitably reminding an English audience of the regime's current mismanagement of the war in southern France. A Yorkist patronage in particular could scarcely have missed the point in 1443 or 1444, and over the following decade the inability to secure Guyenne was a constant theme in charges made, by Richard and others, against the Lancastrian regime (Vale, *English Gascony,* 131 ff.).

In what ways did Bokenham manage his text distinctively? To begin, it seems curious that he associates Agen with Spain rather than with France. As the emperor Diocletian

ded kum	came
In-to spayne that royal cuntre	Into Spain, that royal country,
A cyte he entryd clepyd agennum. (3601–3)	He entered a city called Agen.

To be sure, the Spanish province was created by Julius Caesar and remained Roman until the defeat of the Visigoths in 507 by the Frankish ruler Clovis, so in Faith's time, it would have been legally Roman and ethnically Iberian. Given Bokenham's emphasis on English and specifically Yorkist rights in Spain (see chapter 7), his insistence on the Roman–Iberian history of the region might have been an indirect allusion to those expansionist aspirations, military wishful thinking insofar as it ignores France and conveys the sense of an area up for grabs.

In the sense that Aquitaine had been transferred to the English and was clearly about to be restored to, or reconquered by, the French, the region itself was in process of "translation." Bokenham's treatment of the transfer of Faith's corpse is oddly mixed, considering how much attention and enthusiasm he invests in narrating the translation of Margaret. He makes no mention of the date of the theft, which may have occurred in 866, if it occurred at all (cf. Geary, app. A, II), and he fails even to mention the name of the town, Conques, to which Faith's body is removed and where her cult, with its famous reliquary, remains to this day.

In many legends, the major motive for translation was the failure of the community of origin to honor the body properly. This is specified in the twelfth-century Provençal life of Faith, which characterizes the people of Agen as lazy, sinful, greedy, and materialistic pagans who denounce the saint to their new ruler, Dacian (ed. Hoeppfner and Alfaric, stanzas 4–5). Neglect is also the motive in the translation of one of Ursula's virgins, which Bokenham narrates at length (3468–3502). With Bokenham's Faith, though, there is no such motive; indeed, Bokenham specifies to the contrary that when Faith and her companions die, the Christian community

dedyn alle here dylygence	did all their diligence
Them to beryin wyth greth reverence.	To conduct themselves with great
(3984–85)	reverence.

Nevertheless, he says, it is only a simple memorial (3986), and many years later Bishop Dulcidius performs the translation along with a group of monks and priests. This bishop is, of course, "styryd of devocyoun" (3991) and spurred on by a revelatory dream, yet he is also motivated by civic pride, considering it "ful expedyent" (advantageous or suitable) that his town should possess the relics. An orthodox writer could scarcely oppose a long-accomplished translation; moreover, these devout thieves are Gascons, and Gascons were, in the war with France, loyal to the English administration. Furthermore, if Bokenham's Aquitainian saint is a reminder of the war now winding down and of England's lost territories in France, then his representation may be aiming at reconciling an English audience to the new status quo, by emphasizing an inevitable cycle of gain and loss. In view of the criticisms being made of Richard of York at this time for his inadequate prosecution of the war, such a view would also tend to have an exculpatory effect, and the life of Faith would take its place, albeit a very modest place, alongside the Magdalene prolocutory as part of the duty owed by a poet to a patron.

I F THE MAGDALENE MATERIAL forms the theological, social, and mathematical center of the poem (see chapter 5), the life of Katherine is central in another dimension. Its field of signification is the politics of gender and of the state. The interest of the Katherine story here is its ability, in Bokenham's handling of it, to join the two concerns. Obviously, the story cannot compete with that of Magdalene, which it immediately follows, in theological importance. Therefore it does not compete in poetic elaboration, either, lacking the proliferation of prefatory material and being told in couplets rather than stanzas. Yet the two lives are comparable in length—945 lines for Magdalene and 1,002 for Katherine—and it looks as if Bokenham has chosen other, more obscure, means to signal the importance of his Katherine. It is ninth in the series; the prologue has nine stanzas; and the life has exactly an even one thousand lines (omitting the final "Amen" and thanks to Jesus). It can scarcely be coincidental that in the Pythagorean system of numbers, nine is the symbol of justice and that Bokenham has transformed the legend of Katherine into his most thoroughly politicized legend, precisely and explicitly a plea for justice.

If we use a Platonic definition of justice—balance or equilibrium, whether in the polis or the human body (cf. *Republic*)—then the connection among nine, justice, and the human body is evident. Hugh of St. Victor states the connection concisely: "The music of the human body . . . is constituted in the number 'nine,' since nine are the openings in the human body by which, according to natural adjustment, everything by which the body is nourished and kept in balance flows in or out" (*Didascalicon,* 2.4). The other distinctive feature of nine is that—like ideal justice—it is "incorruptible"; that is, "however often multiplied, it always reproduces itself" (Hopper, 123). As for one thousand, it is the cube of ten, the Pythagorean perfect number or decad. At a deeper philosophical level, numbers both represented and constituted various universal harmonies and proportional structures, particularly since—as a late Middle English treatise observes—"in makyng of the word [world] God disposed al thynges in mesure, nombre, and weight" (Mooney). Numerology is thus fundamental to the thought of many classical and medieval thinkers—not least among them Augustine, who wrote throughout his life about the properties of numbers (Hopper, 78–88). As such, in the late Middle Ages, numerology was often included "as a prominent part of the regular arts curriculum" (Peck, 19) at Oxford and elsewhere.

These numerological considerations become less speculative when we notice that Clémence of Barking's twelfth-century life of Katherine has exactly 2,700 lines (3 × 9 × 100) and that Christine de Pizan's version of Katherine's life occurs in chapter 3 of book 3—the book spoken by Justice—of Christine's *Livre de la cité des dames*. Moreover, as Kevin Brownlee points out, the structure of this book consists of a midpoint tale—that of the author's namesake—preceded by nine lives and followed by nine more (116).

Clearly, the association with justice and Pythagorean number theory is a conventional aspect of the Katherine tradition in the high Middle Ages, on which Bokenham drew for his rendition. Nor is a preoccupation with number limited to lives of Katherine. Eleanor Bulatkin shows that besides the symmetrical proportioning in the Old French *Vie de Saint Alexis* revealed by Anna Hatcher, this poem also displays an arithmetical scheme that serves "as a kind of armature for the inner structure" of the poem, and Russell Peck demonstrates the importance of eight to the fourteenth-century Middle English *St. Erkenwald*. How conscious of number symbolism the university-educated English Augustinian might have been at midcentury is shown by John Capgrave's prolonged meditation on six in his *Chronicle* (2–3). Edward IV, to whom the work is dedicated, entered into his inheritance in 1460, on the death of his father, Richard of York. Capgrave, beginning with 60 as 6 × 10, offers a page and a half of interpretation of six in its various aspects (1 + 2 + 3, 2 × 3, 3 + 3). Obviously, we cannot afford to dismiss numerology as an aspect of the heavily intentional poetics I am discussing here. Particularly in a genre like hagiography, which is about eternal truths, the appeal of numerology, with its cosmic implications, would be considerable.

The life of St. Katherine is the most explicitly gender oriented in Bokenham's series, but not simply because Katherine is an assertive and articulate woman of the ruling class or even because she speaks publicly; other women saints do the same. Katherine's speech, however, directly competes with that of men, for her persecutor, the emperor Maxence, hires fifty famous male orators to confute the Christian princess. The competitive element has already been signaled in the poet's comment about the profundity of Katherine's liberal education:

Was no clerk founde in that cuntre,	No scholar was to be found in that country,
What-evere he were or of what degre,	Whoever he might be or whatever rank,
But that she wyth hym coude comune.	That she couldn't communicate with.
(6395–97)	

In the debate, Katherine appropriates the usually masculine privilege of oratory (as opposed to teaching or the confession of faith), and she surpasses the experts in direct contest with them. This victory of socially subversive female speech calls into question traditional patriarchal notions of order and female subordination even more blatantly than does the typical insolence of the woman martyr. Although this potential inheres in the plot, not every hagiographer foregrounds it as Bokenham does. His treatment can be better appreciated in contrast with that of his contemporary and fraternal colleague John Capgrave.

Capgrave's version of Katherine, weighing in at more than 8,600 lines in five books of Troilus stanza, has evident pretensions to the status of romance. Besides its format imitative of Chaucer's *Troilus,* it includes enormously expanded dialogues and episodes from the heroine's *enfances.* It is a fully developed *vita,* whereas Bokenham chose to write only a short portion of the entire life, the crucial portion, the *passio.*

Sex and gender are prominent concerns for Capgrave certainly, but not only, in the debate episode. In Capgrave's version of the debate, one orator is reluctant to attend, for sexist reasons: "He nedeth not his labour on a woman spende, / he shal on-to hir his discipulis send" (4.1000–1). No woman could possibly be a worthy opponent; the scholar's pupil can take care of the matter. The emperor whips up his scholarly team with a great deal of misogyny and machismo, exhorting them to virile courage and to "lift up your hearts, men!" In a similar vein, the slightly later Italian verse treatment by Bonino Mombrizio has Maxence insult his scholars by saying that they have been shamefully defeated by a "feminucia" (line 759; a trivial woman). Bokenham omits all this testosterone display. One of his scholars does comment that "for so smal a matter" (6705), any one of the fifty orators would have sufficed, but this is not linked to the opponent's sex; it depreciates Christianity, not femininity. Since these fifty are to convert and to accept martyrdom along with Katherine, one suspects that Bokenham wishes to keep them as inoffensive as possible beforehand. Capgrave, far less astute a maker, never deals with the question of what becomes of the scholars' misogyny after their conversion.

Although there is misogyny in Bokenham's legend, it is not on the scholars' part. Rather, it comes from the emperor, whose first word to the saint is the reductively generic "Wumman" (6535). Later, interrogating Katherine in the palace, Maxence remarks that she is no angel but

<table>
<tr><td>"by natur</td><td>"by nature</td></tr>
<tr><td>A wumman . . . , & a frele creatur,</td><td>A woman . . . and a frail creature,</td></tr>
<tr><td>Wych is ever varyaunth & unstable,</td><td>Always changing and unstable,</td></tr>
<tr><td>Fykyl, fals and deceyvable,</td><td>Fickle, false, and deceitful,</td></tr>
<tr><td>As we wel knowyn by experyence." (6629–34)</td><td>As we well know by experience."</td></tr>
</table>

For this reason, Maxence continues, he need not believe Katherine's theology. His tirade serves as a foil to Katherine's calm refutation of misogynist slander— slander familiar to fifteenth-century readers in myriad forms, ranging from ecclesiastical discourse to estates satire and the poetry of John Lydgate. Katherine's rebuttal is not a defense of women, nor does it rely simply on the empirical evi-

dence of her own example. Instead, Katherine calls into question the philosophical underpinning of her opponent's position. Thus Bokenham shrewdly avoids
the ever-contentious "woman question," concentrating instead on impeccable
principles of reason. This call to reason he places in a woman's mouth:

"Who that is reulyd by resoun	"Whoever is ruled by reason
And not by his senswal felyng	And not by his senses
Hath wurthyly the name of a kyng;	Deserves the name of king;
And ther-agayn who-so ne wyl	On the other hand, whoever won't
By resoun be reulyd & by skyl,	Be ruled by reason and logic
But folweth the lust of senswalyte,	But follows sensual impulses,
Thow he emperour, kyng, or kayser be,	Though he be emperor, king, or caesar,
He ne may for al hys lynage	He can't, despite his lineage,
The tytyl avoydyn of servage."	Avoid the label of serfdom [i.e.,
(6644–52)	unfreedom]."

The argument here is more subtle than might at first appear. To be sure, it
represents the conventional Catholic moralism such as found in Chaucer's moral
ballades (and it seems particularly to echo the middle stanza of "Gentilesse"). In
context, however, it turns this moralism to another use. The emperor has just
dismissed a woman's speech because of her sex. Sex is thus exposed as one of the
superficial physical data irrelevant to proper judgment or spiritual truth. It is
connected with the realm of created nature and therefore is accessible only
through an epistemology of experience (as the emperor remarks). In philosophical terms, sex is an "accident" or property, not an essence. The pagan emperor,
however, persists in thinking of sex as an essential quality, a quality a priori determinative of character and behavior. Obviously, we are meant to judge his position as wrong, in both its theoretical premise and its practical application.

The authorial antiessentialism expressed here is perfectly orthodox as far as it
goes. If rigorously pursued, it leads, in the ecclesiastical sphere, to the ordination
of women and, in the political sphere, to the justification of female rule. Although neither Bokenham nor any other hagiographer follows it out to those
implications, nevertheless the more limited contemporary dynastic application
of Katherine's message is clear. The bondage (serfdom) of mere sense perception
causes some people to perceive others only in terms of sex and therefore blinds
them to real issues. In the text, Maxence's error is to reduce doctrinal matters to
the question of the speaker's sex. In contemporary national life, good governance is similarly reduced if succession depends on the sex of the lineal trans-
mitters.

Another question that looms large for Capgrave is marriage. Much of his text
is devoted to lengthy parliamentary debates in which Katherine's barons try to
convince her to marry so that they may be properly governed by a man and the
dynasty may continue without disruption. But Katherine refuses to marry, asserting her own right and ability to rule and proposing a division of labor in
which her decisions will be executed by the men (2.1128–41). It is immediately

evident how convincing the arguments of Katherine's barons are, how reasonable their concern for good government is, and how little misogynistic in any virulent way they are. Indeed, in a clever authorial move, Capgrave co-opts any possible accusation of misogyny by having Katherine herself accused of misogyny; she is said by the barons to have been influenced by the misogynistic and antimarital *Contra Rufinus* of Valerian (2.734–42)! If the exhortation to marriage made by Walter's subjects in Chaucer's *Clerk's Tale* is at all convincing, then so is the exhortation made by Katherine's subjects here, voicing the normative social expectations of their day. Since Katherine's commitment to chastity is not, at first, motivated by religion—she is converted later—it is difficult for the modern reader to avoid seeing her as a kind of proto–Elizabeth I, determined to preserve her single state in order to maintain her political power. But conversion eventually provides a more respectable retroactive reason for Katherine's will to chastity. We see her to have been no ambitious machiavel after all, no mere "uppity woman," but, rather, a saint in the making.

Given the antiwoman potential of this portion of Katherine's *vita* (despite Capgrave's effort to render the masculinist position as palatable as possible), it is not surprising that Bokenham suppresses the marriage theme completely. His Katherine never has to consider marriage, except for the ritual hagiographic proposal by the persecutor (which is never, in any case, seriously considered). What replaces the excised marriage theme is that of politics. I argue that Bokenham transforms his "Katherine" into a minimirror for magistrates and thus an implicit commentary on current affairs.

To be sure, Katherine is not the only one of Bokenham's saints to be associated with politics. At the very end of her legend, Agatha is presented as a liberator of her country, and following Voragine, Bokenham quotes and translates her epitaph, which claims that "fredam she purchasyd to hyr cuntre" (8846). The story does not explain why Agatha deserves this tribute. The sequence of events, though, is that an earthquake that occurs during Agatha's ordeal kills her judges, along with many others, and destroys part of the city. In response to this disaster, the people demand a halt to the martyr's persecution, and the consul Quincian, her persecutor, accedes because "of the peple he drede sedycyoun" (8805). The epitaph also has proleptic meaning, for after her death, when Quincian rides forth to appropriate Agatha's wealth, his horses bolt, trample the tyrant, and throw him into a river, from which his body is never recovered (8861–71). It is a typical Osbernian touch that this wealth of Agatha's, which Voragine refers to only generically as "divitias," is specified now as "hyre patrymonye" (8860), legally hers by right of inheritance from her father. In any case, it is because of Agatha and her personal wealth that the tyrant dies. Doubtless, the women patrons and audience of Osbern's work found this tribute to the independently wealthy woman highly gratifying, likewise the punishment of the upstart who tries to appropriate her personal wealth unjustly.

Bokenham also tried to maximize the political potential inherent in Voragine's characteristically dry version of Agatha's verbal exchange with Quincian when he questions her as to why she, a noblewoman, presents herself as a servile person and she replies that the service of Christ is the highest nobility ("summa ingenuitas"; 171). This very brief exchange is expanded in the English version to twenty lines exploring notions of "servage & ientylnesse" (8456), "sovereyn fredam & lyberte" (8463) and adding the remonstrance that it is a king's duty to serve Christ (8465).

Despite some parallels in Agatha, I have chosen the Katherine legend as the more politically significant, for several reasons. Katherine speaks of equity as well as of liberty; her discussion with the king is much longer than Agatha's with Quincian; she is highly educated, a queen in her own right and an effective public speaker; her cult was far more widespread than Agatha's, especially in England; and she has special historical–legendary connections with England. Let us see, then, how Bokenham was able to domesticate her story.

The harangue that Katherine addresses to her persecutor employs a distinctly, and distinctively, political vocabulary. The passage quoted earlier is surrounded by these lines:

"Wher-fore, syr, beth reuled by equyte	"So, sir, be ruled by equity [justice]
If ye lyst to reioyse yow of lyberte; . . .	If you wish to enjoy liberty; . . .
Wherfore, syr, by counsel of me	So, sir, by my advice
Haboundeth you in verteuous lyberte	Abound in virtuous liberty
Wych evere conservyn wyl your honour."	Which will always conserve your
(6641–55)	honor."

This is a curious vocabulary for a saint. Terms like *liberty* and *equity* are not what one would expect in hagiography, and they stand out in sharp dissonance against the doctrinal background. True, there are hints in earlier versions, but only hints. Although Clémence of Barking has her Maxence say in despair, after the saint has converted his queen and his best friend, "Jo sui serf e nient emperer" (2390), he goes on to explain that he is impoverished because the Christians have deprived him of the people he loves best, his wife and his friend. The *Legenda aurea* has Katherine admonish Maxence in sociometaphorical wordplay about his perceptual limitations: "Sic namque poeta ait: tu si anima rexeris, rex eris, si corpore, servus" (As the poet says: if you are ruled by the spirit, you will be a king, if by the body, a serf). As far as I am aware, no other version of Katherine's life than Bokenham's employs the words *liberty* or *equity* or their equivalent in another language. Nor do any of the three fifteenth-century Middle English versions of the *Secreta secretorum* (ed. Steel), a popular governance treatise in which this special politicized vocabulary might be expected to occur.

But the word *equity* does play an important role in an extremely popular treatise of political instruction that Bokenham could not have avoided knowing well. This is the *De Regimine principum* of Giles of Rome, a work that exists in more than 250 manuscripts in various languages, including a Middle English translation by John Trevisa, which survives in a single copy. Giles's treatise was one of the most widely read of all medieval books among lay and clergy, nobility and bourgeoisie alike—a "best-seller," as Charles Briggs puts it (*English Manuscripts,* 9). Of the fifty-five extant manuscripts of English provenance, one evidently belonged to Richard of York, one was given to Margaret of Anjou as a wedding gift, three were owned by the Austins at York, and many are linked to Norfolk and Suffolk owners both lay and ecclesiastic, including the Paston family (Paston, 2, item 283). Nor should it surprise us, given Giles's status in his order, that several of these manuscripts reveal distinctively Augustinian colophons or apparatus. Both Austins and Benedictines adopted the treatise as a subject for study, and it was in common use as a university textbook before the end of the fourteenth century.

Giles's book is structured according to the cardinal Aristotelian virtues. The first of these is justice, whose aim is "equite and rightfulnesse in workes and dedes" (1.2.5). Two kinds of justice are considered: legal (*legalis*) and equal (*equalis*). It is according to the latter, a distributive type of justice, that everyone gets his or her due. This is, for Giles, the more important form of justice, and so the term *equity* recurs over and over again in those portions of the book devoted to justice—for example, six times in eight lines in a short passage in 1.2.10. The second Aristotelian cardinal virtue is prudence, required if the ruler is to fulfill the Aristotelian role of "natural kingship." Without prudence, the ruler is not a natural lord but, on the contrary, a natural servant, "for as it is declared, primo Politicorum, that som man is kyndeliche a servaunt for a failleth intellecte and understondyng and cannot rule hymself" (1.2.7). Bokenham has clearly loaded Katherine's speech to her persecutor with concepts and vocabulary derived from the treatise of Giles.

Giles does not, however, mention liberty. For this, Bokenham turns from thirteenth-century theory to fifteenth-century practice. As I indicated, one dimension of "liberty" here is phenomenological, as it is with Voragine: the freedom from sense perception that enables penetration to the core spiritual issues. Yet the term *liberty* also participates in another discourse, that of legal history, in which it did not refer to freedom in general, as it does now, but had instead a specific prescriptive and limiting sense. In fifteenth-century usage, *liberty* meant the specific chartered and enforceable rights, privileges, or benefits pertaining to a given legal status, whether individual or corporate. Thus it was possible to speak of the "liberties" of cities, boroughs, ecclesiastical establishments, barons, parliaments, and the like. As Helen Cam remarked, "Magna Carta was a charter not of liberty but of liberties" (183).

The concept of ancient English liberties was deeply ingrained in the popular imagination. This was particularly the case after the Norman conquest, which was often believed to have introduced into England an alien and oppressive social system, that of French feudalism and serfdom. As Christopher Hill shows, the "Norman yoke" theory continued to be invoked through the Civil War by the Puritan left wing in support of its egalitarian claims. Its presence in the Middle Ages can be seen in documents such as the thirteenth-century *Mirror of Justices* or the fourteenth-century *Modus tenendi parliamentum,* both of which aimed to revive former liberties and protect present ones.

But the concept of liberty had even more particular importance in Bokenham's day, and it is interesting that the poet makes Katherine associate it with the king rather than with any of his subjects. What can it mean to urge liberty on a king? S. B. Chrimes points out that in late-medieval English political theory, kings had *libertas* as one of their royal attributes, along with will and grace. The king's *libertas* had been an important concept in the 1399 articles against Richard II, which charged him with perverting the liberty of his predecessors to his own private will.

When Parliament later bestowed on Henry IV "as great royal liberty as all his noble progenitors" possessed before him, the new king tactfully replied that his intention was not to exploit such a liberty but to safeguard the ancient laws and statutes and the traditional rights and liberties of church, lords, cities, and boroughs, for the king has the liberty to do justice and keep the laws. In his opening address at the first Parliament of Henry IV's reign, Bishop Arundel declared it was the king's will to maintain traditional franchises and liberties, with justice and equity for all (Chrimes, *Constitutional Ideas,* 8–9). These principles and this vocabulary were reiterated at virtually every meeting of Parliament over the decades, and they were recorded in both English and French in the careful dance of groups and classes, the constant accommodation of the liberties of each to those of others. Katherine's terminology was thus very much part of contemporary political life and discourse in Bokenham's day, particularly in relation to the dynastic question. Indeed, a deliberate allusion to the many disappointments of Lancastrian rule is far from unlikely, as I show next.

An aspect of the liberties question with which an Augustinian friar was likely to be especially concerned was the relation of royal and ecclesiastical liberties. I mentioned earlier the 1441 case in which John Fortescue acted against an Augustinian house to deny an "ancient liberty" of tax exemption. But this was only one form of ecclesiastical liberty, and it tended to affect the less prosperous establishments. A more urgent issue troubled East Anglian and other clergy during the 1430s and 1440s and was not unrelated to dynastic matters. This was the collection of taxes due from ecclesiastical houses. Well-placed clerics rather than laymen (such as sheriffs), were often favored as collectors because clerics had an administrative staff and a secure place of deposit. However, few ecclesiastics were eager to take on the burden, and many had acquired grants of exemption from this duty during the reign of Richard II. Under Henry VI, the validity of these exemptions was frequently debated in court over a period of months or years while the king's revenue remained uncollected. Thus the problem "was one of the great questions under discussion" (Kemp, 124) during the fifteenth century.

During the 1430s and 1440s, two East Anglian priories—Binham and Wymondham, both near Norwich—were involved in long, notorious disputes over their liberties in the matter of exemption from collection. One of them, Binham, during the 1430s "engaged the attention of the highest officers of the land" (Kemp, 127). Similar cases continued to crop up all over the country during the 1440s. Since principles were rarely debated, the theoretical outcome remained inconclusive, and the empirical solution was to have a sheriff collect the taxes on behalf of a reluctant ecclesiastic. It is easy to see how this issue could become another bit of ammunition in an anti-Lancastrian arsenal, another basis for complaint about the baneful consequences of the 1399 usurpation and Lancastrian lawlessness.

Bokenham's Katherine is not the only hagiographical text of the period to stress traditional liberties. Another is the life of Edward the Confessor, the next-to-last Anglo-Saxon king, who died just before the invasion of 1066 and to whose cult the last Plantagenet king, Richard II, was devoted. Edward's reign was usually portrayed as a utopian interlude, an era of peace under the just laws of a saintly king. Although versions of Edward's life vary considerably in their emphasis on the political dimension of his rule, nonetheless two themes are basic: that Edward married to satisfy his barons' demand for an heir (though the royal couple's vow of chastity subverted the barons' intent) and that Edward canceled a taillage or annual tax, the Danegeld. The most sharply political version of Edward's life (ed. Moore) appears in BL Add. 35298, a fifteenth-century prose manuscript translating Voragine's *Legenda aurea* but adding several lives not included by Voragine. This is the text that Bokenham might have composed (see chapter 1), but whether or not he wrote it, it is contemporary with him and articulates ideas that also surface in his verse legendary, prominent among them the notion of liberty. When Edward is crowned, "then receyvid the comyn people rest and pees and the lordis and the gentilmen reste and wurship and holy churche receyvid then alle his hole lybertees ayen" (fol. 48b, Moore, 78). When he dies, Edward has a prophetic vision whose import is revealed in history: "Then afterward when kyng harolde had broke the othe that he had made to duke william and therefore he was slayne in bateyle then thaye knewe welle that the prophecy of seynte Edwarde was come for then the lyberte a ynglonde made an ende and then came in bondship and thraldom" (fol. 51a, Moore, 95).

Interestingly, the word *liberty,* so important here, does not appear in the other versions, whether prose or verse, of Edward's life included in Moore's volume, or in the *South English Legendary.* It thus provides a small but telling stylistic reason to think that this life of Edward might have come from Bokenham's pen. Whoever composed the Edward, though, it is obvious that when Bokenham has his St. Katherine exhort the emperor Maxence to liberty and equity, her words must strike a chord reverberating far beyond the confines of hagiographic narrative.

The dimension of national politics in the Katherine story may have been present to Bokenham in another way. In one anonymous Middle English version of the early fifteenth century (Kurvinen), the saint is given a genealogy connecting her with ancient British royalty (see figure 10). Her father is said to be Costus, king of Armenia, and he, in turn, is the son of a Roman nobleman, Constantius, by a first marriage to a Greek princess. The saint's grandfather Constantius is called on by Rome to settle a rebellion in Britain. This he does so successfully that he is given in marriage the daughter of King Coel of Britain:

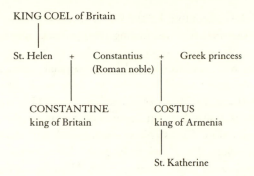

KING COEL of Britain

St. Helen + Constantius + Greek princess
              (Roman noble)

CONSTANTINE   COSTUS
king of Britain   king of Armenia

St. Katherine

FIGURE 10 Genealogy of St. Katherine developed by English historians during the twelfth century.

Helen—"holy seynt Elyne that fond the crosse." The son of this second marriage, Constantine, "be ryght of hys modyr was crowned kyng of Bretayne, that now is called Engelond." In this version of her life, then, Katherine acquires impressive credentials and, for a fifteenth-century British audience, distinctively useful ones. She is given family connections with British royalty as niece to a British king, as well as a connection with St. Helena, who found the true cross. Moreover, this is explicitly accomplished through the maternal line from Katherine's grandfather's second wife, St. Helen.

This link with a British king who rules by matrilineal right appears not in Greek but only in Latin versions of the Katherine legend; nor is it standard in Middle English versions—lacking, for instance, in Mirk, the *SEL,* and the early Middle English *Seinte Katerine.* Amnon Linder suggests that it probably can be traced to the rationalization of a scribal error. The name Costus or Costis, Katherine's father, could be considered in Latin script an abbreviated form of Constantinus, a "correction" that opened the way to an association of Katherine with the Constantinian dynasty. This new theme, Linder suggests, was first explored in a fourteenth-century Franciscan version.

> Through the grafting of Catherine's legend on the myth of Constantine, . . . Catherine was provided with the required noble parentage and with a claim to the government of the East. Her confrontation with Maxentius ceased therefore to symbolize only the conflict between Christianity and paganism, and became a combination of religious and secular political elements. (82–83)

Thus even though Bokenham certainly did not invent the British and political elements of the Katherine story, he further domesticated the material with his pointed political vocabulary.

In fact, the Katherine material could scarcely be better suited to the situation at hand, for it is linked not only to British royalty and matrilineal descent but specifically to the city of York. The Constantinian side of the story is, of course, historical, although Constantine I ("the Great") was not king in England. He was, however, proclaimed emperor in England, at York, when his father, Constantius, died there in 306. Constantine's mother Helena was not English or noble or a wife; she was very likely a lowborn provincial concubine (at the time a perfectly honorable position). Helena is first made an Englishwoman in the twelfth-century histories by Henry of Huntingdon and Geoffrey of Monmouth (Linder, 91), perhaps assisted, as Mulligan notes (260), by the factual and legendary existence of several English pious women with names similar to Helen's.

From these historians the tale of an English Helen married to Constantine passed into general acceptance, appearing in Voragine, Higden, Capgrave, Lydgate, and Mombrizio and eventually forming part of Tudor legitimation propaganda (Mulligan, 266–67). Linder observes that the veneration of Helen in Britain was "particularly connected to local traditions in London, Abingdon—which treasured the famous 'crux nigra,' believed to have been sent there by Constantine himself or his mother . . . —and above all in York" (92). Given Bokenham's display of Yorkist genealogical concern in the Magdalene, we can hardly dismiss the likelihood that the York-related genealogy of his saint is an important, if tacit, dimension of her meaning in his text. And this meaning is intensified by the words Bokenham places in her mouth.

There is nothing explicitly Yorkist in Katherine's words to her persecutor, but in the superheated political atmosphere of the 1440s onward, they would, I believe, have carried partisan implications. The tendency was to identify Richard of York with England's "ancient" liberties, and even though this tendency became quite explicit after 1450, it can scarcely have been entirely absent in the preceding few years. Griffiths remarks that "York's name was certainly worth conjuring with by anyone critical of the king's government in the late 1440s" (*Reign,* 617).

If the leader of Jack Cade's rebellion was moved in 1450 to adopt the name Mortimer—York's forebears—the act makes propagandistic sense only in a climate of popular pro-York opinion and not in Kent alone but in London, too, where Cade's rebels "were welcomed by the mass of inhabitants" (Griffiths, *Reign,* 624).[3] Scofield writes that the insurgents "had voiced the convictions of many people that the Duke of York was the only person who could save the country from disaster" (14). When Richard returned from Ireland, "the oppressed who looked on his coming with hope of reform set about organizing demonstrations and appeals to the duke to enlist his goodwill in destroying the pernicious rule of Suffolk's former henchmen" (Griffiths, *Reign,* 589). Such generalized attitudes are not the creation of a single year—not, at any rate, before the advent of political advertising campaigns in the mass media as we know them today. At that time, they grew over a longer period, encouraged and commented on in literature but developing in response to history as it unfolded and, in some situations, helping shape that history.

Several factors contributed to Richard's early (i.e., pre-1450) reputation as a defender of popular liberties. His performance in Normandy, discussed in chapter

7, contributed strongly to this popular perception. At home, York's factional policy during the 1440s seems to have been to create "an alliance of reforming magnates and the 'people' which might serve as a check on the misguided Henry VI" (P. Gill, 336). In addition, given the widespread abuses committed up and down the country by the affinities or "liveries" of several barons in the circle of royal advisers and given the numerous commercial grievances that also contributed to the unpopularity of the Lancastrian government, it is easy to see how York could present himself as, and be perceived as, a protector of property rights. A contemporary chronicler made exactly that point when describing Richard's entry into London in 1450 on his return from Ireland: "And on the morne that was Wednesday . . . at aftir none and bifore, ther were made cryes in Lundun by the Duke of Yorke and Duke of Northfolke, that no man shuld robbe nor take any good within the cite, nether wythoute, upon peyne of deth" (Kingsford, 297).

Placed in social context, then, the words of Bokenham's Katherine to her persecutor can be heard as a reprimand to contemporary oppressors. It can also be heard, though less explicitly, as a challenge to the English to assert their traditional liberties against the usurping Lancastrians and the marauding barons who supported them. Embedded in a deeply pro-Yorkist text, Katherine's speech could scarcely suggest any potential leader other than Richard of York. Spoken by a cultivated, royal, and heroic woman, her words help validate the claim of the Yorkist matrilineal line.

I N THE MAGDALENE PROLOCUTORY, written about mid-1445, Bokenham tells us that he has completed a number of legends and has just begun that of Elizabeth, whose life

To alle wyvys myht a merour be	May, for all women [or wives], be a mirror
Of very perfeccyoun in sundry degre.	Of the various degrees of true perfection.
(5047–48)	

By 1447, when the legendary was completed and the Elizabeth placed last in the series, Bokenham had evidently expanded his ideas of exemplarity and audience, for at some point after finishing the Magdalene, he revised his opinion about who might learn from the modern saint. Commenting on a particular episode of self-abnegation in Elizabeth's life, Bokenham picks up his earlier mirror image, asking rhetorically,

What wumman koude now obeyin to	What woman could now obey,
Swych a comaundement wythoute offence	Without offense, such a commandment
As ded this myroure of pacyence, lo!	As did this mirror of patience?
(9834–36)	

Scarcely any nun, he answers: "Unneth ony nunne yt mekely wold do" (9837). But by now the full design of the work was in place, and the author intended neither his work nor Elizabeth's example for women only, as he had evidently done earlier when just beginning her legend. In contrasting Elizabeth's behavior with that of his contemporaries, Bokenham now scrupulously rejects the all-too-easy antifeminism implied in limiting his answer to nuns or women. Instead he generalizes to both sexes:

And, to seyn pleyn treuthe, I trowe yt nolde here	And to tell the truth I believe that
Wyth-owtyn murmur & grucchyng also	Neither priest nor monk, canon nor friar
Neythyr prest ner munk, chanoun ner frere.	Would hear it without complaint and grudging,
For both of men & wummen also	For the mold of men and women alike
The molde these dayis is so sore alayde	Is these days so badly alloyed
Wyth froward wyl, that for to do	With stubborn will, that if they
Swyche obedyencys yf thei were asayide,	Were assayed to do such obediences
They wolde compleyn & ben evyl apayid.	They would complain and be ill pleased.
(9838–45)	

This general increase of willfulness is responsible, Bokenham opines, for the current laxity in religious governance, "for dew correccyons ben al put aweye" (9848). Thus the woman saint becomes a "myrour of very obedyence" (9857) to humanity at large and to ecclesiastical personnel of both sexes. In the exemplary behavior of Elizabeth's royal husband, who allows himself to be guided by her piety, we see a model for spouses of either sex who, if not capable of sanctity, may yet lead virtuous lives. Landgrave's role is, of course, standard to the story, but Bokenham's comments are distinctly his own.

That Bokenham focuses here not on the morals of layfolk but, rather, on "re-lygyous governaunce" (9847) may point to disciplinary difficulties in fraternal communities or within his own order. He devotes the next stanza to terminating his digression ("dylatacyoun") on clerical misbehavior:

For peraventur, yf I dyde treuly talke,	For perhaps, if I spoke truly,
Sum folk wolde have greth indygnacyoun.	Some people would be very indignant.
(9851–52)	

The distinctive and well-known moderation of the Augustinian order, and the accompanying privileges, could and often did backfire. A constant problem was the number of "apostates" of the order: those who sought employment or revenue without authorization from their superiors in the order but instead with episcopal, royal, or papal help.

Another problem was that the privileges accorded to Augustinian masters in theology (privileges that Bokenham also held; see chapter 1) sometimes led masters to go beyond the permitted bounds, so that they failed to observe the communal life and the renunciation of private property—"la seule forme spirituelle augustinienne," as Van Luijk (12) points out. Frequent rulings throughout the fourteenth and fifteenth centuries (including one in 1446) attempted to deal with such abuses. Van Luijk (12–13) notes that the masters were nonetheless sufficiently prosperous that in 1451 the order required each master to support a novice. Even though reform was much discussed within the order from the start (i.e., from the unification of various groupings in the so-called Great Union of 1256), the observantine movement "never gained a foothold in the English province" (M. B. Hackett, "Seventh Centenary," 11).

Or Bokenham's dark hints may have been meant for orders other than his own. A tempting and obvious target would have been the mighty abbey of St. Edmunds in nearby Bury, whose abbot

> was a great lord, and lived accordingly. Among other things, he had a private hoard of gold and silver, and a personal array of gold and silver smiths. He also had several personal silk merchants, and a string of the plushest private residences in East Anglia. Abbey officers copied the style of their leader. . . . At any given time, over half the officers and less exalted monks could be away from the monastery, "on vacation." (Gottfried, 238)

A double inversion of traditional power relations is accomplished in this passage: a woman becomes the model for women and men alike; a devout layperson becomes a model for lay and cleric alike. I write "inversion" rather than "subversion," but would it be legitimate to see this inversion as also subversive? It may be tempting to do so, but I think it would be a somewhat skewed perception, for the thrust of the passage, in context of internal Augustinian politics, is clearly for less worldliness and greater commitment to the rule of the order. The mixed life may be well and good, but close attention must be paid to the proportions.

WE HAVE SEEN THAT Bokenham omits a misogynistic motif such as the demon's lament in Margaret or the scholars' antifeminism in Katherine or a potentially sexist one such as the nudity of the protagonist. He also omits gratuitous indignities; thus the urine in which Voragine's Lucy is superstitiously drenched to nullify her "witchcraft" becomes oil in Bokenham's revision. Another telling omission is that of the frequent compliment paid to the female martyr, sometimes by a persecutor, sometimes by an author: that her courage was equal to a man's or that she had a male spirit in a female body. The trope gained authority from its presence in the apocryphal gospel of Thomas: "Simon Peter said to them, 'Let Mary leave us, for women are not worthy of life.' Jesus said, 'I myself shall lead her and make her male'" (cited in P. Brown, *Body and Society,* 113). As if he understood the double edge of this praise, Bokenham never employs it. His women saints, we may infer, succeed as women, requiring no transmogrification into "spiritual men" for their excellence to be grasped.

By the same token, Bokenham preserves and even emphasizes details already present in hagiographical tradition that help create a positive woman-conscious atmosphere. Female collectivity and solidarity, for instance, appear in the nooks and crannies of several lives as part of their skeleton plot. When Christine's head is shaved and laden with coals, the women who observe the act protest against any woman being treated so shamefully. Bokenham has them remonstrate with the judge Zion by saying that in Christine, "all wommen thou confoundyst utirly" (2754). When Katherine is led to her execution, she is followed by a crowd who mourn her and whom she urges not to mourn. In Capgrave, this is a crowd of pagan men and women (whom the saint nonetheless addresses as "moderis and maidenes alle"). Her last words tartly exhort the crowd to weep not for her but for their own sin and error, with threats of hellfire if they do not mend their ways (5.1786 ff.). This also is fairly similar to the treatment in *Seinte Katerine*. But Bokenham's Katherine is followed to her execution by women only—"Many a matrone of hy wurthynesse, / Many a wedwe, & many a maydyn ying" (7280–81). Thus the crowd comprises all three estates of womanhood and degrees of perfection: virginity, marriage, and widowhood. Bokenham's saint addresses these female spectators with no threat or exhortation but speaks to them "benygnely," telling them to rejoice in her good fortune.

Last but not least of the ways in which Bokenham wages his modest struggle against misogyny is his treatment of the body. One of the central arguments of an antiwoman position relies on the relation of soul to body. If man is to woman as soul is to body—and there is no reason to suppose that Bokenham would challenge this ancient isomorphism—then much depends on how the relation of body to soul is defined and on how highly the body is valued. For John Fortescue the relation is one of clear superiority and dominance:

> For the greatest achievements of the spirit nature has given to man a perfect reason, in respect of which she has made the woman the weaker vessel. (*De Natura,* chap. 8)

> The Master of the Sentences, upon the 1st Epistle to the Corinthians, chap. 11, says, "No one doubts that man was made in the image of God not in respect of his body or in any part of his soul indifferently, but in respect of his mind, wherein there can be an apprehension of God, which lies in the superior part of the reason . . . and this mind, on account of its union with the flesh, . . . is called man made after the image of God." And from these words we are rightly to understand that the first man, who was a rational mind, whom the lord placed over the whole creation, was also set over his own body. . . . He was also by his origin set over the woman, who was then contained in him potentially. (*De Natura,* chap. 18)

Fortescue's chapter 63 is entitled "The Pre-eminence of the man over the Woman is likened to the Pre-eminence of the Soul over the Flesh, and of the superior part of the Reason over the inferior," and chapter 64 "combines the different kinds of Pre-eminence taken notice of above." They deploy mainly scriptural and patristic authorities, concluding that "these arguments from analogies have very great force in law, inasmuch as there is a rule of law in harmony therewith, that concerning like matters there is like judgment."

A far more balanced partnership of spirit and flesh is apparent in Bokenham's work. The legendary itself, as I hope to have shown, is itself structured like a body. The embodiedness of the author introduces into the text a real, living, male body, one that grows fatigued, is frightened in Venice, watches the dancing at the countess's on Twelfth Night, and wears spectacles. No disembodied spirit he, with all his genuine piety: as much as his elegant patrons, the friar is a flawed creature hoping to be saved.

In the text, the body's claims are respected—even emphasized, as with Lucy's mother—and the body is valued as "the armor wherein [Jesus'] victory had been won" (Steinberg, 24). The physical humanity of Jesus and his ancestors is foregrounded in the lives of Anne and Magdalene (see chapters 4 and 5), and it is an important feature of the poem that Bokenham does not offer Jesus crucified as his chosen image of redemption but, rather, Jesus incarnated. Finally, the fact that rigorous asceticism is typical of only one legend—Elizabeth's, the only modern saint in the series—suggests that such extreme devotion as hers is for the chosen few, not recommended as a general practice.

All this is what one would expect from an Augustinian, for the rule was a moderate one (see chapter 6). It valued morality and *caritas* rather than extreme ascetic corporeal observances or *contemptus mundi*. Bokenham's treatment of the body was also doubtless influenced by the nascent humanist trend beginning to develop in the papal court at Rome, where what John O'Malley calls a "world-affirming tendency" (*Praise and Blame,* chap. 4) was coming into fashion. The topic of praise for the body soon found its way into sermons preached in the papal chapel, offering an empirical argument for the existence and benevolence of God. To be sure, the dignity of humanity and the beauty of the human body as themes had not been absent from patristic literature, so that in 1357 when Petrarch wrote on this topic (in *De Remediis*), he had several sources to draw on. Nonetheless, the "dignity of man" topos came into vogue among Italian humanists, particularly from the 1430s onward, as part of what Charles Trinkaus calls "the revival of an earlier Christian tradition of anthropocentric theology" (199). Trinkaus also notes the popularity of Augustine among the humanists generally, because of the saint's "noble vision of human dignity" (182), his attention to will and subjectivity (72), and his opposition to naturalistic determinism (57).

As one of the educated elite in the Augustinian order, as an administrator in an order that prided itself on its links with Rome, and as a traveler to Rome, Bokenham would have been well acquainted with these tendencies—an acquaintance consistent with the classicizing aspect of his work already noted in connection with the Claudian translation (chapter 7). To return to the sexual politics I am discussing here: the significance of this early humanistic attitude toward the body is that, given the traditional isomorphism, rehabilitating the body is rehabilitating woman; it is to overcome at least partly the vicious clerical antifeminism that was the legacy of Gregorian reform and that was displayed for political purposes in the succession treatises of John Fortescue.

In history, the martyrological tradition itself provides ammunition against the rigid subordination of female to male. Historically, no one could deny that in the formative period, women played an important role in the spread of Christianity. They were actively recruited to swell the ranks of Christianity, and the earliest period of martyrs was one in which women were able to teach, hold office, and fill leadership roles in the primitive church—a church so primitive, the legend of Cecelia reminds us, that Pope Urban hides out at the edge of town, skulking among tombs like a common criminal (for he was a criminal in the eyes of the Roman state). In the figurative register, if one wishes to gender-metaphorize power relations during the period of martyrs, then obviously Rome had the "masculine" (dominant, violent) role and Christianity the "feminine" (persecuted, physically weaker) role. The "feminine" component represented truth and eventually was victorious—just as the martyrs were.

During the period of persecutions, the value of martyrdom was sharply contested, particularly through the developed critique made by Christian gnostics. Should Christians conceal their belief in order to survive, even commit a tactical lie or make a temporary concession to official demands? Or should they welcome the opportunity to imitate the man who died for them? That the last became normative policy is attributed by Elaine Pagels to three factors: it consolidated the far-flung and disparate Christian communities; it won converts; and it reinforced acceptance of Jesus' full humanity against the troublesome gnostic rejection of it.

The legend of Faith, in fact, stages the conflict between those who welcome martyrdom and those who want to avoid it. Caprasius belongs to a group of Christians who have fled the city for that very reason and who occupy caves in the surrounding hills. Even though Bokenham minimizes this theme (cf. 3776–82), others give it full treatment. Simon of Walsingham, for example, provides an elaborate defense of the fugitives (464–502). We learn that they did not wish to be tainted by witnessing pagan rites; that Jesus advised his disciples to travel from place to place; and that Jesus himself, as an infant, fled to Egypt to avoid persecution. Thus, Simon writes, there should be no reproach to Caprasius and his collective for dishonor or cowardice ("vilté"). Yet despite this exoneration, the narrative proceeds to show a female child giving the correct example to adult males—who do at last return to the city to share her ordeal. In this way, the legend of Faith offers a fictional bridge between literal history and figuralized institutional history: the girl is at once a martyr like those who really suffered and a symbol of the Christian community's disputed but finally triumphant strategy of exemplary suffering.

In a variety of ways, then, hagiography itself shows that the relations among sex, truth, and power are neither a moral imperative nor historically inevitable. If the Austin friar introduced into his legendary a politics of gender and of nationhood, it is because he saw those imbricated politics as consistent with the theology he also aimed to express. Does, or can, knowing all this about Osbern Bokenham and his legendary make the work any more palatable to a modern audience than any other hagiography would be? After all, the essence of martyrology is the sadistic torture of men and women who suffer for their faith, so does it matter whether one text has a more or a less politically conservative motivation than another? Obviously, I think it does matter, and in the last chapter I want to address some of the concerns implied by these questions.

NINE

Last Things and Afterlives

These legends . . . were no more than monkish
extravagances, over which one laughed inwardly;
there were, besides, priestly matters, and the
priestcraft of the book was far worse than its
monkery. The ears burned on each side of my
head as I listened, perforce, to tales of moral martyrdom inflicted by Rome; the dread boasts of confessors, who had wickedly abused their office,
trampling to deep degradation high-born ladies,
making of countesses and princesses the most tormented slaves under the sun. Stories like that of
Conrad and Elizabeth of Hungary recurred again
and again, with all its dreadful viciousness, sicken-
ing tyranny and black impiety: tales that were
nightmares of oppression, privation, and agony. .
. . I sat out this *lecture pieuse* for some nights as
well as I could, and as quietly too; only once
breaking off the points of my scissors by involun-
tarily sticking them somewhat deep in the worm-
eaten table before me.

Charlotte Brontë, *Villette,* Chapter 13

I begin with Brontë's portrayal of Lucy Snowe's revulsion
against hagiography to open my case against the genre with a
vivid experiential account that is not my own, although I am not so formalistic a
reader as to have escaped or repressed a similar response. It is one of the reasons
that as a medievalist, I avoided hagiography until coming across Bokenham by
chance a few years ago. (Chaucer's one surviving effort in the genre, his *Second
Nun's Tale* of St. Cecelia, and the last portion of Christine de Pizan's *Book of the
City of Ladies* were the exceptions to this avoidance, and they did not change my
reluctance to continue.) The material is revolting; it gives us bad dreams; and
I have written in another format about the insidious effect of these stories,

and much else in our reading and our lives, on a woman's consciousness and—probably worse—her unconscious (Delany, "Alibis").

I would have written "so immasculated a reader" just now (borrowing Judith Fetterley's term) except for the implication it would have carried, that men readers do not feel a similar outrage or suffer the same effects or that the torture of saints is not perpetrated against men as well as women. None of these implications, of course, is true. Most saints and virgins are men, and for those who are martyrs, the violation of bodies is just as atrocious as for women. Among the more lurid, we may cite Bartholomew, who was flayed alive; Simon, who was sawed in half; St. Lawrence, who, on his grill, was urging persecutors to eat his roasted flesh; James, who was gradually dismembered; St. Erasmus, who was disemboweled; or Jonan, who had his fingers and toes cut off and then was crushed in a wooden press. On grounds of cultural commonality, I believe that most contemporary male readers of martyrology feel much the same revulsion I do, or as Charlotte Brontë's heroine does, whichever the sex of the martyr victim.

Nonetheless, Lucy Snowe does not protest on behalf of male saints or impoverished saints, either (although there is a relatively small proportion of the latter).[1] Her indignation, instead, is aroused by the ill treatment of highborn women. It is not only misogynous sadism that offends her but also the depreciation of a woman's social status at the hands of her social inferiors. Not surprisingly, this response reveals Lucy's resentment of her own déclassé existence as an unmarried employee in a Belgian girls' school, at which her main persecutor is a woman, the school's proprietress, Madame Beck. Moreover, as a sensible Englishwoman of Protestant cultural background, Lucy is particularly hostile to the "monkery" and "priestcraft" of these baroque Catholic–continental accounts of suffering, venting a long-standing English antipapalism.

It is difficult not to share Lucy's revulsion to some extent, but what are we to make of it? Is it the case that male-authored lives of women martyr saints reveal a perhaps unconscious but nonetheless typical masculinist voyeuristic sadism on the author's part and therefore that they can never be historically progressive? Can the representation of sadistic violence in martyrology be made to serve any positive end, or can the genre itself serve any useful purpose? Is martyrology a special case of pornography?

In its general principles, this discussion occupies theoreticians in various of the arts, particularly feminist critics who confront the representation of violence. From the preceding chapters, my short answer to these questions should be clear. In this chapter, I offer a more developed consideration of the problem, from several perspectives that converge on what strikes me as the prime feature of an ultrafeminist dismissive view of violence: its reductionism. It seems to me that the most provocative, thorough, and illuminating recent work in this area stresses the complexity, even the indeterminacy, of symbolic meaning and representational strategies, of human desire and subject positionality, and of authorial motives and audience response. All this is necessarily ignored by a dismissive censorious view, which assumes the universality of representation—that every image of violence has meant the same thing down the centuries. Again, from my own initial reading of martyrology, I must admit that in one sense it does: a person being abused means exactly that. Yet the uses to which such an image may be put can vary immensely, just as the uses of a particular genre, symbol, trope, or word may vary with factors such as place, historical period, authorial gender, or political position. Even the term *pornography* need not be a univocal negatively charged shibboleth, for as Lynn Hunt observes, "between 1500 and 1800, pornography was most often a vehicle for using the shock of sex to criticize religious and political authorities" (10). Especially in France of the eighteenth century—"the golden age of pornography," as Robert Darnton calls it—pornography became an adjunct to rationalistic and dissident philosophy, often in the service of an antifeudal, anticlerical politics. Not only do hagiographies vary immensely, but even all-female hagiographies vary immensely, and as I shall show, even an all-female legendary by a female author is not necessarily more certifiably prowoman in its effect than is one by a man.

In her introduction to *Gender and Religion,* Carolyn Bynum stresses what (following Victor Turner) she calls the "polysemy" of religious symbols "as not merely reflecting and shaping but also inverting, questioning, rejecting and transcending gender as it is constructed in the individual's psychological development and sociological setting" (8). Religious symbols, she finds,

> are never merely a model of the cultural fact of gender. . . . Even traditional symbols can have revolutionary consequences. For, if symbols can invert as well as reinforce social values . . . , if traditional rituals can evolve to meet the needs of new participants . . . , then old symbols can acquire new meanings, and these new meanings might suggest a new society. (15–16)

Bynum's own essay in the collection (". . . And Woman His Humanity"), a study of female imagery in late-medieval religious writing, shows that "there was, in the later Middle Ages, no clear association of ordinary women and men with saints of their own sex. Some female saints performed miracles predominantly for women, but so did some male saints. Some shrines dedicated to male saints had predominantly female clientele and vice versa" (259).

Bringing a polysemic approach into the visual arts, Arlene Raven queries the political role of representations of violence in that venue. Can such work empower the onlooker by providing a catharsis? Can inflammatory and assaultive imagery "open wounds in order to trigger a healing revolution?" As must anyone seriously treating such questions, Raven looks to history, in terms particularly appropriate to the evaluation of hagiography:

> Remember, history tells us that today's despised martyrs are often worshiped tomorrow as gods. . . . Artists attempting to reveal what must not but may well come to pass if we don't pay attention are sometimes able to create a synthesis of what is and what can be, one that distinguishes between mindless brutality and the moving power of standing before imminent destruction—and saying no. This

is the kind of creative activism Daniel Berrigan advised: "Don't just do something. Stand there." (187–88)

Other artists support this suggestion that the depiction of violence can serve the function of exposure—as, for instance, in political documentaries, photography exhibitions, or art installations about family abuse, prostitution, mental illness, or poverty. Some propose the socially stabilizing sublimating effect achieved by channeling potentially violent behavior into the realm of fantasy and representation.[2]

Film criticism is the arena in which the problematic of gender and power has been most prominently discussed in recent years. E. Ann Kaplan observes that especially in film, feminist semiology has given "increasing attention to *how meaning is produced* in films, rather than to the content, which had preoccupied sociological critics" (23; italics in original). Among the questions she poses are, Is the gaze necessarily male? Why are women drawn to melodrama; that is, why do women find their objectification and surrender pleasurable? Is all dominance necessarily masculine? Her specific answers are less important to me here than her posing of the questions, which suggest various angles at which the question of violence in art can be approached. The distinction between diegesis and discourse that Kaplan reminds us of (18–19) is roughly parallel to the literary distinction between plot and rhetoric. Plot, as I noted often in the preceding chapters, is what the hagiographer is stuck with, but the rhetoric, or discourse ("means of expression . . . conditions of expression") he or she can—in some senses, can only—invent. In a similar vein, Linda Williams writes of Michael Powell's *Peeping Tom* (1960) that it "can be privileged as a progressive horror film, not so much for sparing the life of its 'good girl' heroine as for exposing the perverse structures of seeing that operate in the genre" (93).

Carol Clover's discussion of gender in the post-1980 "slasher" film is relevant to my argument about Bokenham and hagiography. Surely, more than any other figure, the female martyr qualifies as the "Final Girl" of medieval literature, "the female victim-hero":

> She is the one who encounters the mutilated bodies of her friends and perceives the full extent of the preceding horror and of her own peril; who is chased, cornered, wounded; whom we see scream, stagger, fall, rise, and scream again. If her friends knew they were about to die only seconds before the event, the Final Girl lives with the knowledge for long minutes or hours. She alone looks death in the face; but she alone also finds the strength either to stay the killer long enough to be rescued (ending A) or to kill him herself (ending B). ("Her Body," 201; *Chainsaws,* chap. 1).

The hagiographical female hero is always rescued, and she sometimes achieves the death of her persecutor as well, through either her own prayer or a natural event (earthquake, a fall, etc.), which is seen as divine retribution for the persecutor. The saint's "rescue" is spiritual: she is taken up into heaven as a bride of Christ while the persecutor is destined for hell. In Christian terms, she "has the victory over" him. The Christian doublethink required here is obvious: physically, the martyr is not rescued but suffers and eventually dies. This paradox of victory in death is qualitatively no different from any other on which Christianity is built: the human god, the maiden mother, the three in one, and so on. Hagiography is, after all, a distinctively otherworldly enterprise; strip it of spiritual doctrine and you would do better to read romance.

Moreover, the genre is a peculiar blend of fiction and history, or at least virtual history. We know that even though many saints were fictional creations, medieval hagiographers believed that they were writing history—and sometimes they were, for the persecution and martyrdom of Christians did occur. So, although I make no brief for Christianity per se, I think there are limits to how far we can rewrite hagiography as secular literature—which is what we do when we remove its spiritual framework, its entire raison d'être. In its own terms, therefore, and in the terms accepted by every hagiographer, the saint is victorious.

This victory permits another resemblance of the female martyr to the Final Girl: the compromise of conventional gender attributes. As Clover observes, the role allocation could not be more obvious than in the horror film: male persecutor, female victim. Yet "the gender of the Final Girl is . . . compromised from the outset by her masculine interests, her inevitable sexual reluctance . . . , her apartness from other girls. She specifically unmans an oppressor whose masculinity was in question to begin with" ("Her Body," 210). In her book, Clover suggests that what is common to the several types of horror film she studies is that each in its own way collapses the categories of male and female and that this indecision is one source of the excitement and anxiety produced in the spectator (chap. 4).

A similar ambiguity of gender roles may be observed in hagiography. The female martyr—whether virgin or married—models herself on the man Jesus, as does the male martyr. Jesus himself is unlike the masculine norm in that he is unmarried, sexually abstinent, and a victim. The audience, male and female alike, is meant to identify with the martyr of either sex. As in film, a character's sex is no impediment to audience identification. Such sympathy or "identification" places the audience of either sex in a feminized position and, as Clover claims for the horror film, violates its body in a collective experience.

Simultaneously, hagiography often negates traditional gender roles. The female martyr often assumes a number of conventionally masculine prerogatives: she disposes of her financial assets as she sees fit; rejects marriage, parents, or children; is verbally aggressive; gives sage advice to the persecutor; and demonstrates her superior logic, rhetoric, and sometimes supernatural powers. The male martyr can never defend himself physically, any more than a woman can. Meanwhile, the persecutor becomes incapable of rule, certainly incapable of ruling the martyr, usually incapable of ruling his emotions, and often in danger of losing political control as well. The saint further unmans the persecutor by reducing him to a medically pathological condition of madness (either melancholia or hysterical frenzy). In such fashion, Christian hagiography reconstitutes the female martyr as "virago." Thus she and it become "masculine," despite her and its (only apparently and only temporarily) subordinate "feminine" position.

Although Clover nowhere proposes that the slasher film offers a genuine female voice, subjectivity, or positionality, she does doubt that women and feminism are entirely well seved by "the astonishingly insistent claims that horror's satisfactions begin and end in sadism" (*Chainsaws,* 18–19). She suggests that although "one is deeply reluctant to make progressive claims for a body of cinema as spectacularly nasty toward women as the slasher film is, [nonetheless] the fact is that the slasher does, in its own perverse way, constitute a visible adjustment in the terms of gender representations" (*Chainsaws,* 64)—particularly through the fairly recently developed cinematic device of the "Final Girl."

Those who do believe that every act of violence in art, or specifically violence against women, renders that art ipso facto reactionary, are not likely to be convinced by my, or anyone else's, opinions and analyses. To make the argument in another way, then, I consider two other all-female collections, to expose some of the differences in representational strategy that enable a more nuanced evaluation. Before doing so, however, I need to turn briefly to another position that has surfaced in several recent studies of medieval history and literature and from which I would like to distance this book. This view is also considered feminist, but its argument is at the other end of the spectrum from one that would dismiss all representations of violence as simply sadistic and hence without value. On the contrary, the view I have in mind posits the value of passivity, the distinctively female or feminine power of endurance revealed in women's suffering.

E ARLIER I WROTE THAT the martyr is victorious in context of the Christian doctrine for which he or she dies. This seems tantamount to claiming that powerlessness paradoxically confers power. Since my previous work both implicitly and explicitly contradicts that notion and has been criticized for doing so, I want not only to offer a friendly rejoinder to my critics but also to explain why I think this book is consistent with my previous statements.

In 1974 I published an article on Chaucer's *Man of Law's Tale* in which I described Constance, the long-suffering heroine of that tale, as "among the least attractive of Chaucer's women, sharing with patient Griselda the repulsive masochistic qualities of extreme humility and silent endurance. . . . Constance seems to exist in order to suffer. . . . [She is] an emblem of human submission" (*Writing Woman,* 36–37). I then located this emblem in a historical context of peasant rebellion and suggested its ideological utility to the ruling class.

This article was cticicized by several scholars (Clasby; Edwards, "Approaches," 91; Robertson, 146–47; Mann), all making basically the same point: that Constance has spiritual power that supersedes her apparent submission. I do not deny that this was Chaucer's propagandistic intent; indeed, I said so. However, my reading of it was a reading "against the grain," a historicist and

resistant reading that, far from denying the spiritual dimension of medieval literature, attempts to discern its social thrust. It seems to me that these critics'
agenda is to deny this social thrust—that is, to deny the ideological dimension of
literature or religion—and to rehabilitate Chaucer's religious tales for religion
only. But this gesture is a rear-guard action; it is too late for such cautionary la-
beling. Historicism is long out of the closet and cannot be stuffed back in again,
despite such whiplash reactions.

More empirically, I want also to point out how different Chaucer's Constance
is from the saints as traditionally portrayed, by Bokenham and by others down
the ages preceding Chaucer. The women martyr saints fight back in many ways:
they are combative verbally, physically, or supernaturally. They harangue and
threaten, break the law, wish their persecutors dead. In this sense, Chaucer's
Constance is not at all like a martyr saint, but a pale travesty of one.[3] Little is retained of the tradition except the suffering and the favor of God: the spiritual
power.

Again, though, we need to look critically at the function of this spiritual
power. For Bokenham, spiritual power is precisely what qualifies women saints
for political power, for it confers the right to adivse, contest, chastise, and resist
authority. It is also what—extended to women at large—qualifies them for
temporal authority because the example of the saints vindicates the nature of
women by demonstrating their moral and rational capacities.

For Chaucer, by contrast, Constance's spiritual power disqualifies her from
the arena of secular power. We never see her exercising the rule or rights to
which her class position entitles her: she is, after all, an emperor's daughter and
the wife of both a sultan and a British king. The ex-serf Griselda manages, for a
time, to serve as an agent of justice in Walter's kingdom, but the royal Constance occupies herself in "hooly werkes evere, as was hir grace" (*MLT,* 2.980)
and nothing else.

In a similar vein, Caroline Bynum deplores "the impoverishment of twenti-
eth-century images" of suffering. While denying that the history of food absten-
tion she documents forms any kind of model for the present, Bynum nonetheless displaces her focus from the physical to the symbolic when she recommends
that

> we may, more than we realize, need positive symbols for generativity and suffer-
> ing. Our culture may finally need something of the medieval sense . . . that gen-
> erativity and suffering can be synonymous. Perhaps we should not turn our backs
> so resolutely as we have done . . . on the possibility that suffering can be fruit-
> ful. . . . If their images and values cannot become our answers, they can
> nonetheless teach us that we need richer images and values. Perhaps also they can
> point the direction in which we should search. (*Holy Feast,* 301–2)

I find unconvincing this displacement into the symbolic, for as Bynum acknowledges in her phrase "images and values," symbols are far from innocent.
If medieval symbols cannot become our answers, it is difficult to see how they

can point a direction for us. For me, the most lucid acknowledgment of the dilemma addressed here, and the one pointing toward genuine empowerment, remains that of Karl Marx:

> Religious distress is at the same time the expression of real distress and the protest against real distress. Religion is the sigh of the oppressed creature, the heart of a heartless world, just as it is the spirit of a spiritless situation. It is the opium of the people.
> The abolition of religion as the illusory happiness of the people is required for their real happiness. The demand to give up the illusions about its condition is the demand to give up a condition which needs illusions. The criticism of religion is therefore in embryo the criticism of the vale of woe, the halo of which is religion. (Marx, "Hegel's Philosophy," 42)

I hope the reader takes this (as I do) as a statement of philosophical position, not as a recommendation for state force or censorship. My point in adducing the passage is to suggest that to label a reaction against powerlessness as empowerment is, theoretically at least, to abandon the effort for an empowerment that will not be only symbolic.

IN CHAPTER 2, I mentioned a seventeenth-century all-female legendary (ed. Horstmann), of anonymous but probably male and probably clerical authorship, that shows no influence from Bokenham's work and that markedly differs from his in its treatment of the women martyrs who are its subject. Let me describe some of these differences to define another point in the wide range of possibilities.

This seventeenth-century legendary is in a Latinate, Ciceronian prose, and its Catholicism is of an embattled, polemical, Counter-Reformation variety. Its avowed purpose is to encourage identification with and emulation of the heroines, but its lack of art makes this unlikely. There is neither dialogue nor character development. The language is not lacking in rhetorical technique, but it remains dry throughout, abstract even when narrating emotionally charged or horrendous events and never rising to lyrical intensity or to the immediacy of drama.

Why did this author choose to produce an all-female legendary? By his own account, to embarrass men "when they shall beholde fraile women to have taken up so weightie and great Crosses" (3) and, by this competitive means, to exhort men to virtue. Throughout the work the weakness of women is emphasized: "How many men may blush at their more than womannish weaknes . . . when tender ladies have taken such strength and courage throughe love of their lord, to carrie so mightie burdens? Who may not be ashamed at the name of a man, that can not . . . contend in strength and labour with a weake woman?" (3).

Female saints are able to be "above [their] naturall condition strong" (as the author remarks of St. Julitta, a martyr described by St. Basil). A favorite narrative device with this author is to frame a woman's legend within the masculine world of war or ecclesiastical politics or within a story of male clerical or saintly virtue. Thus the history of colonial war that is the setting for Ursula's legend far overshadows the religious motif, and because there is no mention of the scoffing cardinals in Rome, there is no vindication of women's spiritual powers. Winifred's story opens and closes with that of the monk Beuno; Wulfhilde's starts with that of King Alfred; Margaret of Scotland's with King Edward; Mectild's focuses on her brother Alexander. Others are acolytes of the church fathers. Some of the women are extreme ascetics: Walberge, for instance, appears to be a bulimic converted to anorexia. There is a great deal of material about virginity, taken at great length from SS: Cyprian and Jerome, and instructions for virgins and widows as to dress, wealth, and social life. There is also a deep concern for the rigid observation of the church's rules and regulations generally: thus Sexburge's great virtue is to have enforced very strict penalties for violating Lenten abstinence.

The work displays a patriotic theme as well, with a distinctly colonialistic edge. Besides the stories of war and colonialism that contextualize many of the legends, the work pointedly includes both Scottish and Irish saints along with English, because Scotland is part of the island of Britain and Ireland has belonged to England for four centuries.

I trust that this sketch indicates how different in tone, artistry, and attitudes toward women one all-female legendary can be from another. What, then, can be said about hagiography known to have been composed by a woman author? Most of the same things, I propose, that have been said by historicizing scholars about male-authored works: that the uses of the genre and representational choices vary with specific context and purpose.

Conveniently at hand is a woman author of women saints' lives not far removed from Bokenham in time, place, and cultural setting. The Italian-born but Paris-reared conservative courtier Christine de Pizan composed her *Book of the City of Ladies* about forty years before Bokenham commenced his legendary, and we have every reason to suppose that the work of this popular predecessor circulated, in French and in English translation, among cultivated East Anglian readers (see chapter 2). In looking at Christine's legends, I do not want to imply that she is necessarily typical, for other female hagiographers—Clémence of Barking, for instance—might reveal quite different sensibilities. Although this is not the place for a detailed study of Christine's treatment of saints' lives, a brief comparison with Bokenham's version may be instructive.

Christine's female polity is not a democratic collective or even an organically integrated body politic. On the contrary, as we might expect from a writer whose interests were wholly identified with those of the royal–feudal elite in Paris, it duplicates the hierarchical structure and authoritarian model of the social reality that she supported and that supported her. Thus Christine's all-female legendary—the last and shortest portion of her *Book of the City of Ladies* (1405)—begins with the Virgin Mary.

Mary is represented in many ways in hagiography and in other mariolatrous literature: as a toddler dedicated to the temple, as a chaste Jewish maiden, as a devoted mother of a special infant, and as a sorrowful mother of a martyr. Here, however, Mary is invoked as a principle of rule and authority, with jurisdiction and lordship over all created powers ("administracion et seigneurie sur toutes puissances crées"; Curnow, bk. 3, sec. 1, para. 260), second in power only to her son. She is the queen of heaven and therefore queen of the city of ladies, which is to be dominated and feudally ruled by her ("dominee et seigneurie par elle"). Mary is "ceste trest haulte, excellent souveraine princepce" who must be begged ("suppliee") by the other ladies to inhabit the city among those who are so far beneath her and who must be implored not to hold them in disdain or contempt because of their triviality in comparison with her highness ("sans l'avoir en desdaing ne despris pour le regard de sa haultesce envers leur petitesce"). Even Mary's traditional, distinctive humility is treated as a competitive and paradoxically supreme trait, for it is a humility surpassing every other ("qui toutes autres passe"). Likewise, her benignity, "plus que angelique," competes with that of other women and also of angels—a theologically quite debatable claim. Last, Mary is the female figure who in a sense annihilates all other females, for no other woman's goodness is necessary to refute misogyny, given Mary's transcendent goodness:

> O! Dame, qui est celluy tant outrageux qui jamais ose pensser ne gitter hors de sa bouche que le sexe femenin soit vil, consideree ta dignité? Car se tout le demourant des femmes estoit mauvais, se passe et surmonte la lueur de ta bonté a plus grant comble que autre mauvaistié ne pourroit estre. (Curnow, 3.1.261)

> O! Lady, considering your dignity, who is so outrageous as to ever dare to think or say that the feminine sex is vile? For if all the rest of women were bad, the light of your goodness is so enormously surpassing that no other badness could exist. (My translation)

The least one can say here is that such a concession, even a hypothetical one, is unnecessary and that the logic is thoroughly essentialist: all women may be understood in one.

Christine's narrative treatment of her saints is dry, routine, and economically compressed. There is, for example, very little dialogue, a feature especially regrettable in the tale of Katherine, to whom speech is so important. There is also little development of character or event. For instance, Christine omits Margaret's troubled relationship with her parents, Olybrius's first view of the saint, the swallowing by and rebirth from the dragon, and the lengthy interrogation of the demon that is so interesting a part of many versions of this legend. Many of the stories are only a few sentences long, introduced by the legalistic "Item . . . item" (e.g., 271–78, 280–81, 299–304). Clearly, the material rather bores our courtly author. As she tartly remarks, because there are so many holy virgins in heaven, to describe them all would require a long story indeed. Whoever wishes to read more, she advises, need only consult the *Mirouer historial* (*Speculum historiale* of Vincent of Beauvais).

As for Christine's representations of women, Martina is stripped nude, and her lily white flesh astonishes the spectators. This exposure is gratuitous to the plot and could have been omitted, but for Christine, it evidently intensifies the pathos of the saint's ordeal. Furthermore, God is made to appear complicit with the tormentors when he prevents Martina from dying quickly so as to convert the tormentors and onlookers (3.6.269a). Christine's Magdalene has no career as a preacher but is mentioned only as a faithful weeper and the first to have seen the resurrected Jesus. St. Christine does not reject her mother, so we lose both the young saint's intransigence and the mother's poignant plea. Despite Maureen Quilligan's elaborate psychoanalytic explanation of this effacement (223–28), we find it repeated in the legend of Euphrosyne, "laquelle Dieu avoit donnee a Paffonssien [Paphnutius] son pere" (3.13.289). There is no mention of a mother as agent or medium in this gift.

St. Christine's character is further diminished by the omission of the flesh-flinging episode and taunt and her rejoicing at her father's death. The deaths of Christine's twelve handmaidens also are left out because of her stubborn cling-ing to Christianity. Thus it is a much "nicer" Christine that we are offered here, a less theatrically provocative character and one who raises no difficult moral questions. That this is the author's namesake is no coincidence, even though the tendency to flatten out personality and dramatic incident is typical of Christine's style.

The legendary, and the work as a whole, is capped by Christine's well-known advice to ladies to be humble, patient, and subject to their husbands. Virgins are exhorted, much as they had been since patristic days, to keep their eyes lowered, speak infrequently, and avoid men. Widows are conventionally urged toward prudence, devotion, humility, and charity. If we did not know that this was written by a woman—if the hagiographical portion of Christine's book had cir-culated separately, without authorial self-attribution—could we confidently as-cribe it to a woman on the basis of its representational strategies? I doubt it.

My assumption throughout this book is that hagiographers know what they are doing. I suspect that some scholars assume that the doctrinal content of the material, and its predetermined basic plot, necessarily intimidate new authors or reduce them to a passive role. That this is not the case should be evident from the different results just discussed. But we are fortunate to have a more direct glimpse of late-medieval authorial self-consciousness and pride. The following remarks by an anonymous fifteenth-century translator, editor, and reviser of a life of St. Katherine offer precious insight into the flux of textual process in an anything but fossilized tradition:

> After I had drawe the martirdom of the holy virgyn and martir seynt Kateryne from Latyn into englesshe as hit is wryton in legendis that are compleet, ther was take to me a quayere, where-yn was drawe in to englesshe not oonly hire martir-dom but also hir birthe and lyvynge to-fore hir conversion, and how sche was con-verted and spoused to oure lord Ihesu crist.
>
> Netheles the martirdom of the saam virgyn was not allinges so plener in that

quayer as hit was drawe by me before. And therfore to oure lordes wurschip and his holy moders and hyres, I have sett hem to-geder, and maad on of bothe, and departed hem in chapitres & somwhat addet therto moor cleer understonyng in som places. (Nevanlinna and Taavitsainen, 31)

After I had translated the martyrdom of the holy virgin and martyr St. Katherine into English, as it is written in versions that are complete, I was brought a book in which was translated into English not only her martyrdom but also her birth and life before her conversion, and how she was converted and wedded to our lord Jesus Christ.

Nonetheless the martyrdom of that virgin wasn't as fully detailed in that book as in my version. So, to the honor of our lord and his holy mother's and Katherine's, I have combined the two and divided them into chapters and in some places added further information.

Oscar Wilde once said that the only duty we have to history is to rewrite it. The biographers of holy men and women seem to have observed this duty as rigorously as any other writers.

AFTER THE BATTLE OF TEWKESBURY (May 4, 1471), which signaled the final overthrow of the Lancastrians, the jurist and propagandist Sir John Fortescue was imprisoned. Two weeks later, with the murder of Henry VI, Fortescue was released, pardoned, and restored to his estates and to a government position, although not without submitting an abject apology and a profession of loyalty to Edward IV. Fortescue was also required to write a refutation of the treatises he had written ten years earlier against the Yorkist claim to the throne. This task was performed with remarkable brevity and speed, suggesting that the old lawyer had no deep commitment to misogyny. As lawyers often do, he simply produced the case required for the occasion twice, once on each side. Nor was his about-face unique to the period: Gransden mentions Capgrave and Hardyng as other well-known instances of apparent switch from Lancastrian to Yorkist commitment, and the chronicler-chaplain John Rous in the reverse direction on the accession of Henry VII (Gransden, "Politics," 133–38). York's chamberlain, Sir William Oldhall, also transferred his allegiance from the House of Lancaster, a development that Pugh refers to as "a notable instance of the decay of the affinity of the Lancastrian kings" ("Richard Plantagenet," 116).

Fortescue's "Declaracion"[4] takes the form of a dialogue between himself and "a lernid man." Much as in Sir Thomas More's "Dialogue of Service" in *Utopia* (1516), the author has split himself into two narrative personae, one of them bearing his own name. Thus as in More's text, it becomes possible to read the dialogue as an internal debate, with absolute truth on neither side and a good deal of evidence on both.

The learned man requests a statement regarding documents written, allegedly by Fortescue, while Henry—"somtyme king of this lande in ded, though he wer not so in righte"—was in exile in Scotland. Fortescue begins by disclaiming authorship of at least some of these tracts, for "there wore many such wrytinges made in Scotlande, of which sum were made by other men than by me" (523). Next, he cannot remember everything he said, even in the documents he did write, for he has not seen copies of them since returning to England (524). The interlocutor is able to refresh Fortescue's memory. He raises various genealogical complexities from English history, all centering on inheritance through women. Fortescue reinterprets these as the situation now requires, culminating in his assertion of the right of Edward IV to the thrones of England and France, "consyderinge that he is descended of Lyonell the elder brother, and . . . Henry was descended of Johne [of Gaunt] the yonger brother" (531). Case closed.

Not content with specifics, though, the interlocutor asks for a recantation of the principle of female submission to men. Fortescue is at first evasive; he apologizes and offers to help someone else compose a refutation. But the interlocutor persistently encourages him to write the critique himself, reassuring Fortescue that since the earlier writings "were but arguments, and ye no Jugge, but a parcyall man, servant to him for whos favour ye made the arguments, and his cause is now expired and he deed, ye may now honestly and commendably with oute eny note of blame argue to the contrary entent of that ye have doo" (532).

Thus encouraged, Fortescue proceeds to refute his previous antiwoman arguments as economically as possible.

Woman, he says, may be logically considered under the power of man if she is under the power of only one man, and this one man can be the pope; hence she need not be under the power of any other man (533). After a good deal more logical and genealogical pettifoggery, the issues and slanders are cleared up to the satisfaction of the learned man, who now congratulates Fortescue on having done the right thing. The wily jurist has refuted himself and saved face, too.

Few readers will find this minimalist case an adequate refutation of the virtuoso performance in the original treatises. But it is not intended to be adequate to them, only to the king's requirements for reestablishing Fortescue's position. The succession issue had made an antifeminist of Fortescue and then a reluctant refuter of antifeminism, another instance of the sycophantic response that Helen Solterer has written about in connection with another, earlier lawyer's reversal on the woman question, that of Jean le Fevre, author of the late-fourteenth-century *Livre de leesce*.

We might claim, too, that the succession issue made a protofeminist of the Austin friar Osbern Bokenham, although in a less opportunistic register than with Fortescue, for Bokenham had little to gain personally from his position, and there is no evidence that his prowoman stance in the legendary represented a conversion from some previous antifeminism. Nonetheless, Bokenham produced the case he needed in order to serve his patron's interests. Had he wished to make a thorough and principled defense of women's rights, he might have shown women in power: mythical rulers, for instance (as Christine de Pizan had already done), or Queen Matilda of England, since whose abdication in 1148 no woman had ruled England in her own right. Nearer home, he might have done something really innovative, something no one else had done: he might have proposed, as the best Yorkist candidate for the throne, Isabel, Richard's sister and Bokenham's own patron at Clare Castle next door, for Isabel was older by a year or two than her brother and thus first in line of inheritance—if sex were set aside.

It may be tempting to try to extrapolate from the legendary Bokenham's view of women monarchs, but that was not on the agenda in the fifteenth century, and the friar was a sufficiently politic body not to roil the waters needlessly. Even the women readers and patrons named in his legendary bear more ambiguous witness than we might like to believe. True, their textual presence tells us something about the social life and literary tastes of some East Anglian women of the gentry and nobility. Yet even here we must "by indirection find direction out," for their real importance to the text and its author comes by way of their family connections: the family politics and social conflicts in which their husbands, brothers, fathers, and sons were the active participants. These women are able to act as patrons and to have social importance for Bokenham because they are related to Richard or to men in his affinity.

Despite the importance of women to England's economy and social life generally, such ambivalence was the cultural norm. In 1447, three ladies were the sole heirs to deceased magnates, but they were not summoned to Parliament, as was an heir's right. Instead, their husbands or sons were summoned, after the husband or son had come into possession of the late lord's estates (Powell and Wallis, 480). Similarly, when Commons petitioned in January 1442 for the equality of women with men before the law, this was not based on an egalitarian motive but, rather, as a way to prosecute peeresses for treason. Eleanor Cobham, the duke of Gloucester's second wife—she against whom the women of Stokkes had demonstrated in 1428 (see chapter 7) and for whose sake a Kentish woman would be tried and pressed to death in 1443 for criticizing the handling of Eleanor's case (see chapter 1)—was accused of sorcery. The Magna Carta provided only that "no free man be taken or imprisoned . . . except by lawful judgment of his peers or by the law of the land," but no mention was made of women. So although Eleanor had already been tried and sentenced to perpetual house arrest, the precaution was taken for the future (Griffiths, "Trial"; Powell and Wallis, 472).

Not surprisingly, Osbern Bokenham does not make an open subversive claim for women's social rights. The partisanship remains implicit: women have equal access to grace; they have displayed heroic courage, fortitude, and prudence; and they have given sound political advice. Even though their example helps support the distaff-weighted Yorkist claim to rule, no social or political consequence is explicitly drawn. More to the point, the portrait of female heroism is contained in the structure of a powerful male-dominated institution that had no intention of making room for women in its hierarchy of power, any more than it does today. To this institution Bokenham was evidently loyal and in it he occupied a privileged position, though by no means an exalted or influential one.

Nonetheless, the implications of Bokenham's work do strain at the social limits, promising an eventual rupture that the author himself eventually might want to disown. I mean not the prospect of a woman monarch, as happened a century later, but the complete social equality of women, a goal yet to be achieved in most cultures. In this sense, the play of subversion and containment is as central to Bokenham's legendary as it is to the sixteenth-century texts examined by Stephen Greenblatt. We might say about Bokenham's hagiography, as Greenblatt says of Shakespearian drama, that it "registers the possibility . . . of its own subversion" (26) and that "the form itself . . . contains the radical doubts it continually provokes" (45). It accomplishes the former, the possibility of its own subversion, by its authorization of female power, a power manifested in female characters and women patrons. But the radical doubts are still being provoked and still being contained.

WHAT ELSE IS STILL WITH US? Sainthood, certainly. Henry VI himself became an object of cultic veneration, a propaganda figure helping to affirm the legitimacy of another insecure dynasty, that of the Tudors (see Knox and Leslie; McKenna). Today, virtually all religions have their saints, new ones continue to be made or adored, and relics are venerated. Sikh hagiographical literature from the sixteenth through the nineteenth century recounts the lives and miracles of various divinely inspired gurus. Islamic hagiography, some of it contained in a thirteenth-century compilation, includes rich and poor saints, men and women, ascetics, mystics, and martyrs. Thousands of Moroccan Jews make an annual pilgrimage to the town of Netivot in Israel, site of the tomb of Rabbi Yisrael Abuhatzera who died in the 1970s and was believed to possess divinely bestowed curative powers. Since 1992, childless women have flocked to a supermarket in Ashdod, Israel, to sit in a chair once occupied by another rabbi, Yitzhak Khaduri, whose influence is reputed to bring fertility. In Mexico, the head of Pancho Villa was taken from his tomb in Chihuahua in 1926 and has never been recovered. Only in 1990 was the right arm of General Alvaro Obregón, a hero of the Mexican Revolution, cremated and buried with the rest of the body, after seventy-five years on display in Mexico City.

As for the Catholic Church, it sorts through hundreds of candidates' biographies to determine who deserves beatification and canonization. It also deletes from the traditional roster those saints whose credentials or historicity is suspect. As a consequence of the Second Vatican Council (1962–65), the universal calendar of saints was revised, a process completed in 1969. Of the saints portrayed by Osbern Bokenham, those who made the cut were Agnes, Agatha, Mary Magdalene, Anne (now joined, on her feast day, by her husband, Joachim), Cecelia Elizabeth of Hungary, and Lucy. This is not to say there is no discomfort even with this select group: Cecelia has been kept because of her popularity, despite grave doubts; and even though they are part of a group of martyrs whose deaths are probably fictional ("eorum sane passiones fabulosae sunt"; *Calendarium, 72*), Agatha and Lucy have been retained because they are so widely accepted. The others—Dorothy, Margaret of Antioch, Christine, Katherine of Alexandria, Ursula with her companions—are neither sufficiently documented nor sufficiently popular now to keep; the memory of each "expungitur," "deletur," "relinquitur" (is expunged, is erased, is let go). Finally, St. Faith is mentioned nowhere in the official document.

Moreover, for many believers the medieval tradition of hagiography lives in very practical ways. The parents of Thérèse of Lisieux (d. 1897, canonized 1925) considered as the ideal a sexless marriage, modeled on those of Mary with Joseph and Cecelia with Valerian, even though their priest urged them to discontinue the practice of chastity. The Catholic convert and social activist Dorothy Day recalled that the story of a saint—she did not remember which one, but Elizabeth of Hungary would be a likely possibility—filled her with a spirit of "lofty enthusiasm . . . my heart almost burst with desire to take part in such high endeavor" (25).

Such continuity will tempt some scholars to deduce the "timeless universality" of hagiography: on the one hand, either its relative independence from history or, on the other hand—but paradoxically amounting to the same thing—its status as an actual, literal historical narrative. Thomas Heffernan's recent study takes the latter approach. Heffernan observes that because hagiography "has the longest continuous history" of any genre, it "quintessentially illustrates" Fernand Braudel's idea of *longue durée* (17–18). Yet the profoundly historicist agenda of this statement is quickly negated as Heffernan attempts to transfer hagiography from the category of fiction or propaganda to that of biography or, better, of historical narrative whose function is to "chronicle the appearance of the inbreaking of the divine in the world" (97). This is a fundamentally theological and deeply obsolete gesture, glossed though it may be with a sheen of the contemporary. Geertz, Foucault, LeGoff, Zumthor, Braudel, White, and LaCapra all make a brief bow, yet the occurrence of their names cannot disguise the antirationalist, antimaterialist, and finally antihistoricist thrust of Heffernan's project. To validate hagiography as genuine historiography, Heffernan must somehow account for its obvious fictions, and he does so by taking a whip once again to the long-dead horse of "truth versus fiction," with a moralistic and intentional notion of truth. The justification for hagiographical borrowing and inventing is that no hagiographer ever intended to deceive. One might wonder how Heffernan knows this—but never mind. Their method was a consequence of their definition of the real and of their desire to convert an audience to belief and virtuous action. This, of course, is what hagiographers said about themselves, and although it may be refreshing to find a scholar so fully at one with his subject, I think we can learn little about the realities of the genre in this way. Heffernan's apparent belief that Jews are a race (217) is perhaps another facet of his identification with his material.

A more useful meditation on the nature of hagiographical evidence is offered by Jane Schulenburg. She warns that even though legends may give us indirect evidence about family life or monastic practices, about deviant behavior or popular mentalities, still they must be used cautiously because of their gender bias and propagandistic aim. She emphasizes, too, the importance of reading hagiography in conjunction with a variety of historical and documentary sources ("Saints' Lives"; also see Wogan-Browne, "Saints' Lives").

My book confirms both the value and the caution proposed by Schulenburg. The legendary analyzed here does not yield a great deal of direct representational information about the lives of fifteenth-century English women. Its mode of operation is indirect and corroborative rather than revelatory, probably deliberately so, given the absence of contemporary or very recent saints from its array. The real and living women who make a brief appearance—the several patrons named in the text—might be considered in this sense more adequate channels to history than the eponymous heroines. Yet as I just proposed, their presence is due to the social and political activities of their male relatives.

Still, some women in England and France did act in their own behalf, or that of others, far more forcefully than Bokenham's genteel patrons were able or called on to do. I mentioned in chapter 7 the 1428 demonstration at Parliament of the women of Stokkes on behalf of the repudiated Jacqueline of Hainault. The following is another account of female solidarity, a collective enforcement of justice against a criminal, dating from 1429:

> And that yere there was a ryche wedowe i-slayne at Whyte Chapylle; and the same theffe that kylde hyr fledde to Syn Gorgys yn Sowtheworke; and the Fryday nexte folowynge he for-swore the londe [i.e., to go into exile, as an outlaw whom anyone might kill with impunity]; and he was a-sygnyd the same way [i.e., route to a ship] that he slowe the woman, and there wemmen mette with hym and slowe hym in the waye by twyne the Whyte Chapylle and Algate. (Gregory's "Chronicle," in Gairdner, 164)[5]

In the same year, Joan of Arc—inspired by the life of Katherine of Alexandria, among other saints—sought out King Charles VII of France to offer her military leadership in his struggle against the English. Although she was the most famous, Joan was not the only woman of her day to don men's clothing and engage in warfare. In 1450, at Avranches, the despairing English troops were rallied, and the defense supervised, by the wife of the commander, John Lampet. She wore men's clothes during the battle but changed back into women's dress to negotiate the surrender (Ramsay 2.108).[6] In England, Margaret—second wife of the famous warrior John Talbot, daughter of the countess of Warwick, and herself the countess of Shrewsbury—took up arms in pursuit of her estate claims against her rivalrous cousin Lord Berkeley, the male heir. "Margaret, . . . a virago of parts (she was obviously not the wife of a great general for nothing), captured Lady Berkeley . . . and imprisoned her in Gloucester castle" (Lander, "Family," 30). Even in Bokenham's own East Anglia, such conduct was not unheard of. In February 1448, Margaret Paston asked her husband John for crossbows and poleaxes to defend their manor at Gresham (Norfolk) against the usurping Moleyns affinity—who, however, armed with guns, eventually succeeded in occupying and sacking the mansion.

As an indication of female status in the subjective register, consider the following passage from the *Revelationes* (7.23) of St. Bridget: "When they [the shepherds] saw the child, they first wanted to find out whether it was a male or a female, for angels had announced to them that the savior of the world had been born, and they had not said that it was a savioress. Then the Virgin Mary showed to them the nature and the male sex of the child" (K. Wilson, 245).

Compelling here is the gender-conscious biblical criticism: the writer's assumption that the savior might just as easily have been a savioress—and, equally, her belief that the three shepherds to whom the angels announced the savior's birth shared that assumption.

None of the preceding "reality bites" would be remotely deducible from Bokenham's legendary, all-female though it is and notwithstanding that the friar Bokenham had a far healthier attitude toward women, more extensive and more satisfying social relations with them, than such a gentleman as his contemporary William Worcester, the East Anglian author, antiquarian, and estate official. Regarding a boy (perhaps one of his sons) whom he was trying to place at Lincoln's Inn, Worcester wrote: "He hath cost me moche gode and labour and now he ys uppon hys makyng by vertues governance or undoyng to the contrary, and yn especyalle to be not conversant ne neere among wommen as I was kept froo her company xxx yer er ony such were of my councelle, I thank God of yt" (McFarlane, 201). This may stand as the practical consequence of taking to heart the traditional masculinist arguments such as are collected in Fortescue's Latin dynastic treatises.

W
ITH THE VICTORY OF YORK, the woman question temporarily receded, to be revived as a topic for public debate a century later when Mary Tudor took the throne in 1553. By then, England was no longer a continental power, but it would soon be a colonial one, and its monarchy was comparatively stable and powerful. The fifteenth-century episode was neither the first nor the last time that politics, theology, and the literary representation of women intersected. Each instance had a distinct configuration, and not always what one might expect on the basis of simple binary divisions such as male/female or lay/cleric. Nor is genre always a reliable guide. The curiosity here is that hagiography—the medieval genre par excellence, one would think—is adapted to a protohumanist vision of woman and the body, whereas Fortescue's dramatic dialogue—a favored Renaissance discursive form—becomes the vehicle for a scrap heap of antifeminist clichés completely unreflective of the real social position and productivity of women in its own time, the late Middle Ages. By the same token, Bokenham's apparently protohumanist translation of Claudian is

not motivated by love of the classics per se but is bent to a utilitarian and characteristically medieval purpose: allegory. The modalities of making it new are
often contorted and, as in politics, sometimes a case of "one step forward, two
steps back."

IN CONCLUSION, I find that I have inadvertently observed my author's four
causes, much as he outlined them in his opening. If the first, or efficient, cause
is "the auctour, / Which aftyr hys cunnyng doth hys labour" (13–14), I discussed
the author and his circle in chapter 1. The second or material cause, "the begunne matter" (15), was the focus of chapters 2 and 3, concerning the textual traditions within which Bokenham worked: those of Augustine, Chaucer, Gower,
Lydgate, and courtly literature. Structure is the third or formal cause, which
"settyth in dew ordre clause by clause" (18). Chapters 4, 5, and 6, on the collective anatomy of the somaticized text, fall into this category (although the
Chaucer alignment treated in chapter 2 would also qualify as a formal cause).
Finally, the fourth or final cause "declaryth pleynly . . . / what was the entent /
Of the auctour fynally, & what he ment" (21–24), which I have located in the
politics discussed in chapters 7 and 8.

Although I cannot claim that it was my plan to imitate this scheme, I am
pleased it worked out in this way. But at this point, if I feel empathy with my
author, it is less for his programmatic structuring than for the personal passage
he inserts between his life of Margaret and his account of her translation
(869–920). There he takes a ten-day interval, from September 19 to 29, Michael-
mas, 1443, rehearsing the age-old complaints of scholars:

For sykyr myn handys gynne to feynte,	For surely my hands grow weak,
My wyt to dullyn, and myn eyne bleynte	My wit dulls, and my eyes would be blinded
Shuld be, ner helpe of a spectacle. (895–97)	Without help of spectacles.

Carpal tunnel syndrome and contact lenses were far in the future when Osbern Bokenham wrote these words, but as with much else in his legendary, the
words voice an experience we understand and even duplicate when we work.
Like us, too, the poet modishly avails himself of the best in recent technology to
deal with the old complaints: spectacles—which, though invented earlier, apparently became popular during Bokenham's lifetime (if the *Oxford English Dic-
tionary*'s earliest instances, almost all from the fifteenth century, are an accurate
gauge). As suitably as anything else, the friar's spectacles can serve as a kind of
"objective correlative" (T. S. Eliot's phrase) for the dialectic of ancient and modern within which he considered sex and gender, politics and literary genre.
There were authors a lot worse than Bokenham in his time—as poets, moralists,
and propagandists. To say that there are a lot worse in our time as well is less a
tribute to the friar than a rueful comment on history.

Notes

1. Despite the usual translation of Marx's subject as "man" or "men," the German *Mensch* refers to humanity at large, whereas *Männer* would be the sex-specific term.

2. ME *toss* means "to pull apart wool so as to loosen the mass." The "tose and pulle" phrase also appears in Gower's *Confessio amantis*, 1.17. The plant called *teasel* or *fuller's teasel* was used to tease cloth—that is, to raise the nap on woolen fabric. The image is deeply rooted in the economy of late-medieval village life.

3. According to the rule of the Augustinian order, "all revenues or donations made to an individual person must be made common property of the monastery by a written document drawn up in the name of the Prior and his monastery, so that these revenues or proceeds appear to be received in the name of the monastery. After these formalities the Superior may decide to return the things to that particular brother for his personal use" (Mathes, 96).

4. Curiously, Roth's account of Capgrave's career contradicts his documentary evidence. The error is elucidated by Fredeman, 218–19, n. 57. As for Bokenham, Roth admits that it is not clear when he finished his degree. Roth also shows an inconsistency in birth date, giving 1393 in his text but 1392 in his biographical entry (1.515).

5. Harvey mentions Andrew Holes, a royal representative at the papal curia, as an agent helping arrange safe conducts for English delegates at Florence (9). Greatrex claims there were only four English observers, all Carmelites. The assertion is based on the secondhand account of Thomas Rudborne, a Benedictine, who wrote around fifteen years after the events. Greatrex inexplicably and mistakenly calls this long interval "contemporary, almost 'hot off the scriptorial writing board' news for some of his readers" (172).

Gill tells of a Greek in the emperor's retinue who met a group of English en route from Bologna to Florence, eager for news of the council's progress (300, citing Parks, 1.302). Parks adds to the list Robert Sutton, canon of Lincoln. Parks is oddly uninformed about Bokenham, mentioning him only in a single sentence and relying on the Horstmann edition, long out of date when Parks wrote. The division between the Greek and Latin Churches had lasted some four and a half centuries, with union agreed on at the end of June 1439. The news was greeted with public official celebrations in England, but it was soon repudiated by the Greeks, and shortly thereafter, with the Turkish conquest of Constantinople in 1453, it became a dead letter.

6. Maddern challenges the usual characterization of these events as "riots," although much of her argument is *ex silentio:* the absence of coroners' reports of death or injury, or re-

ports of property damage. One of her major criteria for using the term *riot* ("a seizure of power by a normally suppressed populace," 198) seems neither crucial nor even normative. In fact, if power were actually seized, the event would *not* be a "riot" but a coup or revolution. See McRee, who discusses the Norwich riots [*sic*] of 1433, 1437, and 1443.

7. Warner. For a political analysis relating the poem to current events and policies, see Holmes. The poem represents debates that arose in the Parliament of January 1437, and its positions parallel those of cloth exporters, the Staplers, and the duke of Gloucester. Warner notes that in one manuscript, BL Harley 4011, the *Libell* is bound with Bokenham's *Mappula*. This may suggest an anthology based on patriotic themes, as well as a certain kind of audience for the *Mappula*.

8. A few scholars have misinterpreted this entry as referring to Clare College (or Hall), Cambridge. However, Dowsing was at the university a year later, and university documents record no such destruction at Clare College as described in the journal under Clare. For instance, the 1647 *Querela Cantabrigiensis,* or *Remonstrance,* which protests Parliament-authorized depredations against "that ancient and noble Seminary of Learning," lists for Clare Hall only the seizure of "three or foure hundred pounds of Timber" intended for renovations.

9. Horstmann, who edited the *Mappula* and the *Legend,* wrote off Bokenham as the possible author of the earlier collection because some of the saints that Bokenham mentions in the *Mappula* as appearing in his legendary did not appear in the *Gilte legende.* Manuscripts discovered later do include the rest of the saints mentioned by Bokenham, which prompted Sister Mary Jeremy to revive Bokenham's candidacy. Several scholars accept this reattribution. Görlach contends, however, that the extra saints are not part of the original text of the *Gilte legende* but are additions that, he claims (largely on the basis of style), are probably not by the *Gilte legende* translator. Whateley questions that the extra lives are not by the original author of *Gilte legende.* I do not find Görlach's arguments persuasive or sensitive, although this is not the place to dissect them. It seems to me that the question remains unresolved and lacks a strong argument against Bokenham's authorship.

10. The manuscript is dated 1456. In his introduction to Barnardiston's edition, Norman Scarfe says that "on internal evidence [the work] can only have been finished in 1460" (xiii). He does not specify the evidence, and I have been unable to identify it, so I have accepted the manuscript date. The "Dialogue" was also printed as an appendix in Horstmann's edition of the legendary.

Chapter 2

1. For more discussion of Christine's reputation in England and the various fifteenth-century English translations and imitations of her work, see Bornstein; Campbell; Chesney; Mitchell; and the 1440 translation of her *Epistre* by Stephen Scrope.

2. Since every applicant for the *magisterium* had to recruit at least one novice for the order, or pay for the support of one (Roth, 1.171), Burgh could have been Bokenham's recruit, presumably a fairly close personal relationship. Roth identifies Burgh with the Thomas Borough, *lector,* who in 1440 was the prior at Cambridge (1.253, 520).

3. Some Latin versions have *praefecti corniculario,* as does the Metaphrastes version, edited by Kölbing. The term does not appear in Voragine. Chaucer describes Maximus as "an officer / Of the prefectes, and his corniculer," whereas Bokenham, omitting the word *prefect,* seems to follow out the Chaucerian splitting of the phrase into two apparent synonyms.

4. Tynemouth's compilation was originally in calendrical order, starting on January 5, the feast of Edward the Confessor. It was recast into alphabetical order by Capgrave (if indeed he was the fifteenth-century editor) and printed, with additions, in 1516 by Wynkyn de Worde as *Nova legenda angliae.* This version was edited, with an introduction, by Horstmann.

Horstmann mentions another collection of English saints as well, a fourteenth-century manuscript with forty-seven lives, but Tynemouth was apparently not familiar with it. There is some difference in Ursula's origin. The Horstmann text says she is from "Britannia maiori" (i.e., Britain), although Horstmann notes that another manuscript gives "minori" (Brittany). An English version printed by R. Pynson in 1516, the *Kalendre of the Newe Legende of Englande,* says she came from "moche Brytayne nowe callyd Englonde." Bokenham gives her origin as "brytane the lesse" (3147) and her fiancé's as "ynglond" (3160), so he has perhaps deliberately de-Anglicized her, although this is consistent with Voragine, whose version has Ursula from "Britannia" and her fiancé from "Anglia."

5. Duffy, "Holy Maydens," table A, 178. Duffy writes that the legendary of the Suffolk Austin "canon" [*sic*] Osbern Bokenham "reads like programme notes for one of the East Anglian screens we have been considering, and with which he must have been very familiar" (185). Although I mentioned the rood screen, for several reasons I do not think it has much significance in Bokenham's case. East Anglia does account for nearly half the extant rood screens, but only a few can be dated with any accuracy. Constable concludes that "the great majority were executed within the period 1450 to 1530" (143), thus after the legendary. Of the 158 screens that Cotton lists, only fourteen *might* predate 1450. Besides the problems of dating, the content is not as congruent with Bokenham's legendary as Duffy assumes. Cotton observes that "by far the most common subjects" are men—the twelve apostles—whereas most women saints are local (45). Williamson notes that many obscure, uncanonized, local figures are also seen on screens.

More generally, using artifacts to determine cultural habits must be approached cautiously. For instance, Barbara was frequently seen on East Anglian rood screens, but "no medieval church in Suffolk is dedicated to her" (Salmon, 9). Similarly, Ursula appears on screens but has no church anywhere in England. St. Katherine appears frequently in church art, but only two medieval churches in Suffolk, out of sixty-two, were dedicated to her. St. Margaret had twenty, and the now-forgotten Petronilla had, beside her hospital at Bury, a church and two chapels in Suffolk, thus quantitatively surpassing both Barbara and Katherine with respect to edifices. In all, since different artifacts tell different stories, the use of the rood screen seems a tenuous form of evidence for literary works.

6. Machaut, "Dit de la fleur de lis et de la marguerite," ed. Wimsatt; Lydgate, "Margarete," no. 37 (about 1430) in *The Minor Poems of John Lydgate,* pt. 1, ed. MacCracken.

7. See "Apocalypse of the Virgin" in James, *Apocryphal New Testament.* Lydgate also uses the phrase in several of his poems about Mary, including the *Life of Our Lady* (5.338), as does John Audelay, no. 46, line 19.

8. The version of the Latin *passio* that Bokenham probably used gives both "bed" and "grill": "lectum aereum" and "craticulum." The document has been published several times, perhaps most accessibly by Hoepffner and Alfaric; the relevant phrases occur in 2.183. The bed also appears in various church windows, carvings, alabasters, and brasses; cf. Drake; Husenbeth; Mansfield.

9. For Chaucer, Minerva is always the goddess of war or wisdom. In Christine's *Cité,* Arachne is credited with the invention of weaving, and in her *Othea,* Minerva is the goddess of war. And in Augustine's *City of God,* Minerva invents many works but not specifically weaving.

10. Arachne is written "Araigne" in *Ovide moralisé,* 6.1–105, and "Arenie" by Christine (*Cité,* para. 107), whereas Ariadne is written "Adriagne" by Gower (*CA,* 5.5478). Shakespeare later wrote about "Ariachne's broken woof" (*TC,* 5.2.150). J. Hillis Miller takes the similarity of names beyond "partial homonymy" into narrative itself.

11. *Seinte Katerine,* ed. d'Ardenne and Dobson, line 465. The text, composed in about 1220, is not mentioned by Serjeantson as a source for Bokenham's version. The idea, though

not the exact phrase, also appears in the early-fifteenth-century *Northern Homily Cycle* version of Katherine, ed. Sperk: "Here stand ye als ye had no tung" (269–70).

Chapter 3

1. It is curious that Gwynn never mentions Bokenham, for the legendary had been edited three times by 1940, when Gwynn's book came out, and the *Mappula* and the Claudian translation were also available. For the document concerning Giles, see *Analecta augustiniana,* 2.

2. I have used Robertson's translation except where otherwise noted; mine are from *Augustinus opera omnia,* in Migne, *Pat. lat.,* vol. 34.

3. In her edition of the *Legends,* Serjeantson identified this "Galfryd of England" as Geoffrey Chaucer (xxv). Clearly, this is wrong. Geoffrey's treatise *Poetria nova* is explicitly named ("hys newe poetrye"); Geoffrey did come from England; and Chaucer is always referred to, with appropriate respect, by his last name and in the trio of major writers Chaucer/Gower/Lydgate.

4. See Gower, *Vox,* prol. 2; Walton, stanzas 6–8; Lydgate, *Alban,* 1–27 and *Life of Our Lady,* 2.1659; Hardyng in Lansdowne ms., f9, or in Ellis, 31.

5. One of these Margaret amulets is published with hardly any comment by de Herkenrode. However, it is described elsewhere as existing in a fourteenth-century manuscript: cf. Carolus-Barré, 274, n. 64. This article describes a late-thirteenth-century parchment amulet discovered in 1925, and another one of the mid-fifteenth century, both lives of Margaret; a magic-formula one is also described. The medieval word for these items was *brief* or *bref.* See Wogan-Browne's brilliant contextualization of these amulets in "The Apple's Message."

6. In this discussion, I leave aside the unresolved question of whether Thomas Chaucer was indeed the poet's biological son or whether he was the offspring of a union between John of Gaunt and Chaucer's wife Philippa Payne de Roet. Much of my information about Thomas Chaucer is from the biography by Ruud. For the illegitimacy hypothesis, which is based on heraldry and other evidence, see Russell Krauss. Ruud's reasons for accepting Thomas's legitimacy are weak (especially his willingness to trust Thomas Gascoigne on the matter!) and are superseded by Krauss's careful and persuasive, albeit circumstantial, argument.

7. Harriss, *Cardinal Beaufort,* 20. Also on Thomas Chaucer, see Roskell, passim. Ruud discusses a particular parliamentary incident as "evidence of the extremely close relations between Chaucer and the Beauforts. No medieval parliament would have ventured to adopt such a petition [for the king's abdication] on its own initiative, and no medieval speaker would have ventured to present it who was not hand in glove with the great magnates whose policy and ambitions the petition voiced" (37).

Chapter 4

1. Boureau discerns eighty-one tests or ordeals, classified in three levels of seriousness and purpose; they are listed on pp. 118–20. For a historical study of torture in Roman and European law, see Peters.

2. There is the case of St. Winifred, who survives rape and decapitation by a miracle, and see chapter 5 on St. Cecelia's ambiguous death. Winifred's story is told by Bokenham's contemporary John Mirk in the *Festial* as homily 43.

3. In *Muelos,* Weston LaBarre traces this belief from prehistoric times and through many cultures (including Celtic groups), relating it to the practices of head-hunting, brain cannibalism, skull cults, and antler worship. Antlers, as ossified brain exudate or semen, were thought to have special aphrodisiac properties and still are so considered in Chinese medicine. The no-

tion that semen originates in the brain might also illuminate the text-as-body trope, for—particularly in a society whose cultural production is monopolized by men—both writing and bodies could be seen as brain-generated offspring. For a less ancient and more influential locus than LaBarre's, see Plato, *Timaeus,* 91A–B.

4. The Latin *pedamentum* is a stake or prop to support a vine or tree, from *pedo,* "to provide with feet or to set on a firm foundation." In English, *pediment* has two architectural meanings: a base or foundation (coming from Latin *pes,* "foot") and a triangular portion at the front of a building, but the latter is probably a corruption of *periment,* itself perhaps a corruption of *pyramid,* and in any case does not antedate the seventeenth century.

5. d'Ancona, 6. This ambiguity persisted through the Middle Ages, for manuscripts of the Pseudo-Matthew and the *Protevangelium of James* shift between "has conceived" and "will conceive" at key points in the story. O'Connor remarks that such variants "are, for the most part, attempts to rid the text of the doctrine of a virginal conception of Mary, which seems to have belonged to the original" (516, n. 1).

6. Balic. It is because of his championing of immaculate conception that Scotus was known as the "Marian doctor," and his position was called the "opinio scoti," in contrast to the "opinio thomae." In the same volume, Wenceslaus Sebastian claims that the Augustinians began to adopt the immaculist theory after 1340 but not that it was general throughout the order: "The Controversy over the Immaculate Conception from after Scotus to the End of the Eighteenth Century." Besides these articles, I drew on Obermann's discussion in *The Harvest,* 283 ff., and d'Ancona. Burridge concentrates mainly on the twelfth century, showing that at least one polemicist considered the new doctrine as "un produit de l'imagination anglaise" (585).

7. See *MED,* s.v. "labour", n. Meaning 1.(e) is "the fruits of labor, product; a book," and 4.(b) includes several medical and other instances of "labour of birth," among them citations from *The Book of Margery Kempe* and a translation of Boccaccio's *De Claris mulieribus.* The *OED* has an instance from the Paston letters. These instances are by and large clustered in the first half of the fifteenth century, so that it appears that Bokenham is taking advantage of a fairly recent linguistic development. The *OED* does not mention the Claudian translation done at Clare in 1445, which mentions "labours of . . . childyng" (Flügel, line 377; also see chapter 7).

Chapter 5

1. See Garth. In addition, Saxer notes that except for a surge of interest in the twelfth century (due to Crusade activity), England was, along with Italy and Holland, a nation "à faible densité magdalénienne" (270). Only in Germany did her cult expand during the fifteenth century, because of the founding of a religious order of Magdalenes to help prostitutes. The traditional conflation of several biblical Marys was not challenged until the sixteenth century.

2. In some texts, head and penis tip (*caput virgae*) are made analogous, as are mouth and vagina, tongue and clitoris. See Jacquart and Thomasset, *Sexuality and Medicine,* passim; and Pouchelle, *Corps et chirurgie,* 311–12.

3. Connolly cites a sermon on St. Cecelia by the fourteenth-century Italian Dominican Johanes de Biblia. Curiously, Connolly dismisses the organ/inner ear motif as "hardly grounds . . . for the extreme music-centred cult that later grew up around her" (14). Cecelia's cult was apparently invented around 495–500. In her early *passio,* the imagery of her sermon is alchemical, but with Voragine and Bokenham, it was transmuted into financial.

Chapter 6

1. See Hewson. Although Bokenham would almost certainly have known this text by the dominant writer in his order, it is unlikely he would have agreed with Giles on many ques-

tions regarding women. Giles followed Aristotle's opinion that the female seed played no active role in conception, thus opposing the view of Galen, Avicenna, and other authorities that the female seed did have generative virtue. Hewson notes, too (173), that Giles's calculations of gestation are made on the basis of a thirty-day month.

Chapter 7

1. The town could be either Stoke-by-Clare, not far from Clare Priory, or Stoke Neyland, also in Suffolk.

2. The term is, like most period labels, a convenience. On its inaccuracies and inadequacies, see Chrimes, Preface to *Lancastrians, Yorkists*; Kendall, 29–31; McFarlane, "The War of the Roses," in *England in the Fifteenth Century*.

3. "Gregory's Chronicle," in Gairdner, 204. This is not to say that there were no Lancastrian Austins. Capgrave, for instance, supported whoever reigned, earning the opprobrium of the formidable F. J. Furnivall: "Capgrave, being an Englishman, was of course by race and nature a flunkey, and had an inordinate reverence for kings and rank" (Furnivall's foreword to Horstmann's edition of Capgrave's *Life of St. Katherine*, xv).

4. There are four letters from Richard to Charles VII from 1445, dated April 18, June 10, September 21, and December 21. They are published in Stevenson.

5. Alison R. Allan, "Political Propaganda," 201; paraphrasing Scofield, 1.153. Allan notes that under Edward IV, propaganda also referred indirectly to Castile: a prophecy states that Edward will win three crowns before he dies, which Allan reads as referring to Britain, France, and Spain ("Yorkist Propaganda," 180, 191, n. 34). By Edward's time, though, the latter two can scarcely have been realistic foreign policy aims.

6. An English version of Vegetius's fourth- or fifth-century *De Re militari* was commissioned by Sir Thomas Berkeley in 1408 and possibly executed by the same John Walton who produced a versified Boethius for him. See the introduction to Lester's Vegetius. *Palladius on Husbondrie* was translated about 1420 (ed. Lodge). The *Distichs of Cato* were translated by Benedict Burgh between 1433 and 1440, but there had been earlier translations: see Förster. Burgh probably composed this work for his pupil William Bourchier, eldest son of Henry Bourchier and Isabel, Bokenham's patron. Bokenham cites stanza 71 of the work in his Katherine (6577–82). As to the quality of the Claudian translation, I think Cameron overrates it, as it does not read particularly well. Flügel called it "pedantisch, schulmeisterlich" (430) and listed several major mistakes and misunderstandings (431–32).

7. Flügel lists this as a translation error, but clearly it is not, any more than the translator's proud economic patriotism in dressing Britannia in wool, another local and contemporary allusion that Flügel calls "das schlimmste Missverständnis" (the worst misunderstanding of all) even while noting its patriotic motive (431–32).

8. That St. Jerome, a contemporary of Claudian, also polemicized against a Rufinus (who was a disciple of Origen) ensured that this name would become a traditional rhetorical alias for the object of polemics. Matthew of Vendôme attacked his detractors (probably Arnulf of Orléans and his colleagues) under the name Rufinus in his *Ars versificatoria* during the twelfth century.

9. Cameron follows Flügel, 422; it is a completely unconvincing hypothesis, especially since Henry was not, at this time, an enemy of Richard. Moreover, the unworldly Henry—saintly, in the opinion of some—distinctly lacked the malice and ruthlessness of character required for a Rufinus. In proposing Suffolk, Griffiths associates the 1445 Claudian translation with the 1443 appointment of the duke of Somerset as commander in southern France, a position of authority that conflicted with York's. Presumably the connection is that Suffolk would have been the adviser responsible for this decision. The connection seems tenuous, par-

ticularly given the two-year time lag. Moreover, even though Suffolk dominated the council at this time, other historians do not single him out as key to the Somerset appointment (e.g., Pugh, "Richard Plantagenet," 120; or Cora Scofield, who wrote that responsibility for the insult "lay with the Beaufort party," *Life and Reign,* 1.8). Scofield notes further that it was Suffolk who broached to Charles VII the topic of marrying one of his daughters to Richard's son Edward—scarcely a hostile act, even if intended (as Ferguson suggests, 26–27) to "buy off" York in favor of the truce that Suffolk had recently engineered.

It is true that in June 1445 Suffolk warned of the importance of preparedness in Normandy, urged York to act accordingly to avoid "defaute of provision for that londe," and exculpated himself in case of a disaster. This amounts to implicit criticism of York (Allmand, 45, 47, 260). Although Griffiths does not use this to support his identification by bringing the criticism forward to 1445, it makes Suffolk a credible candidate as Rufinus. Still, because Suffolk's criticism remained implicit, whereas Moleyns's was explicit, harsh, and damaging, the latter is the more likely referent.

10. Oldhall was also a particular friend of Henry Bourchier (York's brother-in-law) and, in 1448 and 1450, a benefactor of Augustinian establishments at Walsingham and Thetford (the latter fairly near Clare), endowing them with manors. He was a trustee of John and Agatha Flegge's estate, and of the estates of some of York's other retainers. Oldhall's daughter Mary married Walter Gorges, son of Sir Theobald Gorges. The latter had married the Flegges' daughter Joan. This was a second or third marriage and apparently a January–May match, although Joan predeceased her husband, who died in 1470, leaving a son, Richard, aged twenty-two: see Gorges.

11. There is some disagreement about when Moleyns's charges, and Richard's reply to them, were made public. Pugh dates the dispute to autumn 1445 (124). The later dating offered by Johnson (52–54, 77) is not implausible, but as a literary critic, I should point out that it does depend on the subjective interpretations of a very few words. Johnson first posits a date after December 8, 1445, when Stanlow, the treasurer of Normandy, returned to France, because Stanlow is referred to in the past tense: he "was here." Johnson assumes that "here" refers to England itself rather than to London or court or Parliament or a particular building or official chamber that Stanlow might have vacated. It assumes that Stanlow's absence from "here" means that he has left the country. Next, Johnson dates Richard's reply as coming after the close of Parliament on April 9, 1446, because Richard's text uses the phrase "the same Parliament" rather than "this same Parliament." Johnson argues that Richard would have employed the latter locution had Parliament still been in session when he wrote. Both interpretations are possible but far from conclusive, particularly if the document in its extant version is scribal rather than holograph. However, for my purposes it is not necessary to date Richard's reply exactly, nor even Moleyns's accusations. The purport of the latter can scarcely have been unknown to Richard before they were made public, and Richard's charge that Moleyns had conspired against him in Normandy some months earlier suggests that he had a good idea of Moleyns's position well in advance of his return to England and the eventual production of documents.

12. The member of Parliament for Bristol who submitted the petition, Thomas Young, received from Richard, also in 1451, the manor of Easton in Somerset. Young had been an attorney for Richard while the latter was in Ireland during the previous two or three years. Bean observes that Richard's relationship with Young indicates that Richard himself suggested the parliamentary petition (198). Young was sent to the Tower briefly for his petition.

13. In his introduction to Barnardiston's edition, Norman Scarfe summarizes the reasons that Serjeantson did not assign the "Dialogue" to Bokenham and explains why he believes it is now safe to do so. He also claims that the manuscript "on internal evidence . . . can only have been finished in 1460" (xiii) but does not specify what the evidence is and was unable to

supply any in response to my request. Some scholars suggest that perhaps Richard did not publicly rely on the Lionel of Clarence ancestry until his 1460 appeal to Parliament for recognition of his claim. But Griffiths writes that genealogies displaying Richard's descent from Lionel began to appear as early as 1455–58 and that York's circle may have encouraged their dissemination ("Sense of Dynasty," 35, n. 57). Moreover, the "Dialogue" might anticipate Richard in this, since the priory's own history was closely connected with Lionel. In the absence of contrary evidence, I believe the 1456 date can stand.

In 1538 the house was suppressed and sold into private hands. Mrs. Barnardiston grew up in it in this century, and in 1953 it was sold back to the Augustinians, who occupy it now.

14. This figure is an average. The authors point out that during the eleventh and twelfth centuries, the proportion of female saints was substantially lower but began to increase in the thirteenth century, peaking in the fifteenth at 27.7 percent. Jane Schulenburg confirms the lower figures for the earlier period. Of the 2680 names of historically authenticated saints constituting her sample, 324, or 14.6 percent, were women ("Sexism"). For the period from 1588 to the present, men outnumbered women by two to one (Woodward, 337). Woodward adds that this ratio has changed in recent years because many women founders of religious orders have been nominated.

15. The story is discussed by Beaune, 41–44. I thank Craig Taylor of Worcester College, Oxford, for directing me to her book. Beaune points out that the story appears in the work of William of Malmesbury and several French chroniclers and that in some later versions, Charles the Fat is replaced with Charles the Bald and the female-descent theme omitted. Beaune's chapter 9 provides a thorough review of the evolution of Salic law.

Unfortunately, Beaune mistakes some of the participants, identifying the proposed candidate as "Louis the Child, Lothaire's grandson through the female line" (41). As any genealogy shows, Louis the Child was the son of Arnulf (who succeeded Charles) and the grandson of Carloman, that is, not in the line of Louis at all and not entitled through the female line. The correct lineage is given in Riché, 226.

The Latin document is also briefly discussed by Rigg in "The Legend of Hugh Capet." Rigg is unaware of the Vision of Charles the Fat (cf. 402) and, since he anachronistically refers to "Salic law" as a fourteenth-century phenomenon, also seems unaware of the history of this legend.

16. Perhaps this argument was not used more often because it is so weak. The author of *Fluxo* has both facts and dates wrong. In fact, Matilda was recognized as the heir to Henry I in 1127, but she was an unpopular candidate, for a number of reasons. When Henry died in 1135, the barons switched their allegiance to her cousin Stephen. After a period of armed conflict, Matilda recovered the throne, but she was as unpopular a queen as she was an heir and lost all support. Eventually she withdrew in favor of her son Henry, who in 1153 was recognized as the heir. After Matilda, there was no queen regnant in England until Mary Tudor.

17. I am indebted to Judd for the manuscript references. The manuscripts are Bodleian Ashmole 1114 XI, BL Cotton Tiberius b.XII, and BL Harleian 4763. I have consulted all three, and my paraphrases, quotations, and references are to the Ashmolean unless otherwise specified. Harley 4763 has a beautiful "Arbor de successione regum Franciae" (f. 33a) and a genealogy that shows John of Gaunt but omits Lionel as a son of Edward III. Both Harley and Cotton are impressive-looking documents with many elaborate calligraphic designs.

18. Giesey comments that "of course [Fortescue] did not allege the Salic law" (18, n. 57). However, the arguments of contemporary French theoreticians, especially those of the *avocat du roi* Jean de Terre Rouge (cf. Potter, 244–49) earlier in the century, are quite similar to Fortescue's. Since Fortescue was extremely well read in current legal theory, he doubtless knew Jean's work.

19. In the Douay translation of the Vulgate, 1 Samuel is known as 1 Kings. Even though

its translation is literal, most modern bibles prudishly offer some such equivalent to the Latin phrase as "one male descendant" (Revised Standard Version) or "a single mother's son" (New English Bible).

20. The, or an, earlier version is BL Lansdowne 204, "rythmo Anglicano composita" on vellum, still unedited. Ms. Harley 661—revised, compressed, extended chronologically, and also in Troilus stanzas—may be a presentation copy to Edward IV. Along with an early printed edition, it is the basis for the edition by Ellis. Besides Edward, Hardyng also addresses at various times Henry VI and Richard, duke of York. For a review of the various manuscripts, see Edwards, "Manuscripts and Texts."

21. See Battaglia, who points out, as "a very neglected fact of the country's early history," the survival of matrilineal culture in Britain through the ninth century; among other sources are notices in Bede.

Chapter 8

1. The genealogy appears in "An Exact Exposition of the Orthodox Faith," 4.14, translated by Frederic H. Chase Jr. as John of Damascus, *Writings*. The text was owned by the Austins at York and also by the Carmelite Friars in London and Norwich (see Humphreys). Bokenham also mentions "ierom," perhaps one of the apocryphal gospels then erroneously attributed to St. Jerome or perhaps the saint's (genuine) commentary on Matthew—which does take up the question of patrilineal genealogy in Matthew 1:3 ff. but mentions neither Anne nor Mary.

2. See Brandenbarg; Gibson, 82–84. Ashley and Sheingorn write that "due chiefly to the *Legenda Aurea*, the late medieval Jesus is most significantly a product of a matrilineal descent system, rather than the patrilineal one of the Gospels" (17) but this seems to me to misrepresent Voragine's chapter "De nativitate beatae Mariae virginis," on which I have relied.

3. As with any rebellion, loyalties were not as clear-cut as my quotation might suggest. Griffiths provides a convenient and more nuanced summary: "At the moment of crisis in 1450, London had proved equivocal in its loyalty to Henry VI. Many of the inhabitants were ready to join the rebels and shared their common grievances. It was obvious to the king that they could not be trusted and hence he withdrew to the midlands; this simply had the effect of quickly handing the city over to the rebels and their sympathizers—but only for a few days, until mob rule showed itself for the destructive force it usually was in the later middle ages" (*Reign*, 628).

Chapter 9

1. Weinstein and Bell's chap. 7, including tabulated breakdowns by class, show a majority of about three to one in the proportion of wealthier groups, both lay and ecclesiastical, to poorer ones.

2. It is important to observe the extreme caution and tentativeness with which psychologists report their experimental findings in the areas of sex, pornography, aggression, and violence—qualities usually ignored by ultrafeminists, who often make large and sweeping statements not actually supported by the experiments they cite. What psychologists do appear to agree on is that pornography alone is not a determinative factor in rape or other violence; other factors, such as economic deprivation, anger, frustration, or a history of abuse, carry far more weight. The instance of Scandinavia seems ambiguous at the moment, but that of Japan evidently shows the possible coexistence of uncensored pornography and a low incidence of rape. See Diamond; Russell.

3. It is a curious fact that many of the contributors to the Robertson–Benson collection state or assume that Chaucer's religious tales are, ipso facto, excellent versions, superior to others in narrative interest and literary art. They are not necessarily. The contributors fail to take a diacritical comparative view in their assertions. Revealingly, there appears to be only one reference to Voragine in the entire collection (even though he would not be an instance of superior narrative technique) and none to any other hagiographers.

4. Full title: "The declaracion made by John Fortescu, Knyght, upon certayn wrytinges sent oute of Scotteland, ayenst the Kinges title to the Roialme of Englond." To simplify the general outline, I left out of my account the important issue of the Treaty of Troyes (1420), according to which Henry V was designated "heres et regens regni franciae." It was through this treaty that Henry VI henceforth claimed France, and not through female descent, which French custom would not have recognized. In any case, Henry was not Isabel's heir; rather, the descendants of Lionel were. Thus the Fortescue persona is able, in the "Declaracion," to exclaim (with a surprise I find hard to credit) that at last he understands "how grete nede the councell of the laste Kynge Henry hadd to wryte ayene the title of the enherytaunce of women . . . ; for els by that title the Kynge our soverayne lorde [Edward IV] myght have distroyd inevitably the title whiche the sayd late Kynge hadd in the Roialme of Fraunce" (531). In other words, the Lancastrian dilemma was that the female succession that they denied the Yorkists constituted their own claim to France. By providing a different ground for the claim to France, the Treaty of Troyes solved this problem, freeing the Lancastrians to propagandize against female rule and transmission of rule. Some visual and verbal propaganda consequences of the treaty are discussed by J. W. McKenna.

5. Gregory was a member of the Skinners Company and mayor of London in 1451; he died in 1466. The incident is narrated in several other chronicles, as well as in records of official inquiries into the two deaths. Griffiths refers to the women's action—which also included pinning the parish constables to the ground to prevent their intervention—as "brutal vengeance . . . excess of misplaced female zeal," even though the widow was bludgeoned with a hatchet and dismembered with a knife ("Breton Spy").

6. The incident is narrated in Robert Blondel's *De Reductione Normannie,* in *Narratives,* ed. Stevenson, 206–7. The narration includes (the chronicler's version of) Mrs. Lampet's speech to the troops.

Bibliography

Manuscripts

Bodleian (Oxford) Ashmole 1114 (XI)
British Library Additional 36983
British Library Additional 11814
British Library Arundel 327
British Library Cotton Domitian A. XI
British Library Cotton Tiberius B. XII
British Library Egerton 3031
British Library Harley 661
British Library Harley 4763
British Library Lansdowne 204
Cambridge University Library Dd. XI. 45

Editions and Translations of Works Certainly or Probably by Bokenham

Aspland, Alfred, ed. *The Golden Legend: A Reproduction from a Copy in the Manchester Free Library.* London: Wyman, 1878.
Barnardiston, Katherine W. "Dialogue at the Grave." In *Clare Priory: Seven Centuries of a Suffolk House.* Ed. Katherine W. Barnardiston. Cambridge: W. Heffer & Sons, 1962.
Bokenham, Osbern. *The Lyvys of Seyntys.* London: W. Nichol, for the Roxburghe Club, 1835.
Delany, Sheila, trans. *A Legend of Holy Women.* Notre Dame, Ind.: University of Notre Dame Press, 1992.
Flügel, Ewald, ed. "Eine Mittelenglische Claudian-setzung (1445)." *Anglia: Zeitschrift für englische Philologie* 28 (1905): 255–99, 421–38.
Horstmann, Carl, ed. "*Mappula Angliae* von Osbern Bokenham." *Englische Studien* 10 (1887): 1–34.
———. *Osbern Bokenams Legenden.* Heilbronn: Altenglische Bibliothek, 1883.
Roxburghe Club. *The Lyvys of Seyntys.* London: W. Nicol, 1835.
Serjeantson, Mary, ed. *Legendys of Hooly Wummen.* EETS o.s. 206 (1938).

Other Printed Sources

See the list of abbreviations in the front matter.

Allan, Alison R. "Political Propaganda Employed by the House of York in England in the Mid-Fifteenth Century." Ph.D. diss., Swansea University College, 1981.

———. "Yorkist Propaganda: Pedigree, Prophecy and the 'British History' in the Reign of Edward IV." In *Patronage, Pedigree and Power in the Later Middle Ages.* Ed. Charles Ross. Gloucester: Sutton, 1979.

Allen, Hope Emily. "The *Manuel des Pechiez* and the Scholastic Prologue." *Romanic Review* 8 (1977): 434–62.

Allen, Judson B. *The Ethical Poetic of the Later Middle Ages: A Decorum of Convenient Distinction.* Toronto: University of Toronto Press, 1982.

———. *The Friar as Critic.* Nashville, Tenn.: Vanderbilt University Press, 1971.

Allmand, C.T. *Lancastrian Normandy, 1415–1450: The History of a Medieval Occupation.* Oxford: Clarendon Press, 1983.

Ancelet-Hustache, Jeanne. "Les 'Vitae Sororum' d'Unterlingen." *Archives d'histoire doctrinale et littéraire du moyen age* 5 (1930): 317–517.

Anderson, Marjorie. "Alice Chaucer and Her Husbands." *PMLA* 60 (1945): 24–47.

Ashley, Kathleen, and Pamela Sheingorn, eds. *Interpreting Cultural Symbols: Saint Anne in Late Medieval Society.* Athens: University of Georgia Press, 1990.

Atkinson, Clarissa W. *Mystic and Pilgrim: The Book and the World of Margery Kempe.* Ithaca, N.Y.: Cornell University Press, 1983.

Audelay, John. *The Poems of John Audelay.* Ed. Ella Keats Whiting. EETS o.s. 184, 1931.

Auerbach, Erich. *Literary Language and Its Public in Late Latin Antiquity and in the Middle Ages.* New York: Pantheon, 1965.

Augustine. *On Christian Doctrine.* Trans. D. W. Robertson Jr. York: Liberal Arts Press, 1958.

———. *The City of God.* Trans. Marcus Dods. New York: Random House, 1950.

———. *Confessions.* New York: Airmont, 1969.

———. *De Genesi contra Manichaeos.* Trans. Roland J. Teske. Washington, D.C.: Catholic University of America Press, 1991.

———. *The Literal Meaning of Genesis.* Trans. John Hammond Taylor. 2 vols. New York: Newman Press, 1982.

———. *De Musica.* Trans. Robert Catesby Taliaferro. New York: Fathers of the Church ser., no. 4, 1947.

———. *Opera omnia.* Ed. J. Migne, *Patrologiae . . . Series Latina,* vol. 34. Paris: Garnier, 1844–80.

Aungier, George James. *The History and Antiquities of Syon Monastary.* London: J. B. Nichols, 1840.

Balic, Carlo. "The Mediaeval Controversy over the Immaculate Conception up to the Death of Scotus." In *The Dogma of the Immaculate Conception: History and Significance.* Ed. Edward D. O'Connor. Notre Dame, Ind.: University of Notre Dame Press, 1958.

Barfield, S. "Lord Fingall's Cartulary of Reading Abbey." *English Historical Review* 3 (1888).

Barkan, Leonard. *Nature's Work of Art: The Human Body as Image of the World.* New Haven, Conn.: Yale University Press, 1975.

Barnie, John. *War in Medieval Society: Social Values and the Hundred Years War 1337–99.* London: Weidenfeld and Nicolson, 1974.

Baron, Hans. *The Crisis of the Early Italian Renaissance.* Rev. ed. Princeton, N.J.: Princeton University Press, 1966.

———. *Humanistic and Political Literature in Florence and Venice at the Beginning of the Quattrocento.* Cambridge, Mass.: Harvard University Press, 1955; repr. New York: Russell & Russell, 1968.

Bartle, R. H. "A Study of Private Book Collections in England Between c. 1200 and the Early

Years of the Sixteenth Century with Special Reference to Books Belonging to Ecclesiastical Dignitaries." B. Litt. University of Oxford, 1956.

Battaglia, Frank. "The Matriliny of the Picts." *Mankind Quarterly* 31 (1990): 17–43.

Baybak, M., Paul Delany, and A. K. Hieatt. "Placement 'in the middest' in *The Faerie Queen.*" In *Silent Poetry.* Ed. Alastair Fowler. London: Routledge & Kegan Paul, 1970.

Bean, J. M. W. "The Financial Position of Richard, Duke of York." In *War and Government in the Middle Ages.* Ed. John Gillingham and J. C. Holt. Woodbridge, Suffolk: Boydell Press, 1984.

Beaune, Colette. *The Birth of an Ideology: Myths and Symbols of Nation in Late-Medieval France.* Berkeley: University of California Press, 1991.

Becker, M. Janet. *Blythburgh: An Essay on the Village and Its Church.* Halesworth, Suffolk: Denny, 1935.

Bennett, Michael. "John Audley: Some New Evidence on His Life and Work." *ChR* 16 (1982): 344–55.

Bethell, Denis. "The Making of a Twelfth-Century Relic Collection." In *Popular Belief and Practise.* Ed. G. J. Cuming and Derek Baker. Cambridge: Cambridge University Press, 1972.

Block, K. S., ed. *Ludus Coventriae.* EETS e.s. 120 (1922; repr.1960).

Bloom, Harold. *The Anxiety of Influence.* Oxford: Oxford University Press, 1973.

Boffey, Julia. "Manuscript Evidence for Chaucer's Early Readers." Paper given at the New Chaucer Society Congress, Seattle, 1992.

Bolgar, R. R. *The Classical Heritage and Its Beneficiaries.* Cambridge: Cambridge University Press, 1963.

Bornstein, Diane. *The Middle English Translation of Christine de Pisan's Livre du Corps de Policie.* Heidelberg: Carl Winter, 1977.

Boureau, Alain. *La Légende doreé: Le Système narratif de Jacques de Voragine (+1298).* Paris: Éditions du cerf, 1984.

Bozon, Nicholas. "Saints' Lives Attributed to Nicholas Bozon." Ed. Mary R. Learned. *Franciscan Studies* 4 (1944): 79–88, 171–78, 267–71.

———. *Seven More Poems by Nicholas Bozon.* Ed. M. Amelia Klenke. St. Bonaventure, N.Y.: Franciscan Institute; Louvain: E. Nauwelaerts, 1951.

———. *Three Saints' Lives by Nicholas Bozon.* Ed. M. Amelia Klenke. St. Bonaventure, N.Y.: Franciscan Institute, 1947.

Brandenbarg, Ton. "St. Anne and Her Family." In *Saints and She-Devils: Images of Women in the 15th and 16th Centuries.* London: Rubicon, 1987.

Brewer, Derek. "Two Notes on the Augustinian and Possibly West Midland Origin of the Ancren Riwle." *Notes and Queries* 3 (1956): 232–35.

Brie, F., ed. *Brut.* In E.E.T.S. o.s., 131, 136 (1906; repr. 1960).

Briggs, Charles Fairbanks. "The English Manuscripts of Giles of Rome's *De Regimine Principum* and Their Audience, 1300–1500." Ph.D. diss., University of North Carolina at Chapel Hill, 1993.

Brown, Elizabeth, A. R. "Death and the Human Body in the Later Middle Ages: The Legislation of Boniface VIII on the Division of the Corpse." *Viator* 12 (1981): 221–70.

Brown, Peter. *The Body and Society: Men, Women and Sexual Renunciation in Early Christianity.* New York: Columbia University Press, 1988.

———. *The Cult of the Saints.* Chicago: University of Chicago Press, 1981.

Brownlee, Kevin. "Martyrdom and the Female Voice: Saint Christine in the *Cité des dames.*" In *Images of Sainthood in Medieval Europe.* Ed. Renate Blumenfeld-Kosinski and Timea Szell. Ithaca, N.Y.: Cornell University Press, 1991.

Bulatkin, Eleanor Webster. "The Arithmetic Structure of the Old-French *Vie de Saint Alexis.*" *PMLA* 74 (1959): 495–502.

Burney, E. "The English Rule in Normandy, 1435–1450." B. Litt., University of Oxford, 1968.

Burridge, A. W. "L'Immaculée Conception dans la théologie de l'Angleterre médiévale." *Revue d'histoire ecclésiastique* 32 (1936): 570–97.

Bynum, Caroline Walker. "Bodily Miracles and the Resurrection of the Body in the High Middle Ages." In *Belief in History: Innovative Approaches to European and American Religion.* Ed. Thomas Kselman. Notre Dame, Ind.: University of Notre Dame Press, 1991.

———. *Holy Feast and Holy Fast: The Religious Significance of Food to Medieval Women.* Berkeley: University of California Press, 1987.

———. "Introduction: the Complexity of Symbols" and ". . . And Woman His Humanity: Female Imagery in the Religious Writing of the Later Middle Ages." Both in *Gender and Religion: On the Complexity of Symbols.* Ed. Caroline Walker Bynum, Steven Harrell, and Paula Richman. Boston: Beacon Press, 1986.

———. "Material Continuity, Personal Survival and the Resurrection of the Body: A Scholastic Discussion in Its Medieval and Modern Contexts." In *Fragmentation and Redemption: Essays on Gender and the Human Body in Medieval Religion.* Ed. Carolyn Bynum. New York: Zone Books, 1991.

Calendarium romanum. Rome: Libreria Editrice Vaticana, 1969.

Cam, Helen. *Liberties and Communities in Medieval England.* London: Merlin, 1963.

Cameron, Alan. *Claudian: Poetry and Propaganda at the Court of Honorius.* Oxford: Clarendon Press, 1970.

Cameron, Louis, ed. *The Commonplace Book of Robert Reynes of Acle.* New York: Garland Press, 1980.

Campbell, P. G. C. "Christine de Pisan en Engleterre." *Revue de litterature comparée* 5 (1925): 659–70.

Capgrave, John. *The Chronicle of England.* Ed. F. C. Hingeston. London: Longman, Brown, Green, 1858.

———. *The Life of St. Katherine of Alexandria.* Ed. Carl Horstmann. EETS o.s. 100 (1893).

———. *The Life of St. Norbert (1393–1464).* Ed. Cyril Smetana. Toronto: PIMS, 1977.

———. *Lives of St. Augustine and St. Gilbert of Sempringham.* Ed. J. J. Munro. EETS o.s. 140, 1910; repr. New York: Kraus, 1971.

Carolus-Barré, Louis. "Une nouveau parchemin amulette." *Comtes rendus de l'Académie des inscriptions et belles lettres* (1970).

Catholicon anglicum. An English–Latin Wordbook Dated 1483. Ed. Sidney Herrtage. EETS o.s. 75 (1881).

Cavanaugh, Susan H. "A Study of Books Privately Owned in England, 1300–1450." Ph.D. diss., University of Pennsylvania, 1980.

Cave, C. J. P. *Roof Bosses on Medieval Churches: An Aspect of Gothic Sculpture.* Cambridge: Cambridge University Press, 1948.

Chadwick, Henry. "Origen, Celsus, and the Resurrection of the Body." *Harvard Theological Review* 41 (1948): 83–102.

Champion, Pierre. *La Dame de beauté: Agnès Sorel.* Paris: Champion, 1931.

Chastellain, Georges. *Chronique.* In *Oeuvres.* Ed. Kervyn de Lettenhove. 7 vols. Brussels, 1863–65.

Chatillon, F., ed. *Le Songe du vergier.* In *Revue du moyen age latin* 13 (1957).

Chaucer, Geoffrey. *The Riverside Chaucer.* Ed. Larry Benson. Oxford: Oxford University Press, 1990.

Chesney, Katherine. "Two Manuscripts of Christine de Pisan." *Medium Aevum* 1 (1932): 35–41.

Childs, Herbert Ellsworth. "A Study of the Unique Middle English Translation of the *De*

Regimine Principum of Aegidius Romanus." Ph.D. diss., University of Washington, 1932.

Chrimes, S. B. *English Constitutional Ideas in the Fifteenth Century.* Cambridge: Cambridge University Press, 1936.

———. *Lancastrians, Yorkists and Henry VII.* London: Macmillan, 1964.

Clark, J. P. H. "Image and Likeness in Walter Hilton." *Downside Review* 97 (1979): 204–20.

———. "Late Fourteenth Century Cambridge Theology and the English Contemplative Tradition." In *The Medieval Mystical Tradition in England.* Ed. Marion Glasscoe. Cambridge: D. S. Brewer, 1992.

Clasby, Eugene. "Chaucer's Constance: Womanly Virtue and the Heroic Life." *ChR* 13 (1979): 221–72.

Clay, Rotha Mary. *The Medieval Hospitals of England.* London: Cass, 1909; repr. New York: Barnes & Noble, 1966.

Clémence of Barking. *Life of St. Catherine.* Ed. William McBain. Anglo-Norman Text Society, no. 18. Oxford: Blackwell, 1964.

Clermont, Thomas F. Lord, ed. *The Works of Sir John Fortescue, Knight.* 2 vols., London: 1869.

Cleve, Gunnel. "Margery Kempe: A Scandinavian Influence in Medieval England?" In *The Medieval Mystical Tradition in England.* Ed. Marion Glasscoe. Cambridge: D. S. Brewer, 1992.

Clover, Carol J. "Her Body, Himself: Gender in the Slasher Film." *Representations* 20 (1987): 83–99.

———. *Men, Women, and Chainsaws. Gender in the Modern Horror Film.* Princeton, N.J.: Princeton University Press, 1992.

Coleman, Janet. *English Literature in History, 1350–1400: Medieval Readers and Writers.* London: Hutchison, 1981.

Colledge, Edmund, ed. *A Book of Showings to the Anchoress Julian of Norwich.* Toronto: PIMS, 1978.

Connolly, Thomas. *Mourning into Joy. Music, Raphael, and Saint Cecelia.* New Haven, Conn.: Yale University Press, 1994.

Conroy, Kenneth C. "A Glossary of John Trevisa's Translation of the *De Regimine Principum* of Aegidius Romanus." Ph.D. diss., University of Washington, 1964.

Constable, W. G. "Some East Anglian Rood Screen Paintings." *Connoisseur* 84 (1929): 141–7, 211–20, 290–3, 358–63.

Cooke, William. *The College or Chantry of Denston.* London: Dent, 1924; repr. 1961.

Cornelis, H., ed. *The Resurrection of the Body.* Notre Dame, Ind.: Fides Publishers, 1964.

Cornelius, Roberta D. *The Figurative Castle.* Oxford: Oxford University Press, 1930.

Cotton, Simon. "Mediaeval Roodscreens in Norfolk—Their Construction and Painting Dates." *Norfolk Archaeology* 40 (1987): 44–54.

Courtenay, William J. *Schools and Scholars in Fourteenth Century England.* Princeton, N.J.: Princeton University Press, 1987.

Coville, A. *Evrart de Trémaugon et le songe du vergier.* Paris: Droz, 1933.

Curley, Michael J. "Fifteenth-Century Glosses on *The Prophecy of John of Bridlington*: A Text, Its Meaning and Its Purpose." *Medieval Studies* 46 (1984): 321–39.

Curtius, Ernst R. *European Literature and the Latin Middle Ages.* New York: Pantheon, 1953.

d'Ancona, Mirella Levi. *The Iconography of the Immaculate Conception in the Middle Ages and Early Renaissance.* College Art Association of America, 1957.

d'Ardenne, S. R. T. O., and E. J. Dobson, eds. *Seinte Katerine.* EETS 7 (1981).

Darnton, Robert. "Sex for Thought." *New York Review of Books,* December 2, 1994, pp. 65–74.

Day, Dorothy. *The Long Loneliness: The Autobiography of Dorothy Day.* New York: Harper & Row, 1952.

de Gaiffier, Baudouin. "La Mort par le glaive dans les passions des martyrs." *Subsidia hagiographica* 52 (1971): 70–96.

de Herkenrode, Léon. "Une amulette." *Le Bibliophile belge* 4 (1847): 2–23.

Delany, Sheila. "Alibis." *Event* 22 (winter 1993/94): 12–16.

———. "Bokenham's 'Claudian' as Yorkist Propaganda." *Journal of Medieval History* (1996): 83–96.

———. *The Naked Text: Chaucer's Legend of Good Women*. Berkeley: University of California Press, 1994.

———. "Techniques of Alienation in *Troilus and Criseyde*." In *Chaucer's Troilus and Criseyde: Current Essays in Criticism*. Ed. R. A. Shoaf. Binghamton: CEMERS, 1992.

———. *Writing Woman: Women Writers and Women in Literature, Medieval to Modern*. New York: Schocken Books, 1983.

Delehaye, Hippolyte. *Les Passions des martyrs et les genres litteraires*. Brussels: Société des bollandistes, 1920; repr. 1966.

Derrida, Jacques. *Of Grammatology*. Baltimore: Johns Hopkins University Press, 1976.

———. *Specters of Marx*. New York: Routledge, 1994.

Desmond, Marilynn. "Bernard Silvestris and the *Corpus* of the *Aeneid*." In *The Classics in the Middle Ages*. Ed. A. Bernardo and S. Levin. Binghamton: CEMERS, 1990.

Dewart, Joanne. *Death and Resurrection*. Wilmington, Del.: Michael Glazier, 1986.

Diamond, Irene. "Pornography and Repression: A Reconsideration." In *Take Back the Night: Women and Pornography*. Ed. Laura Lederer. New York: Morrow, 1980.

Dickinson, J. C. *The Origins of the Austin Canons and Their Introduction into England*. London: SPCK, 1950.

Dobson, E. J. *The Origins of Ancrene Wisse*. Oxford: Clarendon Press, 1976.

Doig, James A. "Political Communication and Public Opinion in Lancastrian England, 1399–1450." Master's thesis, Swansea University College, 1975.

Douglas, David C. *The Social Structure of Medieval East Anglia*. Oxford: Clarendon Press, 1927; repr. New York: Octagon, 1974.

Douglas, Mary. *Purity and Danger: An Analysis of Concepts of Pollution and Taboo*. London: Routledge & Kegan Paul, 1966.

Dowsing, William. *The Journal of William Dowsing, Parliamentary Visitor*. Woodbridge: R. Loder, 1786; repr. London: John W. Parker, 1844.

Drake, Maurice, and Wilfred Drake. *Saints and Their Emblems*. London: Laurie, 1916.

DuBoulay, F. R. H. "The Fifteenth Century." In *The English Church and the Papacy in the Middle Ages*. Ed. C. H. Lawrence. New York: Fordham University Press, 1965.

Duffy, Eamon. "Holy Maydens. Holy Wyfes: The Cult of Women Saints in Fifteenth- and Sixteenth-Century England." In *Women in the Church*. Ed. W. J. Sheils and Diana Wood. Oxford: Blackwell, 1990.

———. *The Stripping of the Altars: Traditional Religion in England, c. 1400–c. 1580*. New Haven, Conn.: Yale University Press, 1992.

Edwards, A. S. G. "The Manuscripts and Texts of the Second Version of John Hardyng's *Chronicle*." In *England in the Fifteenth Century*. Ed. Daniel Williams. London: Boydell Press, 1987.

———. "The Transmission and Audience of Osbern Bokenham's *Legendys of Hooly Wummen*." In *Late-Medieval Religious Texts and Their Transmission*. Ed. A. J. Minnis. Woodbridge: Boydell and Brewer, 1994.

———. "Critical approaches to the *Man of Law's Tale*." In Elizabeth Robertson and C. David Benson, eds. *Chaucer's Religious Tales*. Cambridge: D. S. Brewer, 1990.

Ferguson, John. *English Diplomacy, 1422–1461*. Oxford: Clarendon Press, 1972.

Festugière, A. J. "De la doctrine 'origéniste' du corps glorieux sphéroïde." *Revue des sciences philosophes et théologiques* 43 (1959): 81–86.

Fetterley, Judith. *The Resisting Reader: A Feminist Approach to American Fiction.* Bloomington: Indiana University Press, 1978.

Fisher, John. "A Language Policy for Lancastrian England." *PMLA* 107 (1992): 1168–80.

Förster, Max. "Die Burghsche Cato-Paraphrase." *Archiv für das Studium der neueren Sprachen und Litteraturen* 115 (1905): 298–323.

Fortescue, John. *The Works of Sir John Fortescue, Knight.* Ed. Thomas F. Lord Clermont. 2 vols. London: Chiswick, 1869.

———. *De Laudibus legum angliae.* Ed. and trans. S. B. Chrimes. Cambridge: Cambridge University Press, 1949.

Foucault, Michel. "Nietzsche, Genealogy, History." In *Language, Counter-Memory, Practice.* Ed. D. F. Bouchard. Ithaca, N.Y.: Cornell University Press, 1977.

Fox, Denton. "Chaucer's Influence on Fifteenth Century Poetry." In *Companion to Chaucer Studies.* Ed. Beryl Rowland. New York: Oxford University Press, 1979.

Fradenburg, Louise O. "Chaucer and the Middle Scots: Studies in Chaucerian Reception." Ph.D. diss., University of Virginia, 1982.

Fredeman, Jane. "The Life of John Capgrave, O.E.S.A. 1393–1464." *Augustiniana* 29 (1979): 197–237.

Freud, Sigmund. "Family Romances." *Sigmund Freud on Sexuality.* Harmondsworth: Penguin, 1977.

Froissart, Jean. *Des Croniques de france, d'angleterre. . . .* 4 vols. Paris: Anthoine Verard, 1498.

Furnivall, F. J., ed. *Political, Religious, and Love Poems.* EETS o.s. 15 (1866; repr. 1965).

Gairdner, James, ed. "Gregory's Chronicle." In *Collections of a London Citizen.* London: Camden Society 17 (1876).

Garth, Helen Meredith. *Saint Mary Magdalene in Medieval Literature.* Baltimore: John Hopkins University Press, 1950.

Gascoigne, Thomas. *Loci e libro veritatum.* Ed. James E. Thorold Rogers. Oxford: Clarendon Press, 1881.

Geary, Patrick J. *Furta Sacra: Thefts of Relics in the Central Middle Ages.* Princeton, N.J.: Princeton University Press, 1978.

Gellrich, Jesse. *The Idea of the Book in the Middle Ages.* Ithaca, N.Y.: Cornell University Press, 1985.

Genette, Gérard. *Palimpsestes: La Littérature au second degré.* Paris: Éditions du Seuil, 1982.

Gerould, Gordon Hall. *Saints' Legends.* Boston: Houghton Mifflin, 1916.

Gibson, Gail McMurray. *The Theater of Devotion: East Anglian Drama and Society in the Late Middle Ages.* Chicago: University of Chicago Press, 1989.

Giesey, Ralph E. "The Juristic Basis of Dynastic Right to the French Throne." *Transactions of the American Philosophical Society* 51 (1961): 3–44.

Giles of Rome. *Errores philosophorum.* Trans. John O. Riedl. Milwaukee: Marquette University Press, 1944.

———. *De Regimine principum.* Ed. Charles F. Briggs and David Fowler. 2 vols. New York: Garland Press, 1994, 1996. Original ed.: Rome: Stephanus Planck, 1482. Columbia University Special Collections.

Gill, Joseph. *The Council of Florence.* Cambridge: Cambridge University Press, 1959.

Gill, Paul E. "Politics and Propaganda in Fifteenth-Century England: The Polemical Writings of Sir John Fortescue." *Speculum* 46 (1971): 333–47.

Gillespie, Vincent. "Idols and Images: Pastoral Adaptations of *The Scale of Perfection.*" In

Langland: Cambridge Mystics and the Medieval English Tradition. Ed. Helen Phillips. Cambridge: D. S. Brewer, 1940.

Gilson, Etienne. *Christian Philosophy in the Middle Ages.* London: Sheed and Ward, 1955.

Goody, Jack. *The Development of the Family and Marriage in Europe.* Cambridge: Cambridge University Press, 1983.

Gorges, Raymond. "Sir Theobald Gorges, Knight Banneret, 1401–1470." *Proceedings of the Somersetshire Archaeological and Natural History Society* 79 (1933): 64–69.

Görlach, Manfred. *The South English Legendary, Gilte Legende and Golden Legend.* Braunschweig: Universität Carolo-Wilhelmina, 1972.

Gorman, Peter. *Pythagoras: A Life.* London: Routledge, 1979.

Gottfried, Robert S. *Bury St. Edmunds and the Urban Crisis: 1290–1539.* Princeton, N.J.: Princeton University Press, 1982.

Gower, John. *The Major Latin Works of John Gower.* Ed. Eric Stockton. Seattle: University of Washington Press, 1962.

Gransden, Antonia. *Historical Writing in England.* 2 vols. London: Routledge, 1982.

———. "Politics and Historiography During the Wars of the Roses." In *Medieval Historical Writing in the Christian and Islamic Worlds.* Ed. D. O. Morgan. London: University of London Press, 1982.

Gray, H. L. "English Foreign Trade from 1446 to 1482." In *Studies in English Trade in the Fifteenth Century.* Ed. Eileen Power and M. M. Postan. London: Routledge, 1933.

Greatrex, Joan G. "Thomas Rudborne, Monk of Winchester and the Council of Florence." In *Schism, Heresy and Religious Protest.* Ed. Derek Baker. Cambridge: Cambridge University Press, 1972.

Greenblatt, Stephen. "Invisible Bullets: Renaissance Authority and Its Subversion." In *Political Shakespeare: New Essays in Cultural Materialism.* Ed. Jonathan Dollimore and Alan Sinfield. Manchester: Manchester University Press, 1985.

Griffiths, Ralph A. "A Breton Spy in London, 1425–29." Orig. in *Annales de Bretagne et de l'ouest* 86 (1979): 399–403. Repr. in Ralph A. Griffiths, *King and Country: England and Wales in the Fifteenth Century.* London: Hambledon Press, 1991.

———. "Duke Richard of York's Intentions in 1450 and the Origins of the Wars of the Roses." *Journal of Medieval History* 1 (1975): 187–210.

———. *The Reign of King Henry VI: The Exercise of Royal Authority, 1422–1461.* London: Benn, 1981.

———. "The Sense of Dynasty in the Reign of Henry VI." In *Patronage, Pedigree and Power in Later Medieval England.* Ed. Charles Ross. Gloucester: Sutton, 1979.

———. "The Trial of Eleanor Cobham." *Bulletin of the John Rylands Library* 51 (1969): 381–99; repr. in *King and Country.*

Grisdale, D. M., ed. *Three Middle English Sermons from the Worcester Chapter Manuscript F.10.* Leeds: Titus Wilson, 1939.

Gwynn, Aubrey. *The English Austin Friars in the Time of Wycliff.* Oxford: Oxford University Press, 1940.

Hackett, Benedict. *William Flete, O.S.A., and Catherine of Siena, Masters of Fourteenth Century Spirituality.* Villanova, Pa.: Augustinian Press, 1992.

Hackett, M. B. "Note on Bokenham." *Notes & Queries* 206 (1961): 246.

———. "The Seventh Centenary of the Great Union of Augustinians." *Irish Ecclesiastical Record* 87 (1957): 13–24.

Hale, D. G. *The Body Politic: A Political Metaphor in Renaissance English Literature.* The Hague: Mouton, 1971.

Hall, D. J. *English Medieval Pilgrimage.* London: Routledge & Kegan Paul, 1965.

Hammond, Eleanor, ed. "How the Lover Praiseth His Lady." *MP* 21 (1923–24): 379–95.

————, ed. "The Lover's Mass." *JEGP* 7 (1907–08): 95–104.

Hardyng, John. *Hardyng's Chronicle*. Ed. Henry Ellis. London: Woodfall, 1812.

Harper-Bill, Christopher, ed. *The Cartulary of the Augustinian Friars of Clare*. Woodbridge: Boydell Press for the Suffolk Records Society, 1991.

Harriss, G. L. *Cardinal Beaufort: A Study of Lancastrian Ascendancy and Decline*. Oxford: Clarendon Press, 1988.

————. "Marmaduke Lumley and the Crisis of 1446–9." In *Aspects of Late Medieval Government and Society: Essays Presented to J. R. Lander*. Ed. J. G. Rowe. Toronto: University of Toronto Press, 1986).

Harvey, Margaret. *England, Rome and the Papacy 1417–1464: The Study of a Relationship*. Manchester: Manchester University Press, 1993.

Hatcher, Anna Granville. "The Old-French Poem St. Alexis: A Mathematical Demonstration." *Traditio* 8 (1952): 112–58.

Heffernan, Thomas. *Sacred Biography*. New York: Oxford University Press, 1988.

Heinzmann, Richard. *Die Unsterblichkeit der Seele und die Auferstehung des Liebes*. Munster: Aschendorffsche Verlagsbuchhandlung, 1965.

Herrmann-Mascard, Nicole. *Les Reliques des saints*. Paris: Klinckseick, 1975.

Hewson, M. Anthony. *Giles of Rome and the Medieval Theory of Conception: A Study of the De Formatione corporis humani in utero*. London: Athlone Press, 1975.

Hexter, Ralph J. *Ovid and Medieval Schooling: Studies in the Medieval School Commentaries*. Munich: Arbeo-Gesellschaft, 1986.

Higden, Ranulf. *Polychronicon*. London: Longman, 1865–86.

Hill, Christopher. *Puritanism and Revolution*. London: Secker and Warburg, 1958.

Hilton, Walter. *The Ladder of Perfection*. Trans. Leo Sherley-Price. Penguin, 1988.

Hoepffner, E., and P. Alfaric, eds. *La Chanson de Sainte Foy*. 2 vols. Paris: Société d'édition, 1926.

Holmes, G. A. "The 'Libel of English Policy.'" *EHR* 76 (1961): 193–216.

Holmes, George. *The Florentine Enlightenment, 1400–50*. New York: Pegasus, 1969.

Hopper, Vincent Foster. *Medieval Number Symbolism: Its Sources, Meaning, and Influence on Thought and Expression*. New York: Columbia University Press, 1938.

Horrall, Sarah M. *The Lyf of Oure Lady. The M.E. Translation of Thomas of Hales'* Vita. Heidelberg: Carl Winter, 1985.

Horstmann, Carl. *The Lives of Women Saints of Our Contrie of England*. EETS o.s. 86 (1896); repr. New York: Kraus, 1973.

Hugh of St. Victor. *The Didascalicon . . . A Medieval Guide to the Arts*. Trans. Jerome Taylor. New York: Columbia University Press, 1968.

Hughes, Jonathan. *Pastors and Visionaries. Religion and Secular Life in Late Medieval Yorkshire*. Woodbridge: Boydell Press, 1988.

Humphreys, K. W., ed. *The Friars' Libraries*. London: British Library, 1990.

Hunt, Lynn. ed. *The Invention of Pornography: Obscenity and the Origins of Modernity, 1500–1800*. New York: Zone Books, 1993.

Hurry, Jamieson B. *Reading Abbey*. London: Elliot Stock, 1901.

Husenbeth, F. C. *Emblems of Saints*. Norwich: Norwich Archaeological Society, 1882.

Hutchison, Ann M. "Devotional Reading in the Monastery and the Late Medieval Household." In *De Cella in Seculum: Religious and Secular Life and Devotion in Late Medieval England*. Ed. Michael G. Sargent. Cambridge: D. S. Brewer, 1989.

Jacob, E. F. *Essays in the Conciliar Epoch*. 1st ed. Manchester: Manchester University Press, 1943; rev. ed. Notre Dame, Ind.: University of Notre Dame Press, 1963.

————. *The Fifteenth Century, 1399–1485*. Oxford: Oxford University Press, 1961; repr. 1993.

Jacquart, Danielle, and Claude Thomasset. *Sexuality and Medicine in the Middle Ages*. Paris: Presses Universitaires Françaises, 1985; Cambridge: Polity Press, 1988.

James, Mervyn. "Ritual, Drama and Social Body in the Late Middle English Town." *Past & Present* 98 (1983): 3–29.

James, M. R. *The Apocryphal New Testament: Being the Apocryphal Gospels, Acts, Epistles, and Apocalypses*. 1st ed., 1924, corrected, 1980. Oxford: Clarendon Press.

———. "The Catalogue of the Library of the Augustinian Friars at York." *Fasciculus J. W. Clark Dicatus*. Cambridge University, 1909.

———. *Henry the Sixth: A Reprint of John Blacman's Memoir*. Cambridge: Heffer, 1919.

Jankofsky, Klaus. "National Characteristics in the Portrayal of English Saints in the *South English Legendary*." In *Images in Sainthood in Medieval Europe*. Ed. Renate Blumenfeld-Kosinski and Timea Szell. Ithaca, N.Y.: Cornell University Press, 1991.

Janssen, J. P. M. "Charles d'Orléans and the Fairfax Poems." *English Studies* 70 (1989): 206–24.

———. *The "Suffolk" Poems: An Edition of Love Lyrics in Fairfax 16 Attributed to William de la Pole*. Gröningen: Universiteitsdrukkerij, 1989.

Jeremy, Mary. "The English Prose Translation of *Legenda Aurea*." *Modern Language Notes* 59 (1944): 181–83.

John of Damascus. *Writings*. Trans. Frederic H. Chase Jr. New York: Fathers of the Church ser., no. 37, 1958.

Johnson, P. A. *Duke Richard of York, 1411–1460*. Oxford: Clarendon Press, 1988.

Jones, Charles. *Saints' Lives and Chronicles in Early England*. Ithaca, N.Y.: Cornell University Press, 1947.

Judd, Arnold. *The Life of Thomas Bekynton*. Chichester: Moore and Tillyer, 1961.

Kantorowicz, Ernst. *The King's Two Bodies*. Princeton, N.J.: Princeton University Press, 1957.

Kaplan, E. Ann. *Women and Film: Both Sides of the Camera*. New York: Methuen, 1983.

Karl, Louis, ed. "Vie de Sainte Elisabeth de Hongrie." *Zeitschrift für romanische Philologie* 34 (1910): 708–33.

Kemp, Eric Waldram. *Counsel and Consent: Aspects of the Government of the Church as Exemplified in the History of the English Provincial Synods*. London: SPCK, 1961.

Kempe, Margery. *The Book of Margery Kempe*. Trans. Barry Windeatt. Harmondsworth: Penguin; New York: Viking Penguin, 1985.

Kendall, Paul Murray. *The Yorkist Age: Daily Life during the Wars of the Roses*. Garden City, N.Y.: Norton, 1962.

Ker, N. R. "Medieval Manuscripts from Norwich Cathedral Priory." In *Books, Collectors and Libraries*. Ed. Andrew G. Watson. London: Hambledon, 1985.

Kingsford, Charles, L., ed. *English Historical Literature in the Fifteenth Century*. Oxford: Clarendon Press, 1913.

———. *The Stonor Letters and Papers*. 3 vols. and supplement. London: Camden Society, 1919.

Knox, Ronald, and Shane Leslie, eds. *The Miracles of King Henry VI*. Cambridge: Cambridge University Press, 1923.

Kölbing, E. "Zu Chaucers Caecilien-Legende." *Englische Studien* 1 (1877): 215–48.

Krauss, Russell. "Chaucerian Problems: Especially the Petherton Forestership and the Question of Thomas Chaucer." In *Three Chaucer Studies*. Ed. Russell Krauss. Folcroft, Pa.: Folcroft Press, 1969.

Kristeva, Julia. *Powers of Horror: An Essay on Abjection*. Trans. Leon S. Roudiez. New York: Columbia University Press, 1982.

Kurvinen, Auvo. "The Life of St. Catharine of Alexandria in Middle English Prose." D. Phil., University of Oxford, 1960.

Labarge, Margaret Wade. *Gascony: England's First Colony, 1204–1453*. London: Hamish Hamilton, 1980.

LaBarre, Weston. *Muelos: A Stone-Age Superstition About Sexuality*. New York: Columbia University Press, 1984.

Lander, J. R. *Conflict and Stability in Fifteenth-Century England*. London: Hutchison, 1969.

————. "Family, 'Friends' and Politics in Fifteenth-Century England." In *Kings and Nobles in the Later Middle Ages*. Ed. Ralph A. Griffith and James Sherborne. Gloucester: Sutton, 1986.

Lapsley, Gaillard T. *Crown, Community and Parliament in the Later Middle Ages*. Oxford: Blackwell, 1951.

Lasko, Peter. *Medieval Art in East Anglia, 1300–1520*. London: Thames & Hudson, 1974.

Lawton, David. "Dullness and the Fifteenth Century." *ELH* 54 (987): 761–99.

Leader, Damian Riehl. *A History of the University of Cambridge*. Cambridge: Cambridge University Press, 1988.

Le Bel, Jean. *Chronique*. Ed. Jules Viard and Eugène Déprez. Paris: Librairie Renouard, 1904.

Lederer, Laura, ed. *Take Back the Night: Women on Pornography*. New York: Morrow, 1980.

Leff, Gordon. *Bradwardine and the Pelagians: A Study of His* Causa Dei *and Its Opponents*. Cambridge: Cambridge University Press, 1957.

————. *Gregory of Rimini: Tradition and Innovation in Fourteenth Century Thought*. Manchester: Manchester University Press, 1961.

Le Patourel, John. "Edward III and the Kingdom of France." *History* 43 (1958): 173–89.

Lerer, Seth. *Chaucer and His Readers: Imagining the Author in Late-Medieval England*. Princeton, N.J.: Princeton University Press, 1993.

Lester, Geoffrey, ed. *The Earliest English Translation of Vegetius'* De Re Militari. Heidelberg: Carl Winter, 1988.

Lewis, P. S. "War Propaganda in Fifteenth-Century France and England." *Transactions of the Royal Historical Society*, 5th ser., 15 (1965): 1–21.

Linder, Amnon. "The Myth of Constantine the Great in the West: Sources and Hagiographic Commemoration." *Studi medievali* 16 (1975): 43–95.

Lloyd, T. H. *The English Wool Trade in the Middle Ages*. Cambridge: Cambridge University Press, 1977.

Lodge, Barton ed. *Palladius on husbondrie*. EETS 52 (1873): 72 (1879).

Louis, Cameron, ed. *The Commonplace Book of Robert Reynes of Acle*. New York: Garland Press, 1980.

Lowes, J. L. "The Prologue to the *Legend of Good Women* as Related to the French *Marguerite Poems and the Filostrato*." *PMLA* 19 (1904): 593–683.

Luard, H. R., ed. *Lives of Edward Confessor*. London: 1858.

Lucas, Peter J. "The Growth and Development of English Literary Patronage in the Later Middle Ages and Early Renaissance." *The Library*, 6th ser., 4 (1982): 219–48.

Lydgate, John. *Life of St. Alban and St. Amphibel*. Ed. J. E. Vander Westhuizen. Leiden: Brill, 1974.

————. *Lydgate's Life of Our Lady*. Ed. Joseph A. Lauritis, Ralph A. Kleinfelter, and Vernon F. Gallagher. Pittsburgh: Duquesne University Press, 1961.

————. *The Minor Poems of John Lydgate*. Ed. Henry N. MacCracken. EETS o.s. 107 (1910) and o.s. 192 (1933).

————. *The Serpent of Division*. Ed. Henry N. MacCracken London: Frowde, 1911.

MacCracken, Henry N. "An English Friend of Charles of Orleans." *PMLA* 26 (1911): 142–80.

Maddern, Philippa C. *Violence and Social Order: East Anglia 1422–1442*. Oxford: Clarendon Press, 1992.

Mann, Jill. *Geoffrey Chaucer*. New York: Harvester Wheatsheaf, 1991.

Mannyng, Robert. *Handlyng Synne*. Ed. Idelle Sullens. Binghamton: MRTS, 1983.

Mansfield, H. O. *Norfolk Churches*. Lavenham: Dalton, 1976.

Marshall, Anne. "The Role of English War Captains in England and Normandy, 1436–1461." Master's thesis, Swansea University College, 1975.

Martines, Lauro. *The Social World of the Florentine Humanists, 1390–1460*. Princeton, N.J.: Princeton University Press, 1963.

Marx, Karl. "A Contribution to the Critique of Hegel's Philosophy of Right." In *Marx and Engels on Religion*. New York: Schocken Books, 1964; repr. 1971.

———. "A Contribution to the Critique of Political Economy." In *Collected Works*. Vol. 29. New York: International Publishers, 1987; orig. in *Werke*. Vol. 13. Berlin: Dietz Verlag, 1964.

Mathes, F. A. "The Poverty Movement and the Augustinian Hermits." *Analecta augustiniana* 32 (1969): 1–116.

McFarlane, K. B. *England in the Fifteenth Century: Collected Essays*. London: Hambledon, 1981.

McKenna, John. "Piety and Propaganda: Cambridge Cult of King Henry VI." In *Chaucer and Middle English Studies in Honour of Russell Hope Robbins*. Ed. Beryl Rowland. London: Allen & Unwin, 1974.

McKenna, J. W. "Henry VI of England and the Dual Monarchy: Aspects of Royal Political Propaganda, 1422–1432." *Journal of the Warburg and Courtauld Institutes* 28 (1965): 145–62.

McNiven, Peter. *Heresy and Politics in the Reign of Henry IV: The Burning of John Badby*. Woodbridge: Boydell Press, 1987.

McRee, Ben. "Religious Guilds and Civic Order: The Case of Norwich in the Late Middle Ages." *Speculum* 67 (1992): 69–97.

Meale, Carol. "'. . . alle the bokes that I have of latyn, englisch, and frensch': Laywomen and Their Books in Late Medieval England." In *Women and Literature in Britain, 1150–1500*. Ed. Carol Meale. Cambridge: Cambridge University Press, 1993.

———. "Patrons, Buyers and Owners: Book Production and Social Status." In *Book Production and Publishing in Britain 1375–1475*. Ed. Jeremy Griffiths and Derek Pearsall. Cambridge: Cambridge University Press, 1989.

———. "The Text and the Book: Readings of Chaucer's *Legend of Good Women* in the Late Middle Ages." Unpublished paper.

Medvedev, P. N., and Mikhail Bakhtin. *The Formal Method in Literary Scholarship*. Leningrad, 1928; Baltimore: John Hopkins University Press, 1978.

Meekings, C. A. F. "Thomas Kerver's Case, 1444." *English Historical Review* 90 (1975): 331–46.

Meredith, Peter, ed. *The Mary Play from the N. Town Manuscript*. London: Longman, 1987.

Michalski, Konstanty. *La Philosophie au XIVe siècle*. Ed. Kurt Flasch. Frankfurt: Minerva, 1969.

Milburn, R. L. P. *Saints and Their Emblems in English Churches*. Oxford: Oxford University Press, 1949.

Miles, Margaret R. *Augustine on the Body*. Missoula, Mont.: Scholars Press, 1979.

———. "The Virgin's One Bare Breast: Female Nudity and Religious Meaning in Tuscan Early Renaissance Culture." In *The Female Body in Western Culture*. Ed. Susan Rubin Suleiman. Cambridge, Mass.: Harvard University Press, 1986.

Miller, J. Hillis. "Ariadne's Thread: Repetition and the Narrative Line." In *Interpretation of Narrative*. Ed. Mario Valdes and Owen Miller. Toronto: University of Toronto Press, 1978.

Miller, James I. "How to See Through Women: Medieval Blazons and the Male Gaze." In *The Centre and Its Compass. Studies . . . in Honor of . . . John Leyerle*. Kalamazoo: Western Michigan University Press, 1993.

————. "Literature to History: Exploring a Medieval Saint's Legend and Its Context." In *Literature and History*. Ed. I. E. Cadenhead Jr. Tulsa, Okla.: University of Tulsa Press, 1970. Monograph series 9: 64.

Miller, Townsend. *Henry IV of Castile, 1425–1474.* Philadelphia: Lippincott, 1972.

Minnis, A. J. "Theorizing the Rose: Commentary Tradition in the 'Querelle de la Rose.'" In *Poetics: Theory and Practise in Medieval English Literature.* Ed. Piero Boitani and Anna Torti. London: Boydell and Brewer, 1991.

Mirk, John. *Festial.* Ed. Th. Erbe. EETS e.s. 96 (1905).

Mitchell, Jerome. *Thomas Hoccleve: A Study in Early Fifteenth Century Poetic.* Urbana: University of Illinois Press, 1968.

Mombrizio, Bonino. *La Légende de Sainte Catherine d'Alexandrie.* Ed. Alphonse Bayot and Pierre Groult. Gembloux: Ed. J. Duculot, 1943.

Mooney, Linne R., ed. "A Middle English Text on the Seven Liberal Arts." *Speculum* 68 (1993): 1027–52.

Moore, Grace Edna, ed. *The Middle English Verse Life of Edward the Confessor.* Philadelphia: University of Pennsylvania Press, 1942.

Mulligan, Winifred Joy. "The British Constantine: An English Historical Myth." *JMRS* 8 (1978): 257–79.

Munro, John H. A. *Wool, Cloth and Gold: Anglo-Burgundian Trade, 1340–1478.* Toronto: University of Toronto Press, 1972.

Murphy, James J. *Rhetoric in the Middle Ages.* Berkeley and Los Angeles: University of California Press, 1974.

Nevanlinna, Saara, and Irma Taavitsainen, eds. *St Katherine of Alexandria: The Late Middle English Prose Legend in Southwell Minster MS 7.* Cambridge: D. S. Brewer, 1993.

Nolan, Kieran. *The Immortality of the Soul and the Resurrection of the Body According to Giles of Rome.* Rome: Studium Theologicum Augustinianum, 1967.

Norton-Smith, John, ed. *Bodleian Library Ms Fairfax 16. A Facsimile.* London: Scolar Press, 1979.

Obermann, Heiko. *The Harvest of Medieval Theology.* Durham, N.C.: Labyrinth, 1983.

————. *Thomas Bradwardine, a Fourteenth Century Augustinian.* Utrecht: Drukkerei . . . Kemink & Zoon, 1957.

O'Connor, Edward D., ed. *The Dogma of the Immaculate Conception.* Notre Dame, Ind.: University of Notre Dame Press, 1958.

O'Malley, John W. *Giles of Viterbo on Church and Church Reform.* Leiden: Brill, 1968.

————. *Praise and Blame in Renaissance Rome, 1450–1521.* Durham, N.C.: Duke University Press, 1979.

O'Neill, John. *Five Bodies: The Human Shape of Modern Society.* Ithaca, N.Y.: Cornell University Press, 1985.

Owst, G. R. *Literature and Pulpit in Medieval England.* Oxford: Blackwell, 1933; repr. 1966.

Ozment, Steven. *The Age of Reform, 1250–1550: An Intellectual and Religious History of Late Medieval and Reformation Europe.* New Haven, Conn.: Yale University Press, 1980.

Page, William. *History of the County of Berkshire.* London: Dawsons, 1972.

Pagels, Elaine. *The Gnostic Gospels.* New York: Random House, 1979.

Parker, Roscoe E., ed. *The Middle English Stanzaic Versions of the Life of Saint Anne.* EETS o.s. 174. Oxford: Oxford University Press, 1928.

Parker, William. *The History of Long Melford.* London: Wyman, 1873.

Parks, G. B. *The English Traveller to Italy.* 2 vols. Stanford, Calif.: Stanford University Press, 1954.

Paston. *The Paston Letters.* Ed. John Warrington. 2 vols. New York: Dutton; London: Dent, 1924; repr. 1961.

Patterson, Lee. "Ambiguity and Interpretation: A Fifteenth-Century Reading of *Troilus and Criseyde.*" *Speculum* 54 (1979): 297–330.

Pearsall, Derek. "John Capgrave's *Life of St. Katharine* and Popular Romance Style." *Medievalia et Humanistica* 6 (1975): 121–37.

Peck, Russell. "Number Structure in St. Erkenwald." *Annuale mediaevale* 14 (1973): 9–21.

Peters, Edward. *Torture.* New York: Blackwell, 1988.

Petrarch. *Bucolicum carmen.* Trans. Thomas G. Bergin. New Haven, Conn.: Yale University Press, 1974.

Pfaff, R. W. *New Liturgical Feasts in Later Medieval England.* Oxford: Clarendon Press, 1979.

Philippart, Guy. *Les Legendiers latins et autres manuscrits hagiographiques.* Turnhout: Brepols, 1977.

Pizan, Christine de. *The Epistle of Othea. Translated . . . by Stephen Scrope.* Ed. Curt F. Buhler. EETS, o.s. 264 (1970).

———. *Le Livre de la cité des dames.* Trans. Maureen Curnow, "Christine de Pizan's *Le Livre de la cité des dames.*" 2 vols. Ph.D. diss., Vanderbilt University, 1975.

Plato. *Timaeus.* Trans. R. D. Archer-Hind. New York: Arno Press, 1973.

Plucknett, T. F. T. "The Lancastrian Constitution." In *Tudor Studies Presented to . . . Albert Frederick Pollard.* Ed. R. W. Seton-Watson. London: Heffner, 1924.

Pons, Nicole, ed. *L'Honneur de la couronne de France: Quatre libelles contre les Anglais.* Paris: Klinckseick, 1990.

Potter, J. M. "The Development and Significance of the Salic Law of the French." *EHR* 52 (1937): 235–53.

Pouchelle, Marie-Christine. *Corps et chirurgie à l'apogée du moyen age.* Paris: Flammarion, 1983.

———. "Représentations du corps dans la *Légende dorée.*" *Ethnologie française* 6 (1976): 293–308.

Powell, J. Enoch, and Keith Wallis. *The House of Lords in the Middle Ages.* London: Weidenfeld and Nicolson, 1968.

Procter, Francis, and C. Wordsworth, eds. *Breviarii ad usum insignis ecclesiae Sarum.* Cambridge: Cambridge University Press, 1879.

Prudentius. *The Poems of Prudentius.* Trans. H. J. Thomson. 2 vols. Cambridge, Mass. Harvard University Press, 1953.

Pugh, T. B. "Richard Plantagenet (1411–1460), Duke of York, as the King's Lieutenant in France and Ireland." In *Aspects of Late Medieval Government and Society: Essays Presented to J. R. Lander.* Ed. J. G. Rowe. Toronto: University of Toronto Press, 1986.

Quilligan, Maureen. *The Allegory of Female Authority: Christine de Pizan's* Cité des Dames. Ithaca, N.Y.: Cornell University Press, 1991.

Ramsay, James H. *Lancaster and York: A Century of English History, a.d.* 1399–1485. 2 vols. Oxford: Clarendon Press, 1892.

Raven, Arlene. *Crossing Over: Feminism and the Art of Social Concern.* Ann Arbor, Mich.: UMI Research Press, 1988.

Reames, Sherry. *The* Legenda aurea: *A Re-Examination of Its Paradoxical History.* Madison: University of Wisconsin Press, 1985.

———. "A Recent Discovery Concerning the Sources of Chaucer's *Second Nun's Tale.*" *MP* 87 (1990): 337–61.

Redstone, Vincent B., ed. *Memorials of Old Suffolk.* London: Bemrose, 1908.

Reeves, A. C. *Lancastrian Englishmen.* Washington, D.C.: University Press of America, 1981.

Riché, Pierre. *The Carolingians: A Family Who Forged Europe.* Philadelphia: University of Pennsylvania Press, 1993.

Riddy, Felicity. "'Women Talking About the Things of God': A Late Medieval Subculture." In *Women and Literature in Medieval Britain, 1150–1500*. Ed. Carol Meale. Cambridge: Cambridge University Press, 1993.

Rigg, A. G. *A History of Anglo-Latin Literature 1066–1422*. Cambridge: Cambridge University Press, 1992.

———. "The Legend of Hugh Capet: Cambridge English Tradition." In *The Centre and Its Compass. Studies . . . in Honor of . . . John Leyerle*. Ed. Robert A. Taylor et al. Kalamazoo: Western Michigan University Press, 1993.

Riley, Henry T., ed. *Annales Monasterii S. Albani a Johanne Amundesham, monacho*. Rolls Series 28.5.1. London: Longmans, Green, 1870.

Robbins, Rossell Hope, John L. Cutler, and Carleton Brown. *Supplement to the Index of Middle English Verse*. Lexington: University of Kentucky Press, 1965.

Roberts, Michael. *Poetry and the Cult of the Martyrs: The* Liber peristephanon *of Prudentius*. Ann Arbor: University of Michigan Press, 1993.

Robertson, Elizabeth. "Aspects of female piety in the *Prioresse's Tale*." In Elizabeth Robertson and C. David Benson, eds. *Chaucer's Religious Tales*. Cambridge: D. S. Brewer, 1990.

Robinson, Pamela, ed. *Manuscript Tanner 346. Bodleian Library, Oxford. A Facsimile*. Norman, Okla.: Pilgrim Books, 1980.

Rosenthal, Joel T. "Richard, Duke of York: A Fifteenth Century Layman and the Church." *Catholic Historical Review* 50 (1964): 171–87.

Roskell, J. S. *The Commons and Their Speakers in English Parliaments, 1376–1523*. Manchester: Manchester University Press, 1965.

———. "Sir William Oldhall, Speaker in the Parliament of 1450–1." In J. S. Roskell, *Parliament and Politics in Late Medieval England*. Vol. 2. London: Hambledon Press, 1981.

Ross, Woodburn O., ed. *Middle English Sermons*. EETS o.s. 209 (1940).

Roth, Francis. *The English Austin Friars*. 2 vols. New York: Augustinian Historical Institute, 1961.

Russell, Diana E. H. "Pornography and Violence: What Does the New Research Say?" In *Take Back the Night: Women and Pornography*. Ed. Laura Lederer. New York: Morrow, 1980.

Ruud, Martin B. *Thomas Chaucer*. Minneapolis: University of Minnesota Press, 1926; repr. New York: AMS, 1972.

Salmon, John. *Saints in Suffolk Churches*. Bury: Suffolk Historic Churches Trust, 1981.

Samson, Annie. "The South English Legendary: Constructing a Context." In *Thirteenth Century England*. Ed. P. R. Coss and S. D. Lloyd. Woodbridge: Boydell Press, 1986.

Saxer, Victor. *Le Culte de Marie Madgalène en occident*. Paris: Clavreuil, 1959.

Schirmer, Walter F. *John Lydgate: A Study in the Culture of the XVth Century*. London: Methuen, 1962.

Schulenburg, Jane Tibbetts. "The Heroics of Virginity, Brides of Christ and Sacrificial Mutilation." In *Women in the Middle Ages and the Renaissance*. Ed. Mary Beth Rose. Syracuse, N.Y.: Syracuse University Press, 1986.

———. "Saints' Lives as a Source of the History of Women, 500–1100." In *Medieval Women and the Sources of History*. Ed. Joel T. Rosenthal. Athens: University of Georgia Press, 1990.

———. "Sexism and the Celestial Gynaeceum—From 500 to 1200." *Journal of Medieval History* 4 (1978): 117–33.

Scofield, Cora L. *The Life and Reign of Edward IV*. 2 vols. London: Cass, 1923; repr. 1967.

Scott, Margaret. *The History of Dress Series: Late Gothic Europe 1400–1500*. London: Mills & Boon; Atlantic Highlands, N.J.: Humanities Press, 1980.

Sheingorn, Pamela. "'Crystis wyf': Saint Faith in England." Unpublished paper.

Shoaf, R. A. *The Poem as Green Girdle: Commercium in* Sir Gawain and The Green Knight. Gainesville: University of Florida Press, 1984.

Singleton, Charles S. "The Poet's Number at the Center." In *Essays in the Numerical Criticism of Medieval Literature*. Ed. Caroline D. Eckhart. Lewisburg, Pa.: Bucknell University Press; Cranbury, N.J.: Associated University Presses, 1980.

Smalley, Beryl. *English Friars and Antiquity in the Early Fourteenth Century*. New York: Barnes & Noble, 1960.

———. *The Study of the Bible in the Middle Ages*. New York: Philosophical Society Library, 1952.

Sneyd, Charlotte Augusta, ed. *A Relation . . . of the Island of England*. London, 1847.

Solterer, Helen. *The Master and Minerva: Disputing Women in French Medieval Culture*. Berkeley: University of California Press, 1995.

South English Legendary. Ms. Laud 108, Bodleian. Ed. Carl Horstmann. EETS o.s. 87 1887; repr. New York: Kraus, 1973.

South English Legendary. Corpus Christi Ms. 145. Ed. Charlotte d'Evelyn and Anna J. Mill. EETS 235, 236; 1956.

Spalding, Mary Caroline, ed. *The Middle English Charters of Christ*. Bryn Mawr, Pa.: Bryn Mawr College Press, 1914.

Sperk, Klaus, ed. *Medieval Saints' Legends*. Tübingen: Niemeyer, 1970.

Spurgeon, Caroline. *Five Hundred Years of Chaucer Criticism and Allusion*. London: Russell, 1966.

Stahl, Paul-Henri. *Histoire de la décapitation*. Paris: Presses Universitaires de France, 1986.

Steinberg, Leo. *The Sexuality of Christ in Renaissance Art and in Modern Oblivion*. New York: Pantheon, 1983.

Steinmetz, David. "Luther and the Late Medieval Augustinians: Another Look." *CTM* 44 (1973): 245–60.

Stevenson, Joseph. *Letters and Papers Illustrative of the Wars of the English in France During the Reign of Henry the Sixth, King of England*. Rolls series. 2 vols. London: Longman, Green, 1861–64.

———. *Narratives of the Expulsion of the English from Normandy*. London: Longman, Green, 1863.

Stouck, Mary-Ann. "Chaucer and Capgrave's *Life of St. Katharine*." *American Benedictine Review* 33 (1982): 276–91.

Strohm, Paul. "*Passioun, Lyf, Miracle, Legende*: Some Generic Terms in Middle English Hagiographical Narrative." *ChR* 10 (1975): 62–75, 154–71.

Tanner, Norman P. *The Church in Late Medieval Norwich, 1380–1532*. Toronto: PIMS, 1984.

———. *Heresy Trials in the Diocese of Norwich, 1428–31*. London Royal Historical Society, 1977. Camden Society, 4th ser., vol. 20.

Thomas of Hales. *The Lyf of Oure Lady: The Middle English Translation of Thomas of Hales' Vita Sancte Marie*. Ed. Sarah M. Horrall. Heidelberg: Carl Winter, 1985.

Thompson, J. A. F. *The Later Lollards*. Oxford: Oxford University Press, 1965.

Thornton, Gladys A. *A History of Clare, Suffolk*. Cambridge: Heffer, 1930.

———. *A Short History of Clare Suffolk*. Long Melford: Tyrell, 1946, repr. 1983.

Toner, N. "Augustinian Spiritual Writers of the English Province in the 15th and 16th Centuries." *Analecta augustiniana* 2 (1959): 496–504.

Trapp, Damasus. "Augustinian Theology of the 14th Century." *Augustiniana* 6 (1956): 146–274.

Trinkaus, Charles. *In Our Image and Likeness: Humanity and Divinity in Italian Humanist Thought*. 2 vols. Chicago: University of Chicago Press, 1970.

Turner, Ralph V. "*Descendit ad inferos*: Medieval Views on Christ's Descent into Hell and the Salvation of the Ancient Just." *Journal of the History of Ideas* 27 (1966): 173–94.

Tymms, Samuel, ed. *Wills and Inventories . . . of Bury St. Edmund's*. Camden Society, 1850; repr. New York: AMS, 1968.

Tynemouth, John. *Wynkyn de Worde's* Nova Legenda Angliae. 2 vols. Oxford: Clarendon Press, 1901.

Vale, M. G. A. *Charles VII.* London: Eyre Methuen, 1974.

———. *English Gascony, 1399–1453.* Oxford: Oxford University Press, 1970.

Van Dijk, S. J. P., and Joan Hazelden Walker. *The Origins of the Modern Roman Liturgy.* London: Darton, Longman & Todd, 1960.

Van Luijk, Benigno A. L. *Le Monde augustinien du XIIIe au XIXe siècle.* Assen: Van Gorcum, 1972.

Vendome, Matthew. *Ars versificatoria.* Trans. Ernest Gallo. *Proceedings of the American Philosophical Society* 118 (Philadelphia, 1974).

Victoria County History, Norfolk. Vol. 1. Ed. A. H. Doubleday. Westminster: Constable, 1901. Vol. 2. Ed. William F. S. A. Page. Westminster: Constable, 1906; repr. Folkestone: Dawson, 1975.

Victoria County History, Suffolk. London: Archibald Constable, 1907; repr. Folkestone: Dawson, 1975.

Vinsauf, Geoffrey. *Poetria nova.* Trans. Margaret F. Nims. Toronto: PIMS, 1967.

Voragine, Jacob. *Jacobus a Voragine Legenda aurea.* Ed. Th. Graesse. Dresden and Leipzig, 1846.

Walsingham, Simon. "Vie Anglo-Normande de Sainte Foy par Simon de Walsingham." Ed. A. T. Baker. *Romania* 66 (1940): 49–84.

Walton, John, trans. *Boethius's* De Consolatione philosophiae. Ed. Mark Science. EETS o.s. 170 (1927).

Ward, Jennifer. "Elizabeth de Burgh, Lady of Clare (d. 1360)." In *Medieval London Widows, 1300–1500.* Ed. Caroline Barron and Anne F. Sutton. London: Hambledon Press, 1994.

Warner, George, ed. *The Libelle of Englyshe Polycye: A Poem on the Use of Sea-Power.* Oxford: Clarendon Press, 1926.

Warren, Ann. *Anchorites and Their Patrons in Medieval England.* Berkeley: University of California Press, 1985.

Watts, John Lovett. *"De Consulatu Stilichonis*: Texts and Politics in the Reign of Henry VI." *JMH* 16 (1990): 251–66.

———. "Domestic Politics and the Constitution in the Reign of Henry VI, c. 1435–c. 1461." D.Phil., Cambridge University, 1990.

Weinstein, Donald, and Rudolph M. Bell. *Saints and Society: The Two Worlds of Western Christendom, 1000–1700.* Chicago: University of Chicago Press, 1982.

Whateley, Gordon. "A 'Symple Wrecche at Work . . . in the *Gilte Legende.*" In *Legenda aurea: Sept siècles de diffusion.* Ed. Brenda Dunn-Lardeau. Paris: Vrin, 1986.

Williams, Harry F. "Old French Lives of St. Barbara." *Proceedings of the American Philosophical Society* 119 (1975): 156–85.

Williams, Linda. "When the Woman Looks." In *Re-Vision: Essays in Feminist Film Criticism.* Los Angeles: American Film Institute, 1984.

Williamson, W. W. "Saints on Norfolk Rood-Screens and Pulpits." *Norfolk Archaeology* 31 (1955–57): 299–346.

Wilson, E. M. Carus. "The Overseas Trade of Bristol." In *Studies in English Trade in the Fifteenth Century.* Ed. Eileen Power and M. M. Postan. London: Routledge, 1933.

Wilson, Katharine M. *Medieval Women Writers.* Athens: University of Georgia Press, 1984.

Wimsatt, James, ed. *The Marguerite Poetry of Guillaume de Machaut.* Chapel Hill: University of North Carolina Press, 1970.

Wogan-Browne, Jocelyn. "The Apple's Message: Some Post-Conquest Hagiographic Accounts of Textual Transmission." In *Late-Medieval Religious Texts and Their Transmission.* Ed. A. J. Minnis. Cambridge: D. S. Brewer, 1994.

———. "Rerouting the Dower: The Anglo-Norman Life of St. Audrey by Marie (of Chatteris?).” In *Power of the Weak. Studies on Medieval Women*. Ed. Jennifer Carpenter and Sally-Beth MacLean. Urbana: University of Illinois Press, 1995.

———. “Saints’ Lives and the Female Reader.” *Forum for Modern Language Studies* 27 (1991): 314–32.

Wolfe, B.P. “The Personal Rule of Henry VI.” In *Fifteenth Century England, 1399–1509: Studies in Politics and Society*. Ed. S. B. Chrimes, C. D. Ross, and R. A. Griffiths. Manchester: Manchester University Press, 1972.

Woodforde, Christopher. *The Norwich School of Glass Painting in the Fifteenth Century*. London: Oxford University Press, 1950.

Woodward, Kenneth L. *Making Saints: How the Catholic Church Determines Who Becomes a Saint, Who Doesn’t and Why*. New York: Simon & Schuster, 1990.

Woolf, Rosemary. *English Religious Lyric in the Middle Ages*. Oxford: Oxford University Press, 1968.

Woolf, Virginia. *Moments of Being: Unpublished Autobiographical Writings*. Ed. Jeanne Schulkind. London: Hogarth Press, 1972.

Wright, Thomas, ed. *Political Poems and Songs*. Rolls ser., 14.1. London, 1859; repr. New York: Kraus, 1965.

Zacour, Norman. *Jews and Saracens in the Consilia of Oldradus de Ponte*. Toronto: PIMS, 1990.

Index

amulets, 63–64

antifeminism. *See* misogyny

Augustine, 45

   City of God, 45, 117, 120, 125, 153

   Commentary on Genesis, 120-121

   Confessions, 120

   De Doctrina christiana, 49–64, 91,
      95–96

   De Musica, 105, 120

   sermons, 53, 102, 120

Augustinian order, 31, 44, 49, 130,
      180–181, 205 n. 3

   moderation in, 118–121, 140, 180, 183

   recruitment to, 6

   training, 6–7

Augustinianism, 46–49

Baret, John, 5, 15

Bible

   Christian, 58, 73, 92, 124, 160–161

   Hebrew, 76, 87, 121, 149, 151, 152,
      161, 212 n. 19

blazon, 80, 110–112, 115

body, as text or edifice, 26–28, 74–78,
      116, 129, 209 n. 3

body parts

   breast, 106–110, 112–113

   face, 79–81

   feet, 73–74, 78–79, 92–94

   genitals, 72, 82, 93, 97–98, 115, 209 n. 2

   head, 71–73, 208 n. 3

   mouth, 91–93

   tongue, 89, 97–98

   womb, 81–85

Bourchier, Henry, 21, 22

Bourchier, Isabel, 19, 21, 33, 54, 56, 57,
      62, 130, 136, 198

Bozon, Nicholas, 31, 164, 165

Burgh, Thomas, 24, 33, 206 n. 2

Bury St. Edmunds, 5, 6, 9, 13, 15, 130,
      181

Cambridge University, 7, 14, 46, 206 n.
      8

Capgrave, John, 4, 7, 8, 30, 38, 196

   Chronicle, 14

   Life of St. Katherine, 8, 35, 94,
      170–172, 182

Castile, 131–133, 210 n. 5

Catholic doctrine, 70

   calendar of saints, 31, 199–200

   grace, 100–102, 141

   immaculate conception of Mary,
      83–85, 161, 209 n. 6

   incarnation of Jesus, 26, 93–94, 95,
      183

   resurrection, 124–126

   salvation of virtuous pagans, 140–141

   trinity, 87, 141

Chaucer, Alice, 67